PRAISE FOR THE JESUS MYSTERIES

'Rarely have the roots of Christianity been disentangled to such disturbing effect. I shall never be able to read the gospels in the same way again.'

'This is a powerful book, and its impact, like a rolling express train, accelerates as one is carried along, page after page. It makes an absolutely compelling case for the non-existence of the gospel Jesus.'

'A wonderful blend of detective story, historical research and clear thinking. The time for the inner mysteries of Christianity to be brought out of the closet is long overdue, and this book is a powerful and courageous voice for the cause.'

'This is not for readers with a delicate nervous system. The book is shock treatment in paperback.'

'Powerful, provocative and extremely well written. This book is a milestone and if it succeeds, as I hope it does, it will no doubt feel the heat from the academic fire it is fanning.'

'*The Jesus Mysteries* is a powerful book which successfully challenges the history of Christianity bequeathed to us by the Roman Church. Already this book has started to have an impact and this is understandable. *The Jesus Mysteries* is too well researched and controversial to be ignored, so I predict it will provoke discussion and debate for many years to come.'

'As the Jesus Mysteries Thesis becomes more widely known, and if it begins to be accepted, it is clear that the implications are revolutionary. It is likely to become one of the most important religious debates of the twenty-first century.'

TIMOTHY FREKE AND
PETER GANDY

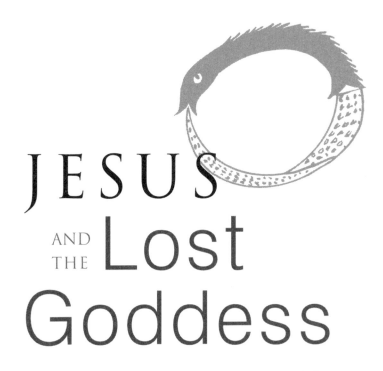

JESUS
AND
THE
Lost
Goddess

THE SECRET TEACHINGS OF THE
ORIGINAL CHRISTIANS

Harmony Books * New York

Published by Harmony Books, New York, New York.
Member of the Crown Publishing Group.

Random House, Inc. New York, Toronto, London, Sydney, Auckland
www.randomhouse.com

HARMONY BOOKS is a registered trademark and the Harmony Books colophon is a trademark of Random House, Inc.

Printed in the United States of America

Library of Congress Cataloging-in-Publication Data is available upon request

ISBN 0-609-60767-7

10 9 8 7 6 5 4 3 2 1

First Edition

THIS BOOK IS DEDICATED
TO THOSE WHO KNOW
THEY DO NOT KNOW.

CONTENTS

ACKNOWLEDGEMENTS

We would like to thank our commissioning editors Carole Tonkinson, Rebecca Strong, Eileen Campbell and Patricia Gift, our agent Susan Mears, our dedicated copy editor Lizzie Hutchins, Tim Byrne for turning our vision of the cover into a reality, Ellen Freke for her positive comments on the manuscript, all at Thorsons and Harmony who have helped and will be helping in publicity and promotion, and last but not least, readers of our previous books, especially *The Jesus Mysteries*, for supporting and encouraging our work.

chapter one

THE GOSPEL OF
Gnosis

'I will reveal to you what no eye can see,
what no ear can hear,
what no hand can touch,
what cannot be conceived by the human mind.'
Jesus, *The Gospel of Thomas*[1]

Life is a Mystery. A Mystery so awesome that we insulate ourselves from
its intensity. To numb our fear of the unknown we desensitize ourselves
to the miracle of living. We perpetuate the nonchalant lie that we know
who we are and what life is. Yet behind this preposterous bluff the
Mystery remains unchanging, waiting for us to remember to wonder. It is
waiting in a shaft of sunlight, in the thought of death, in the intoxication
of new love, in the joy of childbirth or the shock of loss. One minute we
are going about our business as if life were nothing special and the next we
are face to face with profound, unfathomable, breathtaking Mystery. This
is both the origin and consummation of the spiritual quest.

Although the conditions of life have changed continually throughout
history, the Mystery of life has remained the same. This is a book about a

remarkable group of men and women who, some 2,000 years ago, were touched by the Mystery and dared to plumb its depths. Revolutionary free-thinkers who synthesized the available wisdom of the world and articulated perennial truths in dynamic, innovative ways. Creative visionaries who encoded their teachings in extraordinary myths. Explorers of consciousness whose mystical philosophy promised 'Gnosis' – experiential Knowledge of Truth. These forgotten spiritual pioneers could not have conceived of the unparalleled impact they would have on the history of humanity. Who were they? They called themselves 'Christians'.

It was these radical individualists who inadvertently created the most authoritarian religion in history. Their questioning mysticism was distorted, almost beyond recognition, into the dogmatic creed of what they called an 'imitation church'.[2] When this impoverished form of Christianity was adopted as the official religion of the brutal Roman Empire, the original Christians were violently suppressed, their scriptures burned and their memory all but erased. The Roman Church fabricated its own account of the origins of Christianity, still believed today, which dismisses the first Christians as a minor cult of obscure heretics. But it was these brilliant mythographers who authored a story which continues to dominate the spiritual imagination of the Western world. From the archaic allegory of a dying and resurrecting Son of God they fashioned a new and vibrant myth which has captured the hearts and minds of millions: the fable of a Jewish peasant who saved the world: the story of Jesus the Christ.

THE GOOD NEWS

For the original Christians, the Jesus story was a myth used to introduce beginners to the spiritual path. For those wishing to go deeper than the 'Outer Mysteries', which were only 'for the masses', there were secret teachings or 'Inner Mysteries'.[3] These were 'the secret traditions of true Gnosis' which, according to the 'Church Father' Clement of Alexandria, were transmitted 'to a small number by a succession of masters'.[4] Those initiated into these Inner Mysteries discovered that Christianity was not just about the dying and resurrecting Son of God. They were told another myth that few Christians today have even heard of – the story of Jesus' lover, the lost and redeemed Daughter of the Goddess.

Amongst the original Christians the divine was seen as having both a masculine and feminine face. They related to the Divine Feminine as Sophia, the wise Goddess.[5] Paul tells us, 'Among the initiates we speak of Sophia', for it is 'the secret of Sophia' that is 'taught in our Mysteries'.[6] When initiates of the Inner Mysteries of Christianity partook of Holy Communion, it was Sophia's passion and suffering they remembered.[7] Amongst the original Christians, priests and priestesses would offer initiates wine as a symbol of 'her blood'.[8] The prayer would be offered: 'May Sophia fill your inner being and increase in you her Gnosis.'[9] It was Sophia who was petitioned:

> 'Come, hidden Mother; come, you who are made manifest in your works, and give joy and rest to those who are bound to you. Come and partake in this Eucharist which we perform in your name, and in the love feast for which we have assembled at your invitation.'[10]

The eradication of this Christian Goddess by the patriarchal Roman Church has left us all motherless children. Women have been denied a sympathetic rapport with the Divine Feminine. Men have been denied a love-affair with a female face of Deity. Spirituality has become part of the battleground which separates the sexes, when it should be the sanctuary of eternal fellowship. The original Christians, however, practised 'partnership spirituality'. They valued men and women equally, as expressions of God and Goddess. They saw the division of the sexes as a correlate of that primal duality which is the source of creation, a duality that when made one, as in the act of love, brings the bliss of union that they called 'Gnosis'.

For the original Christians the Jesus story appears at the end of a cycle of Christian myths which begins with the ineffable Mystery manifesting itself as a primordial Father and Mother and culminates in the mystical marriage of Jesus and Sophia. The Inner Mysteries reveal these myths as allegories of spiritual initiation, symbolic stories which encode a profound philosophy with the power to transform an initiate from a Christian into a Christ.[11]

For the original Christians the 'gospel' or 'good news' is not a story written in a book. Rather they taught that: 'The gospel is the Gnosis.'[12] The good news is that a complete transformation of consciousness is possible. The good news is that there is a way to transcend suffering. The good news is that there is a natural state of happiness which is our birthright. This is the gospel of absolute freedom. It is not a set of rules which we must follow to become 'good'. It is about discovering our own essential nature, which is good already, so that we can live spontaneously.

This gospel holds out the extraordinary promise that those who understand it 'will not taste death'.[13] But immortality is not access to Heaven as reward for living an upright life. It is the immediate realization, here and now, of our true identity, which was never born and so can never die.

A JOURNEY OF INITIATION

This book is an exploration of the gospel of Gnosis. Our aim has been to present a radical alternative to the traditional picture of who the original Christians were and what they believed. Like all spiritual movements, early Christianity covered a broad spectrum of individuals and schools with differing levels of perception, so we have chosen to focus on what we regard as their best and most enduring insights, which may still be valid for us today.

Why isn't the gospel of Gnosis common knowledge? First, because the Roman Church has spent over 16 centuries systematically destroying the evidence that it ever existed. For much of this time, merely to possess Christian works unacceptable to the established Church was punishable by a cruel death. Thankfully some of these texts have nevertheless survived. In recent decades they have been augmented by fabulous archaeological finds such as the discovery of a library of 'heretical' Christian scriptures in a cave near Nag Hammadi in Egypt. The implications of this find, and the advances in our understanding of early Christianity that it has led to, have yet to be widely appreciated.

Inadequate translation has also played a significant role in disguising the secret teachings of Christianity encoded in the New Testament gospels and alluded to frequently by Paul in his letters. Rendering these works into familiar 'churchy' English lulls us into the reassuring illusion that we have understood what is being said, when in fact we have not even begun to scratch the surface of the real significance of the original Greek. The 'heretical' Christian gospels, on the other hand, are regularly rendered into unfamiliar English, making them sound strange and inaccessible. One translator was even in the habit of remarking that such texts were 'not supposed to make any sense'.[14] Little wonder, then, that an artificial division has been created between the orthodox canon and other Christian gospels. However, when the New Testament Jesus story is understood in its original context, as part of the whole Christian myth cycle, and the 'heretical' gospels are interpreted sympathetically, they can, at last, be seen as expressions of one profound mystical philosophy.

In our examination of these texts we have made one assumption which other commentators often do not make: that our ancestors were not idiots. We have postulated that although they lived in very different physical conditions, they still faced the same great enigmas of existence as we do today and that their answers are potentially as valuable as contemporary views. We have, in short, approached the people we are studying with the respect which they deserve and which they have been denied for nearly two millennia.

Academics have often failed lamentably to understand the spirituality of the original Christians because they have lacked mystical insight. The Gnosis is not an intellectual theory. It is a state of being. It is an inner 'Knowledge' which can never be truly understood from the outside. Trying to comment on the Gnosis without ever having personally experienced its life-changing impact is like writing a travelogue for a country you have never visited. Any native would find it laughably absurd. We approach this work not only with a commitment to rigorous scholarship, but also as life-long students of experiential mysticism. We are not, however, members of any cult or affiliated to any religious organization. This, we feel, makes us ideally placed to take up the challenge of recovering the ancient Gnosis for modern readers.

New ideas can take decades to travel from scholarly circles to the general public. We have attempted to circumvent this process by making the main text of the book as accessible as possible while offering notes for those who wish to see more detailed evidence in support of our ideas or to check our sources.

For us, putting together this book has been much more than an academic study. It has been a revelation. For the original Christians, the process of initiation involved meditating on their myths to tease out the allegorical significance. In writing this book we ourselves have had to undertake a similar in-depth study of Christian mythology. This has been an initiatory experience which has left us transformed in ways we did not anticipate.

It has been a philosophical journey of cosmic proportions. Yet at its conclusion we have found that the secret teachings of the original Christians, although seemingly arcane, are actually about understanding the miracle of life just as it is. We have struggled to penetrate indecipherable riddles.

Yet we have found that, although seemingly complex, these teachings are in essence astonishingly simple. We have time-travelled back into the ancestral mind. Yet although the gospel of Gnosis belongs to a so-called 'dead' spiritual tradition, we have found it to be as relevant and challenging today as it was two millennia ago. Our hope is that this book allows you to also taste something of the ancient and perennial Gnosis for yourself.

chapter two

THE ORIGINAL
Christians

'Much that is written in Pagan books is found also in the books of God's Church. What they share in common are the words which spring from the heart, the law that is inscribed on the heart.'

Valentinus, *On Friends* [1]

It's a strange world. At the end of the nineteenth century the influential Hindu guru Vivekananda was sailing across the Mediterranean Sea on a return journey to England when he had a curious dream. A very old and venerable-looking sage appeared to him, saying:

> 'Do ye come to effect our restoration? I am one of the ancient order of Therapeutae. The truths preached by us have been given out by Christians as taught by Jesus; but for the matter of that, there was no personality by the name of Jesus ever born.' [2]

This extract from Vivekananda's autobiography was kindly sent to us by a reader of our previous book, *The Jesus Mysteries*, because it endorses the revolutionary view of the origins of Christianity that we presented there.

After years of painstaking research we concluded that the traditional history of Christianity was at best hopelessly inaccurate and at worst a pack of lies. The evidence demanded that we think the unthinkable. Christianity was not the cult of a first-century Messiah, but a Jewish adaptation of the ancient Pagan Mystery religion. We could find no evidence that there had ever been an historical Jesus, because the gospel story was a Jewish reworking of ancient Pagan myths of a dying and resurrecting Son of God.[3] We even ventured an informed guess as to who may have authored the original Jesus myth – a sect of mystical Jews called the Therapeutae.[4]

Is it possible that Vivekananda reached the truth by intuitive means a century before us? Perhaps. The psychologist Carl Jung came to believe that the whole of human history could be reconstructed from the contents of one person's unconscious.[5] Yet it requires substantial evidence to validate such a shocking revision of received history. This we provided in *The Jesus Mysteries*.

The main concern of that book was to uncover the true *history* of Christianity. The main concern of this book is to discern the true *meaning* of Christianity. But before we can embark on an exploration of the gospel of Gnosis we need an understanding of the historical context in which it was taught. In the light of our latest research, therefore, we will first review, clarify and expand upon the picture of Christian origins which we presented in detail in *The Jesus Mysteries*.

The traditional history of Christianity has managed to survive for so long, in part, because although it is utterly inadequate to the facts, it is fairly internally consistent and easy to grasp. We have found that the best way to open people to the idea that this supposed history is actually a complete fantasy is to present a rival picture of how Christianity and Christian mythology developed, which is more coherent and plausible. In this book, therefore, this is what we will attempt.

Fundamentally all we are suggesting is that we listen to the losers in the civil war that bedevilled Christianity in the third and fourth centuries between the Roman Church and those it branded heretics and did everything in its power to silence. The traditional history was written by the winners, but we have come to believe that the account of the origins and meaning of Christianity given by those dissident Christians is far closer to the truth.

GNOSTICS AND LITERALISTS

To understand something in a new way, we often need to think using new terms. When writing about the history of spirituality, scholars usually classify people according to the religion to which they are affiliated – Pagan, Jew, Christian, Muslim, and so forth. We would like to suggest that this way of thinking conceals a much more significant classification, which categorizes individuals according to spiritual understanding rather than religious tradition.

From our studies of world spirituality, we have observed that religious movements tend to embrace two opposing poles, which we call 'Gnosticism' and 'Literalism', with particular individuals inhabiting the whole spectrum between the two extremes. This classification is important because Gnostics from different religious traditions have far more in common with each other than they do with Literalists within their own tradition. Whilst Literalists from different religions clearly hold conflicting beliefs, Gnostics from all traditions use different conceptual vocabularies to articulate a common understanding, sometimes called the 'perennial philosophy'.[6] It is not that all Gnostics agree. Different schools argue vehemently with each other, but these differences are minor compared to their shared essential perspective.

To get an accurate understanding of the development of spiritual ideas, we need to view Gnosticism as an identifiable spiritual tradition which transcends the accepted divisions into regional religions. Those who embrace Gnosticism and have been born into a Jewish culture tend to remain within their national tradition and become Jewish Gnostics, while those born elsewhere tend to become Muslim Gnostics, and so on. But all Gnostics need to be understood as essentially parts of one evolving tradition, whatever their race or culture.[7]

The goal of Gnostic spirituality is Gnosis, or Knowledge of Truth. We have chosen to use the name 'Gnostics', meaning 'Knowers', because in the various languages used by different religions, individuals who have realized 'Gnosis' or achieved 'Enlightenment' are often referred to as 'Knowers': *Gnostikoi* (Pagan/Christian), *Arifs* (Muslim), *Gnanis* (Hindu), *Buddhas* (Buddhist).[8]

Gnostics interpret the stories and teachings of their spiritual tradition as signposts pointing beyond words altogether to the mystical experience of the ineffable Mystery. Literalists, on the other hand, believe their scriptures are actually the words of God. They take their teachings, stories and initiation myths to be factual history. They focus on the words as a *literal* expression of the Truth. Hence we have chosen to call them 'Literalists'.

Gnostics are concerned with the inner essence of their tradition. Literalists associate their faith with its outward manifestations: sacred symbols, scriptures, rituals, ecclesiastical leaders, and so on. Gnostics see themselves as being on a spiritual journey of personal transformation. Literalists see themselves as fulfilling a divinely ordained obligation to practise particular religious customs as a part of their national or cultural identity.

Literalists believe that their particular spiritual tradition is different from all others and has a unique claim on the Truth. They obsessively formulate dogmas which define membership of their particular cult.[9] They are prepared to enforce their opinions and silence those who dissent, justifying their actions by claiming that they are fulfilling God's will. Gnostics, on the other hand, are free spirits who question the presuppositions of their own culture. They follow their hearts, not the herd. They are consumed by their private quest for enlightenment, not by the goal of recruiting more adherents to a religion.

Gnostics wish to free themselves from the limitations of their personal and cultural identities and experience the oneness of all things. They therefore have no reluctance in adopting the wisdom of other traditions if it adds something to their own. Literalists use religion to sustain their personal and cultural identity by defining themselves in opposition to others. This inevitably leads to disputes with those outside their particular cult. It is Literalists who fight wars of religion with Literalists from other traditions, each claiming that God is on their side. Literalists' enmity also extends to Gnostics within their own tradition who question their bigotry. Most spiritual traditions have a tragic history of the brutal oppression of Gnostics by intolerant Literalists. Interestingly, it is never the other way around.

We know that we are radically changing accepted terminology and run the risk of affronting some classicists and Christian scholars, but we feel that thinking in these terms enables us to understand the origins of Christianity much more accurately. This way we can circumvent the dead end of looking for a particular 'parent' religion. Christianity certainly adopted many elements from Judaism, as is generally accepted. It was also heavily influenced by Paganism, as is being increasingly realized.[10] But it is best conceived as a product of neither and a reaction against both.

THE THERAPEUTAE AND THE ESSENES

We have come to understand the original Christians as part of a disparate Gnostic tradition flourishing across the whole of the Mediterranean with a common mystical philosophy and a common abhorrence of limited Literalist religion. Strictly speaking, there were no 'original Christians', but rather a continuous stream of Gnostics from different cultures with different experiences of life, all producing their own unique variations on the perennial philosophy. Amongst some Jewish Gnostics a school developed which synthesized Jewish and Pagan mythology to produce distinctive new myths. In retrospect we can see that this was the beginnings of what we now call 'Christianity'.

These proto-Christians were probably the Therapeutae and Essenes, who are described by the Jewish Gnostic Philo, himself probably an initiate of the Theraputae, as two parts of a single school of philosophy. The world they inhabited was dominated by cosmopolitan Pagan civilizations which had been trading, conquering and synthesizing with each other for centuries. As early as the fourth century BCE the Pagan Gnostic Plato had described the peoples of the Mediterranean as like 'frogs around a small pond'.[11] A few decades later the empire of Alexander the Great transformed the ancient world into essentially one culture, and Greek became the international language. Pagan, Jewish and Christian Gnostics all wrote in Greek, thus making their ideas readily available to each other and fuelling an explosion of creative eclecticism. It was an ideal environment for Gnosticism to flourish.

By the first century CE huge numbers of Jews in Judaea and throughout the Mediterranean were fully integrated into sophisticated Pagan society, none more so than Jewish Gnostics, such as the Therapeutae, who regarded themselves as literally 'cosmopolitans' – 'citizens of the cosmos'.[12] Philo writes of being part of an international fellowship of Gnostic philosophers who, 'although comparatively few in number, keep alive the covered spark of wisdom secretly throughout the cities of the world'.[13]

Jewish Gnostics claimed to be inheritors of secret mystical teachings passed down from their own great Gnostic master, Moses.[14] These teachings were so similar to those of Pagan Gnosticism that many Jews claimed that the great Pagan philosophers had originally received their wisdom from Moses.[15] This belief encouraged Jews to enthusiastically embrace the philosophy and mythology of the Pagan Gnostics to augment their own tradition, producing a large number of spiritual treatises which synthesized Pagan and Jewish motifs.[16]

The spirituality of the Therapeutae and Essenes is an example of this fusion of Jewish and Pagan Gnosticism. As well as being followers of their own Jewish master Moses, they were also followers of the great Pagan philosopher Pythagoras, whose disciples had set up communities throughout the Mediterranean world. The Jewish historian Josephus informs us that the Essenes are comparable to the Pythagoreans,[17] enthusing 'all who have tasted their philosophy are attracted to it'.[18] Philo, himself known as 'the Pythagorean',[19] describes the Therapeutae as practising 'the contemplative life', which was a way of describing Pythagoreans.[20] He tells us their wisdom stems from Greece and that 'this kind exists in many places in the inhabited world'.[21]

Following the practice of the Cynic school of Pagan Gnosticism, these Jewish Gnostics called their spiritual tradition simply 'the Way' – a term also adopted by the original Christians.[22] The fourth-century Christian Literalist historian Eusebius saw so many similarities between the Way of the Therapeutae and the Christian Way that he claimed the Therapeutae were amongst the first followers of Christ.[23] But Philo's description of the Therapeutae was written before the time that Jesus is supposed to have been teaching, so he is clearly not writing about disciples of an historical Messiah, as Eusebius believed.[24] Ironically, Eusebius was probably right nevertheless, albeit in an entirely different way from how he intended. The Essenes and Therapeutae did not follow Jesus. They created him![25]

The idea of some sect 'making up' the Jesus myth may seem strange today, but this is because we no longer think of myths in the same way as our ancestors did. To us myths are irrelevant fantasies, but the ancients regarded them as profound allegories encoding mystical teachings. Mythical motifs represented philosophical principles. They were an archetypal vocabulary with which to think. Creating new myths was a way of exploring new ideas.

Reworking old myths and syncretizing them to create new ones was a major preoccupation of the Gnostics. Philo tells us that the Therapeutae were devoted to 'philosophizing and interpreting their ancestral scriptures allegorically, for they think that the words of the literal meaning are symbols of a hidden nature which is made plain only by the under-meaning'.[26] Imaginative mythologizing is also what the later Christian Gnostics specialized in. One of their critics condemns them for using 'allegorical interpretation' to freely 'recompose' Jewish scriptures and

'Greek epic mythology',[27] which are precisely the two sources used to create the myths of Jesus and the Goddess.

Beginning with the Therapeutae and Essenes in the first century BCE, a body of specifically Christian mythology gradually evolved, passing through many stages and revisions, with different Christian schools developing their own myths or their own versions of common myths. Essentially, all of these myths explore two questions which are fundamental to the human predicament: how did we get into this mess and how do we get out of it?!

Jewish Gnostics believed that answers to these questions were encoded in two allegorical myths from the Books of Moses: *Genesis* and *Exodus*. *Genesis* means 'origination'. It was understood as encoding teachings about the descent of the soul into physical incarnation. *Exodus* means 'the way out'. It was seen as encoding teachings about the initiate's spiritual path back to God.[28] The original Christians synthesized these Jewish myths with Pagan myths which also encoded Gnostic teachings about the fall and redemption of the soul to create their own myth cycle which explained both the 'descent' and the 'return'.

The Christian myth of descent or origination is a synthesis and elaboration of the Jewish *Genesis* myth and *Timaeus*, a Pythagorean treatise by the Pagan Gnostic Plato.[29] In his treatise *On the Creation of the World* Philo argues that, understood allegorically, these two works encode the same doctrines.[30]

The Christian myth of the 'return' is a powerful allegory designed to guide us through the stages of initiation which lead to Gnosis. It was created by synthesizing the Jewish myth of *Exodus* with Pagan myths of the dying and resurrecting Godman Osiris-Dionysus. Originally a simple and abstract myth, it was revised and embellished over the course of the first and second centuries CE to become the most influential myth ever created: the Jesus story.

SOURCES OF THE JESUS MYTH

Let's examine the various elements from which the Jesus myth was constructed, beginning, as the original Christians undoubtedly did themselves, with the myth of *Exodus*.

The *Exodus* Allegory

This famous Jewish myth relates the story of Moses leading his people out of captivity in Egypt by miraculously parting the Red Sea. There follows 40 years of wandering in the wilderness in search of the Promised Land, at the end of which Moses dies. It is his successor, Joshua ben Nun, who miraculously parts the river Jordan to lead the Jews to the destined homeland.[31]

The name 'Jesus' itself comes from *Exodus*.[32] In Greek the Hebrew name 'Joshua' becomes 'Jesus'. Today it is normal practice to use Joshua for the hero of *Exodus* and 'Jesus' for the hero of the gospels, which avoids any comparison of the two. At the time, however, it would have been completely obvious that they shared the same name. This is not a coincidence. The Christian Jesus is a mythic development of the Jesus of *Exodus*.

In Hebrew the name Joshua/Jesus is written with the letters *Yod Heh Shin Vah Heh*. The letters *Yod Heh Vah Heh*, known as the Tetragrammaton, were extremely significant to Jewish Gnostics, as they were used to signify the unpronounceable name of God, usually rendered today with added vowels as either Jehovah or Yahweh. As Philo explains, when the middle letter *Shin*, known as the Holy Letter, is added, the name means 'Saviour of the Lord'.[33]

The honorary title 'Christ' is also linked to the *Exodus* myth. Paul tells us that, as well as Jesus, Moses was also 'God's Christ'.[34] 'Christ', which means 'Anointed One', is a Greek rendering of the Hebrew word 'Messiah', which was an epithet for a leader, used of Jewish kings. Although today the name 'Jesus Christ' is inextricably linked to the Literalist figure of the supposed founder of Christianity, in the first century CE the name would have been heard as obviously symbolic, meaning 'The Saviour King'.

Jewish Gnostics, and Christian Gnostics after them, understood *Exodus* to be an initiation allegory. Egypt represents the body. Whilst initiates identify with the body they are 'in captivity'. To 'come forth out of Egypt' was understood as leaving behind the idea of being merely a body and discovering the soul. The ignorant Egyptians represent those 'without Gnosis', who remain identified with their physical selves.

Crossing the Red Sea was understood as symbolizing a purifying baptism, which is the first stage of initiation on the path of spiritual awakening for those who are 'conscious'.[35] Explaining that *Exodus* should be understood 'allegorically', Paul writes:

'Our ancestors passed through the Red Sea and so received baptism into the fellowship of Moses'.[36]

Initiation by baptism begins a process in which initiates must face their doubts and confusion, symbolized by the Jews being afflicted in the desert for 40 years. The next stage of initiation is about the 'death' of the old self, represented by the death of Moses. Moses is mythically reborn as Joshua/Jesus who completes the journey to the Promised Land, representing the 'reborn' initiate who realizes Gnosis.

The basic structure of the *Exodus* allegory, representing the fundamental stages of Gnostic initiation, is the framework upon which the Jesus myth was constructed. The first stage of initiation is one of purification and struggle. In the *Exodus* myth this is the crossing of the Red Sea, which inaugurates 40 years of wandering in the wilderness. In the Jesus story, this stage is represented by Jesus' baptism, followed by his 40 days in the wilderness. The next stage in the process of initiation is the 'death' of the old self which precipitates Gnosis. This is represented in the *Exodus* myth by the death of Moses and in the Jesus myth by the death of Jesus on the cross. The experience of Gnosis is represented in *Exodus* by Jesus crossing to the Promised Land and in the New Testament by Jesus' resurrection from the dead and ascension to Heaven.

Basic Structure of *Exodus* and the Jesus Story as Initiation Allegories

Initiation Process	Exodus	Jesus Story
Purification	Crossing the Red Sea	Baptism by John
Death of the old self	Death of Moses	Crucifixion
Realization of Gnosis	The Promised Land	Resurrection

Acknowledging their debt to the *Exodus* allegory, the original Christians classified people as 'the captive, the called and the chosen'.[37] Those yet to undergo initiation and still trapped in the idea of being a physical body are like the Jews captive in Egypt. Those who have heard the call to awaken and begun the spiritual journey by being initiated into the Outer Mysteries of Christianity are like those Jews who were 'called out of Egypt' to begin the journey to their true home. Those who have undergone the process of purification and spiritual struggle necessary to prepare themselves for Gnosis and been chosen to be initiated into the secret Inner Mysteries of Christianity are like those 'chosen people' whom Jesus leads across the river Jordan to the Promised Land.[38] Initiates who finally realized Gnosis were known as 'those who have crossed over'.[39]

Early Christians were well aware of the parallels between their Jesus Christ and the Jesus Christ of *Exodus*. Justin Martyr, for example, explains that the Christian Jesus will lead his people to the Promised Land just as the Jesus of *Exodus* led his people to the Promised Land.[40] Justin traces the motif of the cross to *Exodus*, where Moses holds up a serpent on a cross and says, 'If you look at this image and believe, you shall be saved by it.'[41] This source is made explicit in *The Gospel of John*, where Jesus is made to announce:

'The Son of Man must be lifted up as the serpent was lifted up by Moses in the wilderness.'[42]

Other, more incidental, mythic motifs found in the Jesus myth also come from *Exodus*. Once he has crossed the river Jordan, the Jesus of *Exodus* selects 12 men to represent the 12 tribes of Israel. After his baptism in the river Jordan, the Jesus of the gospels likewise selects 12 men as his immediate followers.[43] Both motifs refer to the 12 astrological signs of the zodiac.[44] Such a reference is not surprising. The Jews had adopted astrology from the Babylonians whilst in exile in Babylon, eventually becoming renowned throughout the ancient world as astrologers. They even claimed that the Jewish Patriarch Abraham had been the inventor of this ancient science.[45]

In the myth of Moses, at his birth the evil Pharaoh, fearful of a prophesy that Moses would be the cause of his downfall, commits mass infanticide in an attempt to kill him. In the gospel myth of Jesus this becomes the 'slaughter of the innocents' perpetrated by the evil King Herod who, fearful of a prophesy that the true King of the Jews has been born, attempts to kill the infant Jesus.[46] Mary the sister of Moses becomes Jesus' mother

Mary, a correspondence pointed out in many Christian texts, as well as in the Muslim Qur'an.[47]

Like the Jews in *Exodus*, in the gospel story Jesus is called out of Egypt, where he has been in hiding, like the soul within the body. *The Gospel of Matthew* explains that this is to fulfil the prophesy 'Out of Egypt I have called my Son.'[48] Here, as elsewhere in the gospels, we should read 'fulfil the prophesy' as a coded reference to the source of the symbolic motif and its intended allegorical meaning. This is prophesy in retrospect. Jesus fulfils Jewish scriptural expectations precisely because the Jesus story has been constructed from them.

Piecing together previously existing mythological material in a new way was a traditional Jewish technique known as *midrash*.[49] It has long been known to scholars, for example, that the entire passion narrative in the gospels has been created from motifs taken from *Psalms 22, 23, 38* and *39* and from the depiction of the 'suffering servant' in *The Book of Isaiah*.[50]

The Essenes taught that in ancient times the Jesus of *Exodus* had hidden secret teachings, so only those who were worthy could discover them at the appropriate time.[51] They developed a contemporary mythic Christ figure called the 'Teacher of Righteousness', whom they identified with the Jesus of *Exodus*.[52] This figure eventually became the Jesus of the gospels, a mythical reincarnation of the great hero of the most important of all the Jewish Gnostic myths. The secret teachings hidden by Jesus the Christ of *Exodus* are finally made public by the reworked figure of Jesus the Christ in the gospels. This is the 'secret not revealed in former times' but 'now disclosed' of which Paul writes in his letters.[53]

Jewish Messiah and Pagan Godman

These Jewish mythological motifs were syncretized with motifs borrowed from the initiation allegories of the Pagan Mysteries. All of the great Pagan Gnostics, such as Pythagoras, Socrates, Plato and Plotinus, were initiates of one or more of the Mystery cults that were ubiquitous throughout the ancient Mediterranean.[54] Each Mystery tradition consisted of exoteric Outer Mysteries, which involved religious practices in which anyone could participate, and esoteric Inner Mysteries, to which access was gained by undergoing a process of initiation. In the Inner Mysteries the rituals and myths of the Outer Mysteries were revealed as allegories encoding mystical teaching which could lead an initiate to the experience of Gnosis.

The most important characters in these allegorical initiation myths were the lost and redeemed Goddess and the dying and resurrecting Godman. Regional variations on these two mighty figures are found throughout the ancient world. In Egypt they were known as Isis and Osiris, in Greece as Persephone and Dionysus,[55] in Syria as Aphrodite and Adonis, in Asia Minor as Cybele and Attis, in Mesopotamia as Ishtar and Marduk, in Persia as the Magna Mater and Mithras, in the area around Judaea as Asherah and Baal.[56] The Pagan Gnostics were aware that all these different Goddesses and Godmen were essentially two universal mythic archetypes. They sometimes used the general name 'Great Mother' to denote the Goddess and 'Osiris-Dionysus' to denote the Godman.[57]

The myths of the Pagan Godman describe a 'Son of God', born to a virgin on 25 December, who dies at Easter through crucifixion, but who resurrects on the third day. He is a prophet who offers his followers the chance to be born again through the rites of baptism. He is a wonderworker who raises the dead and miraculously turns water into wine at a marriage ceremony. He is a saviour who offers his followers redemption through partaking in a meal of bread and wine, symbolic of his body and blood. These and many more mythic motifs, as we explore in detail in *The Jesus Mysteries*, were incorporated by the original Christians into their myth of Jesus.

The Therapeutae, whom Philo describes as 'like those initiated into the Mysteries of Dionysus', were based in Egypt not far from a lake where there had been major celebrations of the Mysteries of the Egyptian Godman Osiris for centuries.[58] The Essenes were based in Judaea, near the place where Jesus ben Nun was said to have crossed into the Promised Land.[59] From these mythically charged sacred sites, Jewish Gnostics combined the *Exodus* initiation myth of the Jewish Christ Moses-Jesus and the initiation myths of the Pagan Godman Osiris-Dionysus to create a unique synthesis we know as the gospel story of Jesus Christ.

These two sources are made explicit in the two incompatible accounts of Jesus' birth.[60] On the one hand we are given long genealogies tracing the ancestors of his father Joseph to show that Jesus is born in the line of King David, as the Jewish Christ/King was expected to be. Yet on the other hand we are told that actually Jesus' father is God and his mother a virgin, motifs taken from the Osiris-Dionysus myth. By placing these contradictory accounts side by side, the gospel writers made clear, for 'those with ears to hear', the dual mythic identity of Jesus.

By combining the Jewish Messiah with the Pagan Godman, Jewish Gnostics must have felt they were creating the ultimate mystical superhero. They were also, as is characteristic of Gnostics, openly challenging their own Literalist tradition. Jewish Literalists were anxiously awaiting an historical Messiah, who was expected to be a warrior king sent by their tribal deity Jehovah to free them from domination by the Romans. By syncretizing the figure of the Jewish Messiah with the Pagan dying and resurrecting Godman, Jewish Gnostics were not only making Pagan wisdom more readily available to Jews but were also presenting Jews with an entirely different vision of their Messiah.

The Gnostic Jesus does not come to bring political salvation, but mystical enlightenment. He does not lead victorious armies, but dies as a common criminal, which to Jewish Literalists was offensive heresy. Like the Gnostics themselves, he is a free-thinker who breaks the rules, embraces society's outsiders and ridicules the ecclesiastical authorities for their ignorance. By creating and popularizing the Jesus myth, Jewish Gnostics were doing what Gnostics always do – they were confronting the status quo and presenting their own radically alternative vision of life as a journey towards Gnosis.

The Saviour King

At the heart of the perennial philosophy of Gnosticism is a simple but powerful idea, the implications of which we will be exploring throughout this book. It is the idea of God as a Big Mind which contains the cosmos and which is becoming conscious of itself through all conscious beings within the cosmos. The purpose of Gnostic initiation is to awaken in us a recognition of this our shared divine essence.

The Pagan Gnostics mythically represented the idea of the one Consciousness of God that is conscious in all by the image of the 'King'.[61] Plotinus, for example, writes:

'Consciousness is the King. And we are also the King when we are transformed into the King.'[62]

Based on this Pagan image the original Christians created the image of the 'Christ' which, as we discussed previously, is equivalent in meaning to 'King'. Paul describes Christ as 'the consciousness of God'[63] and teaches that we are all Christ's body.[64] When we are 'baptized into union with him' through Gnostic initiation, 'there is no such thing as Jew and Greek, slave and freeman, male and female; for we are all one in Christ Jesus'.

If we replace the word 'King' in the previous passage from Plotinus with the Jewish synonym 'Christ', we can see just how similar Pagan and Christian teachings are:

'Consciousness is the Christ. And we are also Christ when we are transformed into the Christ.'

Pagan and Christian Gnostics imagined the initiatory journey to be about awakening the King within. In the Pagan Mysteries, the initiate was 'enthroned' as a king as part of the initiation ceremonies.[65] Pagan Gnostics of the Cynic school called the realized initiate a 'King' in the 'Kingdom of God'.[66] Likewise, Christian Gnostics taught that when we realize Gnosis we will become 'self-ruled' kings in the Kingdom of God and 'reign over the All'. They imagined the triumphant Christian initiate crowned with a halo of light, declaring: 'The light has become a crown on my head.'[67]

The Evolving Jesus Myth

The Jesus story as we now know it was not created all at once, or by only one person. Nobody sat down surrounded by big piles of books containing Jewish and Pagan myths and proceeded to 'cut and paste' the new myth of the Saviour King together. Rather, it developed bit by bit, as different Gnostics added new motifs and refined old ones, fashioning a progressively more complex allegory in the form of an ever more colourful and emotive story. Later the Jesus story fell into the hands of those with a more political agenda and became distorted and confused, but the underlying initiation allegory which is its foundation remains.

The earliest Christian texts we possess are the genuine letters of Paul written in the first half of the first century. Paul quotes older hymns to Christ, which suggests that he is developing a Joshua/Jesus cult that may have already been in existence, perhaps for centuries. Unlike the New Testament gospels, written some 50–100 years later, Paul does not teach a quasi-historical narrative about Jesus. Paul's Jesus is a clearly mythical figure who does not inhabit any particular time or place. Paul never quotes Jesus and does not portray him as a recently deceased Jewish master.[68] Indeed, he doesn't treat him as someone who had actually lived at all.[69] He writes, '*If* Jesus had been on Earth, he wouldn't have been a priest,' not, '*When* Jesus was on Earth, he wasn't a priest.'[70]

When Paul reveals to us 'the secret' of Christianity, it has absolutely nothing to do with an historical Jesus. The secret he declares is the mystical revelation of 'Christ in you' – the one Consciousness of God in all of us.[71] His Jesus is a mythic figure whose story teaches initiates the path they must follow to realize the Christ within. The only narrative elements of the Jesus myth important to Paul are Christ's baptism, death and resurrection, which he understands as symbolizing the stages of initiation. By identifying with Jesus' baptism initiates are washed clean of their past and begin the quest for Gnosis. By vicariously sharing in Jesus' death and resurrection, they symbolically die to their 'old self' and resurrect 'in Christ'.[72]

In the writings of Paul, then, we find the basic Jesus myth as a three-stage initiation allegory, adapted from the three-stage initiation structure of the *Exodus* Moses–Jesus myth: baptism (crossing Red Sea), the death of Jesus (death of Moses), resurrection (Jesus arrives in the Promised Land). Later Christians will expand this simple allegorical foundation to create the complete Jesus story.

Christian gospels began to be written down at around the end of the first century and the beginning of the second century. These include *The Sophia of Jesus Christ, The Dialogue of the Saviour, The Gospel of Thomas, The Shepherd of Hermas, The Exegesis of the Soul, The Hypostasis of the Archons, The Apocryphon of John, The Secret Gospel of Mark* and *Pistis Sophia,*[73] all now rejected as heretical by the Roman Church.

It is currently accepted amongst most scholars that also written at this time were the anonymous gospels that were later attributed to Matthew, Mark, Luke and John, which turn Paul's timeless Christ myth into a pseudo-historical drama.[74] The evidence for dating these gospels so early, however, is very flimsy. Once we have jettisoned the untenable idea of these texts being eye-witness reports, it seems likely that future scholarship will date them later and later into the second century – and even then with no certainty as to just how similar the gospels of that time were to the versions with which we are familiar today.[75]

The Gospel of Mark is thought to be the earliest of the New Testament gospels, but scholars have shown it to have been created from pre-existing fragments which contain sayings and a non-time/place specific Jesus story to which someone has added a geographical and historical context.[76]

Matthew and Luke based their versions of the Jesus myth on *Mark*, copying sections of it right down to the same Greek particles,[77] while *The Gospel of John* presents a significantly different version of the myth. All of the New Testament gospels contradict each other in many important details.[78] This is because the Gnostics saw their scriptures as initiation allegories and so had no compunction about adapting them to suit their own particular requirements.

The Pagans had for centuries expressed their myths in the form of plays. The Jews had no dramatic tradition, but did write the first Greek historical novel – an allegorical story which portrays Judaism as a Mystery religion.[79] It should not surprise us, therefore, that some 200 years later the Jesus allegory, the central myth of the Christian Mystery cult, was likewise written in the form of a quasi-historical novel.[80]

Historical myths were the Jews' speciality. The *Exodus* initiation allegory, which also appears to have no basis in actual history, is written in the form of a pseudo-historical narrative.[81] When Jewish Gnostics developed their new myth of Jesus the Jewish dying and resurrecting Godman, it was inevitable they would eventually also set this allegory in an historical context. As with the *Exodus* myth, the creators of the Jesus story mixed together mythical figures, such as Jesus and Mary, with a handful of historical figures which were also used to play symbolic roles in the initiation allegory. Unlike *Exodus*, the new Jesus myth could not be set in archaic times, because it was portrayed as a revelation of a new Messiah. It was set, therefore, in the recent past and incorporated figures who were important to Jewish Gnostics, such as the much revered John the Baptist and the much hated Pontius Pilate, the Roman ruler of Judaea.

At the end of the first century CE, when the original Christians were casting the Jesus myth in an historical setting, Israel was in deep crisis. Jews needed an explanation for the terrible events which were befalling them. In 70 CE the Jerusalem Temple, the very heart of Jewish Literalism, had been torn down by the Romans. By 135 CE the whole of Israel would be laid waste and cease to exist for 2,000 years. Jewish Gnostics deliberately set the Jesus story in the years in which the crisis began.

It was precisely at the time that Jesus was portrayed as being born that Rome imposed direct taxation on Judaea, forever ending its independence,[82] and Pilate signalled the irrelevance of Jewish culture by desecrating the Temple in Jerusalem.[83] It was a defining moment in Jewish history, which reached its terrible crescendo in the holocaust of 70 CE. In Israel and the

Diaspora, the first century felt like the 'end days', as indeed it was for the Jews as a sovereign nation. The original Christians therefore really had no choice about when they set their Jesus myth. If the Messiah didn't come at this time, when he was most needed, he just couldn't be the Messiah.

The original Christians portrayed their Gnostic hero Jesus as a harbinger of these turbulent times who came to offer mystical liberation as an alternative to the futile attempts at political liberation which, in retrospect, the Jews could see had destroyed them completely. The Gnostic Messiah Jesus offered defeated and dejected Jews meaning and new hope.

THE CHRISTIAN GODDESS

The myth of the Godman Jesus can only be properly understood alongside the myth of the Goddess Sophia. After so many centuries of patriarchal Christianity it is both shocking and reassuring to discover a Goddess at the very heart of Christianity. She is, like her son/brother/lover Jesus, a syncretic figure created from both Pagan and Jewish sources.

Sophia, whose name means 'wisdom', had been the Goddess of the Pagan philosophers for centuries. Indeed, the word 'philosopher', first used by Pythagoras, means 'lover of Sophia'.[84] Although often pictured today as dry academics, these brilliant intellectuals were actually mystics and devotees of the Goddess. Parmenides, for example, is usually remembered as the founder of Western logic, yet his masterwork is a visionary poem in which he descends to the underworld to be instructed by the Goddess.[85]

Sophia was also an important mythical figure for Jewish Gnostics, such as Philo.[86] Although later rejected by Jewish Literalists, there had always been a Jewish Goddess tradition.[87] At one time Israelites had worshipped the Goddess Asherah as the consort of the Jewish God Jehovah.[88] In the fifth century BCE she was known as Anat Jahu.[89] In texts written between the fourth and first centuries BCE, such as *Proverbs*, *The Sophia of Solomon* and *The Sophia of Jesus the Son of Sirach*, she becomes God's companion and co-creator Sophia.[90]

The Jewish Sophia is the lover and inspiration of the good and the wise. She is 'an initiate in the Mysteries of God's Gnosis' who teaches her followers to become 'friends of God' – the ubiquitous name used by Pagan, Jewish and Christian Gnostics.[91] *The Sophia of Solomon* assures us:

'Sophia shines brightly and never fades. She is readily discerned by those who love her, and by those who seek her she is found. She is quick to make herself known to all who desire her Gnosis.'[92]

The Sophia literature talks of a 'Good Man' – no one in particular – who is the Goddess' envoy on Earth.[93] Moses was pictured as such an envoy. According to the *Exodus* myth, when he passes on his authority to Jesus ben Nun, Jesus also receives 'the Spirit of Sophia'.[94] For the Christian Gnostics, their Jesus is likewise Sophia's envoy, coming to reveal her wisdom which leads to Gnosis. Hence 'the secret' that Paul proclaims is 'Christ in whom is hid the treasures of Sophia and Gnosis'.[95]

In the Sophia literature the Good Man is persecuted by his own people for preaching Sophia's wisdom and condemned to a 'shameful death'. But he is vindicated afterwards and confronts his persecutors as their judge in Heaven, where he is one of the 'Sons of God'.[96] In the hands of Christian Gnostics this Good Man is transformed into Jesus the 'Son of God', who comes, according to the original Christians, 'so that Sophia might be proclaimed'[97] and is murdered by his misguided kinsmen, but is vindicated by his resurrection and ascension to Heaven, where he becomes the divine judge.

As well as basing their version of the Jesus myth on the *Gospel of Mark*, the authors of *Matthew* and *Luke* drew on a now lost gospel, which scholars call Q. *The Gospel of Q* portrays both Jesus and John the Baptist as messengers sent by Sophia.[98] It contains sayings attributed to Sophia, which in the gospels are put into the mouth of her envoy Jesus.[99] Most of these sayings are not Jewish in character, but heavily influenced by the Cynic school of Pagan philosophy.[100] In *The Gospel of Luke* one of these sayings remains attributed to Sophia herself. Referring directly to the myth of Sophia and the Good Man, and so insinuating that he is Sophia's representative on Earth, Jesus attributes to Sophia the pronouncement 'I will send them prophets and messengers and some of these they will persecute and kill.'[101]

Philo describes Sophia as the 'mother of the *Logos*'.[102] The *Logos* is a Pagan philosophical concept with many meanings. For Philo, the *Logos* is the Guide on the path which leads to Sophia and her Gnosis.[103] Philo describes Moses as embodying the *Logos* and as a child of Sophia.[104] Later Christian Gnostics describe their Jesus in the same way. In the Christian Gnostic *Acts of John* Jesus announces: 'In me know the *Logos* of Sophia.'[105]

The concept of the *Logos*, usually translated by the misleading term 'Word', is most familiar from the opening lines of *The Gospel of John*, in which Jesus is described as an embodiment of the *Logos*. This passage, written in the form of an antiphonal hymn, is clearly a quotation from an older work.[106] Everything it says of Jesus the envoy of Sophia had already been said of the Goddess herself in the Sophia literature.[107]

Philo was based in Alexandria in Egypt, the cultural centre of the ancient world and an eclectic melting-pot of different spiritual traditions. Here, taking as his mythological models the Pagan figures of Osiris-Dionysus and the Great Mother, this Jewish Gnostic created his own mythic figures of the Logos and Sophia.[108] A little later these same figures would appear as Jesus and Sophia, the central figures of the myths taught by thriving schools of Christian Gnosticism operating throughout the Mediterranean.

SCHOOLS OF CHRISTIAN GNOSTICISM

By the first half of the first century there were already three distinct schools of Christian Gnosticism, which suggests, once again, that in some form or another Christianity had been in existence for some time. These schools are the Simonians, Paulists and Ebionites. The issue which divided them was the relationship of Christianity to traditional Jewish religion.[109] The Simonians were radical internationalists who rejected Judaism and its tribal deity Jehovah as redundant Literalist nonsense. The Paulists were also internationalists who wanted to free Christianity from close ties with Judaism, but took a more moderate view, seeing Christianity as fulfilling and therefore surpassing Judaism. The Ebionites were nationalists who saw Christianity as a specifically Jewish cult and wanted Christians to conform to traditional Jewish religious customs.

These schools can be considered as different wings of early Christianity. The Simonians were the left-wing revolutionaries who wanted to overthrow Jewish Literalism. The conservative Ebionites saw Christianity as a movement of reform within Judaism. The Paulists, in the centre, considered Judaism to be superseded by Christianity and therefore obsolete.

None of these Christians were practising Christianity as we would recognize it today. Christian Literalism, from which nearly all forms of modern Christianity have evolved, didn't begin to appear until the middle of the second century.

Simonians

The man vilified by later Christian Literalists as the 'father' of Christian Gnosticism was an early first-century Samaritan known as Simon the Magus.[110] Because we have inherited a version of the Jesus myth in which the hero dies in Jerusalem, we assume that Christianity was originally an exclusively Jewish cult. Actually, many early Christians, such as Simon, were Samaritans and there is no evidence to suggest that they set their Christ myth in a Jewish setting. Today only a small number of Samaritans survive, but at the time they far outnumbered the Jews.[111] Samaria had its own distinct religious traditions, also based on the Books of Moses, which rivalled the Jewish Temple cult based in Jerusalem.[112] Writing in the middle of the second century, Justin Martyr, who was himself a Samaritan, tells us that Simon was 'regarded with great reverence by nearly all Samaritans'.[113] This is an amazing testimony to Simon's influence from a source which is nothing but hostile to him.

Simon is said to have been the most outstanding disciple of John the Baptist. The story goes that when John died Simon was in Alexandria, where he had received a Greek education, so another Samaritan Gnostic, Dositheus, became John's successor.[114] When Simon returned home, however, he became the acknowledged master. John, Simon and Dositheus were probably linked to the Essenes, either as envoys or founders of a breakaway school. John teaches in the wilderness, close to where the Essenes were based. Dositheus is said to have come from the same area. Essene teachings show the influence of Persian Zoroastrianism, which would explain why Simon was called 'Magus', a Zoroastrian term for a sage.[115]

Simon was also known as 'Faustus' or 'Honoured One'[116] and described himself as a 'Christ'.[117] His followers regarded him as an embodiment of the 'Great Power', the male aspect of the Mystery of God.[118] He travelled with a spiritual partner called Helen who was seen as an embodiment of the Goddess.[119]

Many important later Christian Gnostics are part of Simon's lineage, including the first-century Samaritan master Menander, the second-century Alexandrian masters Carpocrates, Epiphanes and Basilides, the Syrian master Cerdo, who taught in Rome, and Saturninus of Antioch. The Christian Literalist Irenaeus complains that 'from Simon a multitude of Barbeloites has arisen'.[120] These Gnostics developed myths in which the Goddess, called by them 'Barbelo', was prominent.[121]

The Simonians were enthusiastic eclectics who sought out Gnostic wisdom wherever they could find it. The Literalist Hippolytus tells us that Simon interpreted the words of Moses and the Pagan poets.[122] His followers continued this tradition of open mindedness. Basilides even wrote a book on Hinduism. They had no time for nationalistic Jewish Literalism, whose complex religious rules and regulations they regarded as unnecessary mumbo-jumbo. Faith and love were the only pre-requisites to being saved through the experience of Gnosis.[123]

Simonians waged war on the Jewish Literalists' anthropomorphic image of God as the jealous and despotic tribal deity Jehovah, requiring their initiates to ritually declare their rejection of this false god.[124] These Jewish Gnostics opposed the Jewish Literalists' personification of God for the same reason that Pagan Gnostics mocked the personified gods of Pagan Literalists. For Gnostics, God is the Great Mystery which is the source and essence of all that is. Any idea of God is just that – an *idea*. Confusing the idea of God with the true ineffable nature of the Mystery is idolatry. The image is mistaken for the essence. To Simonians, the Literalist interpretation of the Old Testament portrays the Mystery of God as a Jewish monarch, which is ridiculous nationalist nonsense. Cerdo asserts:

> 'The God proclaimed by the law and the prophets is not the Father of our Lord Jesus Christ. The God of the Old Testament is known, but the Father of Jesus Christ is the Unknowable.'[125]

Paulists

Of all early Christians, Paul was the most revered by later Gnostics. He was the primary inspiration for two of the most influential schools of Christian Gnosticism, set up by the early second-century masters Marcion and Valentinus. Christian Gnostics calling themselves 'Paulicians' ran the 'seven churches' in Greece and Asia Minor that were established by Paul, their 'mother Church' being at Corinth.[126] The Paulicians survived until the tenth century and were the inspiration for the later Bogomils and Cathars.[127]

Marcion was originally a student of the Simonian Gnostic Cerdo, but when he set up his own highly successful school it was Paul he placed centre-stage as the 'Great Messenger'. Even his later Literalist critics acknowledged that Marcion was 'a veritable sage' and that his influence was considerable.[128]

Valentinus tells us he received the secret teachings of Christianity from his master Theudas, who had in turn received them from Paul.[129] Based on these teachings, Valentinus founded his own influential school of Christian Gnosticism, which survived as a loose alliance of individual teachers until it was forcibly closed down in the fifth century by the Literalist Roman Church.[130] The number of second and third-century Valentinians that we can still name is testimony to Valentinus' importance: Alexander, Ambrose, Axionicus, Candidus, Flora, Heracleon, Mark, Ptolemy, Secundus, Theodotus and Theotimus.[131]

Paul was such an important figure in the Christian community that at the end of the second century the newly emerging school of Christian Literalism could not simply reject him as a misguided heretic but felt compelled to reshape him into a Literalist.[132] They forged in his name the (now thoroughly discredited) 'Pastoral Letters', in which Paul is made to spout anti-Gnostic propaganda.[133] Throughout his genuine letters, however, Paul uses characteristically Gnostic language and gives Gnostic teachings, a fact that is deliberately obscured by Literalist translators.

Like later Christian Gnostics, Paul addresses his teachings to two levels of Christian initiates, called *psychics* and *pneumatics*, describing the latter as 'having Gnosis'.[134] Of himself he writes, 'I may not be much of a speaker, but I have Gnosis.'[135] He sees his mission as awakening in initiates an awareness of 'the Christ within' – the one 'consciousness of God' – by 'instructing all without distinction in the ways of Sophia, so as to make each one an initiated member of Christ's body'.[136]

Paul tells us that when he personally experienced Christ it was as a vision of light on the road to Damascus.[137] 'Damascus' was a code word used by the Essenes to refer to their base in Qumran, which suggests that Paul, like Simon, had Essene affiliations.[138] He uses the same language as the Essenes, for example when he describes human beings as being enslaved by the powers of fate, imagined as 'the elemental rulers of the cosmos',[139] the '*archons* of this dark cosmos',[140] from which 'Christ has set us free'.[141]

Paul, like Simon, was an internationalist who wanted to liberate Christianity from any baggage it had inherited from Jewish Literalism. He writes dismissively of the traditional Jewish Law:

'I count it as so much dung. All I care about is knowing Christ, experiencing the power of the resurrection, sharing his sufferings, in growing conformity with his death, so that I may finally arrive at the resurrection from the dead.'[142]

Again like Simon, Paul is adamant that the true God is the ineffable Oneness, not the national Jewish deity:

'Do you suppose God is the God of the Jews alone? Is he not the God of the Gentiles also? Certainly of the Gentiles also, if it be true that God is the One.'[143]

For Paul, Jewish Literalism divides Jews from Gentiles. It is a 'curse' which could be healed by the syncretic figure of the Jewish Messiah/Pagan Godman Jesus.[144] He explains that Jesus 'has broken down the enmity that stood like a dividing wall' between 'Gentiles and Jew', creating 'out of the two a single humanity in himself, thereby making peace. This was his purpose, to reconcile the two in the Oneness of God.'[145]

However, although Paul wants to dump Judaism, he doesn't completely condemn it, as Simon did. He accepts that it is appropriate for those Jews who wish to maintain their indigenous traditions, but maintains that it is irrelevant to Gentiles and Jewish initiates who wish to leave the old ways behind. For Paul, Jesus *fulfils* the laws and the prophets, precisely because he takes us beyond them.

Of Paul's later followers, the Valentinians maintained this more liberal approach. Marcion, however, amplified Paul's criticism of Judaism. He wrote a famous treatise called *Contradictions*, setting out all the differences between the God of the New Testament and the God of the Old Testament. As a way of distancing Jesus from the figure of the Jewish Messiah, Marcionites, and others with a similar perspective, claimed to follow 'Jesus Chrestos' (Jesus the Good) rather than 'Jesus Christus' (Jesus the Messiah).[146] From as early as the middle of the first century through to the fifth century we hear of those calling themselves 'Chrestians' rather than 'Christians'.[147]

Ebionites

The other school of early first-century Christian Gnosticism was the Ebionites or 'Poor Ones'. They were based in Jerusalem, where Paul says he visited them. Ebionites wanted Christian Gnosticism to retain its ties with traditional Jewish religion. They emphasized that Christianity was for Jews and that if Gentiles wanted to embrace it they would have to undergo circumcision and keep all the Laws of Moses.

Paul vehemently attacks Ebionite leaders, calling them 'evil' and 'dogs'. He complains that they 'proclaim a different Jesus' from himself.[148] He ridicules them for arrogantly regarding themselves as 'super-messengers' because of their Jewishness, dismissing them as 'axe-wielding circumcisionaries' who might as well 'go the whole way and make eunuchs of themselves!'[149] Ebonite letters, attributed to Clement of Rome, retaliate with similar ferocity, attacking Paul as inspired by Satan.[150]

Paul's internationalist Christianity flourished amongst Gentiles, but was largely unacceptable to Jews. He reports that only four Jewish Christians worked with him and that he was often attacked by Jews for preaching his heretical vision of the mystical Messiah Jesus.[151] Ebionite Gnosticism, on the other hand, due to its ties with Judaism and insistence on circumcision, made little impact beyond the Jewish community, although it did survive for hundreds of years and influenced the creation of Islam (see Appendix II: 'Gnostic Islam').[152]

The real importance of the Ebionites is not who they were, but the fantasies which were later created about them. Because they were based in Jerusalem, later Christian Literalists claimed that they were the original disciples of the historical Jesus. However, in the second century, when the Christian Literalist Melito of Sardis went to Jerusalem hoping to find the descendants of the original disciples, he found only Ebionite Gnostics, whose Christianity was inspired by 'heretical' scriptures such as The Gospel of the Ebionites, The Gospel of the Hebrews, The Gospel of the Twelve Apostles and The Gospel of the Nazarenes.[153]

Paul happens to mention the names of some Ebionites in his letters. He refers to a particularly conservative leader called James as a 'brother of the Lord'.[154] Later Literalists took this literally and became convinced that not only was there an historical Jesus, but that Paul knew his brother. Actually the title 'brother of the Lord' was used by Christian Gnostics to refer to each other and is not specific to James.[155] The Gnostic Apocalypse of James categorically tells us that James was not literally Jesus' sibling.[156]

Paul also mentions a Cephas. Because the Hebrew name 'Cephas' means the same as the Greek name 'Peter', Literalists assume Paul to be talking about the Simon Peter of the gospels, but actually at the time that Paul was writing, the gospel story as we know it had not been created. Christ was a mystical, timeless figure, not yet the hero of a historical romance set in Judaea, and the character of Simon Peter had yet to be invented. Paul is definitely not writing about the Peter of the gospels. He is extremely critical of the Cephas he mentions, to an extent that would not be credible if he were talking about the historical Jesus' right-hand man – especially when Paul had never met Jesus himself. Paul never mentions any of the gospel events to do with Simon Peter or the times that Jesus is portrayed as being hostile to Simon Peter, even when simply mentioning one of these criticisms would clearly clinch his argument with Cephas.[157]

Free Spirits

What sort of people were the original Christians? Much of what we know of them is recorded by later Christian Literalists. From their critical testimony it seems that, apart from more conservative groups such as the Ebionites, they were characteristically eclectic, egalitarian, rebellious free spirits with a wickedly irreverent sense of humour.

Their attacks on the 'sacred cows' of Jewish Literalism are deliberately provocative. Some schools rework Jewish mythology, recasting all the goodies as baddies and the baddies as goodies. Traditional biblical villains, such as Cain, Esau and the Sodomites, become fearless heroes for standing up to the oppressive Jehovah.[158] The evil snake in the traditional reading of the *Genesis* myth becomes the 'Serpent of Light', an embodiment of Jesus, who encourages Adam and Eve to eat of the Tree of Gnosis.[159] Poking fun at sanctimonious Literalists, Marcion writes:

> 'When Jesus descended into Hell, the sinners listened to his words and were all saved. But the saints, believing as usual that they were being put to the test, rejected his words and were all damned.'[160]

Other Christian Gnostics took a less combative approach, which Christian Literalists found even more infuriating. They viewed the Literalist understanding as a stage that initiates sometimes needed to pass through on the path to Gnosis and, as Gnosis itself could never be expressed in words anyway, saw no problem in simply going along with whatever Literalists said. The Literalist Irenaeus complains that it is impossible to argue with such people because they keep on agreeing with him, although he is sure that in secret they believe something else entirely.[161] When Literalists asked initiates of the Messalian school of Christianity if they believed one thing or another, they would always answer 'Yes', whatever the question. The Literalist Epiphanius records with dismay the following conversation: 'Are you Patriarchs?' 'Yes.' 'Are you Prophets?' 'Yes.' 'Are you angels?' 'Yes.' 'Are you Jesus Christ?' 'Yes.'[162] If nothing else, you have to admire their sense of fun!

Eclectics

Christian Gnostics were enthusiastic eclectics. The Naassene school taught that there was one spiritual system underlying the mythology of all religions.[163] These Christian initiates were also initiated into the Pagan Mysteries of the Great Mother.[164] They praised the great Pagan poet Homer as their prophet and equated their Jewish Godman Jesus with the various mythical faces of the Pagan Godman – Osiris, Attis, Adonis, Pan, Bacchus, and so on. For them the Son of God was 'many-named' and known by different cultures in different ways.[165]

The Sethian school of Christianity practised an adaptation of the Pagan Mysteries of Orpheus.[166] When the Roman emperor Hadrian visited Alexandria in the first half of the second century, he encountered Christians who practised the local Pagan Mysteries of the Godman Serapis and who studied Pythagorean mathematics and astrology.[167] When the Valentinian teacher Marcellina came to Rome, she brought with her 'painted icons, illuminated with gold, representing Jesus, Pythagoras, Plato and Aristotle'.[168] The Literalist Hippolytus wrote that 'whatever variations there may be between the systems of the Simonian and Valentinian Gnostics and that of Pythagoras 'was in name only'.[169]

Alongside the Christian gospels discovered at Nag Hammadi were found works by Plato and works attributed to the mythical ancient Egyptian sage Hermes Trismegistus.[170] The Pagan master Plotinus, who taught in Rome in the middle of the third century, treats Christianity as a rival school of philosophy which, like his own, had developed from the teachings of Plato.[171] Much to his consternation, members of his own school were also initiates of Christian schools. Plotinus writes of 'some of our own friends who fell in with this doctrine before joining our circle and, strangely, still cling to it'.[172]

The closeness of Christian and Platonic Gnosticism is also obvious from the fact that the influential Christian Gnostic Origen and the great Pagan Gnostic Plotinus were both pupils of the Platonist Ammonius in Alexandria.[173] Indeed, if Christian Gnosticism had triumphed instead of Christian Literalism, the Christian 'Old Testament' (as it were), would probably have been the works of Plato, instead of the largely banal Jewish texts we have actually inherited as holy scripture.

Gnostics are eclectics because they understand different spiritual traditions as using different conceptual languages to point us beyond words altogether to the realization of Gnosis. All philosophical ideas are relatively true or false expressions of the Absolute Truth, which is by its nature inexpressible. If we become fixated with the words, as Literalists do, we mistake the message for the meaning and end up eating the menu, not the meal. *The Gospel of Philip* cautions us:

'Names are very deceptive because they turn the heart aside from the real to the unreal. Whoever hears the word "God" doesn't think of the reality, but of what is unreal. Likewise with words such as "Father", "Son", "Holy Spirit", "life", "light", "resurrection", "church", and so on.'[174]

Egalitarians

Following in the tradition of Pagan philosophers such as Antiphon, Epicurus, Diogenes and Zeno, Christian Gnostics were political radicals who preached liberty, equality and fraternity centuries before the French Revolution.[175] Epiphanes, the son of Gnostic master Carpocrates, although he died at the young age of 17, wrote an extraordinary treatise called *On Justice*, in which he condemned property and social authority and declared that all have divinely ordained rights, whether they be free or slaves. 'Where does Justice lie?' he asks. 'In a community of equals,' he answers. He proposes a mystical anarchism which urges us to discover the natural goodness within ourselves and live according to our own essential nature. Being constrained by unnatural man-made laws stops us living in communion with the divine Laws of Life.[176] Anticipating Proudhon's slogan 'Property is theft', he argues:

'When man forgot that community means equality and deformed it by laws, on that day, the thief was born.'[177]

Creating visions of social utopias has always been a part of the Gnostic tradition.[178] Gnostics are 'Idealists' both in the philosophical and political sense of the word. Pythagoreans lived in egalitarian communities, in which property was held in common and women were treated as equal, which inspired the first Christian monasteries.[179] The Stoic school of Pagan Gnosticism developed the idea of the *'Politea* of Zeus' or 'Commonwealth of God', a community of equals living naturally in harmony with the divine order of things.[180] Christian Gnostics from Paul onwards also talk of the 'Commonwealth of God' and the 'Kingdom of God' as an ideal state to which we should aspire.[181]

Christian Gnostics followed the dictates of their own hearts and rejected any external authority. They called themselves 'a generation which knows no tyranny' and 'a kingless generation', addressing each other as 'brother' or 'sister'.[182] They did not develop a fixed ecclesiastical hierarchy, like the Literalists, but cast lots to select who would take leadership roles, such as priest, overseer, reader, and so on.[183] This prevented power from being consolidated in the hands of any one person, as happened later in the Literalist Roman Church, with disastrous consequences.[184]

Much to the horror of misogynistic Christian Literalists, Christian Gnostics dared to treat women as equal to men. Epiphanes writes:

> 'The Father of All gave us eyes to see with, and his only law is justice, without distinction between man and woman.'[185]

Pagan Pythagorean Gnostics were also famous for treating women as equals.[186] In the Jewish Therapeutae school of Pythagoreanism, women were particularly honoured for their 'love of Sophia'[187] and Christian Gnostics continued this tradition. Some schools were named after women, such as Helen, Salome, Mary, Marcellina and Martha. In fact the Pagan philosopher Celsus, writing about Christianity c.170 CE, only knows of gospels written by women or sects named after women![188]

The Literalist Irenaeus regrets that women were particularly attracted to Gnostic Christianity and is appalled that the Gnostic sage Marcus encouraged women to become priestesses and officiate at the Eucharist celebration.[189] The bigoted Tertullian is enraged that women Gnostics dare to 'teach and engage in discussion' and horrified at the idea of them baptizing and acting as bishops.[190]

Paul tells us it was the accepted practice for male Christian Gnostics to travel with a female spiritual partner, whom he calls a 'sister-wife'.[191] Paul himself travelled with a woman called Thecla[192] and he mentions other women – Prisca, Junia, Julia and Nerueus' sister – who worked and travelled in missionary pairs with their 'husband-brothers'.[193] Other man/woman Gnostic teams we know of include Simon and Helen, Dositheus and Helen,[194] Apelles and Philumene,[195] and Zosimos and Theosebeia.[196] The Gnostic sage Montanus, who was renowned for his following of ecstatic women, travelled with two women, Priscilla and Maximilla.[197]

Libertines

Gnostics deliberately violated social norms as a way of deconditioning themselves from their social personae and so becoming aware of their true spiritual identity.[198] For some, such as the Cainite school, this was done through ascetic abstinence. For others, such as the Carpocratian school, this was done through libertine indulgence. Sometimes both of these approaches were adopted by different individuals within the same school.[199]

Carpocrates taught that our ideas of good and bad conduct are only matters of human opinion, not divine decree. He taught his students to enjoy life, including the pleasures of sex that are so often condemned by religious Literalists. His son Epiphanes writes:

'God created the delights of love equally for all humankind. But men have repudiated the very thing which is the source of their existence.'[200]

Such Gnostics saw sexuality as a celebration of the union of God and Goddess, from which all of life springs.[201] They are said to have sometimes practised sacramental nudity in church and even ritual intercourse.[202] The Literalist Epiphanius describes his experience as a young man of 20, meeting two pretty young Gnostic women who invited him to one of their *agapes* or love feasts, which turned out to be an orgy.[203] With the horror characteristic of the deeply repressed, Epiphanius is outraged that these Gnostics believed that they 'must ceaselessly apply themselves to the mystery of sexual union'.[204]

These allegations, which may well be exaggerated, have led to Gnostics being portrayed as completely immoral. Carpocrates was accused of promoting the idea that we should deliberately commit as many 'sins' as possible.[205] Paul complains of such a misrepresentation of Gnostic doctrine even in the first century. Probably referring to the conservative Ebionites, he writes, 'Some libellously report me as saying, "Do evil so that good may come of it."'[206] Actually liberal Gnostics are teaching that moral laws are unnecessary social conventions, because we are actually good by nature.[207] Someone who, through the experience of Gnosis, has discovered their true identity, can live a spontaneous and natural life motivated by the good within them. For conservative Literalists, then as now, such teachings are irresponsible and depraved.

Rejecting the Gnostic idea of 'original goodness', Literalists preached the absolute opposite – the pernicious doctrine of 'original sin'. The

Literalist Timothy writes with disgust about the shameless naturalness of the Christian Gnostics:

'They eat whenever they are hungry. They drink when they are thirsty, at any hour of the day, without regard for the proscribed fasts. They spend their time doing nothing and sleeping. In summertime, when night falls, they lie down to sleep in the open air, men and women together, and they say that this is of no consequence.'[208]

SUMMARY

❖ The original Christians were Jewish Gnostics who were part of an international Gnostic tradition flourishing across the whole of the Mediterranean. Like all Gnostics, they encoded their mystical teachings in the form of allegorical myths. Out of previous Jewish and Pagan myths they created the Christian myth cycle, of which the Jesus myth is a part.

❖ The original Christians synthesized elements from the Jewish allegorical myth of the Christ Moses-Jesus with Pagan myths of the dying and resurrecting Godman Osiris-Dionysus to create the Jesus myth. In its earliest form, found in the writings of Paul, the Jesus myth is a simple initiation allegory. Paul is not concerned with an historical man, but with the mystical 'Christ in you'. Later the Jesus myth was fleshed out as a more complex allegory in the form of a pseudo-history.

❖ None of the early schools of Christianity resemble the Literalist Christianity with which we are familiar today. The original Christians were characteristically eclectic, egalitarian free spirits who treated women as equals and rejected organized religion.

What happened? How did a disparate group of libertine anarchists end up creating a religion that would come to dominate the world by force? How did an allegorical myth composed by imaginative mystics come to be understood as a literal account of the most important events in history?

chapter three

CHURCH OF THE
Anti-Christ

'That which is called the Christian religion existed among the ancients, and never did not exist, from the beginnings of the human race until Christ came in the flesh, at which time the true religion, which already existed, began to be called Christianity.'

Augustine, *Retractions*[1]

It is a common pattern in the history of spirituality that dissident, non-conformist Gnostics find they have unwittingly inspired an authoritarian Literalist religion.[2] Religions characteristically begin with charismatic masters who share their personal understanding of the Gnosis with small groups of spiritual enthusiasts, teaching the perennial philosophy in their own unique way. Over time the number of students grows, until there are too many for them to all have personal access to the teacher. It becomes impractical to carry on as a disparate band of anarchic mystics and those with a more authoritarian nature start to organize things. Before you know it, a new religion has been born. But the more the student/master ratio becomes unbalanced, the more the general level of understanding diminishes. Subtle allegorical teachings become understood in superficial, literal ways. The trajectory is one of inevitable degeneration from the simple but sophisticated teachings of Gnosticism to the shallow but often complex teachings of Literalism. This is exactly what happened with Christianity.

THE LITERALIST HERESY

Once the Jesus myth had been set in an historical context, it was only a matter of time before a group of Christians began to interpret it as a record of actual events. By the middle of the second century a Literalist school of Christianity had begun to emerge in Rome, with autocrats such as Irenaeus as its spokesmen.[3] The Gnostics' understanding of the Jesus story as an initiation allegory leading to salvation through Gnosis was replaced by the Literalists' idea of salvation through belief in an historical Messiah.[4]

Literalists did not claim Christian teachings to be radically different from Pagan philosophy and were well aware of the similarities between the story of Jesus and the Pagan myths of Osiris-Dionysus. But they had one unique eye-catching selling-point – the other Mystery cults had myths that may or may not have referred to actual events in the archaic past, but Literalist Christians claimed that their myth of the dying and resurrecting Godman had recently been realized in real life. This is Literalist Christianity's one claim to uniqueness, which is made by Augustine, the great spokesman of Christian Literalism. As someone who had been a follower of both the Pagan Gnostic Plotinus and the Christian Gnostic Mani before becoming a Catholic, Augustine knew there was nothing exceptional about Roman Christianity but this one incredible idea: 'Christ came in the flesh.'

Christian Literalism was destined to dominate the West with an iron fist for nearly two millennia, but it began as an insignificant sect with a macabre enthusiasm for the imminent end of the world. The Gnostic myth that Jesus would appear at the culmination of time was an allegory expressing the idea that when all souls were reunited with the Consciousness of God there would be a return to the primordial state of Oneness and the cosmic drama would be over. Literalists took this myth literally, developing the grotesque idea that Jesus was about to arrive to destroy the world, rescue a small group of Christian Literalists and condemn everyone else to eternal torment. Thankfully, they turned out to be wrong.[5]

However, replacing the mythical sacrificed Godman with an historical martyr led to Christian Literalism becoming a sort of 'suicide cult' which, much to the horror of the Gnostics, encouraged its members to imitate Jesus by also seeking out a sacrificial death.[6] In the Literalist version of Christian history the Roman authorities are pictured as singling out the Christians for terrible persecution. Actually they were often appalled at Christian Literalists' eagerness to be martyred.[7]

Literalism replaced the enlightened Gnostic sage at the centre of a small group of initiates with a hierarchy of bishops at the head of an expanding evangelical cult. The whole purpose of Gnostic initiation was to bring initiates to spiritual maturity, where they would experience themselves to be completely free of any external authority and become their own 'Christ' or 'King'.[8] Literalists, by contrast, wanted to enlarge their religious powerbase and worked hard to keep their flock securely in the fold. Despite the fact that in *The Gospel of Luke* Jesus teaches, 'Everyone when his training is complete will reach his teacher's level,'[9] the Gnostic idea that Christianity was about oneself becoming a Christ became branded as blasphemous heresy.

The role of the Gnostic master was to undermine all of an initiate's opinions and encourage them to directly confront the Mystery of Life. The role of the Literalist bishops, on the other hand, was to tell people what to believe and to discipline those who disagreed. Free intellectual inquiry was actively discouraged and blind belief became exalted as a spiritual virtue.[10] As long as the Jesus story was understood as myth, Christians were at liberty to interpret it and change it as they felt appropriate. Once it became seen as a biography, the development of intolerant dogmatism was inevitable. Literalists would argue vehemently for centuries over what Jesus actually did and said, as they still do today. But, as the argument is about supposed historical events, they all agree that there is only one accurate version of what really happened. And if only one version is right, that means everyone else must be wrong.[11]

Forged Lineage

From the large number of Christian scriptures in existence, Literalists selected four gospels to form the canon of the New Testament.[12] These gospels were then declared to be the only authentic gospels and all of the other Christian scriptures were denounced as heretical. The four New

Testament gospels are variations on the Jesus myth originally used by different schools of Christian Gnosticism. Putting them together created the illusion of there being four (albeit contradictory) eye-witness accounts of the same historical events.[13] The later triumph of Literalism has left us with the distorted impression that these gospels were always the most popular Christian scriptures, but this is not true. In fact we don't hear anything about *Matthew, Mark, Luke* and *John* until the late second century![14]

To endorse their authority, Literalist bishops fabricated a lineage connecting themselves back to the fictional disciples of the gospels.[15] They turned Paul from the 'Great Messenger' of the Christian Gnostics into a bastion of Literalism by simply forging letters in his name which make him condemn their Gnostic rivals. It's a simple trick, but it worked.[16] It was not until the last few centuries that scholarship became sophisticated enough to see through it.

Literalists also co-opted to their cause later Christian philosophers, such as the second-century writers Athenagoras of Athens, Theophilus of Antioch and Minucius Felix of Africa. These writers actually promoted a philosophical Christianity based around the mythical figures of the Logos and Sophia.[17] Not only were they not Literalists, they were not even particularly interested in the figure of Jesus. Athenagoras claims to go 'minutely into the particulars' of Christian doctrine, yet never mentions Jesus at all.[18] Neither does Minucius Felix, even when an adversary asks him to name someone who has actually returned from the dead. Instead he gives a list of diabolical beliefs and practices that have been wrongly attributed to Christians. These include (along with drinking the blood of sacrificed children and worshipping the genitals of priests!), 'worshipping a man who suffered death as some criminal as well as a wretched piece of wood'.[19] As he comments:

> 'These and similar indecencies we do not wish to hear. It is disgraceful to have to defend ourselves against such charges. When you attribute to us the worship of a criminal and his cross you wander far from the truth.'[20]

Indeed, Minucius condemns Pagan Literalists who 'choose a man for their worship'[21] and Theophilus ridicules Pagan Literalists for believing that Hercules and Asclepius had actually come back from the dead.[22]

Why did Literalists try and adopt to their cause writers who were so obviously promoting something quite different? Because there are no early

Christian writers who defend the idea of there literally being an historical Jesus. There were no historical disciples. There were no early Literalists. They all had to be invented. The earliest Christian whose writings suggest he was a Literalist was Justin Martyr, c.150.[23] But even Justin still saw Christianity as a branch of philosophy and set up his own philosophical school in Rome.[24] After Justin's death, his pupil Tatian abandoned his master's Literalism, suggesting that it was seen as something of an innovation, and regarded the Jesus story as comparable to Greek myths, urging his Pagan readers:

'Compare your own stories with our narratives. Take a look at your own records and accept us merely on the grounds that we too tell stories.'[25]

International Christian Gnosticism

The traditional history of Christianity is that Literalism took the world by storm, whilst Christian Gnosticism remained a minor heretical fringe movement. This is nonsense. Christian Literalism was initially a minor school of Christianity which developed in Rome towards the end of the second century. By this time Christian Gnosticism was an international movement which had spread throughout much of the Mediterranean, flourishing in cosmopolitan cities such as Alexandria, Edessa, Antioch, Epheseus, and Rome.[26]

In Egypt the first Christians we hear of are the Gnostics Valentinus, Basilides, Apelles, Carpocrates and his son Epiphanes. There is no sign of any form of Christianity which resembles Roman Catholicism in Egypt until Bishop Demetrius at the end of the third century.[27] In Antioch the Gnostics Saturninus, Cerdo and Menander had established schools at the beginning of the second century. The Literalist Justin Martyr regrets that in Edessa, eastern Syria, to be a Christian means to be a follower of Marcion. *The Chronicle of Edessa* notes the birth of Marcion, Bardesanes and Mani before it mentions Roman Christianity. Even Rome itself was full of different schools of Christian Gnosticism, such as the Marcellites, Marcionites, Archonites, Valentinians, Sethians, Barbeloites, Montanists and Ophites.

Literalists complained that in Persia all Christians were members of the Marcionite school of Christian Gnosticism.[28] Tertullian bemoaned the fact that Marcion's followers filled 'the whole universe'.[29] At the beginning of the third century the Christian Gnostic sage Bardesanes initiated into his school a Syrian ruler who made Christian Gnosticism the official state cult.[30] The forged *Second Letter to Timothy* has its phoney Literalist Paul complain, 'All Asia has turned against me,' which tells us that in the late second century 'all Asia' was dominated by Gnostic Christianity. *The Epistle of Polycarp* laments that 'the great majority' of Christians embrace the idea of Jesus not existing in the flesh.[31]

The school of the third-century master Mani became a world religion in his own lifetime.[32] Eventually reaching from Spain in the West to China in the East, Manicheism flourished for 1,000 years.[33] Mani was a great eclectic who synthesized the Gnosticism of different religious traditions in an attempt to create a truly international form of spirituality which would 'embrace all humanity'. His followers taught that 'Judaism, Paganism, Christianity and Manicheism are one and the same doctrine.'[34] Mani himself is said to have travelled to India and believed that he was teaching the same Gnostic doctrines as the Buddha. A king of Mongolia and an emperor of China honoured him as the successor of both the Buddha and the Taoist sage Lao Tzu.[35]

The Growth of Christian Literalism

Over the course of the third century, despite the flimsiness of its claims to be the authentic Christian lineage, Literalism grew in popularity in Rome and the West, though Eastern Christianity remained overwhelmingly Gnostic. Eventually, however, it was inevitable that the simplistic certainties and offer of vicarious atonement of Christian Literalism would attract more adherents than Christian Gnosticism, with its puzzling promise of Gnosis through mystical transformation.

As Literalists grew more powerful, so did their vitriolic attacks on all other Christian schools. In response, Christian Gnostics condemned Literalists for establishing an 'imitation Church' which no longer taught the secret Inner Mysteries. Some Gnostics, such as the Valentinians, tacitly went along with Literalism in an attempt to heal the ever-growing rift.[36] Other Gnostics, such as Clement of Alexandria and his successor Origen, embraced the idea of an historical Jesus, but remained Platonists and continued to teach the Gnosis in their Christian school of philosophy.

Christianity grew in popularity as part of a general upsurge of interest in Mystery cults, such as the Mysteries of Mithras. Over a period of

350 years Mithraism developed from a little-known Persian cult into the dominant religion of the Roman Empire, until at the end of the second century CE it was adopted by the emperor Commodus.[37] The Jewish Jesus cult followed in the footsteps of the Persian Mithras cult, growing in popularity from its conception at the beginning of the first century until 350 years later, in the middle of the third century, it had large numbers of followers throughout the Roman Empire and was adopted by the emperor Constantine. Within 50 years Christian Literalism was the party line of a totalitarian state which dictated to its citizens the one religion that they were permitted to follow.[38]

A common Literalist reaction to the idea that Jesus is a mythical figure is the question 'How do you explain the rise of Christianity without it being founded by an inspirational leader?' Mithraism provides us with the answer. Christianity became the dominant religion in the ancient world without there being an historical Jesus in exactly the same way that Mithraism, a few decades earlier, had become the dominant religion in the ancient world without there being an historical Mithras. Mithraism was inspired by charismatic leaders, but none of them was Mithras. In the same way Christianity was inspired by charismatic leaders amongst the original Christians, but none of them was Jesus. In fact the myth of Jesus was partly based on the myth of Mithras. The two stories are so similar that Literalist Christians claimed that in an attempt to confuse the faithful, the Devil had created the Mithras story by mimicking the life of Jesus in advance of his birth![39]

It seems extraordinary that the Roman world embraced the Mysteries of Rome's enemies, the Persians and Jews. But the vast majority of inhabitants of the empire were not Romans, of course, and had little sympathy for them. The cults of Mithras and Jesus spread so successfully precisely because they fed on conquered peoples' resentment of the Romans and represented a form of acceptable dissent. Roman emperors were concerned above all with uniting their disparate colonies. Mithraism, Christianity and other popular Mystery cults were adopted by the state, regardless of their national origins, in an attempt to bring coherence to a fragmenting empire. Christian Literalism was an ideal candidate for the job. It was exactly what a Roman despot like Constantine required – a populist and authoritarian religion which had freed itself of Gnostic radicals.

Although Christian Literalists rejected the Gnostic Inner Mysteries of Christianity, they continued to portray Christianity as a Mystery cult.

Phrases such as 'This is known to initiates' continued to be routinely used, but they were now little more than empty words.[40] As Christian Literalism grew in power it adopted more of the trappings of the Pagan Literalism it replaced. Its ritual processions were identical to those of the Pagan cults.[41] Although Jesus had specifically said, 'Call no man "father",' Christian Literalists adopted the Mithraic practice of calling priests 'father'.[42] In imitation of the Mithraic bishops, Christian bishops wore a 'mithra' or 'mitre' and carried a shepherd's staff. Eventually the Bishop of Rome took up the title *Ponifex Maximus*, the ancient name for the Pagan high priest, a title still held by the Pope today.[43]

The Suppression of Women

Literalist Christianity took as its scriptural backdrop the Jewish Old Testament, with its patriarchal monotheism. It therefore vigorously suppressed the idea that there was a Christian Goddess. But the people's need to relate to the Divine Feminine was too strong to be ignored and the void was quickly filled. In 431 CE a Christian council met at Ephesus, previously the chief site for the worship of the Pagan Goddess, and bestowed the titles of the ousted Goddess upon Mary the mother of Jesus, honouring her as 'Queen of Heaven' and *Theotokos*, 'Mother of God'.[44] Protestant Literalists would later condemn this elevation of Mary, but ironically it was actually a demotion. For the original Christians, Mary had always represented the Goddess Sophia, Queen of Heaven.[45] For the Literalists, she was merely a mortal woman, special only because her son Jesus was divine.

Literalists put an end to Gnostic ideas of equality between the sexes. They interpreted the Jewish *Genesis* myth as literal history, with terrible consequences for women. Women were no longer seen as spiritual partners with men, but the descendants of the evil Eve, because of whose sin 'even the Son of God had to die'.[46] Augustine wrote to a friend:

> 'What does it matter whether it is a wife or a mother, it is Eve the temptress we must beware of in any woman.'[47]

Literalists played down the importance of women in the gospels to endorse their policy of making them second-class human beings.[48] This reversal of attitude towards women in Christianity is symbolized perfectly by the retitling of the fourth gospel. Known to us now as *The Gospel of John*, if it is to bear any name at all it should be *The Gospel of Mary*

Magdalene.[49] This gospel claims to be written by an unspecified 'Beloved Disciple'.[50] It is attributed to John *solely* on the basis of the Literalist Irenaeus, at the end of the second century, claiming he had a childhood memory of being told that the gospel was written by the disciple John.[51] According to the Gnostics, it was written by the Gnostic master Cerinthus at the end of the first century.[52] Modern research suggests that the 'Beloved Disciple' he makes the narrator of the story is not John, but Mary Magdalene.[53] Mary is clearly identified in other Gnostic sources as 'the beloved disciple', 'the disciple that Jesus loved', 'the companion of Jesus', and so on.[54] As scholars have noted, *The Gospel of the Beloved Disciple* has been modified, creating obvious structural flaws, in order to turn the 'Beloved Disciple' Mary into the male figure of John, who was more acceptable to misogynist Literalists.[55]

Attacks on Gnosticism

As their confidence grew, Literalists' attacks on Gnostics became ever more virulent, creating the distorted picture of Christian Gnosticism still prevalent today. In a classic case of psychological projection, the Gnostics were misrepresented as the diabolical heretics that the Literalists had actually become. Although it was Literalists themselves who were preaching an exclusive religion and arrogantly condemning all other faiths as evil, they accused the Gnostics of being 'puffed up' sectarians and named themselves the 'Catholic' or 'Universal' Church. Although Gnostic philosophy teaches 'All is One' and Literalists preach an irreconcilable war between God and the Devil, Literalists portrayed themselves as 'monotheists' and the Gnostics as 'dualists'.[56] Although it was Literalist Christianity that had begun as a suicide cult, teaching its adherents that the way to salvation was to actively seek a martyr's death, its later followers vilified the Gnostics as world-haters.[57]

Christian Literalists turned their caustic polemics equally against Paganism, which was denounced as a barbaric cult of bloody sacrifice. This is deeply ironic given the Christian Literalist belief that God had sacrificed his only Son as the sole way of getting the rest of us off the hook. When taken literally, it is difficult to imagine a more barbaric idea than that! And for all the undoubted barbarism of Pagan Literalists, it was Christian Literalists, not the supposedly primitive heathens, who presided over the collapse of Western culture into the aptly named Dark Ages.[58]

This disastrous collapse was precipitated at the end of the fourth century when Christian Literalism, now the only legal religion in the Roman Empire, launched a brutal crusade to completely eradicate its old rivals, Christian Gnosticism and ancient Paganism. In an orgy of violence, armies of fanatical Christian Literalists tore down the architectural wonders of the Pagan world. They built infernal bonfires of books containing the spiritual wisdom and scientific knowledge of the ages. They subjected to grisly torture and a painful death philosophers, priestesses and scientists – anyone who disagreed. They did not stop until they had cut the head off Western culture, leaving it to wander like an amnesiac in an ignorant stupor. They did not stop until they had cut the heart out of Western spirituality, bleeding it dry of its mystical vitality. The corpse of a religion which remained offered nothing but hope of a better afterlife in return for blind belief in its irrational opinions and unquestioning allegiance to power-crazed popes. This tyrannical empire of the soul extended the arm of the state right into the inner sanctum of every individual, denying the right to spiritual autonomy and compelling all to acquiesce or burn.

Yet despite this ruthless persecution, Gnosticism survived. It can be suppressed but never eradicated. It is the spontaneous expression of the natural inquisitiveness and enthusiastic exuberance of the human soul. It is the unquenchable thirst for truth and the undeniable urge to enjoy. It is the spirit of liberty, equality, love and insight. It is the force of life. It always reasserts itself.

THE GNOSTIC HERITAGE

Whilst by the fourth century the Roman Church in the West had condemned anything Gnostic as heresy, in the Eastern Church, based in Constantinople, the original Christian spirit survived a little longer. Sages such as Basil of Caesarea, Gregory of Nyssa, Gregory of Nazianzum,[59] Evagrius of Pontus and Diodochus of Photice[60] continued to teach the oral tradition of 'private secret teachings' to those initiated into the Inner Mysteries of Christianity.[61] They understood the Bible allegorically, explaining that, ultimately, the secrets of the scriptures can only be revealed 'thanks to the Gnosis'.[62] They emphasized devotion to Mary as the manifestation of Sophia and taught that the goal of Christianity was 'to become God'.[63]

In the West, the spirit of Christian Gnosticism was smuggled back into the mainstream Church via mystical writings attributed to Dionysius, a co-worker of Paul.[64] Today these treatises are generally thought to be the work of an unidentified sixth-century monk who deliberately took the pseudonym 'Dionysius' to claim authority for what would otherwise be condemned as heretical works. The writer is thought to have been a pupil of the Pagan Gnostic Proclus, the last master of the Platonic Academy, which the Christian emperor Justinian had forcibly closed down in 529, ending a prestigious 1,000-year history.[65] However, in the light of our thesis that the Gnostics were the first Christians, it is possible that this view will come to be seen as mistaken and that these texts are at least based on the works of a first-century Gnostic master, as they claim to be.

Dionysius is unconcerned with an historical Jesus. His Jesus is a symbolic representation of the *Logos*.[66] According to Dionysius, there are two Christian gospels, the familiar teachings of the Church and a secret gospel, which is 'symbolic and presupposes initiation' and 'must never be divulged to the uninitiated'.[67] He eulogizes the wonders of the 'divine enlightenment into which we have been initiated by the secret tradition of our inspired teachers'.[68] The narratives and symbols of Christianity have one meaning to the uninitiated and another to the initiated:

> 'Don't suppose that the outward form of these contrived symbols exists for its own sake. It is a protective clothing, which prevents the common multitude from understanding the Ineffable and Invisible. Only real lovers of holiness know how to stop the workings of the childish imagination regarding the sacred symbols. They alone have the simplicity of mind and the receptive power of contemplation to cross over to the simple, marvellous, transcendent Truth the symbols represent.'[69]

These writings were extremely influential. No other works were so frequently translated or had so many commentaries written on them, apart from the Bible and *The Consolations of Philosophy* by Boethius, which was another text through which the spirit of Gnosticism survived in the Dark Ages of Literalism.[70] Condemned for heresy by the Christian emperor Theodoric, Boethius describes languishing in prison, where he is visited by Sophia herself, who instructs him in philosophy. Despite his vision of the Goddess and never mentioning Jesus once, due to the immense popularity of his writings Boethius was later claimed by Christian Literalists as one of their own.[71] As for the man himself, Theodoric had him tortured and then bludgeoned to death for heresy.

Despite the Literalist Church's unrelenting attempts at suppression, some 'heretical' schools of Christian Gnosticism continued to teach. Paulicians survived into the tenth century, Manicheans into the thirteenth and Simonians into the fourteenth.[72] In the Balkans, from the tenth to fifteenth centuries the Paulicians flourished as 'Bogomils', meaning 'Friends of God'[73] – the traditional name for Gnostics first used by the Pythagoreans. The Bogomils even had their own Gnostic Pope.[74] At the anti-Bogomil council of 1211 they were accused of performing 'unholy mysteries like the Hellenic Pagan rites'.[75] One of their Literalist opponents writes with disgust:

> 'They denounce wealth, they have a horror of the Tsar, they ridicule their superiors, condemn the nobles and forbid all slaves to obey their masters.'[76]

In the twelfth century the Bogomils developed into the Cathars or 'Purified Ones'.[77] Catharism was for many years the prevalent form of Christianity in large areas of France, Spain and Italy.[78] The Cathars called themselves 'the Friends of God'[79] and condemned the Literalist Church as the Church of the Anti-Christ. They claimed to be the living inheritors of the true Christian heritage that had persisted in secret and which still had large numbers of adherents 'throughout the world'.[80]

Like the original Christians, the Cathars were vegetarians, believed in reincarnation and considered the Old Testament god Jehovah to be a tyrant.[81] *Pistis Sophia*, an early Christian gospel, explains that Christ taught 'through the mouth of our brother Paul'.[82] The Cathars maintained this tradition, claiming that Jesus was 'not ever in this world except spiritually in the body of Paul'.[83]

The Cathars were respected for their goodness, even by their opponents. The Catholic Bernard of Clairveaux writes:

> 'If you interrogate them, no one could be more Christian. As to their conversation, nothing can be less reprehensible, and what they speak they prove by deeds. As for the morals of the heretics, they cheat no one, they oppress no one, they strike no one.'[84]

Despite this, the infamous Inquisition was set up by the Literalist Church specifically to eradicate the Cathars, which it did with ferocious enthusiasm, burning alive men, women and children. From 1139 onwards the Roman Church began calling councils to condemn the heretics. Pope Innocent III declared that 'anyone who attempted to construe a personal view of God which conflicted with Church dogma must be burned without pity'.[85] In 1208 he offered indulgences and eternal salvation, as well as the lands and property taken from the heretics, to anyone who would take up the crusade against the Cathars. This launched a brutal 30-year pogrom which decimated southern France. Twelve thousand people were killed at St Nazair and 10,000 at Toulouse, to give just two examples.

The inquisitor Bernard Gui instructed that no one should argue with the unbeliever, but 'thrust his sword into the man's belly as far as it will go'.[86] At Béziers, when asked how to tell who was a Cathar and who was not, the commanding legate, Arnoud, replied, 'Kill them all, for God will know his own.' Not a child was spared.[87] In 1325 Pope John XXII observed that many Cathars were fleeing to Bosnia, where the Bogomils were still thriving, as if to the 'Promised Land'.[88] In a grotesque prefiguring of the Nazi terror, Cathars who converted to Catholicism were obliged to wear a yellow cross sewn on their clothes and lost all civil rights,[89] and in eastern Europe the Inquisition used ovens to burn heretics, who were rubbed with grease and roasted alive.[90] If ever proof were needed that the Gnostics were justified in calling Roman Catholicism the Church of the Anti-Christ, here it is.[91]

Yet despite the persecutions, the Gnostic free spirit could not be extinguished. It inspired the great German master Eckhart, who wrote about Sophia and taught that at the heart of Christianity, Judaism and Paganism there were the same mystical doctrines.[92] It inspired the Rhineland mystics Tauler, Suso and Ruysbroek, who also called themselves the 'Friends of God'.[93] It inspired countless groups of non-conformists, such as the Brothers and Sisters of the Free Spirit in Europe, who taught: 'The gospel contains poetical matters which are not true.'[94] In England it inspired the Levellers, Ranters, Diggers and Quakers.[95]

It also inspired many of the great cultural heroes of the West – Dante,[96] Leonardo da Vinci, Michelangelo, Pico and most of the great minds of the Renaissance, who set up a new Platonic Academy;[97] the Protestant Gnostic Jacob Boehme, who received visions of Sophia;[98] poets such as Blake, Milton and Goethe, who created their own Gnostic myths;[99] scientists such as Galileo, Copernicus and Kepler, who revived Pythagoreanism; philosophers such as Descartes, Fichte, Schelling and Hegel, who was accused of being a Valentinian Gnostic.[100]

Christian Gnosticism was reinterpreted for the twentieth century by Carl Jung, who along with Sigmund Freud founded psychoanalysis. Jung wrote to Freud that the Gnostics' Sophia was 'a re-embodiment of an ancient wisdom that might appear once again in modern psychoanalysis'.[101] He asserted, 'It is clear beyond doubt that many of the Gnostics were nothing other than psychologists,' and began to view mental illness as a failed initiation.[102] He wrote:

'All my life I have been working and studying to find these things, and these people knew already.'[103]

In his forties, using as a pseudonym the name of the second-century Christian Gnostic Basilides, Jung wrote his own Gnostic scripture called *Seven Sermons to the Dead*. This remarkable text is addressed to the disquieted dead, who have been failed by Christian Literalism and who appear to Jung, wailing, 'We have come back from Jerusalem where we have found not what we sought.'[104] Jung regarded this work as the wellspring of all his later insights, but although he circulated it amongst his friends, he prohibited its publication until after his death, fearing it would discredit him in the eyes of the scientific establishment.[105]

When the Nag Hammadi library of Christian Gnostic texts was discovered in 1945, Jung's foundation bought one of the collections, now known as the Jung Codex. When translated, these works proved that many of his intuitions about Christian Gnosticism had been remarkably correct. Towards the end of his life he appeared on a television chat show, in which he famously replied to the question of whether he believed in God with the perennial Gnostic assertion: 'I know that God exists. I don't need to believe, I know.'[106]

THE LITERALIST LEGACY

The triumph of Christian Literalism was a spiritual and cultural disaster from which we are still recovering. After the civilized exterior of 'Christian' culture in Germany had been ripped open in the twentieth century by Hitler's Nazis, Jung wrote:

'Christian civilization proved hollow to a terrifying degree: it is all veneer, but the inner man has remained untouched and therefore unchanged. Yes, everything is to be found outside – in image and in word, in Church and Bible – but never inside.'[107]

When Literalist Christianity exiled the Gnostic Inner Mysteries, it lost its soul. It became a bastion of the 'hypocrites' which the Gnostics portrayed Jesus as mocking in their gospel story – ecclesiastical autocrats who imposed their dogmas with threats and maintained their power through violence, politicians dressed up as priests who justified the laying waste of whole continents and the enslaving of millions.[108]

Literalist Christianity is often credited with inspiring positive social reforms in Western society. But the truth is that the driving impetus for humanitarian change has come from humanists and non-conformists. The conservative forces of the established Churches have resisted every step towards greater compassion, from the ending of slavery to the abolition of the death penalty.[109] In recent decades, unable any longer to simply bully us into submission, Literalist Christianity has developed a gentler, more attractive face. Yet its darker side continues to be a nefarious force in the world. A recent report estimated there are at least 8,000 'missionaries' active in Guatemala alone, many of whom openly collaborate with the brutal secret police and the military in their oppression of the indigenous people. Typifying the spirit of Christian Literalism throughout the ages, one preacher from the missionary group El Verbo justified this with:

'The army does not massacre Indians. It massacres demons and the Indians are possessed by demons.'[110]

In many European countries, however, the power of Literalist Christianity is finally waning. Congregations are dwindling dramatically and churches are being sold off as houses.[111] Science is fast becoming the dominant worldview. This has provoked two very different reactions from those unwilling to consign Christianity to the rubbish bin of history – 'Fundamentalists' are desperately endeavouring to retreat to the old certainties, whilst others are attempting to rework the figure of Jesus to fit new times.

Fundamentalism

Fundamentalism is a Protestant continuation of the intolerant and dogmatic traditions of Roman Christianity.[112] Heretics are no longer burned at the stake, thank God, but we have still endured the wrath of Fundamentalists for daring to publish our ideas about the origins of Christianity. Whilst we have escaped death threats, we have received many 'after-death threats'. According to Fundamentalists, Jesus has an eternal torture camp set up specifically to get even with blasphemers such as ourselves.

Fundamentalism emphatically insists that the Bible is literally the word of God and cannot be questioned. This is an attitude that goes right back to the beginnings of the Roman Church at the end of the second century, when Tertullian included 'thirst for knowledge' amongst his list of vices, to be replaced by the virtue of blind faith in scripture.[113] But this fixation on the written word is a form of idolatry. It mistakes the garment for the naked Truth. It confines living insight within the concepts of the past. As Paul says, 'The letter kills, but the spirit gives life.'[114]

Although fanatically concerned about a supposed decline in moral values, Fundamentalists hold up the barbarous Old Testament as a divinely inspired account of the works of the one and only god Jehovah. Let's just have a quick look at the sort of god they are worshipping. In *The Book of Genesis* Jehovah destroys all living things on the Earth by flood,[115] but somehow manages to also find the time to specifically execute one individual man for letting his semen spill on the ground when having sex.[116] In *The Book of Exodus* he inflicts hideous plagues on Egypt for not letting the Israelites leave, despite the fact that it was he himself who 'hardened Pharaoh's heart'.[117] He also kills all the firstborn Egyptian children, assists the Israelites in slaughtering an entire tribe of Amalekites, makes it allowable to beat a slave to death and, after rumours that Israelites have worshipped a rival god, orders faithful Israelites to kill their friends and relatives, leading to the death of 3,000 people.[118]

Not content with this, in *The First Book of Samuel* Jehovah takes vengeance on the people of Gath by giving all the men a fatal dose of haemorrhoids.[119] In *The Book of Leviticus* he condones human sacrifice.[120] In *The Book of Deuteronomy* he orders the Israelites to utterly destroy the people of the cities that he bequeaths to them as their 'inheritance', commanding them 'not to leave anything that breathes alive'.[121] In *The Book of Numbers* he orders a man to be stoned to death for gathering sticks for a fire on the Sabbath, and sends a plague which kills 14,700 people.[122] He also gives the Israelites power to utterly destroy the Canaanites and exterminate the people of Og, advising with regard to captured women and children:

> 'Kill every male among the little ones, and kill every woman who has known a man intimately. But keep alive for yourself all the young girls who have not known a man intimately.'[123]

You can see why the Christian Gnostic Marcion nicknamed Jehovah 'the exterminator'.[124] And when it's not being gruesome, the Old Testament is so culturally foreign and outdated it is just plain daft. *The Book of Leviticus* tells us that we must have no contact at all with a menstruating woman,[125] but it's fine to buy slaves from neighbouring states.[126] Eating shellfish is out, however. That's apparently an 'abomination'.[127] *The Book of Exodus* insists that anyone who works on the Sabbath should be put to death, which I guess means most of us deserve to die.[128] *The Book of Deuteronomy* decrees that a son who will not obey his parents is to be stoned to death by the whole town outside the city gates, so if you're male, and your dad's a Fundamentalist, and you're reading this, you're in big trouble![129]

If you do literally believe that God wrote or personally inspired certain infallible books, as Fundamentalists do, then this is the sort of ridiculous mess you end up in. You can see why Paul regarded the Old Testament as so 'rickety' that it wouldn't 'be around for much longer'![130] It's a shame he was so completely wrong.

Fantasists

At the other extreme to Fundamentalists are what could be called 'Fantasists'. Fantasists are keen to reject traditional forms of Christianity as misconceived, out of date and redundant. They see the gospels as the work of fallible human authors and therefore feel free to dismiss those elements in the Jesus story which they dislike, filling in the gaps from their own imagination to create a 'pick 'n' mix' Jesus who fits their own fantasies.

In recent decades such fantasies have reached epidemic proportions. We have had Jesus going to India and Tibet, Jesus getting married and founding a dynasty of European kings,[131] even Jesus the spaceman who wants us to commit suicide in order to join him on the great Mothership in the sky.[132] You name it, someone out there believes it!

The very first time we gave a lecture on the ideas contained in *The Jesus Mysteries*, we were confounded when a young woman at the back of the audience confidently announced that, impressive as our research was, we couldn't possibly be right because she vividly remembered being Mary Magdalene in a past life. Since then we have come across several more Mary Magdalenes, a man who is sure he lives in a house once inhabited by Jesus when he visited England, and an elderly gentleman whose 'spirit guides' have reliably informed him there were in fact five Jesuses.

Actually there are thousands of Jesuses, because everyone has a different one. And the extraordinary thing is everyone's Jesus looks suspiciously like them. Fire and brimstone types have a fire and brimstone Jesus. Nice liberal pacifists have a nice liberal pacifist Jesus. Jews have a rabbi Jesus. Buddhists have a Buddhist Jesus. Hindus have an avatar Jesus. The great German theologian Rudolf Bultmann called this the 'deep well effect'. Looking for the 'real' Jesus is like looking down a well – all we see is our own reflection.

This is not just an affliction of flaky New Agers – it applies equally to respected historians. In his book *The Quest of the Historical Jesus*, Albert Schweitzer describes scholars as practising plastic surgery on Jesus, who always emerges looking like the surgeon who operated on him.[133]

Docetism

This proliferation of Jesuses is not a new situation. According to the Literalist Hippolytus, all Gnostics had 'their own particular Jesus'.[134] But this was not a cause of conflict and controversy because, for the Gnostics, Jesus was a mythological figure who appeared in the imagination in a form appropriate to the individual, according to their level of spiritual awareness.[135] *The Gospel of Philip* explains:

'Jesus does not show himself as he really is, but he shows himself as people are able to see him. He shows himself to all. To the great he appears great. To the small he appears small. To the angels he appears as an angel, and to men as a man. Hence the *Logos* conceals itself from all. Some indeed see him and realize that they are seeing themselves.'[136]

In *The Acts of John*, John and his brother James see Jesus beckoning to them, but one sees a beautiful man and the other a little child. Later, for one of them the figure becomes 'rather bald-headed but with a thick flowing beard' and for the other 'a young man with an immature beard'.[137] In *The Acts of Peter*, Peter relates, 'I saw him in such a form as I was able to take in.' He teaches a group of widows how to see Jesus:

'See with your mind what you do not see with your eyes. And though your eyes be closed, yet let them open in your mind within you.'[138]

The widows become 'senseless with bewilderment' and all experience Jesus in a different way. Some say they saw 'an old man who had such a presence we cannot describe it to you'. Others say, 'We saw a growing lad,' and others, 'We saw a boy who gently touched our eyes and they opened.' Peter remarks:

'God is greater than our thoughts, as we have learned from these aged widows who have seen the Lord in a variety of forms.'[139]

According to Theodotus, Paul recognized that 'each one knows the Lord in his own way and not all know him alike'.[140] Paul himself famously experienced Jesus as a vision of light.[141] In *The Apocryphon of John*, John also experiences Jesus as light, but in this case containing a metamorphosing image:

'I saw in the light a youth who stood by me. While I looked at him he became like an old man. And then he changed his appearance again and became like a servant. There were not many before me, but an image with many forms in the light. And the image appeared through each. And it took three forms. He said to me, "John why do you doubt? Why are you afraid? You are not unfamiliar with this image, are you? Don't be nervous. I am the One who is with you always." '[142]

The Gnostics' doctrine that Jesus is a symbolic visionary figure is known as docetism. It is misunderstood by Christian Literalists as the bizarre claim that Jesus was some sort of disembodied spook that miraculously appeared to be a man who lived the life described in the gospels. But this crazy idea is just the product of Literalists taking the Gnostics literally. Docetism actually teaches that Jesus is a mutable figure who represents the archetype of the Self and appears in different ways to initiates with different levels of understanding. As *The Gospel of Philip* says with startling clarity, some 'realize that they are seeing themselves'.[143]

The problem is that at first when someone experiences a relationship with their particular version of Jesus they 'recognize him as their brother and regard all the rest as bastards', as Hippolytus puts it.[144] Their Jesus is the real Jesus, everyone else's is an impostor. But once the idea of an historical man is abandoned, competing Jesuses are not a problem. Everyone can look down the well and come up convinced that Jesus looks just like them, and that doesn't conflict with everyone else doing the same. We can all have a different Jesus. The whole point of a mythological figure is that it can be adapted to suit different people and changing times.

What unites Fundamentalists and Fantasists is their obsession with the idea of an historical Jesus. We are suggesting a radical alternative: freeing ourselves from the futile preoccupation with history and returning to the original Christians' understanding of Jesus as the hero of a powerfully transformative allegorical myth.

THE REAL JESUS IS A RED HERRING

We fully understand how difficult it is to doubt the existence of someone whom millions believe to be the most important human being ever to have lived. Many of us have been brought up since childhood with a vivid picture of the historical Jesus. Mention his name and we can almost see him in his rough white robes with long flowing hair and beard. Yet the earliest representations of Jesus actually portray him beardless, with short hair, wearing a Roman tunic.[145] Paul explicitly writes that 'Flowing locks disgrace a man,' so presumably he did not share our modern image of the Christ![146]

The now ubiquitous image of the bearded long-haired Jesus did not become established until the eighth century, when the Eastern Church in Constantinople suddenly produced a 'self-portrait' which had been miraculously created when Jesus wiped his face on a cloth.[147] Not to be outdone, the Roman Church turned up a portrait of a bearded Jesus painted by Luke and later completed by angels. Pilgrims still kneel before this absurd fabrication in the Vatican today, hoping it will in some way bring them to the Truth. The truth is, however, that the picture we have of Jesus is a product of the imagination – our own and that of others before us.

Was there an 'historical' Jesus? The evidence suggests there was not. But to us this emotive issue is really not important. What *is* important is to realize that the Jesus we relate to in our imagination is a mythical 'archetype' through which we can reach the 'Christ Consciousness' within ourselves, because if we are unable to get enough distance from our own fantasies and opinions to see that our picture of Jesus is an imaginative construct, we will never have the self-knowledge necessary to grasp the Gnosis. However, we have to be spiritually ready before we can hear this message as positive rather than negative, as giving us what we have been really looking for rather than taking something away. The teachings of 'the Christ within' are an open secret that only someone who is ripe can really hear.

Many people desperately want to believe in a miraculous saviour who has literally incarnated to rescue them. There is nothing wrong with this. The miracle worker is a stock character of ancient myths, used to inspire hope of something more than the mundane in those unable to see that the whole of life is a staggering miracle. The image of the divine Godman was deliberately designed to appeal to spiritual beginners who have yet to discover that this mythical figure represents their own true identity. Those who are not ready cling to their 'real' Jesus like a life-buoy in the tempestuous sea of existence. To suggest they let go sounds like madness. But the secret teachings of the original Christians were not designed to maliciously deny comfort to simple believers. They are actually offering something infinitely more reassuring than blind belief in historical events. They are offering Gnosis – immediate experiential knowledge of the Truth. The message is not 'Look out, you are clinging to an illusion.' The message is:

> 'Relax. You are not drowning. You can let go, because life is actually completely safe. Just experience Gnosis and all your ignorance will be dispelled. Just know who you really are and you will have absolutely no fear ever again. Discover the Christ within yourself and you will be always One with God.'

SUMMARY

❖ Christian Literalism developed towards the end of the second century as a minor cult with the unique claim that Jesus had literally lived out the Pagan myth of the dying and resurrecting Godman. Literalists fabricated a lineage to link themselves back to the supposed disciples and forged letters of Paul to make him appear anti-Gnostic.

❖ Mirroring the success of the Mysteries of the Persian Godman Mithras, Christian Literalism gradually grew in popularity, becoming the official religion of the Roman Empire in the fourth century. With the full might of the Roman state behind them, Christian Literalists waged a barbaric war against Paganism and Christian Gnosticism, pulling down temples and libraries, burning books and dissidents, and plunging Western civilization into the Dark Ages.

❖ The legacy of Christian Literalism has been a misguided obsession with the historical Jesus. The original Christians, however, taught that Jesus is a mythological figure who appears in the imagination in different ways, according to the understanding of the individual.

If the Jesus story is an allegorical myth, what does it mean? If we have lost the secret Inner Mysteries of Christianity, can we rediscover them? By understanding Chrisianity as part of the broad Gnostic tradition that florished throughout the ancient world, we have been able to discover the true origins of Christianity. Let's now see if, by examining Christian myths and doctrines in the light of Pagan and Jewish Gnostic philosophy, we can recover the gospel of Gnosis.

chapter four

KNOW
your Self

'The Kingdom of Heaven is within you and whoever knows himself shall find it. Know your Self.'

Jesus, *Oxyrhynchus Manuscript*[1]

Above the ancient Pagan sanctuary at Delphi were written the words 'Know your Self.'[2] This injunction was seen as the fundamental challenge of Gnosticism by Pagan, Jewish and Christian Gnostics alike.[3] The 'Gnosis' or 'Knowledge' they sought was self-knowledge. Their spiritual quest was to answer the most obvious of mysteries, which continually confronts each one of us: 'Who am I?'

If we can grasp the Gnostics' teachings about who we really are, then the meaning of the Christian myths of Jesus and the Goddess will become clear. These teachings have little in common with Christianity as it is generally understood today. At first they may seem strange and abstract, but, if you are willing, just open yourself to the possibility of a revolutionary new vision of who you are and what life is. That is the first step on the journey of Gnosis.

BODY - SOUL - SPIRIT

What does it mean to know ourselves? Who are we really? The Gnostics understood a human being as having three aspects: body, soul and spirit.[4] The words 'soul' and 'spirit' are so familiar that we can easily presume we know what we mean by them, but do we? What exactly is a 'soul'? And how is it different from a 'spirit'? Although today these concepts are so woolly as to be almost meaningless, for the Gnostics they had clear and definite meanings.

To explain their teachings, the Gnostics used the image of a circle.

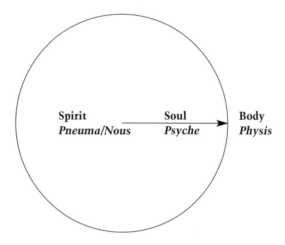

The circumference of the circle represents the physical body, which the ancients called *physis*, from which we get our word 'physical'. This is our outer self.

The radius represents our *psyche*. This is traditionally translated as 'soul', although, as the ancient word 'psyche' has come into common usage since the advent of psychology, it is probably less misleading to leave the term untranslated. In relationship to the outer body, we experience the psyche/soul as our 'inner self'. For the Gnostics, it is a deeper level of our identity than the body.

At the centre is our essential identity, which the ancients called *pneuma* or *nous*. *Pneuma* is usually translated 'spirit', but today this word has become all but meaningless. *Nous* is traditionally translated 'intellect', but this is misleading as we now associate the word 'intellect' purely with rational thought, whereas *nous* is the witness of all experiences, whatever their quality. Plotinus describes *nous* as 'a knowing principle'.[5] It is that in us which knows. It is the subject of every experience, which each one of us calls 'I'. It is the sense of *being* in every human being. It is who we *are*. A more appropriate modern translation for both *pneuma* and *nous* is 'Consciousness'.

Recognizing the Levels of our Identity

We can clearly distinguish the three levels of our identity if we examine the three states we inhabit each day: waking, dreaming and deep sleep. In the waking state, Consciousness extends its awareness from the centre to the circumference, experiencing the psyche and the body. In the dreaming state we abandon the body and retreat into the psyche or soul. In the deep sleep state we withdraw completely into our essence as *nous/pneuma*, spirit or Consciousness. Paradoxically, in this state of being pure Consciousness, because we are not experiencing anything, we are *unconscious*. We remember this state afterwards only as a blissful void in which we exist as the emptiness of Consciousness, conscious of nothing.

States of Awareness	Levels of Identity
Deep sleep	Consciousness
Dreaming	Consciousness–psyche
Waking	Consciousness–psyche–body

The 'common sense' view of ourselves is that we are bodies which are awake, dreaming or in deep sleep. From the outside, we do indeed *seem* to be bodies in one of these three conditions. Gnostics, however, take as their starting-point our own subjective experience of ourselves, not others' experience of us, and in our own immediate experience, we are permanently who we *are*, whilst the body and psyche come and go. We are not a physical body that is sometimes conscious. We are Consciousness that is sometimes conscious of a body.

The modern conception of human identity, articulated by scientific materialism, is that we are a complex physical organism which, in some way we have yet to understand, has an inner life and is therefore conscious.

From this perspective, Gnostic teachings sound like spiritual mumbo-jumbo. But to the Gnostics, it is the notion that matter could somehow be the cause of conscious experience which is truly fantastic and incomprehensible. In *The Gospel of Thomas* Jesus argues:

> 'If the body came into being because of consciousness that is a wonder, but if consciousness came into being because of the body this is a wonder of wonders.'[6]

Science starts with the body and ends with Consciousness, moving from the outside inwards. The Gnostic approach starts with Consciousness and ends with the body, moving from the inside outwards. Science teaches we are as we *appear* to others – physical bodies. The Gnostics teach that we are as we *are* for ourselves – Consciousness. Both approaches have something to tell us about the human predicament. The ancients saw them as complementary, not in opposition. Science deals with appearances and has taught us much about how we *appear* to be. Gnosticism deals with what we *are*.

The Gnostics take us back to basics and explain the complexity of the human predicament from these simple beginnings. There is nothing more obvious than the fact that we are conscious of experiences. Our essential identity is the experiencer, *nous*, spirit, Consciousness. The flow of experience which Consciousness witnesses is the psyche or soul. For the Gnostics, therefore, our fundamental condition could be described as Consciousness aware of experience, *nous* aware of *psyche*, spirit aware of soul.

The Body is in the Soul

From the outside it appears as if the psyche or soul is in the body. We seem to see it when we look into someone's eyes – the 'windows of the soul'. When Gnostics talk about how things *appear* objectively, they go along with this common notion of the soul as a sort of intangible, more rarefied body which is trapped inside the physical body. But when they talk on a deeper level about how things *are* subjectively, the psyche or soul is conceived of as an ongoing *event* witnessed by Consciousness. It is the totality of our experience, which includes the experience of the body.[7] This turns inside-out the notion that the psyche somehow inhabits the body. As Plotinus teaches, 'The psyche is not in the body, rather the body is in the psyche.'[8]

To the modern materialist mindset this can seem a bizarre idea, yet it is an important insight on the path of Gnosis. We can begin to understand it if we carefully examine our own raw experience. Through the experience of sensations – seeing, hearing, touching, tasting and smelling – we know the body in what we think of as the objective world. Yet sensations themselves are subjective events in the psyche. Most children have at some time wondered whether other people actually experience the same thing as they do when they see 'green' or 'orange'. No one knows the answer to this simple question. Why? Because sensual experiences exist within the psyche and we have no direct access to the psyches of others.

From the point of view of the body, looking inwards from the circumference, we appear to be a physical organism which has an inner life – a psyche – and is therefore conscious. From the point of view of the centre, we are Consciousness experiencing psyche, which, at the circumference, includes the body in the form of sensations.[9] The psyche-body is what we *appear* to be. Consciousness is what we *are*. Porphyry writes:

> 'What lesson have we learned from those who best understand the human condition? Surely, that you must not think of me as this person who can be touched and grasped by the senses, but my true self is remote from the body, without colour and without shape, not to be touched by human hands.'[10]

We opened this book with the perennial Gnostic promise, attributed to Jesus in *The Gospel of Thomas*:

> 'I will reveal to you what no eye can see,
> what no ear can hear,
> what no hand can touch,
> what cannot be conceived by the human mind.'[11]

What is the one thing – in reality not a *thing* at all – which cannot be seen, or heard, or touched, or conceived of? It is that which witnesses the seeing, hearing, touching and conceiving: Consciousness itself. The great revelation of Gnosticism is that our essential identity is Consciousness.[12]

THE ONE CONSCIOUSNESS OF GOD

The Christian Gnostic Clement of Alexandria writes: 'The greatest of all lessons is to know your Self, for when a man knows himself he knows God.'[13] For the Gnostics, the quest for self-knowledge is identical with the quest to know God, because when we discover our deepest identity, we discover we *are* God.[14]

What can this possibly mean? It seems a bizarre idea because we are used to the Literalist picture of God as some sort of omnipotent patriarch who is boss of the cosmos. For the Gnostics, however, God is omnipresent Consciousness within which everything exists as an idea. This one universal Consciousness expresses itself through all conscious beings. So, although we may all seem to be separate individuals, as Plotinus teaches, 'at the innermost depths'[15] of each of us 'there is one Consciousness, unchanging and the same'.[16] This is our shared essential identity. It is the hidden root of the tree of which we are all branches.[17]

Using the analogy of the circle of self, the Gnostics imagine us like many radii emanating out from a common centre. The one Consciousness of God is represented by 'the centre shared by all the radii', explains Dionysius.[18] God is an 'indivisible point' which is 'the source of all', 'the root of the entire circle of existence', teaches Simon Magus.[19] 'You will find Him in yourself, like that little point,' proclaims the Christian master Monoimos.[20]

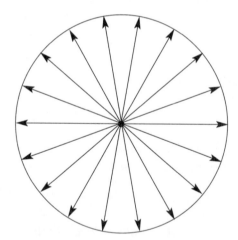

Centre: One Consciousness

Radii: Many psyches

Circumference: Many bodies

The radii, representing individual psyches, terminate at the circumference in individual bodies. But at the centre is a shared essence. When we look outwards to the psyche-body we each appear separate, but actually our centre is *the* centre. As Plotinus teaches, if we 'hold through our own centre to that centre of all centres', we will discover that our consciousness is the one Consciousness of God.[21]

Monoimos imagines an essentially indivisible essence appearing to have many faces and many eyes.[22] Plotinus offers us the same image, writing, 'Imagine something full of faces, gleaming with living faces.'[23] Each line which extends from the centre of the circle has its source in the one Consciousness of God, and its fruition in a distinct human form, which is an image or face of God.

The One Appearing as the Many

But if we are all one in God, why don't we experience ourselves as God? To answer this question we must first understand the paradoxical nature of Consciousness. Imagine for a moment the centre of the circle without any of the radii. It is Consciousness without anything to be conscious of and, therefore, unconscious. In a poetic attempt to capture this paradox, Gregory of Nyssa and Dionysius call it the 'dazzling darkness'.[24] Just as light is darkness when it has no objects upon which to reflect, so Consciousness is unconscious when it is witnessing no experiences.[25] The one Consciousness of God is the dazzling darkness. It appears as the light of Consciousness when it has something to illuminate. What it illuminates is an infinite number of psyches – sequences of experience – represented by the radial lines. Plotinus explains:

> 'All beings may be thought of as centres uniting at one central centre. The centres appear as numerous as the lines starting from them, and yet all those centres constitute a unity. Thus we may liken conscious beings in their diversity to many centres coinciding with one centre. They are all one because they share the same centre, but appear to be many because of the many radial lines which lead from the centre.'[26]

The one Consciousness of God appears to be many individual consciousnesses because when it looks out to the circumference along a particular radius, the common centre appears to itself to be the centre of that particular radius. As Consciousness witnessing an individual psyche – the centre in relationship to a particular radius – we *appear* as individual beings. As the dazzling darkness – the centre in itself – we *are* the universal Being the Gnostics call God.

The Absolute Mystery and its Apparent Qualities

Our shared essential identity is an ineffable Mystery. It is not a *relative* mystery which one day might be solved. It is a Mystery by its very nature. The 'Mystery of God', to use Paul's phrase, is the Absolute Mystery.[27] The Gnostics represent the Mystery by a point because, by definition, a point has no dimensions. In itself it has no characteristics. We can only call it the 'centre' in relationship to the circle that issues from it. Likewise, the 'indivisible point' which is the one Consciousness of God in itself has no characteristics. We can only call it 'Consciousness' in relationship to psyche, because in itself it is the dazzling darkness.

Yet despite this the Gnostics often talk of the Absolute Mystery as if it did have qualities. They not only call it 'Consciousness', but also 'the One'. Platonists describe it as 'the Good, the Beautiful and the True'. Valentinus calls it 'Love'.[28] When these mystics recount their experiences of spiritual awakening they do not relate a cold encounter with the qualityless and unknowable, but an ecstatic revelation of an all-consuming unity and an all-embracing compassion.

We can understand how the essentially ineffable appears to have qualities by considering waking up from deep sleep. We might say that the deep sleep experience was peaceful and blissful, or describe it as a void in which we have no separate existence. But whilst we are in deep sleep there is no deep sleep experience. We are not conscious of any of these qualities, since we are unconscious. Deep sleep in itself is an Absolute Mystery, but from the conscious perspective we can say that, relative to the waking world, it appears to have certain qualities.

In the same way, the Mystery in itself, like a point, is completely beyond description. But from the human perspective, on the circumference of the circle of self, the Mystery appears to be our centre. Relative to our experience, it appears as Consciousness. Relative to our existence as separate beings, it appears as the One. Relative to our desires, it appears as the Good towards which, knowingly or unknowingly, we all aspire. Relative to our feelings of happiness and sadness, it appears as perfect Bliss. Relative to our experience of rejection and acceptance, it appears as unconditional Love. Relative to our feelings of attraction or repulsion, it appears as incomparable Beauty. Relative to our states of confusion and clarity, it appears as the simple Truth.

Our essential nature, then, that we have so far described using the language of psychology as 'Consciousness' and the language of theology as 'God', could equally be described in the language of philosophy as 'Oneness', or in the language of ethics as 'goodness', or emotionally as 'love', or aesthetically as 'beautiful', and so on. But when we reach beyond all such necessarily inadequate descriptions, we can only say that, in truth, at the heart of each one of us there lies the same Mystery. As Plotinus puts it, 'All consciousnesses are the various members of *THAT*.'[29]

Incarnation

The psyche contains a spectrum of experience, from rarefied ideas near the centre of the circle of self to concrete sensations at the circumference. Here the radii that have emanated from a common centre confront each other as apparently separate beings. Here the private dream which is each radius becomes a shared dream that we call 'the world', in which we seem to exist as separate physical bodies. Before we are 'born' as a physical body we exist as consciousness and psyche, as we do in dreams before we wake up in the morning. When we are born, just as when we wake, we bring into manifestation the denser level of our psyche. Plotinus teaches:

> 'The experience we call birth is the coming into being of the lower phase of the psyche which we call the physical body.'[30]

As newborn babies we have no concept of who we are. We therefore come to conceptualize ourselves as who everyone says we are – the visible body. We identify with how we appear to others, rather than how we are for ourselves. The Gnostics call our apparent identity the *eidolon*, which means 'image'. The *eidolon*, like a reflection in a mirror, is who we appear to be, but not who we really are. In modern spiritual jargon the *eidolon* is the 'ego'. In the Christian text *Pistis Sophia*, it is called the 'counterfeit consciousness'.[31] Basilides calls it the 'parasitic psyche'.[32] Plotinus calls it 'the intruder'.[33] Our word 'idea' – an image in the mind – comes from the same root as the word *eidolon*. The *eidolon* is the 'I am the body' idea. We have identified ourselves with this idea, rather than the Consciousness within which the idea arises. We have mistaken the image for the essence.

This is the tragi-comedy of the human predicament. We are all God, but most of us think of ourselves as a somewhat shoddy person. We have completely identified with the body we appear to be on the circumference of the circle of self and have no awareness of our essential nature as Consciousness at the centre. When we identify with the body, we attempt to gratify and protect the particular person we mistake ourselves to be. We seek what is good for this limited idea of who we are, regardless of the consequences to others and the entirety. Thus the wise, loving, impersonal presence that is the Mystery of God becomes an ignorant, selfish, separate person.

The Gnostic path of self-knowledge is discovering that the *eidolon* is not our true Self and progressively becoming aware of our essential nature as Consciousness. It can be imagined as the process of moving our point of identification from the circumference of the circle of self up the radii to the centre and realizing ourselves to be what we have been all along: Consciousness. The Gnostics teach that this is a journey of many lifetimes. Just as each night we go to sleep to wake up reinvigorated the next day, so at the end of a lifetime we die and reincarnate, manifesting ourselves as a new body in the world, the wiser for our previous experience. In this way, life by life, we progressively move further along the road of realization.

THE PATH OF SELF-KNOWLEDGE

The Gnostics divide human beings into categories according to their level of self-awareness. Paul, Valentinus and other Christians use the terms *hylics, psychics* and *pneumatics*.[34] *Hylics*, or 'materialists', identify themselves with the body – the circumference of the circle of self. *Psychics*, or 'soulists', identify with the psyche or soul – the radius. *Pneumatics*, or 'spiritists', are aware of themselves as spirit or Consciousness – the centre.

In Pagan, Jewish and Christian Gnostic traditions there are two basic stages of initiation which lead initiates progressively through these states of being. Christians called the first the *psychic* or 'soul' initiation, because it initiates the journey from being a *hylic* to becoming a *psychic*. They called the second the *pneumatic* or 'spirit' initiation, because it initiates the journey from being a *psychic* to becoming a *pneumatic*.

Psychic initiates were taught the exoteric teachings or Outer Mysteries of Gnosticism, which were openly available to all those interested in joining a particular Gnostic school. *Pneumatic* initiates went on to be taught the secret esoteric teachings or Inner Mysteries. Literalist

Christianity is the product of *psychic* initiates, uninitiated into the Inner Mysteries, making a religion out of the Outer Mysteries. This is why the secret *pneumatic* teachings of Christianity, which we are exploring, seem so remote from Christianity as it is generally understood today.

The *pneumatic* teachings were kept a secret because the spiritually immature can easily be so baffled that they dismiss them as incomprehensible nonsense. *Psychic* initiates were not taught the secret Inner Mysteries for the same reason that we do not tell children the secrets of sexuality until they are old enough to understand them. Such knowledge too early is simply confusing and could even be harmful. The Christian master Ptolemy explains: 'These things are not openly spoken of, for not all people are ready for Gnosis.'[35] Paul states:

> '*Psychics* don't grasp things which concern the consciousness of God. They seem like foolishness to them, because they are *pneumatically* discerned. *Pneumatics*, however, understand everything.'[36]

Psychic initiates can also easily misinterpret *pneumatic* teachings. The danger with telling those who are still completely enmeshed in identification with the *eidolon* that they are really God is that this will lead to inflation rather than transcendence. The ego starts to believe it is the Lord of the Universe. The history of religion is full of such ego-mania passed off as spirituality.

Soul Initiation

Although today the words 'spirit' and 'soul' are used interchangeably, for the ancients the conceptual differentiation between spirit and soul was the foundation of the initiatory structure underlying Gnostic spirituality. The *psychic* or soul initiation was about exploring soul/experience. The *pneumatic* or spirit initiation was about discovering the experiencer – spirit/Consciousness, the ground of all experience. Together these two levels of initiation created the conditions for the realization of Gnosis, which was their common fulfilment.

The process of awakening starts with an experience the original Christians called *metanoia*. This term, which is found throughout the New Testament, is traditionally translated 'repentance', a word now so loaded with religious connotations that it is difficult to hear what it really means. *Metanoia* is not about apologizing to God for breaking the rules or about performing prescribed penitential acts. It means 'a change of heart'.[37] It is deep dissatisfaction with the way we have been and the sincere desire to be different. It is the turning-point in our lives, when we realize we can't go on investing in our separate ego, because we intuitively know that life is actually about spiritual awakening. *Metanoia* is the signal that we are ready to embark on the process of soul initiation.

Dionysius describes this stage of initiation as being about 'purification'.[38] Both Pagans and Christians marked it with a 'baptism' – an initiation ritual involving immersion with water, symbolizing being cleansed. During this stage of initiation, initiates are instructed in ethics, which teaches them to live a good and selfless life and so helps them to gradually purify themselves of the selfish ego.

The *psychic* initiate understands self-knowledge to be about earnestly examining our faults and failings, so that we can become a better person. To use modern spiritual jargon, the *psychic* initiation is primarily about 'personal growth' through 'working on ourselves'. The underlying purpose is to lessen our identification with the *eidolon*, so that we can transcend it altogether in the *pneumatic* or spirit initiation.

Psychic initiates understand the injunction 'Know your Self' as the call to personal self-knowledge: 'Know what your personality is like.' *Pneumatic* initiates hear it afresh, as meaning: 'Know who you really are.' The *psychic* or soul initiation is about working on ourselves to become a better person. The *pneumatic* or spirit initiation is about coming to understand that we are not a person at all. We are impersonal Consciousness or spirit.

Spirit Initiation

The Pagan Gnostics call the two levels of initiation *catharmos*, meaning 'purification', and *paradosis*, meaning 'transmission'. In the first stage initiates are purified through ethical teachings. The second stage of initiation involves the transmission of esoteric philosophy.[39]

Today the word 'philosophy' is associated with dry academic theories, but the ancients did not see it in this way. For them, philosophy was not an intellectual exercise. It was a spiritual practice.

Philosophy is a rigorous examination of the mysteries of who we are and what life is. It questions our deepest assumptions and fundamentally changes how we perceive ourselves and our lives. It is a process of using the reasoning mind, which is an aspect of psyche, to guide us beyond thoughts altogether, to Consciousness itself. It disperses the confusion which obscures the Mystery of God. Clement of Alexandria teaches: 'Philosophy purges the psyche and prepares it for Gnosis.'[40]

Under the transforming impact of mystical philosophy initiates learn to 'disengage' completely from the psyche or soul, and so no longer identify themselves with anything they appear to be within their experience, instead identifying with the experiencer.[41] This state of 'contemplation' is getting back to the primal simplicity of being the conscious witness of the unfolding events that make up the psyche. When we do this, we are no longer actors in the drama of our lives. That is only how we appear within the psyche. We are not living our lives at all. Life is living through us. We are Consciousness aware of the Mystery spontaneously expressing itself as a sequence of experiences. We are not a person who does this or thinks that. Thoughts and actions arise in our experience and we enjoy the show.

The downside of believing we are the body is the inevitability of its demise. Fear of death is often what motivates spiritual exploration. The quest for self-knowledge is the search for a deeper identity which can survive physical death.[42] When we enter the state of contemplation, this is exactly what we discover. The process of *pneumatic* initiation is 'the purification of the unbornness', as the Christian Gnostic Zostrianos puts it with startling clarity.[43] At the end of this process we realize we are Consciousness itself, which will witness the death of the body, as it witnessed its birth, but which can never die, because it was never born.

In the Greek used by the original Christians, the word usually translated as 'salvation' also means 'preservation'. 'To be saved' is 'to be preserved', or 'made permanent'.[44] When the original Christians talk about 'being saved', they are talking about realizing the permanence of our essential nature. When we discover we are the permanent presence of Consciousness, not the temporary ever-changing psyche-body, we know that we are truly safe.

The Journey to God

The Gnostic path of self-knowledge can be thought of as a journey to God, for it comes to the same thing. Hermes Trismegistus, the legendary Egyptian sage whose mystical works were studied by the original Christians, teaches:

'Pure philosophy is spiritual striving through constant contemplation to attain Gnosis of God.'[45]

The process of initiation changes initiates' understanding of God. In truth, they *are* God, but whilst this is unknown, or a theory only, they experience their own essential identity as a superior being outside themselves. Whilst they think of themselves as a person, they experience God as a Big Person. As they come to understand themselves impersonally, they also come to understand God in impersonal terms. In the realization of Gnosis they finally come to know themselves to be indistinguishable from the Mystery of God.

Hylics either don't bother to think about God at all, or have a religious relationship with what they imagine to be the ultimate external authority figure. In the *psychic* stage of initiation, this gives way to a softer conception of God as a wise parent who nurtures us on our personal journey through life's trials and tribulations. Picturing God as a big person allows us to have an intimate relationship of love, devotion and friendship with the ineffable Mystery, which could otherwise seem remote, abstract and inaccessible.

In the Pagan tradition there were many different gods and goddesses, who were understood to be particular faces of the Oneness through whom initiates could relate to the Mystery. Drawing on this Pagan tradition, the Christian Sabellius compares the Holy Trinity – Father, Son and Holy Spirit – to *personas*.[46] A *persona* was a mask worn by an actor in the ceremonial pageants of the Pagan Mysteries. It is the root of our word 'personality'. In the same way that our personality or *persona* both masks and represents our ineffable essential nature, so the various images with which we picture the Divine are God's *personas*, which mask and represent the Mystery.

As *pneumatic* initiates we come to understand our own nature in impersonal terms and so no longer imagine God as a big person, but in impersonal terms such as the One, the Good and so on. As we approach the realization of Gnosis we progressively transcend duality and so all relationship with God is subsumed by the Oneness. There is no longer God and devotee, only the Mystery of God in love with itself. As Hermes Trismegistus writes, 'The goal of Gnosis is to become God.'[47] In *The Gospel of John*, Jesus proclaims that his mission is to make his disciples one with God as he is one with God, so that 'all is perfectly One'.[48]

THE REALIZATION OF GNOSIS

The process of Gnostic initiation has more twists than the plot of a Hollywood blockbuster. Initiates on the Christian Way set off to fulfil the injunction: 'Know your Self.' As their awareness grows, so their idea of who they are is transformed and transformed again.[49] In the *psychic* stage of initiation they discover that they are not the physical body. In the *pneumatic* stage of initiation they discover that they are not the personal psyche either. In the realization of Gnosis they understand that they are not even the impersonal witness. They are not a *self* at all. They are the Absolute Mystery.

The realization of Gnosis is the fulfilment of both the *psychic* initiation of personal transformation and the *pneumatic* initiation of personal transcendence. Initiates realize the Oneness of all that is and the complete illusion of their existence as a separate individual. This completes the *pneumatic* initiation of transcendence. Yet they continue to *appear* to be a separate individual – to others and to themselves – just as they have always done. Through the realization of Gnosis, however, the apparent person is perfected, which fulfils the *psychic* initiation of personal growth.

The Gnostics called the Mystery of God 'the Good'. They teach that when we realize Gnosis, we will discover that our essential identity is the Good. We won't need to *become* good. We will spontaneously act well as a natural expression of our being.[50] We will no longer identify with the *eidolon* and so will be literally selfless. We will know we are one with all that is, which is the experience of all-embracing love. We will know that all that happens is the will of God, which is the experience of unconditional acceptance and unshakeable faith. We will be intoxicated with wonder at what has been staring us in the face the whole time, but which we have been too preoccupied to notice: life is an awesome, incomprehensible miracle.

Gnosis is the knowledge that all is One. But this does not mean we suddenly experience the world as an amorphous blob. Rather, we understand that the essential Oneness necessarily expresses its infinite potential as the rich variety of life. Realizing that we are not a person does not mean we suddenly become some sort of disembodied nobody. Rather, we know we exist on many levels. We are the Mystery expressing itself as Consciousness witnessing psyche, within which we appear to be a person living a life in the world.

The Christian Way is not about withdrawing from the world, or the personality, into some abstract, impersonal void. It is about progressively expanding our awareness back to its source in the Mystery and being all that we are. Gnosis is consciously knowing in our everyday lives that we exist simultaneously in the states of waking, dreaming and deep sleep. Usually we move our awareness each day from the centre of the circle of self to the circumference and back again, passing through the states of waking (circumference), dreaming (radius) and centre (deep sleep). Through the process of initiation, we learn to maintain in our waking lives on the circumference the awareness of also being the radius and the centre.

As we explore the deep psyche in the *psychic* stage of initiation, reaching further and further back along the radius towards the centre, the magical quality that we associate with dreams starts to break out in our everyday experience. Mundane reality becomes strangely mythic and meaningful, ridiculing the ideas of the cosmos as some sort of grand machine run by blind cause and effect. In the *pneumatic* stage of initiation, as we learn to stand right back inside ourselves and be the ineffable witness of our experience, reality becomes completely dream-like. The person we took ourselves to be is a character in a drama we are witnessing. We exist outside the whole play of time, invulnerable and immortal.

The realization of Gnosis is becoming aware of being the dazzling darkness of the Mystery. We subsume ourselves in this wonderful absence of experience each night in the state we call 'deep sleep'. It is the glorious rest of stillness without movement. The One with no other. Pure subjectivity, without objectivity. Essence with no appearance. It is the primal paradise of union.

The realization of Gnosis is being aware that this state of Oneness is not just something we sink into when we relinquish Consciousness. It is possible to be conscious of Oneness by becoming aware that the state we think of as 'deep sleep' is actually the ground of all experience. The reason we aren't aware of it is because it is not an experience. We habitually focus on *what* we experience, rather than *that* we are experiencing. But when we focus on the permanent presence that witnesses our ever-changing experience, we become conscious of Consciousness.

Although in deep sleep itself there is no experience, when we emerge from deep sleep we sometimes remember it as pure bliss. This is because, as we have already explored, from the perspective of duality, the One is experienced as Love, Beauty, Bliss – the Good. When we maintain an awareness of the One whilst experiencing the multiplicity of appearances we call 'life', we are conscious of the rich variety of our ever-changing experiences, whilst simultaneously bathing in the permanent bliss of our ineffable being.

THE ESSENCE OF CHRISTIANITY

The original Christians encoded their teachings in their allegorical myths. Before examining these myths in detail, let's end this chapter by looking at the most important of all Christian mythological figures and what he represents in the light of the philosophy we have been exploring. That figure is, of course, the Christ.

The Christ Within

Christ represents the one Consciousness of God at the centre of the circle of self which is our essential shared identity. *The Treatise on the Resurrection* sees us 'radiating like rays from the Saviour'.[51] For Paul, 'the Christ within' is our common essence. We are 'the members of the body of Christ',[52] he explains, for in reality 'there is one Consciousness and one body'.[53] In *A Prayer of the Apostle Paul*, Paul prays to Jesus, 'It is you who are my Consciousness.'[54] Dionysius urges us to experience 'a communion with Jesus who is transcendent Consciousness'.[55]

Pagan and Christian Gnostics call the one Consciousness in all of us 'the *Logos*'.[56] *The Gospel of John* equates Jesus with the *Logos* that is 'the true light which illuminates everyone who comes into the world'.[57] Hermes Trismegistus explains:

'That in you which sees and hears is the *Logos* of the Lord. It is the Consciousness of God the Father.'[58]

Clement of Alexandria elucidates the idea that Jesus is the 'Son of God' by explaining, 'The Son is the Consciousness of the Father.'[59] The Father is the Mystery – the dazzling darkness of unconscious Consciousness. Jesus represents the potential for Consciousness made actual in every conscious being. The Christian master Marcus has Jesus declare:

'I am the Son of the Father who is beyond all existence. While I, his Son, am in existence.'[60]

To know the Mystery of God, we must come to know our shared identity, which is symbolized by Jesus. Hence in *The Gospel of John* Jesus teaches: 'No one comes to the Father but by me.'[61] This phrase is endlessly plastered over church notice-boards and has probably been the source of more bigotry than any other religious dogma. For the original Christians, however, it does not mean that the only way to God is to be a Christian, in the exclusive cultish sense of the word. As *The Gospel of John* makes clear from its introduction, which equates Jesus with the *Logos*, 'No one comes to the Father but by me' means that the way to the Mystery of God is via his Son, the *Logos*.[62] We know the Mystery through its manifestation as Consciousness.

Resurrection from the Dead

Having understood the symbolic nature of the Christ, we are now in a position to understand the most important motif in Christian mythology, which the original Christians used to express the essence of their message. This is the image of the resurrected Christ, which represents the realization of Gnosis. In the Greek language, in which they wrote, the word for resurrection, *anastasis*, also means 'awakening', so the idea that resurrection represents spiritual awakening was obvious.[63] The 'resurrection of Christ' symbolically represents 'awakening the Christ within'.

Later Christian Literalists taught that an historical person called Jesus literally died and resurrected for us, and that if we believe this we will go to Heaven when we die, whilst if we disbelieve we will be condemned to torment in Hell. This has nothing to do with the understanding of the original Christians, however. They taught that we each need to resurrect for ourselves, because we are all dead and in Hell right now!

As usual, the Gnostics turn our 'common sense' view inside-out. The underworld – Hades or Hell – is usually taken to be the place souls go after death. But for the Gnostics, the world we presently inhabit is the underworld, where we exist as the spiritually dead.[64] Plato writes: 'I have heard from the wise that we are now dead and the body is our tomb.'[65] The Pagan Gnostic Olympiodorus teaches: 'When separated from the body the psyche lives in reality, for here she dies.'[66]

With characteristic irony, the Gnostics also describe the state of being identified with the physical body, which we normally think of as being awake, as falling asleep. Our 'normal' state is not being alive and awake – it is being asleep and dreaming we are in Hell. Plotinus explains that to incarnate 'is to descend into Hades and there fall asleep'.[67] The Christian *Secret Book of John* urges, 'Be wakeful so that you come out of heavy sleep and take off the clothes of Hades.'[68] The Christian text *The Concept of our Great Power* urges, 'You are asleep and dreaming. Wake up.'[69]

We think we are alive, but really we are dead. We think we are awake, but really we are asleep and dreaming. We think we know who we are and what life is, but really we are lost in illusion. We need to resurrect. We need to wake up. We need Gnosis. Quoting a pre-existing hymn, Paul writes:

> 'Awake, sleeper. Rise from the dead,
> and Christ will illuminate you.'[70]

We are all the dead Christ and need to resurrect to our true identity. This is the essence of Christianity. The purpose of Christian initiation is to awaken within us an awareness of our essential nature as the Christ. Then we will be a 'Christian' – a conscious member of the 'body of Christ'. Paul writes:

> 'We are only on the *pneumatic* level if God's consciousness dwells in us. Those who don't possess the Christ consciousness are not Christians.'[71]

If we awaken to Christ consciousness, we will know Heaven to be an ever-present reality. Heaven is the centre of the circle of self, where we permanently exist as the Christ. Hell is the circumference, where we mistake ourselves to be separate egos and so temporally exist as the spiritually dead. Heaven and Hell are both here and now, depending on whether we are spiritually dead or resurrected. In *The Gospel of Thomas* Jesus teaches: 'The kingdom of the Father is spread out upon the Earth and people don't see it.'[72] But Paul explains:

> 'When anyone is united to Christ there is a new world. The old order has gone. The new order has already begun.'[73]

SUMMARY

❖ Christianity is about the quest for self-knowledge. Human identity has three aspects: spirit, soul, body – Consciousness, psyche, physicality. Essentially, we are Consciousness witnessing psyche. The body exists within the psyche as sensation.

❖ Self-knowledge and knowledge of God are the same thing, because our shared essential identity is God. We are the one Consciousness of God believing itself to be many separate persons.

❖ The path of self-knowledge is a process of initiation, through which we learn to disengage from the *eidolon* or ego – the 'I am the body' idea – and discover our immortal nature as Consciousness.

❖ The *psychic* or soul initiation is about perfecting the person we appear to be. The *pneumatic* or spirit initiation is about being the impersonal Consciousness we are. The realization of Gnosis is the fulfilment of the previous two stages of initiation and the culmination of the path of self-knowledge, in which we realize everything and everyone to be an expression of the Mystery of God.

❖ The figure of Christ represents the one Consciousness of God which is our essential shared identity. The Christian message is that we are spiritually dead and need to resurrect to our true identity, which is Christ.

Having explored the essence of Christian Gnosticism, let's now see how these teachings were encoded in evocative myths of Jesus and the Goddess. These two figures, which dominate Christian mythology, represent the fundamental duality of witness and experience, Consciousness and psyche, spirit and soul.

chapter five

THE LOST
Goddess

'I was sent forth from the Power.

I am the honoured one and the scorned one.

I am the holy one and the whore.

I am the mother and the daughter.

I am called Sophia by the Greeks and Gnosis by the foreigners.

I am the one whose image is great in Egypt

and the one who has no image among the foreigners.'

The Goddess, Perfect Consciousness[1]

We come to Gnosis 'through analogies and abstractions', teaches Plotinus.[2] Myths are the 'analogies' through which an initiate is first introduced to Gnostic teachings in the psychic or soul stage of initiation.[3] Philosophy is the process of 'abstraction' through which initiates come to understand what these myths really mean in the *pneumatic* or spirit initiation.[4]

Yet we should not think of myths as merely stories for spiritual beginners, which become redundant once the teachings they encode are understood. It is rather that beginners take them at face value, while mature initiates have a deeper understanding. For the ancients, myths were a symbolic language with which they could explore spiritual ideas that continued to be relevant throughout the whole process of initiation. Decoding the allegorical meaning of a myth is not, therefore, about explaining the myth away, but about taking it to new levels.

The great thing about myths is that they are always pregnant with more meaning. They are a focus for contemplation through which initiates can continually deepen their understanding. They are also a mnemonic, helping initiates to remember what they have learned and ensuring that the teachings survive. As long as the myths are told, the teachings remain, hidden within for those 'with eyes to see' and 'ears to hear'.

Myths also do something which philosophy rarely does – they engage the heart. They put abstract thoughts into the form of a particular story, and it is particulars that stir the emotions. If we are told that there are thousands starving to death right now, we may start thinking about a solution. But if we are shown one particular starving child, we will be moved with compassion. Likewise, myths have the power to fill us with feeling, just as the Jesus myth has done for millions over the centuries.

The Gnostics were well aware that their mythical figures were the product of the imagination. The Pagan poet Ovid writes: 'The gods are created by poets.'[5] The Gospel of Philip explains: 'Men make gods and worship their creation.'[6] But seeing mythical figures as 'unreal' is to miss the point. Mythical figures are images of ineffable archetypes appearing in the psyche. 'Archetype' is a word that was first used by Philo and later taken up by Carl Jung.[7] Archetypes are primordial ideas that structure reality. They appear to us in the form of symbolic images. As Jung explained, a single archetype may appear in the form of a variety of symbols.[8] Such images are more than subjective fantasies. They are the vocabulary of the psyche itself, through which the initiate can communicate with their own inner depths.

In the process of initiation, as we progressively move our point of identification back up the radius of the circle of self, we experience deeper and deeper levels of the psyche.[9] We move beyond superficial imaginings and enter into archetypal mythic states of awareness. We all experience such states in powerfully vivid dreams. As initiates mature, they begin to experience this level of awareness in their waking life. This is characteristically in the form of what Jung calls 'synchronicities' – strange, meaningful coincidences. Intriguing patterns emerge in what were previously random events. Mundane life becomes transformed into a mythic adventure in which initiates have the feeling of being led by some invisible force. They begin to feel the presence of mythical figures in their lives, with whom they develop a personal relationship. These mythic figures, embodying deeper levels of the self, become inner guides on the journey of awakening. Such figures are not 'unreal'. They are powerful psychic realities, as many Christians know from their personal relationship with Christ.

Jung developed a therapeutic technique based on the spiritual practices of the ancient Gnostics called 'active imagination', in which the patient enters into an 'objective' relationship with the images found in their inner world. Jung himself experienced meeting an 'inner teacher' called Philemon, of whom he wrote:

> 'Philemon and other figures of my fantasies brought home to me the crucial insight that there were things in the psyche which I do not produce, but which produce themselves and have their own life.'[10]

Jung captured the ancient understanding of myths when he wrote: 'Dreams are private myths. Myths are public dreams.'[11] In the same way that in dreams all the various characters can be understood as representing different aspects of the dreamer, so in myths all the characters represent different aspects of each one of us. Understanding this prevents the error of identifying women with the Goddess and men with the Godman, which leads to unintended sexual stereotyping. The myth of the lost Goddess, for example, is not designed to tell us about women, but about the human condition. The Godman and the Goddess represent two aspects of our identity, regardless of whether we are male or female.

Although the wisdom that myths explore is timeless and universally human, the images used reflect the values and conditions of the time. Images that seemed appropriate or even radical 2,000 years ago can now seem alien, dated and 'politically incorrect'. We can understand much about the ancient world by studying the forms in which myths were expressed, but that is not the purpose of this book. Christian mythology is full of motifs that may easily offend our modern sensibilities, but we will attempt to peer through the images of the day to the perennial wisdom that it encodes, to be tolerant of the form to understand the essential mystical message.

Although today we tend to dismiss myths as historical curiosities, we are still an extremely symbol-literate society. Look at a few quality adverts and you will soon see how much can be conveyed using just a handful of symbolically charged images. Our difficulty in understanding ancient myths is not that we no longer think symbolically but that we use a different symbolic vocabulary from our ancestors. Mention a 'light sabre' or 'the force' and most of us would understand the allusion to the movie *Star Wars*, but obviously one of the original Christians would have no idea what we were talking about. Likewise, we do not share the common fund of symbols current in the ancient world, and so the allusions of early Christians are often lost on us and seem arcane, although at the time they would have been obvious. To understand their myths as they did themselves, we must uncover the symbolic allusions they incorporated in their works.

We will begin this process by examining the Christian myth of the lost Goddess, which is the partner myth to the Jesus story.[12]

THE MYTH OF SOPHIA

Christ represents Consciousness. His lover/sister the Goddess represents psyche. Christ represents the centre of the circle of self. The Goddess represents the radius. The radius is a line with two ends. One is rooted in the centre of Consciousness and the other lies on the circumference, representing the body in the world. The Goddess is, therefore, thought of as having two aspects, sometimes known as 'higher Sophia' and 'lower Sophia' or 'incorruptible Sophia' and 'mortal Sophia'.[13] The first represents psyche in a state of Gnosis, united with Consciousness at the centre of the circle of Self. The second represents the psyche fallen into identification with the body on the circumference.[14]

As in the Pagan Gnostic tradition, the Christian Goddess is known by many names. Most commonly she is called Sophia, meaning 'wisdom', which is the name we will generally use to refer to her. However, she is also known as Psyche, Zoë, meaning 'life', Achamoth, from the Hebrew for 'wisdom',[15] and other names that we no longer understand, such as Barbelo.

There are many versions of the myth of the lost Goddess, which is one of the oldest Christian myths.[16] Later we will explore the cosmological level of this myth, which relates how the cosmos came into existence. To begin with, however, we will take a look at the same story on the human level, in which the lost Goddess represents the psyche of each one of us. We will examine an abridged form of a version of the myth found in a text called *The Exegesis on the Soul*. It is an allegory for the fall of the psyche or soul into identification with the body and its redemption from the evils of incarnation through the saving power of Consciousness, represented by the psyche's lover. In this version of the story the Goddess and her lover are given no names. In most Christian myths, however, they are identified as Sophia and Christ, and we shall use these names in our analysis of the myth.

In true eclectic Gnostic fashion, *The Exegesis on the Soul* expands on its mythological narrative by quoting from both the Jewish Old Testament and the works of Homer, the 'Pagan Bible'.[17] We will look at these references when we come to decode the myth. But let's first take it at face value as a vivid fable with a powerfully erotic tone[18] which evokes the familiar human experience of being lost, all alone, in a menacing world.

'In olden times wise people gave the psyche a feminine name, because she is feminine in nature. She even has a womb. Originally she was a virgin, living alone with her Father. But when she was born into a body, she fell into the hands of bad men who passed her between them. Some raped her. Others seduced her with gifts. She became a prostitute, although she secretly hoped that each man she embraced would be her husband. Afterwards she was always filled with regret, but as soon as she escaped from one man, she just ran to the next. Each of them made her live with him and service him in bed, as if he were her master. Overcome with shame, she no longer dared to leave her abusers, even though they lied about respecting her and were constantly unfaithful. Eventually they all abandoned her completely. She ended up like a forlorn widow without assistance or sustenance. They left her with nothing except the results of having sex with them: dumb, blind, sickly, feebleminded children.

Then her Father visited her and saw her sighing and suffering with remorse. She begged him, "Save me Father. Look what has happened to me. I know I ran away from home, but please bring me back to myself again." She began raging and writhing like a woman in labour trying to give birth. But a woman doesn't have the power to beget a child alone. So her Father promised to send from Heaven his first-born son, her brother, to be her bridegroom. She gave up whoring and washed off the foul odours of her former abusers. She prepared herself in the bridal chamber, filling it with sweet perfume, and waited for her true husband. She no longer frequented the market-place, having sex with whomever she fancied. She waited for him, anxiously asking, "When will he come?" She was frightened because, since she had left her Father's house, she couldn't remember how her brother looked. Yet, like any woman in love, she even dreamt about her lover at night.

Eventually her bridegroom came to take her as his bride, just as her Father had said he would. Their marriage was not like the earthly type in which, after sex, the man and woman behave as if some irritating physical burden has been relieved and turn over without looking at each other. In this marriage, the two united to share a single life. Gradually she recognized her bridegroom, which filled her with happiness. She wept and wept when she remembered her former widowhood. She made every effort to make herself beautiful, so that he would be pleased to stay with her. She knew she must forget all her false lovers and devote herself to her true king. And so they both enjoyed each other, and when they made love she received his seed and bore good children.'[19]

AN INITIATION ALLEGORY

Sophia's fall, repentance, redemption and marriage represent the *hylic*, *psychic*, *pneumatic* and Gnostic states of awareness.

The *Hylic* State

The myth starts with Sophia as a virgin living alone with her Father. This represents the pristine psyche united with Consciousness, before the process of physical incarnation.[20] Then Sophia runs away from home and undergoes many misfortunes, symbolizing the psyche's birth as a body in the world and the suffering inherent in the bodily state. Unaware of her true nature, she is taken advantage of. She looks for love in all the wrong places, becoming a whore and exchanging love for money. Although she longs for her true lover, she lives with the false bridegroom, representing the ego, and is too frightened to leave. Finally she is abandoned like a lonely widow, left with only her feeble children, representing her bad egotistical thoughts. As it says in *The Naassene Psalm*, 'Hemmed in by evil, she knows no way out. Misled, she has entered a labyrinth.'[21] This represents the confused and fearful *hylic* state of spiritual unconsciousness.

Psychic Initiation

At this stage Sophia's Father visits her and she experiences *metanoia* – a change of heart, repentance.[22] This represents the turning-point in the initiate's journey. When all feels lost, suddenly there is the sense of the divine presence, regret at having been misled and a call for help. The text comments:

> 'As long as the psyche keeps running about everywhere copulating with whomever she meets and defiling herself, she suffers her just deserts. But when she perceives the straits she is in and weeps before the Father and repents, then the Father will have mercy on her. He will make her womb turn inwards again, so that the psyche regains her true nature. When the womb of the psyche turns inward, it is baptized. It is immediately cleansed of external pollution, just as garments, when dirty, are put into the water and turned about until their dirt is removed and they become clean. The cleansing of the psyche is to regain the newness of her former nature. That is her baptism.'[23]

This stage in the story represents the *psychic* initiation of purification, symbolized by baptism. In the fable, Sophia gives up whoring and washes away the odours of her defilers. The turning of her womb inwards symbolizes initiates ceasing to be preoccupied with their outer bodily desires and instead working on their inner self to purify themselves of egotism.

Pneumatic Initiation

Sophia longs to give birth to something good, but cannot do this alone. She needs to discover her true lover, who is her brother Christ. Likewise, the initiate longs to be a good person, but can only really do this by knowing their essential identity, which is goodness itself. Like Sophia preparing herself for her bridegroom with sweet perfume, initiates practise goodness, awaiting the realization of the Good. Yet this is a time of doubt and anxiety. Sophia has been so long from her Father's house that she can no longer remember the brother-lover she is waiting for. Still she is consumed by anticipation, even dreaming of her lover at night. At this stage, initiates are likewise filled with doubt and anticipation. Although they are eagerly awaiting a revelation of their true nature, they do not know what that is.

When Sophia is finally ready, her lover comes and she realizes she must abandon all her previous lovers, devoting herself to her true king. This represents the *pneumatic* initiation in which initiates let go of identification with the ego and its demands, and focus on their true nature as Consciousness, symbolized by the king or Christ.

The Mystical Marriage

The myth of Sophia climaxes with the bride and bridegroom making love together, united as one in a mystical marriage. This image is an important mythological motif for the original Christians, because it represents the realization of Gnosis.

The journey of awakening is a process of expanding our awareness from the body on the circumference of the circle of self up the radius of psyche to the centre of Consciousness. As Plotinus explains:

'In the advanced stages of contemplation, rising from body to psyche to consciousness, the object contemplated becomes a more and more intimate possession of the contemplator. When we reach consciousness itself, there is complete identity of knower and known.'[24]

Consciousness is our *being*. When we focus on *that* we are, rather than on *what* we are experiencing, Consciousness is both subject and object. We become conscious of Consciousness. We know ourselves. When we reach the centre of Consciousness the knower (Consciousness) and the known (psyche) are one. This is the mystical marriage. This is self-knowledge. This is Gnosis.

Silvanus urges us to ignore the body and person we have *become* and be aware of *being* what we eternally are:

'When you entered into a bodily birth, you were begotten. Become aware of *being* inside the bridal chamber! Be illuminated in Consciousness!'[25]

The Exegesis on the Soul relates that Sophia's mystical marriage with her brother-lover results in her 'rebirth'.[26] The text compares this to the resurrection of Jesus in the Jesus myth, which, as we have already discussed, also represents the realization of Gnosis:

> 'It is fitting that the psyche regenerates herself and becomes again as she formerly was. This is the resurrection from the dead. This is freedom from captivity. This is the upward journey of ascent to Heaven. This is the way back to the Father.'[27]

In the mystical marriage Sophia is returned to the state of communion with the Father that she enjoyed before her fall. So she 'becomes again as she formerly was'. Yet she left a daughter and returns a bride. She has matured through the process of incarnation. It has not simply been a silly mistake from which she needed rescuing. Her state of innocence with the Father at the beginning of the myth represents the dazzling darkness of the Mystery, the state of unconscious unity which we experience as deep sleep. Her mystical marriage with her lover-brother Christ represents the state of conscious Oneness which can only result from undergoing the journey of incarnation and awakening.

The mystical marriage symbolizes a state of enlightenment that cannot be understood from the outside. *The Gospel of Philip* states:

> 'Bridegroom and bride belong to the bridal chamber. No one shall be able to see the bridegroom with the bride unless he become such a one.'[28]

Self-knowledge is not a spectator sport. The only way to know Christ – our shared essential identity – is to become a worthy bride – a mature initiate.

Paul urges us to make Jesus our 'husband'.[29] Just as Sophia bears the good children of her divine lover, so Paul explains that 'when we have become identified with Christ', we have 'found a husband in him who rose from the dead, so that we may bear fruit for God'.[30]

In the Pagan Mysteries, initiates also symbolically became brides of the Godman in a mystical marriage. They were veiled like brides and had the veils removed during their initiation to symbolize removing the barrier of illusion between themselves and God. Using the same imagery, Paul writes:

> 'Because for us there is no veil over the face, we reflect, as in a mirror, the light of the Lord, and are thus transfigured into his image.'[31]

The Image of God

The comparison of the psyche to a mirror which reflects an image of the light, representing God/Consciousness, is an important Gnostic metaphor. *The Gospel of Philip* teaches:

> 'You can't see yourself in water or a mirror without light. Nor again will you be able to see yourself with light but no water or mirror. Therefore it is right to baptize with both water and light. But the light is the anointing.'[32]

The *psychic* stage of initiation – the baptism of water – can be imagined as a process of stilling the waters, or cleaning the mirror of psyche, or removing the veil of illusion, to reflect the light perfectly. The *pneumatic* initiation – the baptism of light – is realizing we are the light of Consciousness which illuminates the appearances in the mirror of psyche. This baptism/initiation is called 'the anointing' because it begins the process whereby we realize ourselves to be the universal Consciousness of God, symbolized by the 'Christ' or 'Anointed One'.

We are essentially Consciousness – the light – witnessing psyche – the water. As long as the water is disturbed, we will see a multiplicity of images, just as when we watch the sun reflected as myriad flashes on the rippling sea. This is our normal state of awareness. We are caught up in the reflected appearances and are unaware of the light of Consciousness itself. But when the waters are still, or the mirror is clean, the light is reflected perfectly, without refracting into multiplicity. When we look into the mirror of the perfected psyche, the light of Consciousness sees itself. The two are made one. Simon Magus explains:

> 'The One Power, motionless and unborn, appears as a reflection in the moving waters below. When the image is perfected it will become like the blessed infinite stillness above.'[33]

The One Power – the universal Consciousness of God represented by Christ – is our shared essence. It is reflected in the moving waters of psyche, giving rise to the appearance of multiplicity. But when the waters are stilled and the image is perfected, the mirror reflects the light to the light. It shows the stillness that it is stillness. It reveals to the unborn infinite blessedness its unborn infinite blessed nature.

Pythagoras teaches: 'You will honour God perfectly if you make your psyche God's image.'[34] When we look in the mirror of perfected psyche we see nothing but God. We see a universe permeated by goodness, love, bliss, beauty and Consciousness. We see that all is One. We see what we are. This is the mystical marriage.

ORIGINS OF THE CHRISTIAN GODDESS

As with all Christian mythology, the myth of the lost Goddess is a synthesis of pre-existing Jewish and Pagan myths. Let's examine some of these sources.

Jewish Sources

The Exegesis on the Soul draws attention to some of the Jewish mythological motifs which it develops in the myth of Sophia. It quotes *Jeremiah*, in which God proclaims to Israel, as if to the lost Goddess:

'You prostituted yourself to many shepherds and then you returned to me. Take an honest look and see where you prostituted yourself. You became shameless with everyone. You did not call on me as kinsman or as Father or author of your virginity.'[35]

Likewise, in *Ezekiel* God announces:

'You built yourself a brothel on every lane, and you wasted your beauty, and you spread your legs in every alley, and you multiplied your acts of prostitution. You prostituted yourself to the sons of Egypt, those who are your neighbours, men great of flesh.'[36]

The Exegesis on the Soul decodes the allegorical meaning of this text:

'What does "the sons of Egypt, men great of flesh" mean, if not the world of the body and the realm of the senses and the affairs of this Earth, by which the psyche has become contaminated?'[37]

The Exegesis on the Soul also points out the resonance between the myth of Sophia and the *Genesis* myth. In *Genesis* Adam represents Consciousness and Eve represents psyche. In the beginning there was originally a primordial human being, Adam, from whom God took 'one side' and created Eve (not a 'rib' as it says in traditional translations!) This represents the projection of psyche from Consciousness. The two are essentially one, but appear as opposites. The psyche (Eve) leads Consciousness (Adam) into identification with the body. This is symbolized by the Fall from Eden. The mystical marriage repairs the primal separation of Adam and Eve, Consciousness and psyche. *The Exegesis on the Soul* quotes Paul's teaching, 'They will become a single body,'[38] and comments:

> 'They were originally joined one to another when they were with the Father, before the woman led astray the man, who is her brother. This marriage has brought them back together again and the psyche has been joined to her true lover.'[39]

In another Jewish text, *Proverbs*, the two fundamental states of the psyche are represented by Lady Wisdom and Lady Folly. According to Philo, Lady Folly is like a whore who leads those who listen to her to Hell. Lady Wisdom, however, is compared to an invitation to a wedding and a faithful wife – images which refer to the motif of the mystical marriage.[40]

The Myth of Helen

As with the Jesus story, the most important source for the Christian Goddess myth is Pagan mythology. *The Exegesis on the Soul* compares the Christian myth of Sophia to Homer's initiatory tales *The Iliad* and *The Odyssey*, in which Helen has been abducted and must be rescued.[41] According to the Pythagoreans, Helen is a symbol of the psyche and her abduction represents the fall of the psyche into incarnation.[42]

Euripides tells us that it is only Helen's *eidolon*, or image, which has been captured by the Trojans.[43] The real Helen is safely in Egypt, which for Pagan Gnostics symbolizes the primordial heavenly home of the gods, not the body, as it does to the Jews.[44] The real Helen represents the higher aspect of the psyche, which is forever safe. Her captured *eidolon* represents the lower aspect of the psyche, which has fallen into incarnation. According to Plato, the poet Stesichorus lost his sight as punishment for writing that the real Helen had been captured and only regained it when he recanted.[45] This is again an allegory. As long as we think that the real Self is the body, we are spiritually blind. When we realize that our real Self has never been born, we regain our spiritual sight.

The Helen myth was important to the first Christians. Drawing on this allegory and the Christian myth of the lost Goddess, Simon Magus describes himself as a 'Christ' who had come to rescue the lost Goddess, in the form of his spiritual partner 'Helen', whom he found living as a prostitute in a brothel in Tyre.[46] For the Simonians, Simon and Helen represent the Supreme Power and Sophia.[47] Simon's fellow teacher Dositheus also travelled with a spiritual partner called Helen. Likewise Simon's successor Meander claimed to be a 'Christ' come to rescue the Goddess lost in the world.[48] Deliberately imitating the myth of Jesus and the Goddess, these Gnostic masters identified themselves with the role of the saviour come to reveal Gnosis to their lost followers, symbolized by Helen/Sophia.

Plato's *Phaedo*

In *Phaedo* Plato gives us an account of the fall and redemption of the psyche which was undoubtedly drawn on by the original Christians when they created their own version of the myth of the lost Goddess:

> 'The psyche is dragged by the body into the region of the changeable, where she wanders in confusion. The world spins around her and she is like a drunkard under its influence. But returning to herself, she reflects. Then she passes into the realm of purity, eternity, immortality and unchangeableness, which are her kindred. When she is herself and not obstructed or hindered she is ever with them. When she ceases from her erring ways and is in communion with the unchanging, she is herself unchanging. This state of the psyche is called Sophia.'[49]

The Myth of Aphrodite

The Pagan myth of the Goddess Aphrodite tells fundamentally the same tale as the later Christian myth of the lost Goddess. Like Sophia, Aphrodite has a pristine and a fallen nature. Plotinus explains that in essence she is 'Aphrodite of the Heavens', but 'here she has turned whore'.[50] He writes, 'Zeus represents consciousness and Aphrodite his daughter who issues from him is psyche,'[51] commenting:

'The nature of the psyche is to love God and long to be at one with Him in the noble love of a daughter for a noble Father. But coming to human birth and lured by the courtships of this sphere, she takes up with another lover, a mortal, leaves her Father and falls. But one day, coming to hate her shame, she puts away the evil of Earth, once more seeks her Father and finds peace.[52] The psyche's true good lies in devotion to consciousness its kin. Evil to the psyche lies in frequenting strangers.[53] But suppose the psyche has attained the highest, or rather it has revealed its presence to her. Then as long as the presence holds all distinctions fade. It is like the merging of lover and beloved. Once she has this she would not trade it for anything in the whole universe.'[54]

The Myth of Eros and Psyche

The myth of Eros and Psyche again contains the same fundamental motifs as the Christian myth of Sophia.[55] Psyche obviously represents the psyche or soul. She has fallen asleep in hades, representing physical incarnation. She is rescued from the world of the spiritually dead by Eros who, like Jesus, is God's firstborn Son and the 'Revealer of Light', representing the one Consciousness in all.[56] The Christian text *On the Origin of the World* explains:

'Just as from a single lamp many lamps are lit, but the lamp is not diminished, in the same ways Eros is dispersed in all created beings, but is not diminished.'[57]

Eros means 'love', so the message of the myth of Eros and Psyche is quite clear from the names of the characters: Psyche is rescued by Love. The myth climaxes with their marriage, after which Psyche becomes immortal. As in the Christian version of the myth, this mystical marriage represents the realization of Gnosis, in which initiates know their immortal essence.

The myth of Eros and Psyche is related in Lucius Apuleius' book *The Transformations of Lucius*,[58] which is itself an allegory of the author's initiation into the Mysteries of the Goddess. It tells how he was turned into an ass, symbolizing identification with the body. In this state he overhears the tale of Psyche and Eros, which is being told by an old woman to a young bride who has been abducted by a gang of robbers. Here we have the same motifs again. Allegories within allegories. You see what sophisticated mythographers these people were!

The Myth of Demeter and Persephone

The most influential of all the myths of the Goddess in her two aspects is the myth of Demeter and Persephone, taught in the Mysteries of Eleusis.[59] The Pagan Gnostic Sallustius tells us that this myth is an allegory for the descent of the psyche into incarnation.[60] Olympiodorus likewise explains, 'The psyche descends after the manner of Persephone.'[61] Lucius Apuleius talks of the 'dark descending rites' and 'luminous ascending rites' of Persephone,[62] writing of his own initiation:

> 'I approached the confines of death, and trod on the threshold of Persephone, and being carried through all the elements, I came back again to my pristine condition.'[63]

The Literalist Christian Hippolytus describes the teachings of the descent and ascent of the psyche as the mystery revealed to those 'admitted to the highest grade of the Eleusinian rites' and states that initiates of the Naassene school of Christian Gnosticism had developed their teachings specifically from this source.[64]

Plato tells us the name 'Persephone' comes from *sophe* and means 'wise', so it derives from the same root as 'Sophia'.[65] Persephone, who was known as Kore, meaning 'Daughter' or 'Girl', represents the fallen psyche. In the Christian *Acts of Thomas*, the psyche is called Kore.[66] Demeter means 'Mother'. She is the Celestial Queen who represents the pure psyche.

In the myth, Demeter's daughter Persephone is abducted by Hades, god of the underworld.[67] This represents the fall into incarnation. Before they were initiated, initiates into the Mysteries of Eleusis had to imitate the grief felt by Demeter and Persephone at their separation.[68] This represents the experience of *metanoia* which results from the initiates' grief at having become separated from their deeper nature and lost in the world. Hermes goes to the underworld to rescue Persephone and reunite her with her mother Demeter. This represents rescuing the psyche from identification with the circumference of the circle of self and reuniting it with its true nature at the centre.

Hades secretly gives Persephone pomegranate seeds to eat, however, and because she eats these seeds she must return to the underworld for a third of every year. The pomegranate seeds represent the seeds of future lives which we create in this life, which bring us back into human incarnation to continue the journey of awakening. They represent what the ancients called our 'fate', which in modern spiritual jargon is generally known as our 'karma'.[69] The motif of returning to the underworld for 'a third of the year' is an allusion to the threefold nature of the Self: Consciousness, psyche, body. A third of our identity – the body – is in the underworld.

The figures of Demeter and Persephone were developed by the Greeks from ancient Egyptian mythology. Porphyry tells us that the Egyptian Isis is equivalent to both Demeter and Persephone.[70] In some stories Isis was said to have become a prostitute in Tyre, like Helen.[71] In Egyptian mythology the higher and lower aspects of the Goddess are represented by Isis and her sister Nephthys, the wife of the evil god Set, who, like Hades, represents the material world.[72]

These Egyptian myths are the earliest sources of what was to become the Christian myth of the lost and redeemed Goddess Although this perennial story has been expunged from Christianity, it survived in the form of fairy tales such as *Sleeping Beauty*. As her name suggests, Sleeping Beauty is an image of the psyche fallen asleep in the world. The story portrays her as a princess cursed to sleep forever, imprisoned in a dark castle surrounded by deep impenetrable forest, but finally rescued by her lover, the hero prince.[73]

THE GODDESS IN THE GOSPELS

In the Christian myth of Sophia, the Goddess, representing the psyche, is the central figure, whilst her brother-lover, representing Consciousness, is an incidental character. In the Jesus myth it is the opposite. The Godman is the central character. Yet the myth of the lost Goddess forms an important subtext to the Jesus story, which would have been obvious to Christian initiates familiar with both allegories. The Sophia myth makes clear the nature of Jesus' mythical mission – he comes to rescue his sister-lover Sophia, the psyche lost in identification with the body. 'Christ came for her sake,' states *The Tripartite Tractate*.[74]

Virgin and Prostitute

In the gospels the Virgin Mary and Mary Magdalene represent the higher Sophia and the fallen Sophia. They are called by the same name to emphasize the fact that mythologically they are aspects of the same figure. As in the Sophia myth, the first Mary is a virgin, like Sophia when she was living with her Father, and the second is a prostitute who is redeemed by her lover Jesus, like Sophia when lost in the world.

The Goddess as mother and prostitute is alluded to in the genealogy created for Jesus by *The Gospel of Matthew*.[75] As we would expect, this genealogy follows the patriarchal line, but breaks this pattern to specifically mention four famous Jewish 'fallen women'. Tamar was a temple prostitute. Ruth indulged in shameless sexual exploitation. Baathsheba was committed for adultery with King David. Rahab was the madam of a brothel.[76] In the *Exodus* allegory, when Jesus/Joshua arrives in the Promised Land he rescues the prostitute Rahab, symbolizing the psyche, from the walled city of Jericho, symbolizing the body.[77] By specifically naming Rahab as one of Jesus Christ's ancestors *The Gospel of Matthew* points to the mythological resonance between this story and the gospel story of Jesus redeeming the prostitute Mary Magdalene.

Mary Magdalene, representing Jesus' sister-lover Sophia, is the 'Beloved Disciple' who is consistently portrayed in Christian texts as having a particularly close relationship with Jesus. *The Gospel of the Beloved Disciple* (aka *The Gospel of John*), portrays Jesus and Mary as so close that, during the Last Supper, she is lying in his lap.[78] *The Gospel of Philip* relates that Jesus 'loved her more than the other disciples, and often used to kiss her on the lips'.[79] In *The Gospel of Luke* Mary wipes her hair on Jesus' feet.[80] According to Jewish law, only a husband was allowed to see a woman's hair unbound and if a woman let down her hair in front of another man, this was a sign of impropriety and grounds for mandatory divorce.[81] This incident, then, can be seen as portraying Jesus and Mary either as man and wife or as libertine lovers with scant regard for moral niceties.

Images of the Awakening Psyche

Women play a prominent role throughout the Jesus story, particularly in *The Gospel of the Beloved Disciple*, and all of them represent Sophia in her various states of awakening.[82] *The Exegesis on the Soul* portrays Sophia at her most desperate as a barren old woman. It is in this state that she experiences *metanoia* and calls out to the Father to rescue her.[83] In the Jesus story this aspect of Sophia is represented by Elizabeth, the mother of John the Baptist. She is a partner figure to the Virgin Mary.[84] Mary is young and unimpregnated. Elizabeth is old and barren. In this condition, like Sophia, she calls out to the Father for help, representing the barren psyche in which the call for help arises. The answer is John the Baptist, who represents the *psychic* initiation of purification through baptism with water, which is the start of the Gnostic path of self-knowledge.[85]

Throughout his mission Jesus has various encounters with women who are Sophia figures and symbolize the progressive states of awakening of the psyche. In one incident Jesus prevents an adulterous woman from being stoned to death by pointing out that none of her accusers are themselves blameless.[86] This is an allusion to the fallen Sophia being abused by her adulterous lovers. The woman in this story is a helpless victim surprised to be rescued. This represents the early stage of awakening in which the embodied psyche is a recipient of unasked for assistance from the essential Self, which it experiences as 'grace'.

In a further incident, Jesus meets an adulterous Samaritan woman, representing the fallen Sophia. Jesus reveals to the woman that he is the Christ and offers her the 'waters of life'.[87] This story takes the relationship between Sophia, representing the psyche, and Jesus, representing Consciousness, a step further. Here, Jesus directly offers the teachings which lead to Gnosis, represented by the waters of eternal life, and reveals that he is the Christ. This represents a state in which initiates glimpse their true nature for the first time, and understand the possibility of self-knowledge. The scene is set at Jacob's Well, which is designed to reinforce the allusion to the Sophia myth. In Jewish mythology, Rebecca, the mother of Jacob, draws water from this well, which Philo tells us represents receiving the wisdom of Sophia.[88]

In the next episode, we meet two important Sophia figures, Martha and her sister Mary. Their brother Lazarus has died, but they believe that if Jesus had been present he could have saved him. Moved by their faith, Jesus goes to the cave in which Lazarus is buried and miraculously raises him from the dead. In this remarkable little story Lazarus represents the *hylic* state of being spiritually dead in the underworld. He is brought back to life by the power of the Christ, representing Consciousness, through the faith of Martha and Mary, representing the *psychic* and *pneumatic* stages of awakening.

The motif of Martha and Mary representing these two levels of awareness is found in another vignette. When Jesus comes to their house, Martha is angered that whilst she is busying herself with serving, Mary simply sits at Jesus' feet and listens to his teachings. Jesus tells her:

> 'Martha, you are worried about so many things, but only one thing is important, which Mary has chosen, and it will not be taken away from her.'[89]

Mary and Martha represent the 'active and contemplative life': the *psychic* state of active good works and the *pneumatic* state of philosophical understanding leading to passive witnessing.

Another significant episode also happens whilst Jesus is visiting the house of Lazarus, Martha and Mary. Martha is again serving, whilst Lazarus, now returned from the dead, sits at the table. Meanwhile, Mary takes 'very costly ointment' and anoints Jesus, thus formally making him the 'Anointed' or Christ/King.[90] These events represent the stage of awakening in which initiates are no longer spiritually dead in the *hylic* state, which is represented by the resurrected Lazarus eating at the table. They are engaged in the *psychic* process of awakening, represented by Martha, who is serving, and have progressed sufficiently in the *pneumatic* level of awakening to clearly recognize their true identity as Consciousness, represented by Mary anointing Jesus as the Christ/King.

Jesus is portrayed as having expelled 'seven demons' from 'Mary called Magdalene'.[91] The number seven is significant. In the Gnostic mythical schema, the cosmos has seven levels, represented by the sun, moon and five visible planets.[92] These were sometimes imagined as demonic forces which entrap us in materiality.[93] Above these is the *ogdoad* or 'eighth', represented by the starry skies, which is the mythological home of the Goddess.[94] The Gnostic journey of awakening from incarnation is sometimes conceived of as mounting a sevenfold ladder to the *ogdoad*. That Mary has been freed from seven demons represents Jesus having helped her to ascend the seven rungs of the ladder to the heavens.[95]

At the culmination of the Jesus story, it is Mary Magdalene who finds Jesus' empty tomb and to whom the resurrected Christ first appears.[96] This represents the fulfilment of the process of initiation. For the Gnostics the body is a 'tomb' in which we exist as the spiritually dead. Mary finding that the tomb is empty represents the understanding that we are not the physical body. Her encounter with the resurrected Christ represents the realization that our essential nature is the one Consciousness of God.

After this Mary represents the wise psyche, truly worthy of the name 'Sophia'. As *The Dialogue of the Saviour* puts it, Mary is now 'a woman who completely understands'.[97] In *The Gospel according to Mary* the resurrected Jesus imparts the Inner Mysteries of Christianity to Mary, who reveals these secret teachings to the other disciples. They then go forth to preach 'the gospel according to Mary'.[98] Despite the misogyny of the Christian Literalists, the tradition of Mary Magdalene as the *apostola apostolorum*, the apostle to the apostles, remains Catholic doctrine to this day.

Motifs of the Mystical Marriage

According to the Christian Gnostics, there are many allusions to the mystical marriage in the Jesus story. The most important is the Eucharist ritual, which is based on the ancient rites of the mystical marriage in the Pagan Mysteries.[99] In the Mysteries of Eleusis, the Goddess Demeter was represented by bread and the Godman Dionysus by wine. The original Christians, likewise, associated bread with Mary and wine with Jesus, who is called 'the true vine' in *The Gospel of John*.[100] The Literalist Epiphanius records with horror that initiates of the Colyridian school of Christianity celebrated the Eucharist in the name of 'Mary Queen of Heaven', writing:

> 'They adorn a chair or a square throne, spread a linen cloth over it, and, at a certain solemn time, place bread on it and offer it in the name of Mary; and all partake of this bread.'[101]

In the act of ceremonially eating the bread and drinking the wine, the Godman and the Goddess, representing Consciousness and psyche, commune in the mystical marriage.[102] It is obviously significant that as Jesus officiates at the Last Supper Eucharist celebration, the 'Beloved Disciple' Mary Magdalene rests intimately in his lap.

Earlier, Jesus miraculously turns water into wine at a marriage ceremony at Cana, which according to Christian Gnostics represents the mystical marriage.[103] Water becoming wine is an archaic symbol representing the ecstatic intoxication of spiritual transformation. The creators of the Jesus story borrowed this motif from Pagan mythology, in which the Godman Dionysus turns water into wine at his marriage to Ariadne.[104] In the Christian version of this tale Jesus is not portrayed as the bridegroom. However, in the New Testament Jesus refers to himself, and is repeatedly referred to by others, as 'the bridegroom'.[105] Right at the beginning of *The Gospel of John*, for example, John the Baptist hails Jesus as 'the bridegroom'.[106]

As well as these references to the mystical marriage in the narrative of the Jesus story, it is alluded to in some of the teaching stories told by Jesus to his disciples. For example, it is the mythical backdrop for Jesus' parable of the wise and foolish virgins who are awaiting the arrival of the bridegroom.[107] The wise virgins have plenty of oil for their lamps, but the foolish virgins do not, and while they are going to get more oil, the bridegroom comes. The bridegroom is Christ. The virgins represent Sophia in her wise and foolish states. Olive oil was a familiar symbol in the ancient world for wisdom and was associated with the Goddess. In the story there are one bridegroom and many virgins because the bridegroom represents our shared essential nature as Consciousness (the common centre of the circle of self), and the many virgins represent the multiplicity of psyches (the many radii).

Jesus also alludes to the mystical marriage motif in his tale of a king who invites guests to the marriage of his son. Some guests don't come or abuse his servants. The king therefore invites everyone, good or bad. One of the guests, however, does not wear a wedding suit and is thrown out into the darkness where 'there is much gnashing of teeth'.[108] This parable teaches that, although many will make fun of the Gnostic path and reject its envoys, we are all invited to participate in the mystical marriage, representing the realization of Gnosis. But we must be sure to be appropriately prepared, through the process of purification undertaken in the initial *psychic* stage of initiation. Otherwise, like the guest without a wedding suit, we will be cast into the darkness of Hell. For the original Christians this meant that if we did not awaken to Gnosis in this lifetime we would reincarnate back here in the underworld of the spiritually dead, where, as we all know from personal experience, there is indeed 'much gnashing of teeth'!

In one intriguing non-canonical Christian tale, Jesus takes Mary Magdalene up a mountain, whereupon one side of him becomes a woman with whom he makes love.[109] Going up a mountain is a perennial image for walking the spiritual path to Heaven. The image of Jesus producing a woman from his side is an allusion to the *Genesis* myth in which Eve is created from one side of Adam, representing Consciousness objectifying itself as psyche. In the Christian parable, Jesus (Consciousness) shows Mary (fallen psyche) the magical woman (higher psyche), who is Mary's original nature. Jesus then makes love with the woman, representing the consummation of the mystical marriage in which Consciousness and psyche commune in the realization of their essential Oneness.

SUMMARY

❖ The Christian myth of the lost Goddess is the partner myth to the Jesus myth. Jesus and the Goddess represent Consciousness and psyche, or spirit and soul. The Goddess is portrayed as having two aspects, representing the pure psyche and the embodied psyche. These two aspects can be thought of as the two ends of the radius of the circle of self, one connecting to Consciousness at the centre and the other to the body at the circumference.

❖ The myth of Sophia tells the story of the fall of the psyche into incarnation and her redemption by her lover-brother, representing Consciousness. Sophia's fall, repentance, redemption and marriage represent the *hylic*, *psychic* and *pneumatic* states of awareness that an initiate passes through on their journey towards the realization of Gnosis.

❖ The myth of Sophia forms the subtext to the Jesus story. The most important Sophia figures in the gospels are the two Marys, Jesus' virgin mother and prostitute lover, representing the higher Sophia and the fallen Sophia.

It is easy for most people to accept that the unfamiliar story of Sophia is a mythical allegory, not a miraculous biography of the Daughter of God who literally came to Earth and was abused by various men before being rescued by her brother. For many of us it is not so easy to accept that the over-familiar Jesus story is also not to be taken literally. Despite the fact that this story of the Son of God who is born of a virgin, works miracles and comes back from the dead is far more supernatural and incredible than the comparatively believable tale of Sophia, we hang on to the idea of its historicity through the powerful force of habit. But it is not history. It is something better. It is myth.

chapter six

THE ASCENT FROM
the Cave

'The drama of the archetypal life of Christ describes in symbolic images the
events in the conscious life – as well as in the life that transcends consciousness – of a man who has been transformed by his higher destiny.'

Carl Jung, *The Psychology of Religion East and West*[1]

The Jesus myth is a sophisticated initiation allegory, the hidden depths of
which are not immediately obvious to those not conversant with the symbolic language of the ancient world. The Christian Gnostic Ptolemy explains:

'The scriptures are ambiguous and the truth can not be extracted
from them by those who are ignorant of tradition.'[2]

As we have no living lineage of Gnostic masters to reveal to us the secret
Christian tradition, we will have to decode the meaning of the Jesus myth
piece by piece, like some symbolic jigsaw puzzle. Fortunately, despite the
fact that it has become garbled and distorted over time, the key allegorical
elements of the story are still clearly visible.

The following is not intended as some sort of definitive interpretation, however. By their very nature, myths are open to many interpretations. Indeed, they are intended to be continually reinterpreted in the light of our expanding awareness. From the texts which have survived we can see that the Christian Gnostics constantly reworked and reinterpreted their mythology. There is no static body of myths with a fixed meaning. To understand the Jesus myth, therefore, we must enter into the creative process of allegorical interpretation, as did the original Christians, and see what insights it can reveal to us.

THE IMITATION OF CHRIST

According to the Valentinians, Paul cleverly designed his teachings about Jesus to be understood in different ways by *psychic* and *pneumatic* initiates. To *psychic* initiates he preached the story of the saviour, because 'they were capable of understanding this'. But to *pneumatic* initiates, he proclaimed Christ *pneumatically*, giving an interpretation of the myth as a spiritual allegory.[3]

The genius of the expanded Jesus story found in the New Testament is that its authors have continued this tradition, creating a myth that can be understood on two levels, depending on the awareness of the initiate. To *psychic* initiates it relates the story of the divine redeemer who has come to rescue them. They identify with Jesus' disciples, to whom the saviour imparts his *psychic* teachings, which are primarily about faith and ethics.[4] Jesus dies and resurrects into eternal life on their behalf, as a promise that they too will be blessed with eternal life. For *pneumatic* initiates, however, Jesus is a universal 'Everyman' figure whose initiations, struggles and triumphs represent every initiate's initiations, struggles and triumphs on the path of awakening. *Pneumatic* initiates identify with Jesus himself – the perfect initiate whose symbolic life is the archetypal story of every spiritual seeker.

The familiar name 'Jesus of Nazareth' is probably a later distortion of 'Jesus the *Nazarene*', because there is no record of anywhere called Nazareth at the time that the Jesus myth was being put into an historical and geographical context.[5] According to the Mandean Gnostics, *nazarene* means 'initiate'.[6] So, the gospel myth is the story of 'Jesus the Initiate', the saviour who rescues us by his example.

By imitating the allegorical story of Jesus the perfect initiate, we are led through the process of initiation until we realize Gnosis and become a Christ. Paul explains that in his 'poor human flesh' he is 'completing the full tale of Christ's afflictions' and declares: 'I have shared Christ's crucifixion.'[7] He reminds his students, 'The person we once were has been crucified with Christ.'[8]

As with comparable ancient works of spiritual fiction, from Homer's *Odyssey* to Lucius Apulius' *The Transformations of Lucius*, the Jesus story is a symbolic parable which contains other incidental parables that enlarge and complement the basic themes of the myth. The underlying narrative structure, onto which the mythological subplots are laid, consists of Jesus' baptism, death and resurrection, which represent the levels of Gnostic initiation. These are the only narrative elements of the Jesus myth which are important to Paul and are clearly the foundation upon which the later allegorical pseudo-biography of Jesus was created.

Jesus' baptism by John the Baptist (John the Initiator) represents the *psychic* initiation of purification. His death represents the *pneumatic* initiation, in which initiates die to the false ego-self. His resurrection represents the realization of Gnosis, in which initiates resurrect/awaken from spiritual death here in the underworld and are 'reborn' or 'unborn' into eternal life through the knowledge that their essential nature is disembodied Consciousness, symbolized by the Christ.

Allegorical Structure of the Jesus Story

Psychic Initiation	Baptism
Pneumatic Initiation	Crucifixion
Realization of Gnosis	Resurrection

Initiation Rituals

In the Pagan Mysteries, mythic narratives were enacted as vast ritual pageants through which initiates were transformed, just as we are transformed today by evocative films.[9] Although not on the grand scale of the Pagan Mysteries, the evidence suggests that the original Christians may also have ritually re-enacted elements of the Jesus myth as part of their initiation process. Certainly Christian 'mystery plays' which dramatized the allegorical life of Jesus existed in the Middle Ages. These could well be the continuation of an ancient tradition of ceremonial re-enactment. Many modern Christian communities, particularly in Catholic countries, still annually perform a mock crucifixion, burial and resurrection, with powerfully emotive effect on participants and spectators.[10] An obvious example of re-enactment which most Christian sects still practise is the rite of baptism.

In his *Letter to the Galatians* Paul reminds Christian initiates: 'Jesus Christ upon his cross has been openly displayed before your eyes.'[11] Not even the most enthusiastic Literalist could believe that the Galatian Christian community, living hundreds of miles from Judaea in what is now Turkey, could have been in Jerusalem to witness the supposed historical crucifixion of Jesus.[12] Possibly Paul is saying that the Galatian initiates have been given some sort of literary exegesis on the nature of the Christ from Jewish scripture.[13] Or perhaps in the first century Christians were, like contemporary Pagans, re-enacting the death and resurrection of the Godman as an initiatory spectacle?[14]

Like the Pagan rites they imitated, Christian rituals were clearly intense, ecstatic events, leading the Pagan philosopher Celsus to comment:

'The Christians excite their initiates to the point of frenzy with flute music like that heard among the priests of the Goddess Cybele.'[15]

The original Christians may even have been practising self-mutilation to increase their symbolic identification with the Christ image, for Paul tells us that he 'bears the marks of Christ upon his body'.[16] Such practices were certainly common in the Pagan world. Devotees of the Great Mother Goddess, for example, received a holy seal by being burned with red-hot needles or being tattooed.[17] The Christian master Clement of Alexandria suggests this may have also been a Christian practice, writing: 'The Lord reveals the Mysteries and marks his worshippers with His seal.'[18] It is reassuring to find one element of original Christianity which we can be grateful has now been abandoned!

For the original Christians, rituals were a way of identifying themselves with Jesus. Paul tells us that the ritual of baptism, for example, is about being 'baptized into union with Christ Jesus'.[19] Such rituals were designed to be transformative experiences, not just empty formalities. *The Gospel of Philip* teaches:

'If someone goes down into the water and comes up without having received anything and says, "I am a Christian," he has borrowed the name at interest. Someone who experiences the Holy Spirit, however, has received the name as a gift. This is the way it happens to someone who experiences the Mystery.'[20]

Through the process of initiation, including dramatic re-enactments and other symbolic ceremonies, initiates underwent the transformations of awareness symbolized by the events in the Jesus story until they realized Gnosis and resurrected/awakened by transcending the separate self and knowing themselves to be expression of the Christ – the Consciousness of God.

Addressing 'my children for whom I work until the Christ is formed in you', Paul teaches:

'You are all Sons of God through faith in Jesus Christ, for those who have identified with Christ through baptism have assumed his identity, for in Christ we all have one and the same identity.'[21]

In the Pagan Mysteries, the myths of the Godman were not understood as historical accounts of actual events which initiates should *believe*, but as allegories in which initiates could *participate* and so experience personal transformation. The Pagan philosopher Sallustius writes of the myth of the dying and resurrecting Godman Attis:

'The story of Attis represents an eternal cosmic process, not an isolated event in the past. As the story is intimately related to the ordered universe, we reproduce it ritually to gain order in ourselves. We, like Attis, have fallen from Heaven. We mystically die with him and are reborn.'[22]

In the same way the original Christians, such as Paul, did not mistake the Jesus story for history, as do Literalist Christians today. They knew it to be an allegory, through which they could 'mystically die and be reborn' with their Godman Jesus. For, like the Pagan devotees of the Godman Attis, the original Christians also believed that they had 'fallen from Heaven' and that the secret teachings encoded within the myth of the Godman could reawaken in them a memory of their primal home.

THE WAY DOWN

Let's begin our investigation of the allegorical meaning of the Jesus myth with the account of his miraculous birth. It deals with the 'way down' into incarnation and therefore lays the mythological foundation for the rest of the story, which will deal with the process of initiation, the 'exodus' or 'way out'.[23]

The Fallen Star

Jesus' birth is heralded by a star. For the original Christians, a whole body of teachings using stellar symbolism would have been implicit in this simple motif. The ancient world was obsessed with astrology and the stars, so such teachings were ubiquitous and familiar.[24] We live indoor lives and are blinded to the wonders of the starry night skies by the phosphorescence of ever-present street lights. For the ancients, however, the glittering firmament inspired a sense of profound awe. The Pagan philosopher Cicero writes:

> 'If anyone cannot feel the power of God when he looks upon the stars, then I doubt whether he is capable of feeling at all. From the enduring wonder of the heavens flows all grace and power. If anyone thinks it is mindless then he himself must be out of his mind.'[25]

For the Gnostics, the stars were an obvious source of imagery with which to express their mystical teachings. Whilst everything on Earth is in a state of perpetual flux, the stars revolve through the heavens in fixed and unerring courses. They were therefore equated with the heavenly gods, the permanent archetypes of which the world is a mutable expression.[26]

The Gnostics taught that although we appear to be mortal human beings, we are actually immortal gods or, to use the Jewish equivalent, heavenly angels. In *The Gospel of John* Jesus quotes Jewish scripture to teach: 'You are gods.'[27] The Pagan sage Heraclitus, from whom Hippolytus claims the Christian Gnostics derived their doctrines, writes: 'Gods are mortal men, and men are immortal gods.'[28] On the circumference of the circle of Self we appear to be human beings, but at the centre we are gods or angels – psyches in a state of Gnosis.

The ancients compared our essential godlike nature to an eternal star, ever luminous in the heavens. This stellar metaphor had been in use from as long ago as the Egyptian Pyramid Texts, written in 3000 BCE. It came to be a favourite image of the ancient Gnostics.[29] Plato writes:

'When the Creator had compounded the whole he divided it into as many psyches as there are stars and allotted each psyche a star. And the one who lives his appointed time well will travel again to this state and live a blessed life according to his true nature.'[30]

Plotinus, likewise, teaches that we are all 'eternal stars', explaining, 'A star is the representative generated by each psyche when it enters the cosmos.'[31] When being initiated into the Pagan Mysteries, initiates asserted: 'I am a star shining out of the depths.'[32] The Christian *Gospel of Truth* likewise teaches: 'Speak from the heart, for it is within you that dwells the star that does not set.'[33] In *The Gospel of Matthew* Jesus teaches his disciples: 'You are the lights of the cosmos.'[34]

In the embodied state we are like fallen stars. Drawing on the teachings of Pagan Gnostics such as Heraclitus, the original Christians compared us to sparks of stellar light which have become temporarily imprisoned by matter, a metaphor for the idea that we are Consciousness trapped in identification with the body.[35]

The star in the gospel story is therefore a symbol of Jesus' essential nature, which has fallen to Earth from Heaven, representing physical incarnation. But the baby Jesus is no ordinary child. He is destined to be the saviour of humankind. Like the ancient Egyptian Godman Osiris, Jesus is known as 'the shepherd of white stars'.[36] His mission is to free the sparks trapped in identification with the body, to remind us of our true angelic or godlike nature, symbolized by an eternal star, to guide us, like a shepherd with his flock, to the safety of our true home in the 'Kingdom of Heaven'.

The Cave of the Cosmos

According to *The Gospel of Luke* Jesus is born in a *katalemna*, which means 'cave' or similar temporary shelter.[37] *The Infancy Gospel of James* gives us a vivid account of Jesus' birth, relating, 'A great light appeared in the cave so that eyes could not bear it, and then when the light withdrew a baby appeared.'[38] The bright star which heralds Jesus' birth, representing his true eternal nature as Consciousness, has come into incarnation in a cave.

The Pagan Godman was likewise born in a cave.[39] The motif of the cave was popular in the ancient world. It represents the underworld which, for the Gnostics, is the material cosmos in which we presently live as the spiritually dead. Being 'born in the cave' represents incarnation as a body in the cosmos.

According to Minucius Felix, the Goddess Persephone was imprisoned by Hades in a cavern, representing the psyche imprisoned in the cosmos.[40] The Pagan sage Empedocles describes psyches falling into a cave.[41] In *The Republic* Plato famously describes the human condition as one of being imprisoned in a cave, where we mistake the shadows cast by the light outside for reality.[42] In *The Cave of the Nymphs* Porphyry decodes the allegorical teachings found in the myths of Homer, explaining, 'The cave represents the cosmos. The Pythagoreans, and after them Plato, showed that the cosmos is a cavern.'[43] Plotinus, likewise, tells us, 'In the cave of Plato and the cave of Empedocles I see the cosmos.'[44] Writing about 'the encavement of the psyche', he states, 'The body is the psyche's prison or tomb and the cosmos is its cave or cavern.'[45]

Plotinus describes Greek philosophy as teaching 'the ascent from the cave and the gradual advance of the psyche to a truer and truer vision'.[46] He tells us that Christians also teach 'the ascent from the cave', but in an unnecessarily complex way.[47] From the perspective of Christian Literalism it is hard to imagine what Plotinus could be talking about. Few traditional Christians would describe their faith as being about 'the ascent from the cave'! But Plotinus is right. Jesus is a star born into a cave, representing Consciousness becoming physically incarnate in the cosmos. Through the process of initiation, represented by Jesus' life, he dies to his separate self and resurrects to eternal life. Whereupon the cave, now his tomb, is found to be empty. He is no longer trapped in identification with the body. He has ascended from the cave, back to the kingdom of the starry heavens.

The Virgin of Light

The image of the Virgin Mary giving birth to Jesus in a cave would have been seen by the ancients as a mythical allusion to the virgin Goddess of Justice, who is pictured seated at the entrance of the cave of the cosmos, sending psyches into physical incarnation.[48] Parmenides teaches: 'The Goddess sends psyches from the invisible into the visible and back again.'[49]

To understand this important figure we must understand the Gnostics' mythology of the afterlife. At death the Goddess is pictured as judging psyches according to how they have lived their lives and sending them either up the right-hand path out of the cave of the cosmos to Heaven or down the left-hand path to Hell.[50] *The Gospel of Matthew* presents us with the same basic motif in the parable of the sheep and goats, in which Jesus teaches that humanity will be separated into two types, the sheep on the right, destined for Heaven, and the goats on the left, destined for Hell.[51]

As we have explored previously, the original Christians do not understand Hell in the same way as the later Literalist Christians. Literalists teach the horrendous idea that after one life some of us will be doomed to burn in the underworld forever. Christian Gnostics, like Pagan Gnostics before them, teach that *this world* is the underworld.[52] We come here many times, progressing through many lives in an ongoing process of spiritual maturation which reaches fruition in the realization of Gnosis. Those who do not realize Gnosis in this life are reincarnated here to continue their spiritual schooling. This is symbolized by the left-hand path to Hell.[53] Those who do realize Gnosis in this life know their essential nature to be the Mystery of God, so they don't continue to make the error of identifying with a physical body. This is symbolized by the right-hand path to Heaven. *The Sophia of Jesus Christ* teaches:

> 'Whoever knows the Father in pure Gnosis will depart to the Father and repose in the unborn Father. But whoever knows him defectively will depart to the defect.'[54]

To the Gnostics, the two paths represented remembering and forgetting. The right-hand path of remembering our true nature leads to Heaven. The left-hand path of forgetting our true nature leads back into the cave of the cosmos. Pagan Gnostics imagined that those who took the left-hand path were given a 'draught of oblivion' to drink, after which they found themselves reincarnated in a physical body.[55] Christian Gnostics, likewise, compared our present state to one of forgetfulness, sleep, drunkenness and death, from which we need to awaken through Gnosis.[56]

In Pagan mythology, the Godman presides over the right-hand path of liberation and the Goddess presides over the left-hand path of reincarnation. We find exactly the same motifs in Christian mythology. Jesus sits on the right hand of the Father, representing the right-hand path of liberation. The Christian Goddess was known as 'Her of the Left-hand' and represents the left-hand path back into the cave.[57]

The Virgin Mary, who gives birth to the Godman in the cave of the cosmos, represents the process of incarnation – the 'way down' into the underworld. Jesus, who at the end of his mission resurrects and ascends back to the heavens in glory, represents the path of spiritual awakening – the 'way out'. Theodotus teaches:

'He whom the Mother generates is led into death and into the cosmos, but he who Christ regenerates is transferred to life.'[58]

In *Pistis Sophia*, the Virgin Mary is described by Jesus as 'the likeness of the Virgin of Light', who judges each psyche and reincarnates it into 'a body which is the record of the sins which it has committed'.[59] If we sin we will be judged by the Goddess of Justice when we leave the cave at death and cast again into a physical body to work through the fate we have accrued. Plotinus explains:

'Each human being, as life follows life, is allotted a fate shaped by all that preceded it.'[60]

In Pagan mythology this was represented by the Goddess spinning the hero's fate.[61] It was a Christian tradition that the Virgin Mary 'earned her living by spinning'.[62] She represents the virgin Goddess who spins the fate of Jesus, the Christian hero figure, sending him into incarnation in the cave of the cosmos, of which she is the overseer.

The Goddess of Justice assigns each psyche a fate designed to help that individual become conscious of the errors they have made in previous lives and so progressively awaken. The Gnostics imagined this as a just process in which we suffer what we previously made others suffer. Plato writes: 'When the sinner has returned to our world once more, he must infallibly pay the penalty and be done by as he did.'[63] Plotinus teaches: 'A person once did what they now suffer.'[64] In *The Gospel of Matthew*, Jesus similarly warns: 'What you do to others will be done to you.'[65]

'The body is a prison in which the psyche is incarcerated, kept safe, until the price is paid,' explains Plato.[66] In *The Gospel of Luke* Jesus similarly teaches his disciples to beware of being 'handed over to the Judge' who will cast them 'into a prison from which no one gets out until they've paid the last penny'.[67] *Pistis Sophia* tells us that this parable refers to the Goddess, who casts us back into the 'prison' of physical incarnation, where we must work through the fate we have accumulated through our ignorance in previous lives.[68]

This underworld cave in which we are incarnated is both a hellish prison in which we are temporarily exiled from Heaven and a womb in which we have the opportunity to spiritually mature. If we have lived a good life but not realized Gnosis, in our next incarnation the Goddess of Justice will assign us a life in which it will be easier for us to spiritually awaken. *The Book of the Saviour* teaches:

> 'In its next birth, the good psyche will not be given the draught of oblivion, but will be cast back into a body which will not be able to fall asleep and forget. It will be ever pure in heart, seeking after the Mysteries of Light until it has found them, by order of the Virgin of Light, so that the psyche may inherit the light for ever.'[69]

The figure of the Virgin of Light is equivalent to the higher Sophia, who represents the disembodied aspect of the psyche in communion with Consciousness at the centre of the circle of self. As our judge at death, who creates our future fate according to our just deserts, she represents our own higher nature which, aware of our presently limited awareness, fashions a life for us that will give us the opportunities we need to awaken.

THE PSYCHIC INITIATION

The Gospel of Mark, the earliest version of the Jesus story, begins with Jesus' baptism by John the Baptist. John is born at the summer solstice in Cancer. Jesus is born six months later at the winter solstice in Capricorn.[70] In Pagan mythology, the sign of Cancer represents the path into the cave of the cosmos and the sign of Capricorn represents the way out. Porphyry writes:

> 'Cancer is the gate through which psyches descend, but Capricorn is the gate through which they ascend.'[71]

John represents the gate of Cancer, the way down into the cave of the cosmos. He presides over the experience of *metanoia*, which is the turning-point, the beginning of the *psychic* initiation and the return journey. Jesus represents the gate of Capricorn, the way out of the cave, back to Heaven, the *pneumatic* initiation and the realization of Gnosis.

Between his baptism and his crucifixion, representing the *psychic* and *pneumatic* stages of initiation, Jesus takes on the role of the saviour of *psychic* initiates. He performs miracles, gathers disciples, teaches parables and gives teachings appropriate to initiates on the *psychic* level of awareness. Let's now examine Jesus' ethical teachings and some of the mythically charged imagery in this transitional section of the Jesus story.

Elemental Initiations

Like the Pagan Gnostics before them, the original Christians imagined the process of initiation as a series of elemental 'baptisms' which lead us through the levels of our identity, which they equated with the four ancient elements: earth, water, air and fire.[72] These are nothing to do with the elements of modern chemistry, but are equivalent to the four fundamental states of matter: solid, liquid, gas and radiation. Fixed physicality is represented by earth, ever-changing psyche by water, invisible consciousness by air and the Mystery, hidden in everything like energy, by fire.

The *psychic* initiation is the baptism of water, through which initiates are cleansed of identification with their earthly self. The *pneumatic* initiation is the baptism of air, in which initiates come to know their ineffable essence as Consciousness. The realization of Gnosis is represented by the baptism of fire, in which initiates' sense of being separate from the Mystery of God is finally extinguished in the all-consuming light of the dazzling darkness. In *The Book of the Great Logos* Jesus offers initiates the opportunity to be born again through these three baptisms/initiations of water, air and fire.[73]

In *The Gospel of Matthew*, John the Initiator (John the Baptist) is portrayed as offering the initiation of water. This represents the Gnostic master offering initiates the *psychic* initiation of purification, symbolized by being washed clean with water. John is said to bring 'the remission of sins'.[74] This refers to the process of working on ourselves to become a better person, which is the goal of the *psychic* level of initiation.

John predicts that Jesus will bring the other two initiations, saying:

'I now bathe you in water to bring about *metanoia*, but the one coming after me is stronger than me. I'm not big enough to carry his shoes. He will bathe you in sacred *pneuma* and fire.'[75]

The initiation of *pneuma,* meaning 'breath', represents the initiation of air. *Pneuma* also means 'spirit' or 'consciousness'. The initiation of air is the *pneumatic* initiation, which is about realizing our identity as Consciousness. The initiation of fire is the realization of Gnosis. Jesus teaches that without first undergoing the *psychic* initiation of water and the *pneumatic* initiation of air, this realization is impossible. *The Gospel of John* has him proclaim:

> 'Truly, I tell you: anyone who isn't born of water and *pneuma* can never get into the kingdom of God.'[76]

In *Matthew* and *Luke,* John the Baptist says that Jesus will initiate using a 'winnowing fan' to separate the seeds from the husks.[77] A winnowing fan is a type of corn sieve. It was a traditional symbol in the Pagan Mysteries, used in initiation rituals to symbolize separating the essential Self, the seed which is to be kept, from the *eidolon* or ego, the husk which is to be destroyed.[78]

In *The Gospel of John,* John the Baptist declares of Jesus: 'He must grow greater. I must become less.'[79] To prepare for the *pneumatic* initiation, initiates must progressively cease identifying with the personal self, purified in the process of *psychic* initiation represented by John, to make way for a growing awareness of their essential identity as impersonal Consciousness, represented by Jesus the Christ.

The 12 Disciples

The first thing Jesus does when he begins his teaching mission, deliberately echoing the Jesus of *Exodus,* is to surround himself with 12 disciples representing each of the 12 tribes of Israel.[80] Jewish Gnostics understood the 12 tribes to be a reference to the 12 signs of the zodiac. The idea of 12 tribes is not a specifically Jewish mythological motif. Plato teaches: 'There are 12 feasts to the 12 gods who give their names to the 12 tribes.'[81]

The image of 12 disciples with the Godman at their centre echoes the 12 constellations which revolve in the heavens around the pole star.[82] In the Pagan Mysteries 12 initiates wore masks representing the zodiac signs and danced around a central initiate, symbolizing the Godman and the pole star.[83] Christians also practised such ritual dances. *The Acts of John* describes an initiatory ceremony in which Jesus' 12 disciples, representing the constellations, perform a dance around their master, who represents the pole star, at the centre.[84] Jesus teaches that the true nature of suffering can be understood by comprehending the circle dance which he leads. What does he mean?

The ancients conceived of the turning wheel of the zodiac as the 'wheel of suffering' or 'wheel of necessity' or 'wheel of fate'.[85] Hermes Trismegistus explains:

'It is man's lot to live his life according to the fate determined for him by these circling celestial powers.'[86]

By identifying with the physical body, which is governed by the laws of cause and effect, we have become prisoners on the 'wheel of necessity'. We are bound to the 'wheel of suffering' and must endure the consequences. The only escape is to realize our true impersonal identity as Consciousness at the still centre of the turning wheel, represented by the Godman and the pole star.

Astrological determinism was immensely popular in the ancient world. Gnostics, however, were at pains to emphasize that the stars are not the *cause* of events here on Earth, but rather archetypal patterns in the heavens which *correspond* to events on Earth, and so help us understand the ebb and flow of fate. The Christian Gnostic Theodotus writes that the stars 'are not the cause of things, but a sign of what is taking place'.[87] Plotinus teaches:

'The circuit of the stars indicates definite events to come but without being the direct cause of what happens.'[88]

Because each of the constellations of the zodiac spends six months of every year below the horizon and six months above, the zodiac was also seen as representing the wheel of reincarnation, which carries us through a recurring cycle of life and death. As Pythagoras explains:

'Revolving around the wheel of necessity, the psyche is transformed and confined at different times in different bodies.'[89]

The process of initiation was designed to free initiates from the wheel by revealing their essential identity at the still centre. Proclus teaches that those initiated into the Mysteries of Persephone and Dionysus 'pray that they may cease from the wheel'.[90] In his exegesis on the myth of Jesus' birth, Theodotus writes:

'A strange and new star arose doing away with the old astral decree, shining with a new unearthly light, which revealed a new path of salvation. The Lord himself, humanity's guide, came down to Earth to transfer from fate to his providence those who believed in Christ.'[91]

The role of Jesus is to liberate us from the wheel of suffering by helping us understand that we are the Christ, the still centre of the turning wheel.

Jesus and his Twin

In Christian mythology the disciples are symbols of the *eidolon*, or ego. Actually, of course, we are all *eidolons*, or images of the Christ. In the ancient world the *eidolon* and Consciousness – the false self and the true Self – were imagined as 'twins'. To make it clear that the disciples Thomas, Judas and Simon Peter are to be understood as *eidolon* figures, they are all represented as Jesus' twin brother.

'Thomas' means 'twin' in Aramaic. In *The Book of Thomas the Contender*, Jesus, representing Consciousness, instructs his disciple and twin brother 'doubting Thomas', representing the incarnate self, in the path of self-knowledge:

'Brother Thomas, while you are in the world for a time, listen to me, and I will reveal to you the things you have been thinking about. Since it has been said that you are my twin and true companion, examine yourself and learn who you are, in what way you exist, and how you will come to be. Since you will be called my brother, it is not fitting that you be ignorant of yourself.'[92]

The authorship of *The Gospel of Thomas* is attributed to Didymos Judas Thomas. 'Didymos' means 'twin' in Greek. Giving the disciple both the names Didymos and Thomas means there is no mistaking the message. The author is 'Judas the Twin'.[93] According to *The Gospel of Matthew*, Jesus had a brother called Judas.[94] These are mythological hints that we should understand Judas, Jesus' betrayer, as the twin or *eidolon* of Jesus.[95]

The Gospel of Matthew also tells us that Jesus has a brother called Simon, which is a mythological allusion to the fact that the disciple Simon Peter represents the *eidolon*.[96] Simon Peter, representing the ego, is portrayed as ignorant and foolish in comparison with the enlightened Mary Magdalene, representing the awakening psyche.[97] Whilst Mary faithfully shares Jesus' suffering with him at the cross, Peter denies Jesus three times.[98] When Mary shows him Jesus' empty tomb, Peter wanders off in confusion while Mary remains weeping, so it is to her that the resurrected Jesus appears.[99] In *The Gospel of Mary*, the misogynistic Peter resents the fact that the resurrected Jesus has given secret teachings to Mary and not to him.[100]

One modern scholar summarizes the characterization of Simon Peter in *The Gospel of Matthew* as 'confused, cowardly, without understanding, disliking suffering, giving with a view to future gain, impetuous, impulsive and unstable, stingy in forgiving, overestimating his ability, and denying his master miserably'.[101] At one point Jesus even calls him 'Satan'.[102] It is ironically appropriate that a fictional character presented in such a negative light and symbolizing the false self should be claimed as the founder of the Literalist Roman Church!

Signposts to the Truth

Throughout his teaching mission Jesus is portrayed as performing various miracles. Such tales were the standard ingredients of fictional spiritual biographies in the ancient world. Then as now, the spiritually immature seem not to notice the immense and overwhelming miracle that is life itself, and so are attracted to the spiritual path by tales of little miracles.

The Gnostic master's role is to awaken us to the obvious miracle of existence, which confronts us in every moment. But those not yet ready to hear this message are given tales of magic that excite them with the possibility of life being more than they have previously taken it to be. Which of course it is. Much more. Miracle tales inspire us with a sense of mystery, and as life is all Mystery these little mysteries can take us a little closer to the Truth.

The Greek word usually translated 'miracle' in *The Gospel of John* means 'sign' or 'symbol'.[103] Jesus' miracles are a 'sign' of his spiritual power, which attracts *psychic* initiates who are impressed by supernatural feats. To *pneumatic* initiates, however, Jesus' miracles are 'symbols' which point to his true mission, which is to lead us to an appreciation of the great miracle of life itself through the realization of Gnosis.[104]

For example, Jesus gives eyesight to the blind. In the Pagan Mysteries beginners were known as *mystae*, meaning 'those with eyes closed', and enlightened initiates were known as *epopteia*, meaning 'those who can see'. Jesus represents the master who has the power to open initiates' spiritual eyes to the Truth that they are presently too blind to see.

Like Moses, who summons heavenly *manna* to feed his hungry followers, Jesus also miraculously feeds many thousands of his disciples from very little food.[105] The miraculous food represents Gnostic philosophy, which may seem abstract and insubstantial, but has the miraculous power to give the psyche all the nourishment it needs to truly come to life.

Jesus raises the dead. This represents being rescued from spiritual death here in the underworld. *The Gospel of John* relates that, when Jesus had gone off to resurrect Lazarus, 'Thomas, which is called Didymus, said to his fellow disciples, "Let us also go, that we may die with him."'[106] This curious statement only makes sense when the episode is understood allegorically. Both 'Thomas' and 'Didymus' means 'twin', so the 'twin' or *eidolon* wants to go to the cave where Lazarus is to be resurrected and 'die with him'. Here, once again, we get the typical Gnostic inversion of life and death. In this episode, Lazarus represents the initiate dead in the tomb of the world, whom Jesus will bring back to spiritual life. The words of the 'twin' gives us the other side of the picture, which is that this entails the initiate 'dying' to their false self, as Jesus is represented as doing on the cross. Thomas is urging us, his fellow disciples, to also undertake initiatory death and resurrection along with Lazarus.[107]

Originally the sequence of the miracles performed by Jesus undoubtedly had symbolic significance, but they are now so garbled that a pattern is hard to discern. Scholars have pointed out, for example, that *The Gospel of Mark* contains what were at one time two different sets of miracle stories. Both start with a miraculous crossing of water and end with a miraculous feeding.[108] Each of these sequences of miracles may well have originally been an initiation allegory, starting with a baptism motif (the miraculous crossing of water) and ending with a motif representing the receiving of the teachings (the miraculous feedings).

Scholars have also observed that *The Gospel of John* echoes a pattern of miracles in the Jewish *Sophia of Solomon*, which in turn is based on miracle motifs in the *Exodus* myth. In *The Gospel of John*, this pattern of six 'ordinary' miracles and one 'extraordinary' miracle climaxes in the miracle of Jesus' resurrection. This probably symbolizes the spiritual journey through the seven layers of the cosmos to the Goddess in the *ogdoad*, or eighth,[109] the final step being represented by Jesus' ascension into Heaven.

Psychic Teachings

In the New Testament gospels Jesus' teachings are often extremely enigmatic and given in the form of allegorical parables, which Jesus says he will explain later, although he rarely does.[110] He persistently claims to be the great revealer, but he actually reveals nothing.[111] This is because the Jesus story is part of the Outer Mysteries of Christianity, designed for *psychic* initiates. The secret teachings of the resurrected Christ, which are designed to be taught to *pneumatic* initiates of the Inner Mysteries, are found in other Gnostic gospels, such as *Pistis Sophia*, *The Book of the Saviour*, *The Book of the Great Logos according to the Mystery*, *The Book of Ieou*, and so on. *Pistis Sophia*, for example, claims to give the post-resurrection teachings that Jesus proclaimed for 12 years after his resurrection.[112]

Where Jesus does give teachings in the gospels, they are ethical teachings designed for those on the *psychic* level of initiation. Essentially the Gnostic creators of the Jesus story use their hero to replace the barbaric 'eye for an eye' mentality of Jewish Literalism, which leaves everyone blind, with their 'gospel of love'. Gnostics' ethics are not about outer observances. Jesus does not institute a new set of moral rules and regulations for us to obey. He simply encourages us to love more. In *The Gospel of John* he imparts to his 'friends' his one and only commandment: 'This is my commandment to you: love one another.'[113]

This is a continuation of the tradition found in Paul, who teaches that all ethical precepts are fulfilled if we simply follow the one commandment 'Love others as yourself.'[114] In his *Letter to the Corinthians*, he offers up a beautiful hymn to love, declaring:

> 'Although I speak with the tongues of men and angels, if I don't love,
> I am just a brash trumpet or a tinkling bell. Even if I have the gift
> of prophesy and the faith to move mountains, if I don't love I am
> nothing. I may give everything I have to feed the poor, and my body
> to be burned, but if I don't love it won't benefit me at all.'[115]

For Gnostics, God is love. Plotinus teaches: 'The Supreme is Love itself.'[116] *The First Letter of John*, likewise, teaches: 'God is Love and those that live in God live in Love and God lives in them.'[117]

Love is what overcomes separateness and unites us to the Mystery which is Love. It is the essence of the ethical teachings taught to *psychic* initiates because it is the antithesis of selfishness. Becoming more loving is the surest way to transcend the ego. Basilides teaches us to 'love everything because everything exists in relation to the Whole'.[118] We are all One and so should love our neighbour as another expression of our shared essential Self. We should live together in harmony, through unconditional compassion and radical selflessness, because we are all members of the body of Christ.

The teachings on love attributed to Jesus are so familiar it is easy to miss just how radical they are. We should love our enemies. We should repay evil with kindness. We should not fight back when we are attacked. We should completely forgive those who wrong us. We should offer more than is asked of us.[119] We should not lend money, but rather give it away to someone we know we won't get it back from.[120] In the light of all this, the history of Christian Literalism, from the Crusaders and the Inquisition to the modern Vatican bankers and wealthy TV evangelists, is a tragic betrayal of the gospel of love proclaimed by the original Christians.

Jesus the Gnostic Rebel

Jesus is the mouthpiece of the Christian Gnostics. Through him they convey their vision of what life is and how to live it. Not surprisingly, then, Jesus is portrayed as an egalitarian who rejects external authority and has no time for Literalist religion, just like the Gnostic authors themselves.

Jesus is a rebel. He provocatively flouts Jewish sacred law and customs. He 'works' on the Sabbath. He hangs out with fishermen, publicans, tax collectors and whores. His equal treatment of women is an outrage. He enters into discussions with women and welcomes them as close disciples. He even talks with foreign women, such as the Samaritan at Jacob's Well.

Paul describes Jesus as 'born of a woman under the law to set us free from the law'.[121] The figure of Jesus is a creation of Jewish Gnostics and so is portrayed as a Jew, who is 'born under the law'. But he comes to 'set us free from the law' by offering Gnosticism as a mystical alternative to Jewish Literalist religion. He does this by constantly undermining the religious authorities. In *The Gospel of Mark*, he accuses them of 'neglecting the commandments of God in order to maintain the traditions of men'.[122] In *The Gospel of Matthew* he denounces them, saying, 'Truly, I say to you, publicans and whores will enter the kingdom before you.'[123] In *The Gospel of Luke* he berates them:

> 'Woe to you, teachers of the law, for you took away the keys to Gnosis. You do not enter in yourselves and you obstruct those who want to enter.'[124]

Expressing the Gnostics' distaste for the tyrannical Jewish god Jehovah, in *The Gospel of John* Jesus even tells the Jews that their 'Father' is not God but the 'Devil'.[125]

In the same gospel, a Samaritan woman asks Jesus about the difference between the Samaritan religious law that God should be worshipped in the mountains and the Jewish law that God should be worshipped in the Temple in Jerusalem. Jesus' response encapsulates the mystical message the Christian Gnostics are using their Godman figure to proclaim:

> 'The hour is coming when you will worship the Father neither in the mountains or in Jerusalem. The true worshipper worships the Father in consciousness and truth, for this is the worship which the Father wants. God is consciousness and those that worship him must worship him in consciousness and truth.'[126]

The Gnostic authors of the gospels portray Jesus as giving such controversial teachings that the Literalist religious authorities have him put to death. The authorities' justification is that Jesus has proclaimed himself to be the Son of God.[127] The Gnostic claim to be the Son of God or an incarnation of God has maddened Literalists of every persuasion throughout history. For Gnostics this is the denial of the ego and the affirmation of the reality that there is nothing but God. It is absolute humility. Literalists are incapable of understanding this and hear the claim as affirming the divinity of a particular ego, which is an unacceptable affront to their own egos.

It is for the supposed blasphemy of declaring the highest truth of Gnosticism that the Jewish priests conspire to have Jesus put to death. This motif is more than an affirmation of Gnostic wisdom and a condemnation of Literalist ignorance, however. It is a mythical allegory. For, when initiates realize that their true identity is the Son of God, it is time for the *eidolon* they previously took themselves to be to die.

THE PNEUMATIC INITIATION

Jesus' crucifixion and resurrection represent the *pneumatic* initiation and the realization of Gnosis. For those able to read the symbolic language, when Jesus arrives at Jerusalem, he is shown as having completed the *psychic* initiation. He triumphantly rides a donkey while crowds of admirers hail him as their king. The donkey was a familiar image in the Pagan Mysteries, representing the lower 'animal' self.[128] Riding the donkey symbolizes that Jesus, the archetypal initiate, has fulfilled the goal of the *psychic* stage of initiation by mastering his lower nature. He has been anointed as the King/Christ by Mary Magdalene and is now lauded as 'King of the Jews'. But the goal of the Gnostic path is not to make the *eidolon* the king of this world, but to see through the illusion of the separate self and discover our essential nature as the Mystery of God. So Jesus is not the 'King of the Jews'. This title will be affixed over his dying body on the cross, because it is the King of the Jews who must die, for Jesus to be reborn as the Christ, the King of the Cosmos.

Jesus' mission starts in Galilee and ends in Jerusalem. The name 'Galilee' means 'a rolling wheel'.[129] According to Iraneaus, for the Christian Gnostics, 'Jerusalem' is a code word for 'the Mother'.[130] Mythologically, therefore, Jesus, the archetypal initiate, begins his journey on the 'wheel of suffering'. Through the process of initiation, he climbs the mythical ladder to the Mother Goddess in the *ogdoad*, at the mouth of the cave of the cosmos.[131] He is now ready to break out from confinement in the cave through the *pneumatic* realization that, in truth, he was never imprisoned.

The Death of the *Eidolon*

Jesus' death represents the death of the initiate's *eidolon* – the 'I am the body' idea. His resurrection represents the initiate's revival from spiritual death here in the underworld through the realization of their heavenly essence. Mythically, Jesus' death and resurrection are the same event. When the ego dies, we are immediately resurrected as the Christ, the Consciousness of God.

The idea that the crucifixion represents the death of the *eidolon* is made explicit by non-canonical gospels in which an *eidolon* figure is crucified instead of Jesus, while Jesus watches and laughs at the foolishness of his oppressors.[132] The 'laughing Jesus' is a bold representation of Consciousness witnessing the death of the *eidolon*, safe in the knowledge of its immortal nature. In *The Paraphrase of Shem* it is a figure called Soldas, representing 'the earthly Jesus', who is crucified.[133] According to Basilides it is not Jesus who is crucified, but Simon of Cyrene, who is portrayed as carrying Jesus' cross in the New Testament.[134] Simon was the original name of Peter who, as we have already seen, is an important *eidolon* image. As usual, giving the two characters the same name equates them mythically.

These Christian motifs are based on Pagan myths in which it is the Godman's evil brother, representing the twin or *eidolon*, who tries to kill the Godman but ends up dying himself. In Caananite mythology the evil Mot slays his brother Aleyin, the Son of God, who then resurrects and kills Mot. Just like Jesus on the cross, Mot's last words to his Father are: 'My God, My God, why have you forsaken me?'[135] In Egyptian mythology it is the evil Set who, having killed his brother Osiris, is sacrificed on the 'slave's post', whilst Osiris returns from the dead.[136] In Euripides' *The Bacchae* King Pentheus, whose name means 'One who suffers', represents the *eidolon*. He tries to kill the Godman Dionysus, but ends up himself meeting his death by being lifted up on a tree.[137] Mani, likewise, taught that Satan wanted to crucify Jesus but ended up being lifted up on a tree and crucified instead.[138] This idea is alluded to in the Jesus story when Judas, having instigated the process that will lead to Jesus' death, realizes what he has done and hangs himself.[139] Jesus and his twin brother Judas, representing Consciousness and the *eidolon*, are both 'hung on a tree', but Jesus resurrects and Judas does not. The true Self cannot die. Only the false self dies. Mythologically, when Judas dies, the Christ resurrects. By dying to what we are not, we come to life as what we are.

All these mythic motifs are expressing the same fundamental idea: to commune with the Oneness of God, we must stop identifying with the separate self. Judas' remorse and suicide represent initiates recognizing that they have been embroiled in endless suffering caused solely by identification with the *eidolon* and so committing 'ego suicide' by ceasing to think of themselves as a separate person. In *The Apocryphon of James* Jesus teaches:

'None of those who fear death will be saved, for the kingdom of the heavens belongs to those who put themselves to death.'[140]

Initiates of the Pagan Mysteries imagined initiation as a 'voluntary death' after which they were 'resurrected from the dead'.[141] Initiates of the Christian Mysteries were likewise taught to die as a separate self so that they would resurrect as the Christ. In *The Gospel of Matthew* Jesus proclaims:

> 'If anyone wants to follow me, he must leave his self behind. He must take up his cross and come with me. Whoever cares for the safety of the self is in danger. But if someone lets himself be lost for my sake, he will find his true Self.'[142]

To find our true Self we must take up our cross and crucify the ego. Paul teaches: 'Those who are in Christ have crucified the physical nature.'[143] Self-crucifixion is not some sort of deranged ascetic practice but a symbol of an egoless state of awareness to be cultivated continually. Abiding by Plato's famous description of the 'true philosopher' as someone who 'makes dying his way of life',[144] Paul teaches, 'I die every day.'[145]

We are not being encouraged to develop a morbid obsession with our mortality. We are being offered a profound way of truly coming to life and living without fear. If we willingly sacrifice the idea of ourselves as a physical body, we will discover our true immortal identity. We will know that death is impossible. We can never not be, since we are *Being* itself. By dying as a separate self now, we put an end to death forever. Valentinus teaches:

> 'From the beginning we are immortal children of eternal life. We choose to die so that we can annihilate death completely.'[146]

Becoming the Witness

When we confuse what we *are* with what we *appear* to be, we create the false self, the image or *eidolon*. In the *pneumatic* initiation, initiates disidentify with the *eidolon* by cultivating the state of contemplation in which they discriminate themselves as the experiencer from everything they are experiencing. Jesus' crucifixion symbolizes this process of discriminating Consciousness and psyche, which have become so disastrously confused. As Basilides teaches:

> 'Jesus' suffering came about for no other purpose but to separate what had been mingled.'[147]

The Gospel of Philip tells us: 'It was on the cross that Jesus was divided.'[148] Jesus resurrects as the Christ, the Consciousness of God, when he divides his essence from his appearance and knows himself to be Consciousness witnessing psyche, not the *eidolon*. Paul explains:

> 'The *Logos* of God is living and active and sharper than any two-edged sword, and cuts so deeply it divides psyche from Consciousness.'[149]

In the state of contemplation the idea of being a separate self is completely abandoned. The person we took ourselves to be is seen as a part of the stream of experience being witnessed by impersonal Consciousness. In this state, we are no longer subject to suffering and death, for we know that only the body can suffer and die, and the body is only a temporary appearance in the permanence of Consciousness.

The Acts of John explains that although Jesus suffered, yet he suffered as one who was 'a stranger to this suffering'. Jesus explains, 'I distinguish the man from my Self.'[150] He does not identify with the *eidolon* and, therefore, although he *appears* to suffer, he does not. He teaches: 'See through suffering and you will have non-suffering.'[151]

For initiates who know their true identity as Consciousness, the horrors of our waking world are no more than a dream, which those bound to the wheel of suffering mistake for reality. *The Gospel of Truth* explains:

> 'People are ignorant of the Father, who they cannot see. This has inspired fear and confusion, leaving them uncertain and hesitant, torn to shreds by division. They are caught in many vain illusions and empty fictions, which torment them like sleepers prey to nightmares. They flee they know not where. Or remain at the same spot when trying to go forward, chasing after who knows what. They are giving or receiving blows in battle. Or falling from a great height. Or flying through the air without wings. One minute it is as if they are meeting their death at the hands of some invisible murderer, without anyone chasing them. The next it seems as if they were murdering their neighbour and their hands are full of blood. When they wake up they see that all those dreams were nothing. This is the way it is with those who, as if waking from sleep, have cast ignorance aside. They no longer see the cosmos as real, but like a dream at night. They value Gnosis of the Father as if it were the dawn. Whilst they are ignorant, everyone acts as if they were asleep. Coming to Gnosis is like waking up.'[152]

We are presently like sleepers caught up in a horrific nightmare that disappears when we awake/resurrect through the realization of Gnosis. By realizing that life is a dream in Consciousness, we cease identifying with the *eidolon*, our dream persona. We then find ourselves to be Consciousness witnessing the joys and horrors of life, knowing that they are not happening to what we *are*, but only to what we *appear* to be.

Plotinus questions just how far this ability to be the disengaged witness of life can go. Talking of the enlightened master who has attained Gnosis and, therefore, discovered the source of all happiness, he writes:

> 'If a person who has attained happiness meets some turn of fortune that he would not have chosen, there is not the slightest lessening of his happiness. But suppose he himself were to be offered as a sacrificial victim?'[153]

The Jesus myth explores exactly this scenario. How would an enlightened being react to being tortured and executed? Would they still maintain their inner peace in the face of the worst imaginable circumstances? The Christian answer is the confronting image of the 'laughing Jesus' who watches all of life's unfolding dramas, safe in the knowledge that the whole thing is a passing dream and that he is the eternal dreamer.

When we know ourselves to be Consciousness, we know we are the eternal still centre around which moves the cosmos of unceasing change. In *Pistis Sophia* the enlightened initiate declares:

> 'Even if the physical world moves, I shall not move. Even if it is destroyed, I shall not be destroyed. For the light is me and I am the light.'[154]

When we know ourselves to be Consciousness we are no longer an object in the world, we are the light which illuminates creation. *The Gospel of Philip* promises:

> 'Those who receive the light can not be seen nor seized. No one will be able to persecute them, even if they live in this world.'[155]

Simon Magus, likewise, teaches: 'Someone who knows the Great Power becomes invisible.'[156] This is not a promise of being able to perform some supernatural magical feat. It is a statement of the Gnosis.

Conquering the Cosmos

After the crucifixion, when Mary Magdalene goes to the cave tomb of Jesus, she finds it empty. Jesus has escaped the cave of the cosmos. *The Treatise on the Resurrection* teaches:

> 'The Saviour swallowed death. You must be perceptive, for by this I mean that he laid aside the corruptible cosmos. He exchanged it for the incorruptible eternal realm. He raised himself up, having swallowed the visible by means of the invisible, and gave us the way to our immortality. This is why Paul said we have suffered with him, and arisen with him, and ascended with him.'[157]

Jesus has 'swallowed the visible cosmos' by realizing himself to be 'invisible' Consciousness, within which the cosmos has its existence. If, as Paul urges, we can understand the mystical meaning of this allegory and imitate Christ, then we will also discover we are immortal. According to Valentinus:

> 'When we destroy the cosmos and we ourselves are not destroyed, then we know we are lords over the whole of creation and over all decay.'[158]

If we see the illusory nature of what we think of as 'objective reality', we will 'destroy the cosmos'. Yet we will find that we are not destroyed. The person we took ourselves to be may now appear to be only a character in a dream, yet our sense of *being* will remain real and indestructible. We will know ourselves to exist eternally, unborn and undying.

The Gospel of Philip expresses these teachings by reversing the image of Jesus being crucified, proclaiming: 'Jesus crucified the cosmos.'[159] Paul also talks of 'the cross of the Lord Jesus Christ by which the cosmos has been crucified'.[160] To free ourselves from imprisonment within the cave of the cosmos, we must follow Jesus' example and 'crucify the cosmos'. This represents freeing ourselves from the idea of the cosmos as an objective reality and understanding it to be an ever-changing dream within the constancy of Consciousness.

The Treatise on the Resurrection announces, 'The cosmos is an illusion! The resurrection is the revelation of what *is*.'[161] We think of ourselves as passing through the cosmos, which is the permanent reality. But when we resurrect/awaken, we discover that we are the permanent reality of Consciousness, through which the cosmos passes. We do not exist within the cosmos. The cosmos exists within us. We are Consciousness conscious of the cosmos. When we realize this we can declare triumphantly, as Jesus does in *The Gospel of John*: 'The victory is mine. I have conquered the cosmos.'[162]

In the Jesus story this victory is represented by the tearing of the veil of the Temple in Jerusalem at the moment of Jesus' death.[163] The Temple veil was an 80-foot high Babylonian tapestry representing the cosmos. The Jewish historian Josephus tells us it was 'a panorama of the entire heavens'.[164] Pagans also imagined the heavens as a veil or tapestry.[165] In Pagan myth the Goddess Persephone wove the heavens as a tapestry. Porphyry tells us: 'The heavens are called by the ancients a veil.'[166] The Christian text *On the Origin of the World* teaches: 'Sophia is like a veil which divides humanity from the things above.'[167]

The Goddess at the entrance of the cave in the *ogdoad*, represented by the starry heavens, is the boundary between humanity and the Mystery of God.[168] Our individual consciousnesses are represented by the stars. But this is not our ultimate identity. Stars are perforations in the blackness through which shines the light which lies beyond the veil, just as eyes are windows through which we can glimpse the Consciousness of God which lies beyond the body. All stars shine because of the one light. All individual consciousnesses are the flaring forth of the dazzling darkness.[169]

Jesus starts the story as a star fallen into the Goddess' cave of incarnation. In his death, resurrection and ascension, he passes through the stargate of his individual consciousness to the 'Treasury of Light' beyond. The Temple veil is ripped in two as he conquers the cosmos and frees himself from the underworld cave. He tears apart the veil of ignorance and illusion to reveal the Mystery of God, our ultimate shared identity. To fulfil the Gnostic injunction 'Know your Self', we must imitate Jesus and die to the insignificant smallness of our petty ego and resurrect into the infinite grandeur of our deepest Self, which is the Self of All.

Waking the Dead

The promise of Christianity is that, like Jesus, we can all resurrect from the dead. Literalist Christians came to interpret the resurrection as an historical event that would happen at the end of time, when all believers would rise bodily from their graves.[170] But this rather macabre vision was not that of the Christian Gnostics. Writing derisively of the Gnostic understanding of the resurrection, the Literalist Tertullian tells us:

'They interpret the coming forth from the grave as escaping the cosmos, because the cosmos is the dwelling place of the dead. That is, of those without Gnosis of God. It is even interpreted as the escape from the body itself, because the body, like the grave, keeps the psyche shut up in the death of this worldly life.'[171]

For the original Christians, the resurrection is a mythical not a literal event, which represents a spiritual rather than a physical transformation. The Naassene school of Christian Gnosticism taught:

'The dead shall leap forth from their graves, meaning from their earthly bodies, regenerated spiritually, not physically. This is the resurrection that takes place through the gates of Heaven. All those who do not pass through remain dead.'[172]

The Literalists taught that those who understand the message of Jesus will one day resurrect in their physical bodies. The original Christians taught the complete opposite. It is precisely those who do *not* understand the Christian message who will return to a physical body. The resurrection is spiritual awakening. It is those who do not awaken in this life who will not pass 'through the gates of Heaven' and so 'remain dead' by reincarnating here in the underworld.

The resurrection is not a future event. It is the awareness of our true identity as Consciousness. This can only happen right here and now. The future and past are *imaginings* in Consciousness. The now is the *presence* of Consciousness. We can only be aware of Consciousness in the present moment. *The Treatise on the Resurrection* explains:

'The resurrection is the transformation of things, and a transition into newness. Flee from the divisions and the fetters, and already you have the resurrection.'[173]

If we abandon the idea that we are a separate person, we will find we are already resurrected. We will become what we are, and what we have always been. *The Treatise on the Resurrection* urges us:

'Realize that you are resurrected already. Are you – the real you – something that can decay? Why don't you examine yourself and see that you have risen?'[174]

SUMMARY

❖ The Jesus story is designed to speak in different ways to *psychic* and *pneumatic* initiates. For *psychic* initiates, it tells the story of Jesus their saviour. For *pneumatic* initiates, the story is an allegory in which Jesus is an Everyman character who represents each initiate on their journey of awakening/resurrection.

❖ The fundamental structure of the myth is comprised of Jesus' baptism, death and resurrection, representing the *psychic* initiation, the *pneumatic* initiation and the realization of Gnosis.

❖ The myth is an account of 'the ascent from the cave' of the cosmos. At the being of the tale Jesus is incarnated into the cave by the Goddess Justice, represented by the Virgin Mary. At the end of the tale Jesus' resurrects from his cave tomb and ascends to Heaven, freeing himself from the cave of the cosmos.

Christian Literalists have managed to maintain their ludicrous view of the Jesus story as a biography of the historical Son of God by reading it in isolation from the rest of Christian mythology. To truly understand the Jesus story in the way the original Christians intended, we must see it as the culmination of the epic Christian myth cycle, which takes us on a journey from the beginning of the beginning to the end of time.

chapter seven

CONSCIOUSNESS CONCEIVES
the Cosmos

'Everything manifests from two emanations. Consciousness and thought. Male and female. In essence they are one. When separated they appear as two.'

Simon Magus[1]

The Christian myth cycle is a mythological explanation of where we come from and where we are going.[2] It begins with the myth of origination and ends with the myth of the return. There are many different versions of the Christian myth cycle, with no fixed system.[3] Rather, the original Christians were engaged in an ongoing exploration of mystical metaphysics which encouraged and incorporated imaginative new ideas.[4]

To understand the Christian myth cycle we need to first understand the philosophy which informs it. This seeks to explain the greatest mysteries of all: the arising of something from nothing, the nature of God, the creation of the cosmos and its purpose. As mystics throughout the ages testify, it is notoriously difficult to communicate and comprehend these subtle and abstract ideas. Analogies never quite work and frequently conflict. But don't be put off. We are thinking at the edge, where the shoreline of sense meets the wild ocean of Mystery.

THE MYSTERY MADE MANIFEST

Pagan and Christian myths of origination imagine God as a Big Mind which thinks, or imagines, or articulates, or dreams the cosmos into existence.[5] The Christian teacher Ptolemy describes the first event in the origination of the cosmos as the 'stillness' of the 'Primal Parent', which *The Secret Book of John* describes as 'pure, immeasurable Consciousness',[6] stirring to issue a 'thought'.[7]

Consciousness is the fundamental concept at the heart of Gnostic metaphysics because it is the prerequisite for existence. We can understand this from our own direct experience, because were we not conscious, nothing would exist for us, nor would we exist for ourselves. Yet the ultimate source of all cannot be Consciousness, since before it thinks the first thought Consciousness must be conscious of nothing and therefore unconscious. Plotinus explains:

> 'Consciousness is always inseparable from that which it is conscious of. Eliminate the object of Consciousness and Consciousness disappears with it. So what we are seeking cannot be Consciousness, but must be something that rejects the duality inherent in Consciousness. That which is prior to duality must be something on the further side of Consciousness.'[8]

If Consciousness arises with its object, it cannot be the ultimate source. Plotinus asks: 'Who has begotten such a child as "Consciousness"?'[9]

There is no answer to this question. The ultimate source of all is the Absolute Mystery. Because it comes before Consciousness, it is not something we can be conscious of. It is, therefore, utterly unknowable. The Gnostics are unsure whether it is even wise to use the word 'God' as a name for the Mystery. *The Secret Book of John* explains: 'It is not right to think of it as divine or something like that, for it is superior to God.'[10] Dionysius writes:

> 'If we want to truly understand God we have to go beyond all names and attributes. He is both God and not-God.'[11]

Dionysius attempts to gesture towards the ineffable Mystery with ultimately unintelligible phrases such as 'Consciousness beyond consciousness' and 'the dazzling darkness'.[12] Plotinus cautions that we should add 'as it were' to every description we attempt of the Mystery.[13] 'Strictly speaking we should not even say that it *exists*,'[14] he explains. What exists only does so within Consciousness, so that which is before Consciousness is what Plotinus calls 'the Mystery beyond being'.[15]

Because the Mystery exists before the duality of knower and known the ancients call it the One. The Egyptians talk of 'the undifferentiated One'.[16] Their spiritual heirs, the original Christians, talk in *The Tripartite Tractate* of 'the inconceivable, ineffable, incomprehensible, unchanging One'.[17] Plotinus explains:

> 'The One is neither some thing, nor a quality, nor a quantity. Neither Consciousness nor psyche. It is not moving or standing still. It is not in place or time.'[18]

Yet even to think of the Mystery as the One is misleading, for it is also the Nothing. It is impossible to conceptualize it. Basilides teaches that we should not even call it 'the Mystery', since 'this is to make an assertion' about what is 'beyond every description'.[19] Using language reminiscent of the Hindu *Upanishads*, on which he wrote a tractate, he talks simply of '*THAT* beyond being'.[20]

Plotinus asks, 'What is this principle best defined as "indefinable"?'[21] He instructs us that to answer this question we must negate every concept we may form of it and then also negate the negation![22] As Dionysius explains, 'It is beyond every limitation and also beyond every denial.'[23]

Attempting to describe this indescribable Mystery which is (and isn't!) before the beginning, Basilides writes:

> 'Nothing existed. Not even nothing. The truth, naked of opinion and conceptualization, is that there was not even the One. And when I say "there was", I don't mean that anything *was*. When I use the expression "There was absolutely nothing" I am just giving some sort of indication of what I am trying to talk about. Nothing was. Neither something nor absence of something. Not the One. Not the impossibility of complexity. Not the imperceptible or the inconceivable. Neither man nor angel nor God. In short there was not anything for which human beings have ever found a name.'[24]

Does that mess with your head or what?! Do you *get* the non-idea with which the Gnostics are trying to explode us out of our conceptual prison?

Well, in Gnostic mythology, the process of creation begins when this Great Mystery desires – as it were – self-knowledge.

God and Goddess

The basic narrative which underlies the myth of origination begins like this. The Mystery is the dazzling darkness of Consciousness, conscious of nothing. To become conscious of itself it makes itself simultaneously a subject and an object.[25] As Simon Magus explains, the Mystery 'became manifest to itself from itself and so passed into a state of duality'.[26] The unknowable knows itself by manifesting as the knower and the known. The looker and the looked at. Witness and experience. Consciousness and psyche. Spirit and soul.

These are different ways of describing what the original Christians call 'the primal syzygy'.[27] The word 'syzygy' means 'yoked together'. A syzygy is one thing in two states, a pair of concepts which arise simultaneously. The primal syzygy is the archetype of all subsequent dualities of complementary yet irreconcilable opposites.[28]

The ancients represented this fundamental duality mythologically as God and Goddess. When the Mystery looks at itself, God looks at Goddess. Zostrianos calls the Christian Goddess Sophia 'the introspection of God'.[29] According to *The Sophia of Solomon*, Sophia is a 'reflection' of God, an 'image' of God, a 'mirror of God's active power'.[30] She is God's psyche. She is the appearance of his essence.

The Mystery and the primal syzygy God–Goddess form a mythic trinity. The idea of the Mystery in three aspects goes back to ancient Egypt.[31] Plotinus knows it as 'Plato's Trinity',[32] which is the One, Consciousness and psyche.[33] Christians often anthropomorphize the Mystery as the 'Father' and Consciousness as the 'Son', creating the 'Holy Trinity' of Father, Son and Sophia. Valentinus was the author of a now lost treatise called *On the Three Natures* in which he was said to have been the first Christian to develop a theology based on the trinity of Father, Son and Holy Spirit, in which the Holy Spirit represents the Goddess.[34]

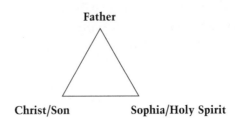

The Christian tendency to give the Mystery a gender can be confusing, because the Mystery is specifically beyond all such dualities.[35] However, Christians emphasize that 'the Father' is not really male.[36] Marcus describes the Mystery as 'the Father who is inconceivable and beyond being, neither male nor female'.[37] Simon Magus speaks of a bisexual Oneness 'generating itself, making itself grow, seeking itself, finding itself, being mother of itself, father of itself, sister of itself, spouse of itself, daughter of itself, son of itself'.[38] In *Trimorphic Protennoia*, a Christian text, a divine voice announces: 'I am androgynous. I am both Mother and Father, since I copulate with myself.'[39]

The One and the Many

In Simon Magus's version of the myth of origination, the ineffable Silent Power (Mystery) emanates the Great Power (God) and the Great Thought (Goddess). Simon teaches:

> 'There are two emanations, without beginning and end, which spring from the one root, which is the invisible, inapprehensible Silent Power. One of these appears from above and is male in nature. It is the Great Power – the universal Consciousness which orders all things. The other appears from below and is female in nature. It is the Great Thought which produces all things.'[40]

The Gnostics teach that: 'In the beginning everything existed unconsciously within the One'[41] then 'Consciousness stirred and ordered them.'[42] In an attempt to picture its unimaginably mysterious essence, Consciousness (Great Power) imagines itself as an infinitely complex conceptual matrix (Great Thought), which shapes the ineffable potential of the 'undifferentiated One' (Mystery), into the appearance of a 'cosmos', which means 'beautiful order'.[43] The essential Oneness manifests itself as the apparent multiplicity of the universe.[44]

God	Goddess
Essence of the Mystery	Appearance of the Mystery
Mind	Thought
Potential	Manifestation
Ineffable Consciousness	Psycho-physical cosmos
Oneness	Multiplicity

Paradoxically, when the dazzling darkness of the Mystery arises as the primal syzygy Consciousness–psyche it simultaneously realizes Gnosis and falls into a state of ignorance. As Consciousness it knows its Self, but as psyche it identifies with its many self-images. When Consciousness objectifies itself as psyche, it necessarily perceives only its ideas of itself. It is impossible for ineffable Consciousness to picture its essential nature. It can only ever see what it imagines itself to be. By manifesting itself, it obscures its true nature, which is the Absolute Mystery. It can't objectify itself as it *is*, because it is pure subjectivity. Psyche is subjectivity that mistakes itself for an object. It is mind that thinks it's a thing.

Using Simon Magus' analogy of the circle of self which we explored previously, we can imagine the Mystery as emptiness within which Consciousness arises as a centre. The one centre of Consciousness emanates the circle of psyche, which manifests as the immeasurable variety of the cosmos, represented by the infinite number of points on the circumference. When ineffable Consciousness at the centre witnesses its multitude of forms, it falls into identification with each image or *eidolon*. Thus the one centre appears to itself as many separate individuals at the circumference. Consciousness dreams the dream of the cosmos and identifies with all of the different characters within the dream.

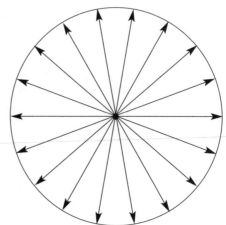

Centre: One Consciousness

Radii: Many psyches within the one universal psyche

Circumference: Many physical bodies within the one physical body of the cosmos

The Goddess is universal psyche which appears to be many individual psyches. She is the Oneness appearing to be multiplicity. We can understand these teachings by imagining the Mystery as a fathomless ocean of potentiality. In a state of stillness the ocean is one transparent, undifferentiated whole. This is equivalent to the stillness of deep sleep, in which Consciousness has no object and is therefore unconscious. When Consciousness stirs, the surface undulates. There is 'movement on the face of the deep'. This agitation of the surface represents psyche. Plotinus explains: 'Consciousness is continually itself. With movement within it we are in the realm of psyche.'[45] In *The Gospel of Thomas* Jesus calls the primal syzygy 'stillness and movement'.[46] Consciousness is either still or in movement. Psyche (consciousness-in-movement) can, in turn, be understood in two ways, either as the moving surface of one sea or as an infinitive number of individual waves. The one moving surface of the water represents universal psyche. Individual psyches are the individual waves. We are unique movements on the shared still depths of Consciousness.

THE EVOLVING COSMOS

To know itself the Mystery arises as the primal syzygy – subject and object

– which results in partial Gnosis and partial ignorance. As subjective Consciousness it knows its Self, but as psyche it mistakes its self for its many objective self-images.[47] As a continuation of the initial impulse towards self-knowledge, that part of Consciousness which has become identified with each psyche-body is in the process of completing the journey of Gnosis by progressively awakening to its true nature.

We can understand this fundamental duality by seeing how it manifests in each of us. We appear to be an evolving psyche-body on a journey of awakening, but our essential nature is ineffable Consciousness. Knowing our essential nature is the realization of Gnosis, because as Consciousness we already exist permanently in the state of Gnosis. Whilst we identify with the psyche-body, however, we experience only relative states of ignorance.

Plato describes these two states as 'being' and 'becoming'.[48] Consciousness is *being*. We experience this as the sense of *I AM*. It is unchanging, qualityless presence. It is what we *are*. Psyche, on the other hand, is what we *experience*. It is an unfolding succession of changing appearances. It is impermanence. It is perpetually in the process of *becoming* something else. The Mystery as Consciousness is *being* what it is. Consciousness witnesses itself as a psyche-body in the process of *becoming* aware of what it is. We are being witnessing becoming.

Another name for the 'becoming' is 'time'.[49] Pagan and Christian Gnostics call time 'a moving image of eternity'.[50] Time is the Mystery striving to imagine a perfect self-image. Time is the journey from ignorance to Gnosis. Time is imperfection longing to be the Good and progressively improving. Time is the relative reaching towards the Absolute.[51] Time is the gradual reconciliation of the two poles of the primal syzygy.

Time is the evolving cosmos, which is 'ever labouring to bring about the ideal, planning to lead all to an unending state of excellence', as Plotinus puts it.[52] In nature this manifests as the evolution of ever more sophisticated physical bodies to express the potentiality of Consciousness. In human society this is expressed in the utopian dream of creating Heaven on Earth. In each individual it is expressed by the impulse towards the Good which manifests as the desire to become a kinder, wiser person. As Basilides teaches, 'All things hasten from worse to better.'[53]

Mythologically, God represents eternal being and Goddess represents temporal becoming. God represents the essence of the Mystery which consciously knows its nature. Goddess represents the appearance of the

Mystery – the 'image of God' – which is continually being perfected. She is the cosmos on a journey of awakening in which we are all participants. She is the great dream of life within which our separate self has a walk-on part. Yet although we seem to be only a fleeting appearance, our common essence is the divine dreamer. We are co-creating this shared dream, which reflects our wisdom and foolishness back to us to help us wake up.

Aspects of the Primal Syzygy

Consciousness	Psyche
Being	Becoming
Gnosis	Journey from ignorance to Gnosis
Eternal Perfection	Evolution over time

THE END IS THE BEGINNING

According to Plato, the ultimate aim of the Mysteries was to instruct initiates in the 'way of return'.[54] The myth of origination is an explanation of how we got into our present predicament and a map to guide us on the return journey home to our essence and source. This is because 'The way down and the way up are the same', as the Christian master Dositheus teaches, quoting a famous line from the Pagan sage Heraclitus.[55]

Phrases such as 'way down and way up' are just metaphors, of course. Different Gnostic masters teach using different metaphors, but they are all basically saying the same thing. Some encourage us to ascend to the heights of Heaven. Others exhort us to descend into the silent depths.[56] To the modern mind, perhaps the best metaphor is of going within ourselves. In *The Gospel of Philip* Jesus calls the Father 'the One who is innermost of all'.[57]

Often many metaphors are deliberately used together to avoid the danger of Literalism. The Pagan Gnostic Porphyry teaches: 'Endeavour to ascend into yourself.'[58] In *Pistis Sophia* Jesus, likewise, describes the journey as 'upward and inwards'[59] to the 'interior of interiors',[60] promising to teach his disciples 'about all the things of the heights, from the outer to the inner and from the inner to the outer'.[61]

It doesn't matter whether we think of ourselves as going within, ascending to Heaven or plumbing the depths. What matters is actually making the return journey. How do we do this? We go back by retracing our steps. We undo the process through which Consciousness creates the cosmos and gets lost in identification with the appearances.

We are unaware of our ineffable essence because we have obscured it with limiting ideas. We have created a conceptual pseudo-reality in which we are prisoners. To set ourselves free we must stop habitually focusing on our psyche – the conceptual matrix – and become conscious of being Consciousness. By focusing exclusively on the psyche we lose all awareness of our true nature, because our true nature exists before psyche, not within psyche. It is not a concept. It is Consciousness.

Plotinus writes:

'Those who take the upward path divest themselves of all they have put on during their downward journey, just as those participating in the Holy Mysteries undergo purifications, and take off the garments they have previously worn, until they enter naked. We must then pass on upward, removing all that is other than God, until in the solitude of ourselves we behold the source of life, Consciousness, Being. When someone experiences this vision, they are filled with an overwhelming love, a passionate longing to dissolve into communion with *THAT*. What a wonder and delight!'[62]

Every child that is born is God asking, 'Who am I?' and every lifetime is a unique attempt at finding an answer, yet at our common centre we already are what we are. In the stillness of our essence there is no coming or going. No incarnation. No evolution. No realization. Only blissful Gnosis. The Mystery knowing itself. Love making love with itself. Beauty delighting in itself. Truth true to itself. Being being itself.

The purpose of the secret teachings of the original Christians is to guide us on our journey of *becoming* until we reach the destination, which is consciously *being*; to help us stop identifying with the psyche-body and become aware of our deeper nature, as the mysterious source of all.[63] This fulfils the primal aspiration which inspired Consciousness to create the cosmos. When we know we are the Mystery, the Mystery knows itself.

The Beginning is Now

The Gnostic path of self-knowledge is a journey back to the Mystery that is the source of all, but this is about plumbing the depths of Consciousness, not about going back in time. As Plotinus teaches, because of their narrative form, myths necessarily separate in time things which belong together.[64] Every step in the unfolding sequence of events through which the Gnostics imagine creation to occur is happening instantaneously in this moment. Consciousness is continuously conceiving the cosmos. So the beginning is not in the distant past. The beginning is now. And the end is also now, whenever we reach back to the beginning – beyond concepts to Consciousness.

Alcmeon the Pythagorean writes: 'Men die because they cannot join the beginning and the end.'[65] In *The Gospel of Thomas*, when Jesus' disciples ask him, 'Tell us how our end will be,' he replies:

'Have you discovered the beginning, then, that you look for the end? For where the beginning is, there will the end be. Blessed is he who takes his place in the beginning, for he knows the end and will not experience death.'[66]

When we return our awareness from the appearances to the source, we know our unborn essence. We witness the temporary, embodied self emerging and passing away again, like a fleeting thought from the unfathomable Mystery. We know we are not the limited thought, but the unknown thinker. We appear as the manifest. But we *are* the Mystery. We are not anything we can possibly think ourselves to be. We are *THAT*.

In *The Gospel of Thomas* Jesus proclaims: 'Blessed is he who is what he was before he was created.'[67]

SUMMARY

❖ In the beginning, desiring self-knowledge, the Mystery looks at itself (as it were!), becoming both subject and object. This duality which arises from the unconscious unity of the dazzling darkness is the primal syzygy: Consciousness and psyche.

❖ The Mystery, Consciousness and psyche form a Holy Trinity, represented mythologically by the Mystery, God and Goddess. In the Christian tradition this becomes Father, Christ and Sophia, or Father, Son and Holy Spirit.

❖ Consciousness conceives the conceptual matrix of universal psyche, creating a 'beautiful order' or 'cosmos' from the infinite potentiality of the Mystery.

❖ As Consciousness, the Mystery knows its Self and is in a state of Gnosis. As psyche, it mistakes itself for its many self-images and is in a state of ignorance, from which it is in the process of awakening. As apparently separate individuals, we are Consciousness identified with a particular *eidolon* or image. We are a part of the evolving cosmos.

❖ Gnostic mythology tells the story of the beginning and the end, but both are actually here and now. Consciousness creates the cosmos in the permanent present, which is also our opportunity to reach back to the beginning and complete the journey of self-knowledge.

Having explored the philosophical ideas which underlie the Gnostic vision of the source and purpose of the cosmos, let's now examine their mythological elaboration into the epic Christian myth cycle.

chapter eight

THE FATHER'S
Secret Plan

'This is the Father's secret plan, his will and desire determined beforehand in Christ, which he will put into effect when the time is ripe: That the whole cosmos, all in Heaven and on Earth, be brought into unity with Christ.'

Paul, *Letter to the Ephesians*[1]

Any lingering remnants of the simplistic Literalist picture of Christianity are quickly dispelled by the study of the complete Christian myth cycle. It shows Christianity to be an enigmatic product of the ancient mind which is both profound and gloriously strange. We will look at an abridged version of the myth cycle taught by Ptolemy, a master from the Valentinian school.[2] It relates the myth of the fall and redemption of the Goddess Sophia, but on a cosmic rather than personal level. Earlier we decoded the Sophia myth as an allegory for the fall into incarnation of our individual psyche. Ptolemy's myth of Sophia is an allegorical exploration of the fall into multiplicity and incarnation of the universal psyche.

THE CHRISTIAN MYTH CYCLE

Ptolemy begins his myth with the Primal Parent emanating a succession of archetypes which form the blueprint for all that will subsequently come into existence. The Christians called these archetypal structuring principles *aeons*, or 'eternals'.[3] The Gnostics reasoned that Consciousness conceives the cosmos in the way that it does because that pattern is already latent in Consciousness.[4] It is already a 'cosmos' or 'beautiful order' of non-manifest *aeons* or archetypes. Christians called the ineffable cosmos of archetypes the *pleroma* and the manifest psycho-physical cosmos of appearances the *kenoma*.[5]

Although routinely ignored by scholars as being utterly incomprehensible, when understood from the mystical perspective we have been exploring in this book, the Christian system of *aeons* can be seen to be a profound attempt to articulate the archetypal structure which underlies existence. We explore the meaning and relationships of the *aeons* in Appendix I, 'Blueprint for Reality'. Here, however, we will immediately engage with the narrative of the Christian myth cycle, which is a drama in three acts.

Act I: The Archetypal Drama

In the beginning the Primal Parent emanates the *aeons* (archetypes) which make up the *pleroma* (archetypal cosmos). The first *aeon* is Consciousness. It is blissfully aware that its essence is the Mystery. It has Gnosis. All the subsequent *aeons*, however, are too distant from the Primal Parent to have this immediate knowledge of their source. They long to have Gnosis of their essence and origin.[6] Consciousness wants to share its Gnosis with the other *aeons* by explaining to them that the Primal Parent is without beginning and beyond understanding, but the Primal Parent stops it doing so. As a result, the *aeons'* collective desire for Gnosis builds and builds, until it is finally expressed by the last of the *aeons*, called Sophia.

Sophia tries desperately to understand the Mystery of the Primal Parent, but she is attempting the impossible. By trying to conceive of the inconceivable, she creates ignorance or error.[7] Theodotus explains: 'The *aeon* which wished to know that which is beyond knowledge brought into being ignorance.'[8] According to *The Gospel of Truth*, by attempting to conceptualize the Mystery, which is 'inconceivable, uncontained and superior to all thought', Sophia inevitably instead conceives 'error', which 'like a dense fog makes it impossible to see'. Mistaking her ideas for reality, Sophia becomes trapped in error or ignorance, a prisoner in a conceptual world of her own making. *The Gospel of Truth* comments:

> 'Without having learned to know the Truth she took up residence in the imagined form, which was a substitute for Truth.'[9]

Lost and bewildered, Sophia experiences fear and other negative emotions which 'are all rooted in her lack of Gnosis'.[10] She prays for help to the Primal Parent, who responds by dividing off from Sophia her 'thinking and consequent emotions' with a barrier called the Cross.[11]

The Cross marks the limit of the *pleroma*. Sophia's ignorance is exiled from the *pleroma* to create the *kenoma*, the cosmos of appearances.[12] The Primal Parent then emanates two new *aeons* called Christ and Holy Spirit. Now that ignorance has been banished from the archetypal cosmos, Christ imparts Gnosis to Sophia and all the other *aeons* of the *pleroma*. The *aeons* then joyously integrate their different natures into the Christ, who becomes the embodiment of the wholeness of the *pleroma*, perfected in the state of Gnosis.

Act II: The Cosmic Drama

Ptolemy personifies Sophia's ignorance as the fallen Goddess figure Achamoth. Ejected from the *pleroma*, she is pictured alone in the darkness of the *kenoma*. Achamoth represents Consciousness or 'spiritual essence' that has identified with appearances. To liberate this Consciousness, Christ sets in motion a rescue operation of truly cosmic proportions.

Christ stretches out along the Cross which divides the *pleroma* and the *kenoma* and wakes the lost Achamoth from her spiritual sleep so that she experiences *metanoia* and begins to search for the light of the *pleroma*, her original home. Then, as an embodiment of the *aeon Logos*, the archetypal organizing principle, Christ gives order to Achamoth's chaotic formlessness. He fashions her *metanoia* into animate psyche and her ignorant passions into inanimate matter. He then oversees the process whereby Achamoth creates the Demiurge, or 'craftsman', from psyche and the Demiurge in turn uses psyche and matter to create the psychophysical cosmos. The universe is thus a manifestation of ignorance and *metanoia*. It is lost Consciousness in the process of repenting or turning back.

The Demiurge has no knowledge of the Primal Parent, Christ or Achamoth, and so believes himself to be the Lord of the Universe. He does not understand that Christ and Achamoth have been acting through him to create the cosmos of appearances as a copy of the *pleromic* archetypes. The Demiurge is a product of Achamoth's ignorance so, not surprisingly, he is an ignorant creator god of a cosmos which is ignorance made manifest.

The cosmos of appearances is formed into eight heavens, or psychic planes of reality, which are imperfect manifestations of the eight principal *aeons* of the *pleroma*. Achamoth inhabits the *ogdoad*, or eighth heaven, just outside the *pleroma*. Below her, in the seventh heaven, is the Demiurge, who is responsible for creating the six subsequent heavens and their angels.

As he is incapable of replicating the eternity of the *aeons*, or 'eternals', 'in his delusion the Demiurge makes an image of the infinite by laying it out in vast epochs of time'.[13] Within time he creates the physical cosmos and its inhabitants. This includes human beings, into whose forms, without the Demiurge knowing, Achamoth places the trapped spiritual essence as 'seeds' of Consciousness, so that through living a human life, they can mature, until they are ready to receive Gnosis by awakening to their true *pleromic* or heavenly nature. This is the purpose of creation. This has been the secret plan all along.

The three levels of human identity are thus all derived from Achamoth, which is why the original Christians called her the Mother. Our spiritual essence is part of the Consciousness trapped when she was expelled from the *pleroma*. Our psyche is created from her *metanoia* and our physical body from her fear and ignorance.[14] It is, then, the inherent nature of physicality to be ignorant and fearful. It is the inherent nature of psyche to be in the process of *metanoia* – transformation or evolution. And it is the inherent nature of our spiritual essence to be 'in the cosmos but not of it', as Jesus teaches.[15]

Act III: The Human Drama

Jesus, the hero of the gospels, is an image of the Christ *aeon* on the human level. His mission is to fulfil the plan of the Christ by bringing Gnosis to the seeds of Consciousness lost in the cosmos of appearances. The Jesus myth narrates the redemption of Mary Magdalene by Jesus, which echoes on the human level the archetypal tale of the redemption of Sophia-Achamoth by the Christ.

According to Ptolemy, as seeds of Consciousness planted in human bodies by Achamoth, we come to Gnosis by being initiated into the 'Mysteries of the Mother', which are the Inner Mysteries of Christianity. When we realize Gnosis we will be reunited with our Mother Achamoth in the *ogdoad* at the entrance of the cave of the cosmos. When all the seeds of trapped Consciousness have realized Gnosis and are gathered back into the Mother, the cosmos of appearances will be perfected.

In the same way that the perfected *pleroma* has already been embodied by the Christ *aeon*, the perfected appearances will be embodied by the Holy Spirit *aeon*. The over-familiar name 'Holy Spirit' is more intelligible if translated 'Purified Consciousness'. She represents 'Consciousness' or 'spirit' which was lost in ignorance but which has become 'purified' or 'made holy' by the process of evolution and now recognizes its true nature. When Christ oversees the formation of the cosmos of appearances, he initiates a process of evolution that will eventually transform Achamoth, the lost Goddess, into Holy Spirit or Purified Consciousness, the archetype of the redeemed Goddess.

The *aeons* Christ and Holy Spirit are emanated by the Primal Parent as two poles of one syzygy. The Christ archetype is fulfilled before the creation of time, when all the *aeons* of the archetypal cosmos realize Gnosis. The Holy Spirit archetype, however, must await the end of time before she is fulfilled, when all of the seeds of Consciousness trapped in the cosmos of appearances realize Gnosis.

The climax of the Christian myth cycle comes when both archetypes are fulfilled. Holy Spirit will then commune with her lover Christ in a mystical marriage, symbolizing the Mystery in a complete state of Gnosis. All that needs to happen before this grand finale can be celebrated and the purpose of creation fulfilled is for the spiritual essences lost in ignorance to awaken. When we all wake up by achieving individual self-knowledge, the Mystery will achieve universal self-knowledge.[16]

The Basic Narrative

Ptolemy's epic narrative encodes mythologically the philosophical ideas we explored in the last chapter. The Primal Parent represents the Mystery. Christ and Achamoth represent the primal syzygy – Consciousness and psyche. The expulsion of Achamoth from the *pleroma* represents the objectification of Consciousness as psyche. When Achamoth forms the *kenoma* or appearances, the Christ *aeon*, representing Consciousness, arises. This represents the idea that Consciousness arises from the dazzling darkness of the Mystery only with the objectification of psyche which gives it an object to be conscious of.

Achamoth represents the Mystery's futile attempt to know itself objectively through thoughts. Christ represents Consciousness which has Gnosis. Achamoth represents that part of Consciousness lost in identification with appearances. Achamoth placing the trapped spiritual essence as seeds into human bodies represents Consciousness identifying with each individual *eidolon* or image.

We are those embodied seeds of Consciousness and when we all awaken to our true identity Achamoth will be redeemed as Holy Spirit, representing the fulfilment of the evolution of the cosmos towards archetypal perfection. The fulfilment of the *pleroma* in the figure of Christ when Achamoth is ejected into the *kenoma* represents the Mystery in a state of partial Gnosis and partial ignorance. The mystical marriage of Christ and Holy Spirit at the end of time represents the Mystery in a state of complete Gnosis.[17]

ALL GOD'S IDEA

On a superficial reading, the Christian myth cycle gives us a very negative view of the cosmos we inhabit. Actually, however, this is not the message at all. True, the creation of the cosmos by the foolish Demiurge is the final stage of an ongoing attempt to redeem Sophia's ignorance. But Sophia's ignorance is deliberately encouraged by the Primal Parent at the very beginning of the myth, when it prevents the *aeon* Consciousness from sharing Gnosis with the other *aeons*.[18] What seems to be an error is actually the will of God – a necessary part of the divine plan which will eventually turn out for the best.[19]

The Primal Parent allows Sophia's ignorance because the only way to knowledge is through ignorance.[20] The purpose of manifestation is for the unconscious Oneness of the dazzling darkness to be conscious of itself. But the One can only be conscious of itself by appearing to be two. Consciousness requires the duality of subject and object, and objectification creates ignorance. Ignorance is a stepping-stone to Gnosis.

Conscious Oneness is not a regression to the absolute Oneness of the dazzling darkness, but an evolution towards the recognition that the apparent duality is actually a syzygy – one essence necessarily appearing to be two.[21] Gnosis is Consciousness, which requires the apparent duality of subject and object, aware of the essential Oneness. It is the realization of unity through duality. The primal syzygy at the beginning of creation is the One appearing to be two. The mystical marriage at the fulfilment of creation is the two knowing themselves to be One.

The Christian myth cycle narrates the journey from the unconscious unity of the dazzling darkness to the conscious realization of unity through duality which is Gnosis. It is an epic adventure which necessitates the creation of the magnificent multi-dimensional cosmos we inhabit, the purpose of which is to bring 'all in Heaven and on Earth' into a state of 'unity with the Christ', representing universal Gnosis. This, according to Paul, is 'the Father's secret plan'.[22]

SUMMARY

❖ The psycho-physical cosmos of appearances is an imperfect image of the ineffable archetypal cosmos. Its purpose is to be a context within which the seeds of Consciousness trapped in ignorance can mature until they are ready to realize Gnosis. We are those seeds.

❖ Although superficially Christian mythology seems to portray the cosmos as the work of the foolish Demiurge, necessitated by Sophia's error, actually everything happens as part of the 'Father's secret plan', which is to bring all to conscious unity in Christ.

❖ Gnosis is Consciousness of the Oneness. Consciousness requires the duality of subject and object. Gnosis, therefore, is the realization of the essential Oneness through the apparent duality. This is symbolized by the mystical marriage of Christ and the Goddess.

The central mythological figures throughout the Christian myth cycle are Christ and the Goddess, in their various guises, representing the perfect essence and the evolving appearances. Let's see how our understanding of the familiar gospel story of Jesus Christ is transformed when we view it in the light of the whole myth cycle of which it is a part.

chapter nine

THE IMAGE OF
Christor

'It is inherent in our faith that in the end we will all attain Oneness through Gnosis of God's Son, becoming fully initiated human beings, equal to nothing less than the *pleroma* of Christ.'

Paul, *Letter to the Ephesians*[1]

The Christian myth cycle is the story of the quest for Gnosis. It is the extraordinary tale of the Mystery of God's search to know itself, of which our search to know ourselves is an echo. It is a grand initiation allegory whose three acts give us the same basic motifs on three levels – archetypal, cosmic and human. On the archetypal level, Sophia is redeemed by the Christ. On the cosmic level, Achamoth is redeemed by the Christ as the *Logos*. On the human level, Mary Magdalene is redeemed by Jesus, the embodiment of the Christ/*Logos*. It is on the human level that the great drama will be fulfilled. Only when all the seeds lost in ignorance have realized Gnosis will the journey, begun when the Mystery first stirred into Consciousness, be completed.

The Christian Myth Cycle: An Allegorical Drama in Three Acts		
Archetypal	*Pleroma*	Redemption of Sophia by Christ
Cosmic	*Kenoma*	Redemption of Achamoth by the Logos
Human	World	Redemption of Mary Magdalene by Jesus

Sophia's search for her origins and essence and her encounter with her ignorance and fear form the archetypal template for the *psychic* initiation. In this stage of initiation, like Sophia, we set off optimistically to understand the Mystery, but find ourselves actually having to face our ignorance and fear. Ptolemy tells us that Sophia's spiritual quest appears to be motivated by love of the Primal Parent for whom she is searching, but actually it comes from fear caused by her lack of Gnosis.[2] In the same way, our spiritual quest may seem to be motivated by love of God or Truth, but actually it is driven by fear generated by not knowing who we really are and what life is all about. Without an understanding of the essential Oneness of all things, we are lost, alone, vulnerable and frightened.[3] It is this which motivates the spiritual quest.

On the archetypal level, Sophia in the *pleroma* is separated by the Cross from her ignorant 'thoughts and emotions' that form the cosmos of appearances. This is the archetype of the *pneumatic* initiation, in which initiates distinguish their essence from their appearance. This motif is echoed on the human level in the Jesus myth by the crucifixion, which likewise represents the *pneumatic* initiation. Having been separated from her ignorance, the Christ reveals Gnosis to Sophia and she becomes integrated with the other *aeons* of the *pleroma* into the Christ. In the same way, through the realization of Gnosis, initiates are awoken from the dream of separateness and realize their shared essential identity, symbolized by the Christ.

On the cosmic level, Achamoth plays out the same initiatory journey in the *kenoma* as Sophia has in the *pleroma*. Christ awakens Achamoth from her spiritual sleep, which represents the inexplicable moment initiates are first touched by something beyond their normal awareness and glimpse the wider reality. Her subsequent experience of *metanoia* and her spiritual search represent the *psychic* initiation. Christ then separates Achamoth's essence from her ignorant passions, as has already happened with Sophia, which again represents the *pneumatic* initiation.

Christ as the *Logos* transforms Achamoth's ignorance into the psycho-physical cosmos within which the seeds of Consciousness that are trapped in appearances can come to the realization of Gnosis. This allows the archetypal initiatory drama to be played out on the human level, represented by the story of Jesus, the saviour of *psychic* initiates and the perfect example for *pneumatic* initiates. The allegorical story of Jesus and Mary echoes the initiatory pattern which was first played out archetypally by Christ and Sophia in the *pleroma*.

The Christian myth cycle explains why Jesus has to come to our rescue and who he really is. Ptolemy teaches: 'The cosmos was constructed and the saviour came to this level to save the psyche.'[4] Whether on an archetypal level, cosmic level or human level, the whole Christian myth cycle is about redeeming the psyche – that part of Consciousness which has become identified with appearances. Jesus is an image or embodiment of the archetypal Christ, whose mission he comes to fulfil by rescuing the seeds of spiritual essence lost in the cosmos of appearances.

This is what Paul means when he teaches that Jesus 'is the *pleroma*', that the '*pleroma* dwells in him', that 'in him the *pleroma* of God lives',[5] that 'it has pleased the Father that in him should dwell the whole *pleroma*',[6] that through 'Gnosis of the depths of Christ's love, which is actually beyond knowing', we may ourselves 'attain the *pleroma* of being, the *pleroma* of God himself'.[7] In the end, Paul writes enthusiastically, we will all experience Gnosis of 'the *pleroma* of Christ'.[8]

According to Ptolemy, Jesus becomes merged with the Christ archetype at his baptism. In the gospel story, when Jesus is baptized the voice of God announces: 'This is my beloved son, with whom I am well pleased,'[9] and the Holy Spirit descends in the form of a dove.[10] From the Christian myth cycle we know that the Holy Spirit is a pseudonym of the Goddess. Heracleon and Ptolemy tell us that the dove symbolizes 'Sophia, the Mother above'.[11] The dove was a widespread symbol of the Goddess in the ancient world and was adopted by Christians as a symbol of Mary.[12] Christians of the Ophite school teach that at his baptism 'Christ and Sophia, the one enfolding the other, descended upon Jesus and he became Jesus Christ'.[13] We are all images of Christ, but Jesus represents the idea of the perfect image, a human being who embodies the universal Consciousness, represented by Christ, and perfected psyche, represented by the redeemed Goddess. Hence Paul teaches: 'Jesus is the Power of God and Sophia of God.'[14] He comes to fulfil the mission of the Christ and

Sophia/Achamoth, which is to bring all the lost seeds of Consciousness to Gnosis.

THE CAVE

The gospel story begins with Jesus being born in a cave and climaxes with him ascending from the cave. Earlier we suggested that the Christian image of the cave was derived from Plato's famous allegory of the cave in *The Republic*. From the Christian myth cycle we can now clearly see that this is true. In Plato's analogy, the human predicament is compared to being imprisoned in a dark cave, where we mistake as reality the shadows on the walls, which are cast by people walking to and fro in the sunlight of the outside world. For Plato, the people in the outside world represent the archetypal ideas which structure the appearance of reality and their shadows represent the world of appearances we inhabit. In the Christian myth cycle this becomes the archetypes of the *pleroma* manifesting as the imperfect images of the *kenoma*.[15] *On the Origin of the World*, a Christian text, describes the Goddess as a veil which divides the light of the *pleroma* and the darkness of the *kenoma*.[16] Human beings exist in the darkness of the *kenoma*, mistaking shadows playing on the veil for reality. The shadows are cast by the light of Consciousness illuminating the real archetypal world of the *pleroma*.

In Plato's analogy, the aim is to escape the cave and enter the real world of light which lies beyond.[17] We are shackled in the cave by our identification with the body. The one who sets himself free is a true philosopher, or 'lover of Sophia'. In Christian mythology, Jesus, the ideal initiate, is the 'lover of Sophia' who dies to the *eidolon* on the cross, ascends from the cave and enters the 'Treasury of Light' – the *pleroma* or Kingdom of Heaven.

In *The Republic*, Plato wonders what would happen to someone who, having escaped the cave and discovered the real world, returned to set his fellow prisoners free. He concludes that the prisoners would not be at all pleased to be told that they were caught up in an illusory world of shadows:

> 'If it were possible to lay hands on the man who tried to release them and lead them up, would they not kill him?'[18]

This is, of course, exactly the fate the gospel writers choose for Jesus, who, in his role as the saviour of *psychic* initiates, comes to set us free from imprisonment in the cave of illusion. The mob that he would redeem turns against him and has him killed.

The False Father

In the cave at Jesus' birth are Mary and Joseph. In our previous analysis of the Jesus myth we saw that Jesus' mother represents the Pagan Goddess of Justice at the entrance of the cave of the cosmos. From Ptolemy's myth we can now see that in Christian mythology this figure is Mother Achamoth, sitting at the mouth of the cave of the *kenoma* in the *ogdoad*, from where she oversees the process of reincarnating the spiritual essences into human bodies to continue their journey of Gnosis.

Just below Achamoth in the seventh heaven is the Demiurge, the false god. With Mary in the birth cave is Joseph, the false father of Jesus the Son of God, who represents the Demiurge or 'craftsman'. In the New Testament Joseph is described as a 'craftsman'.[19] According to *The Gospel of Philip*, 'It is Joseph the craftsman who made the cross.'[20]

After his crucifixion, Jesus is buried in the tomb of Joseph of Arimathaea. The repetition of the name 'Joseph', as with the two Marys, is not accidental, but is designed to equate the two characters mythically. Thus, Joseph finds the cave in which Jesus will be born, makes the cross on which he will be crucified and provides a cave to be his tomb. Jesus, the archetypal initiate, representing each one of us, is born, meets his fate and dies in the material realm – the cave of the *kenoma* – ruled by the Demiurge. But actually we are 'in the cosmos but not of it'. Our real father is not the Demiurge, representing the limitations of psycho-physical existence. Like Jesus, we are children of the ineffable Mystery of God.

Ptolemy portrays the ignorant Demiurge as having no knowledge of his Mother Achamoth, Christ or the Primal Parent and so arrogantly proclaiming: 'I am God and there is no other God but me.' In so doing Ptolemy deliberately equates the Demiurge with Jehovah, the god of Jewish Literalism, who famously announces the same preposterous nonsense in *The Book of Isaiah*.[21] By equating Jehovah with the Demiurge, the original Christians harmonized Jewish and Platonic mythology. They made Jehovah the creator of the cosmos, as he is in Jewish scripture. But they made him equivalent to Plato's figure of the Demiurge, the mediator between the One and the cosmos. For Plato the Demiurge is not a negative figure, but the original Christians pointedly distanced themselves from Jewish Literalism by deliberately portraying the Demiurge Jehovah as an ignorant deity under the higher authority of Christ and Achamoth.

In the New Testament, Jesus is portrayed as *seeming* to be the chosen Messiah of Jehovah. *The Gospel of Matthew* and *The Gospel of Luke* give us two (completely contradictory!) genealogies which trace Jesus' lineage back through Joseph to King David, so that Jesus appears to be from the line of David, as Jehovah's Messiah was expected to be.[22] But actually Jesus is not the son of Joseph and he is not the Messiah of Jehovah the Demiurge. Indeed, he comes to overthrow Jehovah's tyrannical rule in the name of the true God of Love. He comes to replace the laws and prescriptions of Jewish Literalism with the freedom of Gnostic realization. He comes to teach that although our psyches and bodies are under the jurisdiction of the Demiurge who created them, our spiritual essence was given us by our Mother Achamoth and is beyond the control of Jehovah and his entourage of cosmic powers. We are of the *pleroma*.[23] We belong to the Kingdom of Heaven.

In the Jesus myth, the figure of Pontius Pilate also represents the Demiurge. Some Christians taught that Pilate made an image of Jesus which was crucified instead of Jesus himself.[24] This myth encodes the teachings that it is the Demiurge, the craftsman, who creates Jesus' body, the *eidolon* or image, which is what is actually crucified on the cross. Through the death of the *eidolon*, Jesus defeats the Demiurge and his forces, which have temporarily imprisoned him within the cave of the cosmos. Paul teaches: 'On that cross he discarded the cosmic powers and authorities like a garment.'[25] Paul also reminds initiates who have symbolically died and resurrected with the figure of Jesus:

> 'Did you not die with Christ and pass beyond the reach of the elemental powers of the cosmos?'[26]

THE CROSS OF LIGHT

The Christian myth cycle transforms our understanding of Jesus' crucifixion, revealing it to be a symbolic reflection of archetypal events. The Cross, sometimes known as the 'Cross of Light', is the name of the boundary between the *pleroma* and *kenoma*. Ptolemy calls the Cross 'redeemer and emancipator'.[27] It is the creation of the Cross which exiles Achamoth into the *kenoma* and so saves Sophia from being consumed by her ignorance and fear. It is the Cross which the Christ reaches across to redeem Achamoth. In the Jesus myth it is through dying on the cross that Jesus frees himself, and therefore all who follow his example, from the cave of the cosmos. Thus, first on the archetypal level, then on the cosmic level and finally on the human level, the Cross is the means of redemption in the Christian myth cycle.

Jesus suspended on a cross echoes the archetypal Christ suspended on the Cross of Light. Christ is the embodiment of the *pleroma*. As such he is securely on one side of the Cross which divides the *pleroma* from the *kenoma*. But through the ignorant passions of Sophia, some part of Consciousness, and therefore of Christ, has become trapped on the other side of the Cross. Christ is, therefore, suspended on the Cross of Light, in the *pleroma* as the Christ and in the *kenoma* as the lost seeds of spiritual essence. This mythic motif is based on Plato, who taught that the 'Son of God' is 'suspended crosswise in the universe'.[28]

Christ, representing universal Consciousness, embodies all the archetypes of the *pleroma* united through Gnosis and is, therefore, a symbol of the whole made up of many parts. Christ is the one Consciousness which appears as the many separate seeds of Consciousness which are trapped in ignorance and seeking liberation through living a human life. The Oneness of the Christ is fragmented when it passes beyond the Cross of Light into the *kenoma*. Drawing on imagery from the myth of the Pagan Godman Osiris, (and his Greek alter-ego Dionysus), *The Book of the Logos* imagines this as the Christ being dismembered into many limbs.[29]

In the Jesus myth the Father sacrifices his Son on the cross. If taken literally, this is a grotesque notion. In the context of the whole Christian myth cycle, however, we can understand this motif as an archetypal event.[30] The Father (Mystery) sacrifices his Son (Consciousness) through crucifixion/dismemberment, so that we (the many seeds of Consciousness) can experience life. Our existence as individuals is bought at the price of the Christ's crucifixion. Our deaths as separate individuals through the realization of Gnosis are his resurrection. Christ is crucified on the Cross of Light that divides the *pleroma* and the *kenoma* – the one essence and the multiplicity of appearances. Jesus is crucified to reunite the two. The way down and the way back are through the Cross.

The Seamless Garment

The image of the Christ divided on the cross representing the one Consciousness of God divided into multiplicity is symbolically alluded to in the Jesus myth when the soldiers who have crucified Jesus divide up and cast lots for his clothing.[31] *The Gospel of Luke* narrates:

'Jesus said, "Father, forgive them. They don't know what they are doing." And they parted his garment and cast lots.'[32]

Jesus' garment represents psyche which clothes Consciousness. We also find this image in *The Hymn of the Pearl*. In this allegorical Christian tale, at the end of his quest the hero puts on a garment of light, representing perfected psyche, and declares:

'The garment seems to me like a mirror of myself. In it I see all in all. I see that we are distinctly two yet one. I see Gnosis.'[33]

In this passage, psyche is represented both by the mirror in which Consciousness sees itself and by the garment that it wears. The perfect mirror reflects the light perfectly. The perfect garment is one with its wearer.

Understood macrocosmically, Jesus on the cross represents the Consciousness of God and his garment represents the psyche of God. According to *The Gospel of John*, Jesus' garment is 'seamless', which represents the pristine Oneness of universal psyche. In this gospel it is the garment, rather than Jesus, that is divided up. This is perhaps a better allegory than that found in *The Book of the Logos*, because although it appears that Consciousness is divided, it is actually forever One. It is psyche which is divided, not Consciousness. Consciousness appears to be a multiplicity because it witnesses many separate flows of experience – many psyches.

It is significant that the soldiers cast lots for the pieces of Jesus' garment. In *The Republic*, Plato portrays disembodied psyches awaiting reincarnation throwing lots to see which of the lives available will be their next life. In the Jesus myth this becomes the soldiers who 'don't know what they are doing' (psyches without Gnosis) at the foot of the cross (below the Cross of Light in the *ogdoad* from where the Mother sends back psyches into human incarnation) throwing lots for which will be their particular fragment of Jesus' seamless garment (which particular part of universal psyche/experience will be theirs to live out).

Re-Membering Christ

The Acts of John gives us more fascinating insights into the meaning of the Cross of Light and its relationship with Jesus' cross at Golgotha. It relates that John could not bear to watch Jesus being crucified, so he fled to a cave on the Mount of Olives. The image of a cave with olive trees growing outside is, once again, an allusion to the *ogdoad*, the place of the Goddess at the mouth of the cave of the cosmos, outside which grows the olive tree of wisdom.

Suddenly darkness comes over the Earth and Jesus appears to John as light. He teaches him that although the people of Jerusalem believe they are watching Jesus being crucified, they are only watching the *eidolon* or image of Christ. The archetypal Christ is the light of the *pleroma*, which is illuminating the underworld cave to enlighten John. Jesus shows John the 'Cross of Light' and explains:

> 'This Cross of Light is sometimes called *Logos* by me for your sakes, sometimes Consciousness, sometimes Jesus, sometimes Christ, sometimes a door, sometimes bread, sometimes seed, sometimes resurrection, sometimes Son, sometimes Father, sometimes spirit, sometimes life, sometimes faith, sometimes grace. But as to what it is in itself – it is the marking off and delimitation. This is not that wooden cross which you will see when you go down from here; nor am I the man who is on the cross. I am who you now cannot see, but only hear. I was taken to be what I am not. I am not what for many others I was. What I am is known to me and no one else.'[34]

'In the Cross of Light' John sees many people who all share 'one form', whilst around the Cross stand a great crowd of separate individuals. The individuals around the Cross are the spiritually dead – the seeds of Consciousness still lost in the ignorance of the *kenoma*. Those who are 'in the Cross' represent the spiritually resurrected. They have 'one form' because they have seen through the illusion of separateness and realized their essential Oneness with all that is. They have died to the *eidolon* and been reborn as the Christ. They are the limbs of the dismembered Christ that have been reunited. Jesus explains, 'Not every limb of Him who came down has been gathered together,' but he assures John that when the time comes:

> 'Those who presently don't hear will become as you are, and will no longer be what they are not, but exist above the cosmos as I do.'[35]

When all those around the Cross recognize their true nature, then the Christ will be reunified. We are in the process of 're-membering' Christ. But until all the lost seeds of Consciousness spiritually awaken and recognize their essential shared identity, the Christ will not be completely reunified. Jesus tells John: 'As long as some do not call themselves mine I am not what I am.'[36]

The Ankh

The Christian myth cycle suggests that the original source of the Christian image of the cross is the ubiquitous Egyptian cross the ankh. This ancient symbol was so important to Christians that they tooled it into the leather cover of one of the collections of gospels found at Nag Hammadi. The basic ankh is a circle above a 'T' cross. The crosses that were used for crucifixions were 'T'-shaped and in Jewish mythology Moses lifts up a serpent on a 'T' cross in the desert, which was understood as a pre-echo of the image of Jesus on the cross. For these reasons, the early Christians thought of the Christian cross as 'T'-shaped.[37] The ankh, therefore, would have been seen as the cross of Jesus below a circle. The circle is a symbol of wholeness and nothingness. It represents the archetypal potentiality of the *pleroma*. The ankh shows the *pleroma* as delineated by the horizontal axis of the cross, just as it is in Christian mythology. Below the circle, the *kenoma* is cut in two by the descending vertical axis of the cross, representing the Mystery made manifest through duality. The ankh is expressing the idea of syzergy – the One as two.

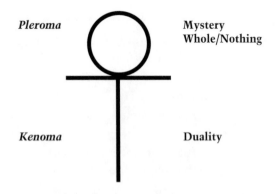

Pleroma		**Mystery** **Whole/Nothing**
Kenoma		**Duality**

The Ancient Egyptian Ankh
Prototype of the Christian Cross of Light

JESUS AND THE LOST GODDESS

Mirrors were constructed in the shape of an ankh, with the cross as the handle and the circle as the mirror.[38] The circle and the cross represent that which is whole and that which is divided – the essence and the appearances, the Mystery and the manifest, the *pleroma* and the *kenoma*. Understanding the relationship between the poles of this fundamental duality is the key to the realization of Gnosis. And what is that relationship? It is one of reflection. The image is a reflection of the archetype. The appearances are how the essence looks to itself. Wanting self-knowledge, the One becomes two. The Mystery becomes the viewer and the mirror. It creates a concept of what it is. It *reflects* on itself. From these two – thinker and thought – comes the cosmos.

THE MYSTICAL MARRIAGE

In the Christian myth cycle Sophia is the last archetype of the *pleroma* and Achamoth inhabits the *ogdoad* at the edge of the cave of the *kenoma*. The two aspects of the Goddess exist either side of the Cross of Light.[39] When the Christ *aeon*'s mission is complete and all the lost seeds of spiritual essence are retrieved, the two aspects of the Goddess will be made one.

In the Jesus story, the Virgin Mary and the redeemed prostitute Mary Magdalene, representing Sophia and Achamoth, are both pictured at the foot of the cross on which Jesus is crucified. In *The Gospel of the Beloved Disciple* (aka *Gospel of John*), from the cross Jesus unites the two Marys. To the Virgin Mary he says, 'Mother, this is your child,' and to Mary Magdalene he says, 'There is your mother.'[40] 'From that hour on' the two Marys share the same house. Like Demeter and Persephone at the end of the Eleusian myth, the two aspects of the Goddess are finally reunited. With which Jesus announces: 'It is finished,' and dies.[41]

In the Christian myth cycle, the uniting of Sophia with Achamoth precipitates the mystical marriage of Jesus and the Goddess in 'the bridal chamber' of the *pleroma*.[42] In the New Testament this is symbolized by the tearing of the veil of the Jerusalem Temple at the moment that Jesus dies on the cross. The veil covered the secret inner sanctum of the Temple, the 'holy of holies', which represents the bridal chamber – the *pleroma*. *The Gospel of Philip* explains:

'The bridal chamber is hidden. It is the holy of holies. The veil at first conceals how God arranged things to be, but when the veil is rent, the things inside are revealed.'[43]

As we explored previously, the veil represents the Goddess. When Jesus dies, the Temple veil is torn. The hymen is rent. The two are made one. The mystical marriage is consummated.

This sexual imagery connecting the holy of holies in the Temple with the 'bridal chamber' was not a Christian innovation. A Jewish Talmudic tradition states:

'When Israel used to make the pilgrimage, the priests would roll up the veil between the temple and holy of holies and show them two cherubim entwined there, one with the other, and say: "Behold! Your love for God is like the love of male and female."'[44]

The Hebrew word for 'knowledge' is *daath*, which also means 'sexual union'.[45] Gnosis truly is 'knowledge' in the Biblical sense! It is the coming together of the opposites in such intimacy that they become one. It is God and Goddess making love and so restoring the primal unity of the Mystery. It is the One being two becoming One.

SUMMARY

- ❖ The Christian myth cycle is an initiation allegory which gives us the same basic initiation motif on three levels. On the archetypal level Sophia is redeemed by the Christ. On the cosmic level Achamoth is redeemed by the Christ as the *Logos*. On the human level Mary Magdalene is redeemed by Jesus, the embodiment of the Christ-*Logos*.

- ❖ Jesus embodies universal Consciousness and purified psyche, represented by Christ and the Goddess, both of which 'enter' him at his baptism. He comes to fulfil their mission by freeing the seeds of Consciousness trapped in ignorance.

- ❖ The cave of the cosmos into which Jesus is born and from which he ascends is the *kenoma*. The Virgin Mary represents Mother Achamoth sitting at the entrance of the cave of the *kenoma*. Jesus' false father Joseph represents the Demiurge or craftsman, the false god.

- ❖ The cross on which Jesus is crucified is an image of the archetypal Cross of Light which divides the *pleroma* and the *kenoma*. The Virgin Mary and Mary Magdalene at the foot of the cross on which Jesus is crucified are images of Sophia and Achamoth at the foot of the archetypal Cross of Light across which the Christ is 'suspended'.

- ❖ From the cross Jesus unites the two Marys as mother and daughter. This represents the reunion of Sophia and Achamoth. The uniting of the two aspects of the Goddess precipitates the mystical marriage, which is the fulfilment of Jesus' mission. In the Jesus myth this is symbolized by the veil of the Temple being torn in two, representing the tearing of the hymen.

When we grasp the vast scope of the whole Christian myth cycle, the idea of taking the Jesus story as a biography appears ridiculous and facile. It reduces the mythologically complex and philosophically sophisticated Christian vision of life to a question of blind belief in the historicity of a one-off supernatural event. Actually, Christianity is ultimately not concerned with Jesus at all. He is an image of the Christ. And the Christ is an image of the Mystery. And the Mystery is what we *are*. Christianity is about what we are. It is about the Mystery of Consciousness.

We have explored the mythic significance of Jesus and the two Goddesses, Sophia and Achamoth. There is one other important mythological figure in the Christian myth cycle. That is the Demiurge, the villain of Christian mythology, who was known as the 'God of the Blind'.[46] Let's now explore some of the extraordinary teachings encoded in the story of how the Demiurge creates the cosmos, which includes powerful insights into the perennial philosophical problems of free will and fate, and the origins of evil.

chapter ten

THE GOD OF THE
Blind

'Evil is thought to abound on Earth. But if you could see the plan of Providence, you would not think there was evil anywhere.'

Boethius, *The Consolations of Philosophy*[1]

The Demiurge represents the ego. In the same way that the ego is an *eidolon* or image of our true identity as Consciousness, Achamoth 'creates the Demiurge as an image of the *aeon* Consciousness'.[2] The original Christians equate the Demiurge with Jehovah, portrayed by the Old Testament as jealous, angry, vindictive, self-obsessed – a perfect symbol for the ego. Hence modern Jungian psychologists have named the neurosis of egotistical self-inflation the 'Jehovah Complex'.[3]

The Demiurge has an inflated sense of his own importance because he has no knowledge of his Mother Achamoth or Christ or the Primal Parent. In the same way the ego has a ridiculously puffed up idea about its significance, because it has no knowledge of the greater psyche of which it is a part, its essential nature as Consciousness, or the great Mystery of which it is an expression. The Demiurge doesn't know that Achamoth has put seeds of spiritual essence into his human creations. He is lost in his own fantasies about why he has created the cosmos and has no understanding of the true purpose of creation, which is to free the Consciousness trapped in ignorance. Likewise, the ego is lost in its own silly personal fantasies of what life is about. It has no understanding of the real purpose of life, which is for us to awaken to our true essence.

The original Christians use the figure of the Demiurge to provide a mythological answer to the important philosophical question of how an imperfect cosmos full of suffering, pain, injustice, cruelty and other evils can arise from a source of perfect love and goodness. The explanation given in the Christian myth cycle is that the Primal Parent is not the creator of the cosmos, the Demiurge is, and the imperfections of the cosmos reflect his imperfections. In the same way, understood allegorically, this myth explains how human beings can be so heartless and small-minded when their eternal essence is the infinite love of God. The Christian answer is that our natural goodness is eclipsed by an impostor – the ego.

Despite his inadequacies, however, the Demiurge is not evil. He is created from Achamoth's *metanoia* – her change of heart or repentance. Although he seems to be the problem, he is (albeit unknowingly) part of the solution. It is through the cosmos, created by the Demiurge, that the seeds of Consciousness lost in ignorance can be redeemed. In the same way, on the human level, the ego – the idea of ourselves as a separate individual – is a necessary stepping-stone in our evolution towards Gnosis. We don't undermine a child's ego, but encourage the development of a self-image. Human beings beginning the process of spiritual maturation need the ego which shapes their world, just as Achamoth needs the Demiurge who shapes the cosmos. Yet ultimately we must transcend the ego to discover our true essence as Consciousness, which is represented in Ptolemy's myth by the liberated seeds transcending the Demiurge and uniting with the Christ.

The Demiurge, like the ego, is ignorant and foolish rather than evil, but through his foolishness he creates the forces of evil. In Ptolemy's myth, when the Demiurge fashions the cosmos, he creates the Devil and his wicked angels from the 'Mother's grief' and 'confusion'.[4] The Demiurge (ego) gives form to the nebulous negative emotions of Achamoth (psyche) and in so doing creates the Devil (the shadow or negative self).[5] The Devil/shadow is the Demiurge/ego's bungled attempt to cope with difficult unresolved emotions. This view of evil as arising from psychological disorder is so remarkably modern that it is clear why Carl Jung regarded the Christian Gnostics as proto-psychologists.[6]

On a superficial reading of the Christian myth cycle, then, it looks as if the Demiurge is responsible for the evils of the cosmos we inhabit. The allegorical message seems to be that it is the ego (or the shadow-self it creates) which causes human beings to act badly. On the *psychic* level of understanding this is indeed the message. But on the *pneumatic* level the myth cycle encodes deeper and more confronting teachings, which undermine the idea of personal volition and, therefore, the concept of responsibility, altogether.

FREE WILL AND FATE

Ptolemy uses the figure of the Demiurge to give some important allegorical teachings about free will. When the Demiurge creates the cosmos he thinks he is acting from his own volition, but actually he is an unknowing instrument of a higher power. 'The Demiurge thought he was creating the cosmos himself, but in reality it was Achamoth through him.'[7]

Achamoth (psyche) acts through the Demiurge (ego). Yet Achamoth is not the source of her intentions and actions any more than her wayward son is the source of his. The creation of the cosmos is Christ's plan to redeem the seeds of Consciousness trapped in ignorance. It is Christ, representing the universal Consciousness of God, who is actually the source of the actions which issue through Achamoth and the Demiurge. Allegorically, this teaches that whilst the ego, like the Demiurge, imagines itself to be a godlike creator who freely wills its own thoughts and actions, it is universal Consciousness which is the ultimate source of every appearance within every psyche, including every action apparently performed by every individual ego. The ego is not the source of anything. It is part of the phenomena being witnessed by Consciousness.[8]

The ego is the idea of ourselves as an autonomous agent, acting separately from the whole. But if all is One, then everything is happening as One. What we think of as 'our' actions arise spontaneously from the Mystery. Because they pass through psyche as intentional thoughts, we say, 'I intended to do that.' But although 'our' actions may appear to be the result of 'our' free will, actually they issue from the will of God.[9]

On the Christian Way the *psychic* initiation is about progressively perfecting the *eidolon* – the self-image – by understanding the self as an integral part of the whole. The *pneumatic* initiation is about transcending the illusion of personal autonomy altogether and being Consciousness passively witnessing the unfolding Oneness, which includes all of 'our' thoughts and actions.[10] When we do this, it is not that we discover we are just programmed automata with no free will. It is that there is no 'us' to be free or otherwise. There is the Mystery witnessing the Oneness.

The Christian sage Monoimos teaches that God is the centre of the circle of self from which everything issues, and advises:

> 'Stop searching for God outside yourself. Look for him within. Examine who says, "My God, my consciousness, my understanding, my psyche, my body." Investigate the source of your experiences of sorrow and joy, love and hate, waking up though you don't will it, and sleeping though you don't will it, and falling in love though you don't will it. If you closely investigate these things you will find him in yourself. The unity in variety. Like a central point. Thus you will find in yourself a way out of yourself.'[11]

If we follow Monoimos' advice and look within, the idea of ourselves as autonomous agents becomes obviously absurd. If we simply pay attention to the coming and going of thoughts, it soon becomes apparent that they rise up from the darkness of the unconscious Mystery, regardless of our will. We cannot stop them. And it is meaningless to say we 'cause' our thoughts. We can only consider ourselves the cause if we have first thought, 'I will think so and so,' but this is infinitely regressive, as we are not the cause of that thought. And as our actions issue from our thoughts, if our thoughts are not our own, then our actions are not our own either.

The truth is we witness our thoughts and the actions which issue from them. Thoughts emanate from we know not where. The psyche is a virgin mother because it never sees what causes it to give birth to the thoughts and images which arise within it. Plotinus teaches:

> 'Just as the spoken word is an echo of the thought in the psyche, so thought in the psyche is itself an echo from elsewhere.'[12]

Philo teaches that we are 'egotistical and Godless' if as separate individuals we 'think ourselves equal to God by believing we are acting when in truth we are passively experiencing'. What we think and do is the fruition of what God has 'sowed and planted in the psyche' and it is 'impious for us to say we do the planting'.[13] Paul proclaims: 'The life I now live is not my life, but the life which Christ lives in me.'[14] In *The Gospel of John* Jesus teaches:

'I am not myself the source of the words I speak to you. It is the Father who dwells in me doing his own work.'[15]

The Christian sage Bardesanes teaches that the three theories about volition – that our lives are completely determined, that we are subjected to the rule of fate and that we are free – are all 'partly true and partly false'. As a physical body we are all governed equally by the laws of nature. As a psyche we are all governed differently by our justly deserved fate, which decrees our various experiences of life. As Consciousness we are each as free as we let ourselves be. Consciousness is utterly free and so are we, therefore, to the degree that we realize our true nature.[16] We are determined, fated *and* free, relative to the different levels of our identity. But ultimately all issues from the will of God. Bardesanes teaches:

'Nature has to do with the body. Fate with the psyche. Freedom with Consciousness. None is absolute. God alone is the absolute.'[17]

MISSING THE MARK

Although everything is happening as One, the fact that our actions occur via the ego is significant. For the original Christians, that creation happens via the Demiurge explains how an imperfect world can arise from a perfect source. In the same way, that actions happen via the ego explains how it is that God can seem to act imperfectly through us. When we act, the perfect goodness of our authentic nature becomes distorted by the ego, so that natural qualities manifest as selfish vices. Plotinus explains:

'The natural urge to live degenerates into ugly passions. Courage becomes ferocity or cowardice. The natural yearning for the Good becomes the pursuit of the semblance of beauty. Power at its lowest produces wickedness, for wickedness is a misguided desire to know Consciousness.'[18]

The Greek word *hamartia*, traditionally translated 'sin', is a term originally used in archery and means simply 'to miss the mark'.[19] For the original Christians, to sin is not to do evil, with all its absolute Catholic connotations, but to mess up, to fail to express our true nature and instead do something stupid. Our true nature is the Good. When the ego gets in the way, the Good's perfect idea becomes our 'sinful' action. What we do misses the intended mark.

For the original Christians, the imperfections of the cosmos are due to the foolish Demiurge, the cosmic ego. In the same way, our imperfections are due to our ego. Because of the Demiurge, the perfect archetypal cosmos manifests as the flawed cosmos of appearances evolving from imperfection to perfection. Because of the personal ego, God's perfect idea of a human being (the archetypal Man) manifests as *us* – flawed human beings on a journey of evolution to manifest our perfect essence.

So the Christian myth cycle teaches that from the absolute point of view no one is responsible for anything and from the relative point of view it is ignorance or error, in the form of egotism, which is the source of all our problems. The cause of the terrible things which human beings do is not some force of absolute evil which they willingly serve – a diabolical idea which Christian Literalists would have us believe. No. It is simply lack of Gnosis which causes human beings to act badly. 'Bad' people are aspects of the Oneness who are convinced they are the separate ego and so end up hurting themselves and others in a misguided attempt to serve their own selfish interests.

When we are aware of the Oneness, guilt and blame are irrelevant. When we know the Good, we no longer see evil and evil-doers, just ignorant people who are, as Plotinus puts it, 'like immature children' as yet unaware of the goodness of their essential nature and the unity of all things.[20] We are all One, so when some lost soul expresses their ignorance of the Oneness by acting badly towards others, it is like some demented fool hitting themselves with their own fist. When the apparent evil-doer is then vengefully vilified by other self-righteous lost souls, it is like the same fool roundly condemning their fist for its evil nature and punishing themselves with a blow from their other fist.

THE INEVITABILITY OF EVIL

If everything is happening by God's will, we cannot ultimately blame the Demiurge for the imperfections of creation. God and God alone must be responsible for all the evident evils of the world. Yet the Gnostics teach that the essence and origin of all is the Good. Dionysius writes: 'The most important of God's names is "the Good".'[21] In *The Gospel of Matthew*

Jesus, like Plato, proclaims: 'The One alone is Good.'[22] But how can this be true?

The secret teachings of the original Christians do not give an explanation for the individual evils which each one of us confronts in our own particular lives. From stubbing one's toe to the horrors of the Holocaust, suffering cannot simply be explained away by philosophy. But Gnosticism can and does account for the inevitability of evil, demonstrating its relative nature and its positive role in the greater goodness of things.

The Gnostic answer to the question 'Why is there evil?' is that without it there would be nothing at all. Evil is an unavoidable by-product of the process of origination itself. Consciousness is only possible with the duality of subject and object. Implicit in this primal duality is every other duality, including good and evil. The One is the Good. When it arises as the two, it inevitably becomes the good and the bad.

Actually it would be more accurate to say that the One is absolutely beyond description, but it appears to us, living in the duality of good and bad, as the Good. As Plotinus teaches, it is the 'Good, not for itself but for others'.[23] The undivided state is neither good nor bad. But from the divided state it appears as the Good.

The One realizes its nature as subjective Consciousness when it objectifies part of itself as psyche. In the same way, it realizes its nature as the Good when it manifests as the syzygy good and bad. The inevitability of evil is implicit in the first stirrings of Consciousness, when it separates itself from itself as objectified psyche. The Christian myth cycle narrates how this 'error' is amplified by Sophia in the *pleroma* and Achamoth in the *kenoma*. Finally, imperfection is made manifest as concrete reality by the Demiurge.

The root of all evil is duality, separation, objectification. The essence of all goodness is the urge to resolve duality into unity, which we experience as love. According to the creation myth taught by the Pythagoreans, in the beginning a cosmic egg, representing the Oneness of potentiality, split in two halves, representing the primal duality. What arose from the egg was Eros, or love.[24] When the One divides itself, the impulse that arises is to reunite, and that impulse towards unification is love.[25] Without evil (separation) there would be no love (reunion). Good and evil arise together. *The Gospel of Philip* teaches:

'Light and darkness, life and death, good and evil, are pairs of mutually dependent siblings who only exist in relationship with each other.'[26]

The *Letters of Clement* describe good and evil as the right and left hands of God.[27] A Mandean text teaches: 'Light and darkness are brothers, emanating from the one Mystery.'[28] The Ebionite school of Christianity portrays the Devil, the embodiment of evil, as the brother of Christ, the embodiment of the Good.[29] The Devil is the divider who entraps us in the illusion of separateness. Christ is the uniter who frees us to realize the essential Oneness.

The Devil is not an irredeemable embodiment of absolute evil, however, because there is no absolute evil. The only absolute is the Good. Evil exists relative to the absolute Good. Being is absolutely Good. Experience is relatively good and bad. For the One, everything is absolutely Good. For the parts, everything is relatively good or bad. Plotinus teaches: 'What is evil for an individual is a good thing in the universal system.'[30] And what appears to be relatively good for one part of the whole is relatively bad for another. As the philosopher Antiphon jokes darkly:

'Incontinence is bad for the incontinent but good for the doctors. Death is bad for the dying but good for the undertakers.'[31]

The original Christians symbolized the cosmos by a snake eating its own tail – which is good for the head and bad for the tail!

The *kenoma* appears to be both good and bad, yet it is essentially good because it is the journey towards the Good. What seems like evil has a positive role to play in the process of evolution. There is good and bad, but that is good. Bad experiences can be important turning-points on the journey of awakening. Often the spiritual quest is suffering driven. We are trying to get away from a situation we don't want. Suffering and joy are the 'stick and carrot' which goad and cajole us along the path of life. In *The Consolations of Philosophy*, Sophia teaches:

'All fortune, whether pleasant or unpleasant, is meant either to reward and encourage the good or punish and correct the bad.'[32]

Children see their parents as alternately good and bad, depending on whether they are being praised or censured by them. But in reality caring parents are always being good to their children, regardless of whether they temporarily appear to be harsh or soft. The original Christians portray the source of life as a Father-Mother because, in the same way, life is parenting us to spiritual maturity. And, as most of us know from personal experience, it is often life's reprimands that benefit us the most. Sophia explains:

> 'What I want to say is such a paradox that I am hardly able to put it into words. For bad fortune is often of more use to someone than good fortune. Good fortune always seems to bring happiness, but deceives you with her smiles, whereas bad fortune is always truthful because by changing she shows her true fickleness. Good fortune deceives, but bad fortune enlightens.'[33]

In the world of duality sooner or later everything must turn into its opposite. Day becomes night. Living things die. Good fortune turns to bad fortune. Good fortune deceives us into investing our happiness in necessarily transitory appearances, which must ultimately disappoint. What appears to be bad fortune, on the other hand, can inspire us to seek out a deeper source of joy by discovering the perpetual bliss of our permanent essence. What appears bad to us is actually tough love. The apparent evils of life are the Good in disguise.

SUMMARY

- ❖ The Christian myth cycle is an initiation allegory in which Christ represents Consciousness, Achamoth represents psyche and the foolish, arrogant Demiurge represents the ego.

- ❖ In the cosmos, 'evil' manifests through the Demiurge, who creates the Devil from the Mother's grief and confusion. In the individual psyche, 'evil' manifests through the ego, which creates the shadow, or negative self, from unresolved negative emotions.

- ❖ The Demiurge believes himself to be creating the cosmos of his own free will, but it is actually Achamoth working through him and Christ acting through her. In the same way the ego mistakenly believes itself to be an autonomous agent, but actually everything is happening as the unfolding Oneness, expressing the will of God.

- ❖ An imperfect world arises from the perfect source because creation happens via the Demiurge. In the same way, when we act, the perfect goodness of our authentic nature becomes distorted by the ego, so that natural qualities manifest as selfish vices, making us 'sin' or 'miss the mark'.

❖ God is the Good. Evil is inherent in the process of origination, however, because when the One arises as the two, it inevitably manifests as the syzygy good and bad. The root of all evil is duality/separation. Goodness is the urge to resolve duality into unity, which we experience as love.

❖ Apparent evil has an ultimately positive role in the evolution of the cosmos of appearances.

The purpose of all the extraordinary teachings encoded by the original Christians in their mythology is to guide initiates to the realization of Gnosis. Having explored the hidden allegorical meaning of the myth of Sophia, the myth of Jesus and the overall Christian myth cycle, let's finally attempt to articulate, in so far as language allows us, the essence of Gnosis.

chapter eleven

THE MYSTICAL
Marriage

'Through Gnosis we are purified of diversity and experience the vision of unity. Those who have realizsed Gnosis know the source and the destination. They have set themselves free by waking up from the stupor in which they lived, and become themselves again.'

Valentinus, *The Gospel of Truth*[1]

What is Gnosis? This is a hard question to answer, because to realize Gnosis is to embrace paradox.[2] Our logical mind may find this impossible, but life itself has no problem in being paradoxical regardless. Life is the ineffable made manifest, the One appearing to be many, the permanent present perpetually changing. 'Here the impossible union of spheres of existence is actual,' as T. S. Eliot writes.[3]

Life is paradoxical by its very nature, and so are we. As a body we are in the cosmos, but as Consciousness the cosmos is in us. Gnosis is looking in 'two directions at once', as Plotinus explains, and simultaneously being aware of our essential identity as the Mystery and our appearance as a person. It is a mystical marriage in which the two aspects of our syzygistic nature commune as one, for as Jesus teaches in *The Gospel of Thomas*:

'When you see the two as one, so that the male and the female are united, then you will enter the kingdom.'[4]

Our present problem is that we are 'intent upon the fragment and severed from the Whole', as Plotinus puts it.[5] We are aware of being a person, but not of being the Mystery. The purpose of the Christian Way is to bring us to an awareness of the One, the Good, God, Mystery – however we choose to describe the indescribable. The *psychic* initiation teaches us how to live as a human being with compassion for all beings, because we are all parts of the One. The *pneumatic* initiation teaches us to transcend the separate self and become aware that essentially we *are* the One. Let's examine in more detail these two initiations and how they combine to lead us to the realization of Gnosis.

THE PSYCHIC INITIATION

The *psychic* initiation takes us on a journey from being a selfish individual to becoming a conscious expression of the Oneness of God who naturally expresses love for all. It teaches us to live well in the world by manifesting our essential nature, which is the Good. We presently appear to be partly 'bad' because we mistakenly identify with the *eidolon*, the separate self. In so doing we set ourselves apart from the Whole and become a self-serving somebody competing to achieve what is good for us, not co-operating to fulfil what is good for all. As Plato writes, 'Attachment to self is the constant source of misdeeds in every one of us.'[6] Plotinus explains, 'Evil has its source in self-will.'[7]

For Christian Literalists we are born in sin and need reforming by being made to follow a strict code of shoulds and should nots as laid down by the religious authorities and apparently approved by God himself.[8] Should we fail to live up to God's expectations, we could well find ourselves spending the whole of eternity suffering horrendous punishments. The approach of the Christian Gnostics is the complete opposite of this. Ptolemy explains our essential nature can't possibly be damned, no matter what we do:

'Consciousness cannot be corrupted, regardless of the behaviour it has to pass its time in the company of. A piece of gold does not lose its beauty when it is put into filth, but keeps its own nature, since the filth can't harm the gold. What leads one to the *pleroma* is not behaviour but the seed that was sent here as an infant and grows to maturity in this place.'[9]

We don't get into the *pleroma* – the Kingdom of Heaven – as a reward for obeying the rules, but by recognizing that this is already the eternal home of our essential Self. We are 'spiritual not by behaviour but by nature, and will be preserved no matter what'.[10] We are saved not because of how we act, but by being what we are.

For Gnostics, therefore, becoming good is not about obeying some written moral code, but about purifying ourselves of the egotism which obscures our natural goodness. To do this we must become conscious of our covert selfish motivations, which are rooted in our identification with the ego. *The Gospel of Philip* explains:

> 'As long as the root of evil is hidden, it is strong. But if it becomes known, it dissolves. If we ignore it, it takes root in us and brings forth its fruit in the heart. It takes us captive so that we do the things we don't want to do and don't do the things we want to do. It exerts this power because we have not recognized it.'[11]

For Gnostics, it is not what we do but *why* we do it that counts. Certain actions are not intrinsically good and others intrinsically bad. It is the motivation which makes an action good or bad.[12] According to Irenaeus, the Gnostics teach: 'Actions are not good or bad in themselves, but only in accordance with human conventions.'[13] Paul writes: 'As a Christian, I am absolutely convinced that nothing is impure in itself.'[14] This challenges us not to blindly go along with how everyone else thinks we should live, but to find the Good within and decide for ourselves what is right and what is wrong. We must 'test everything and retain the good', as Paul says.[15]

Traditional ethical laws and religious customs may be helpful guidelines for beginners on the path, but as we spiritually mature they become increasingly irrelevant. The more we awaken, the more we naturally exhibit our essential goodness, and the need to follow any sort of ethical code is completely superseded. According to Clement of Alexandria:

> 'Outward observances cease to have any value for those whose whole being is brought into an abiding harmony with that which is eternal. They rest in the contemplation of God, which is and will be their unfailing blessedness.'[16]

As our realization of Gnosis deepens we 'no longer abstain from evil because of fear of punishment or do good from hope of promised reward', but naturally express the Good, living spontaneously 'out of love', for someone aware of the Oneness cannot help but express unqualified love for all beings.[17]

Paul writes, 'Love is the *pleroma* of the law,'[18] meaning love is the perfect archetype of which moral codes are inadequate images. He explains that when we have 'identified with Christ' – the universal Consciousness which is our essence – we are 'discharged from the law, to serve God in a new way, the way of spirit, in contrast to the old way, of the written code'.[19]

The purpose of the *psychic* initiation is to help us transcend ethical *ideas* about how to be good and discover the essential loving goodness which we *are*, so that we can live spontaneously from the heart. Clement boldly proclaims:

> 'All the actions of those possessed of Gnosis are right actions, and the actions of those not possessed of Gnosis are wrong actions, even though they conform with a code.'[20]

Whilst we still identify with the ego, all our actions are ultimately selfish, whatever the outward appearance of righteousness. When we stop identifying with the ego, our actions are God's actions, undistorted by the illusion of separateness. We find ourselves unerringly expressing the 'will of God', which, as Basilides teaches, is simply 'to desire nothing, to hate nothing and to love all'.[21]

Irenaeus is outraged that Christian Gnostics proclaim that the realization of Gnosis sets them free to act spontaneously, regardless of moral conventions. He writes indignantly:

> 'They maintain that they have attained to such heights that they are, therefore, free in every respect to act as they please, and have no fear of doing anything.'[22]

But the spiritually awake are impervious to the condemnation of religious moralists such as Irenaeus. As Paul explains, because they are 'no longer under the control of their lower nature, but directed by Consciousness',[23] they 'can judge the worth of everything, but can't be judged by others'.[24] They are indeed, as Irenaeus says, free and without fear.

THE PNEUMATIC INITIATION

Whilst the *psychic* initiation teaches us how to live as an apparent part of the One, the *pneumatic* initiation reveals to us that essentially we *are* the One. This is done through transformative philosophy. But in the same way that Gnostic ethics is about love, not laws, Gnostic philosophy is about revelation, not theories. Gnostic philosophers use ideas to propel us beyond ideas to their source in the Mystery. They use words to 'wake people from their thinking to the vision', as Plotinus puts it.[25]

Pythagoras defines the goal of philosophy as 'knowledge of being'.[26] Clement teaches that the objective of philosophical contemplation is 'knowledge of being itself'.[27] Plotinus explains: 'The highest concern of philosophy is being.'[28] Philosophy helps us cultivate an awareness of something so obvious we usually ignore it and yet so wonderful it is infinitely mysterious: that we exist. It teaches us to be conscious that we are conscious and so not missing out on the greatest miracle of all – that we are a witness to the whole incredible show.

Philosophy undermines the conceptual mindset that we have unconsciously inherited from our culture and mistaken for reality.[29] It reasons us back to basics, taking us from the complexity of the world to simple underlying principles.[30] Eventually we arrive at the idea of the primal syzygy – the Mystery manifesting as Consciousness and psyche. As Paul teaches, this understanding acts like 'a two-edged sword' which 'cuts so deeply it divides Consciousness from psyche'.[31] It enables us to distinguish ourselves as the experiencer from what we are experiencing and so 'disengage' from the psyche-body, entering a state the ancients called *theoria*, meaning 'contemplation', or *hesychia*, meaning 'stillness', in which we identify with the ineffable witness of our unfolding psychophysical experiences.[32]

To deepen this awareness of being Consciousness we must ignore all our thoughts, feelings and sensations and focus on the empty presence within which they rise and fall, entering what Dionysius calls the 'mysterious darkness of unknowing' in which we 'transcend consciousness by knowing nothing'.[33] In this state Consciousness turns back on itself to commune with the dazzling darkness – the mysterious Oneness from which the primal duality of Consciousness and psyche arises. Plotinus explains that 'the transcending of Consciousness in the individual is identical with the first moment of creation'.[34] He teaches:

'The vision is not something that must be entered into but something present before all else, before Consciousness made any movements at all.[35]

The Christian text *Allogenes* gives us a mythical account of the process of *pneumatic* initiation through which we commune with the 'Unknowable One'. Allogenes, whose name means 'foreigner', is a stranger in the world on a return journey to his true home. The Goddess guides him in making an 'ascent', which is 'inwards', until he reaches 'stillness at the level of being' – the state of contemplation in which he can become aware of the dazzling darkness of the Mystery.[36]

The Goddess teaches Allogenes that there is nothing he can *do* to bring about 'a primal revelation of the Unknowable One', since what obscures the realization of the Oneness is the idea of himself as an autonomous agent separate from the One. He must, therefore, completely disidentify with the active personal ego and be passive, impersonal, witnessing Consciousness. She explains:

'To receive a primal revelation of the Unknowable One, withdraw to the rear of activity. Become perfectly still in that place. Any desire to be an active agent will cause you to fall from the inactivity of the Unknowable One.'[37]

The Goddess warns Allogenes that even thinking he has come to know the One will obscure the Mystery of Consciousness with an idea:[38]

'Do not know the Unknowable One, for that is impossible. If by means of an enlightened thought you seem to know him – be ignorant of him!'[39]

The Goddess is encouraging Allogenes to enter a state of deep meditative contemplation by withdrawing his awareness from the circumference of the circle of self towards the centre of Consciousness. In so doing he is, in effect, approaching the state of deep sleep whilst remaining conscious. This can be a helpful practice because it acquaints us with the unfamiliar silent depths of our being, but we cannot remain indefinitely in such a state of retreat. The other side of our syzygistic nature will call us back to body awareness. As we spiritually mature, however, we become simultaneously conscious of our everyday experience and of communing with the Unknowable One. Plotinus teaches:

'Does Consciousness see in part now one vision and now the other? No. In reality, Consciousness has the power of thought eternally, and also the power of suspending thought and looking to the One in another way.'[40]

When we 'look in both ways at once' we know who we are. We are the Whole become conscious of itself through a part. We are the One seeming to be some-one. We are universal Being appearing to be a human being. We are the Mystery of God dreaming it's a person. We are the One-in-many-forms on a journey from the dazzling darkness of unconscious unity, through the separate ego's experience of conscious variety to the enlightened sage's conscious awareness of unity in variety.

THE LOVE AFFAIR OF LIFE

Gnosis is becoming aware of our divinity, but not by rejecting our humanity. It is true that the Gnostic masters portray human incarnation in a negative light as a form of imprisonment from which we need to escape, but that is only half the story. They also portray it in a positive light as an opportunity to spiritually awaken that we should embrace.[41] If we understand the paradox at the heart of the Gnosis we can see that these apparently contradictory teachings are actually complementary, because both are true. To know the One we must escape from identification with the separate self, yet this process of spiritual awakening can only happen to an individual.

Gnosis is not retreating from life, it is valuing human incarnation as a precious opportunity to commune with the Oneness through the multiplicity, to discover the Good through the good and bad, to find Love through separation. Gnosis is not being the One *instead* of a separate individual, but *as well*. It is living as God and man, after the mythical example of Jesus.

Far from rejecting the world as a worthless illusion, Gnosis is participating fully in the process of redeeming the *kenoma* by transforming it into the perfect image of the *pleromic* archetypes, for, as the Christian Gnostic Marsanes teaches, 'In every respect the sense-perceptible cosmos is worthy of being saved in its entirety.'[42] Gnosis is playing a part in creating Heaven on Earth by collectively dreaming a perfect dream of unity and love, instead of the present nightmare of division and strife.

Christian mythology sees this ideal as being realized at the end of time, when all the seeds of Consciousness realize their true identity and the whole of the *kenoma* is united in Gnosis. This state of *Absolute* Gnosis is, then, something we can only realize together. We are all One and we can only realize that Oneness as One. This means that until we all realize Gnosis, no one can. Unless all beings are freed from ignorance and suffering, none can be fully free of ignorance and suffering. Individually, our realization of Gnosis is a relative experience of the Absolute Mystery. It is not a state of having awakened, but a process of continually awakening to deeper levels of Self-discovery. We can never reach the Good, so things can always get better.[43]

As individuals in time, Gnosis is a temporary recognition of our eternal nature. The ground of all experience is constant, but our experience of it fluctuates. Gnosis is always something we are growing towards or falling away from. Whilst we are (relatively) aware that all is One, everything happens perfectly of itself. Without the interference of the distorting ego we don't 'miss the mark'. We are borne along by the natural flow of life. When we look in the mirror of psyche, all we see is God. The world is permeated with intelligence and abundant with love. But sooner or later our self-orientation pulls us back into identification with the *eidolon*. We persevere with the *psychic* process of personal transformation to prevent this come down occurring so often, and so deepen the *pneumatic* awareness of Oneness. The Christian Way is to progressively perfect so that we can increasingly transcend.

Pythagoreans call the levels of initiation 'the active life' and 'the contemplative life.'[44] The Christian Way is being 'at once an active and contemplative image of God', as Theodotus puts it.[45] It is living both the active life of perfecting the evolving *eidolon* and the contemplative life of being the eternal essence, as complementary aspects of an ongoing process of spiritual awakening. It is not about passing through the *psychic* and *pneumatic* levels to the realization of Gnosis, because Gnosis is not about arriving anywhere. It is an ongoing process of transformation and transcendence, becoming and being, actively perfecting and passively appreciating.

The original Christians symbolized the realization of Gnosis by the mystical marriage of Jesus and the Goddess because Gnosis is living life as a love affair of complementary opposites. It is marrying together the *psychic* path of transformation with the *pneumatic* path of transcendence. It is celebrating each moment as a new beginning on a never-ending journey of self-perfection, and as a perfect end in itself. It is embracing the paradox that we are all Christ and each one of us is a separate lost soul. It is understanding that we are the Whole become conscious through a part, so that the Absolute may be relatively aware of itself. It is being universal Mind peering through the pinhole of a particular personality onto the cosmos we have collectively created.

The Authoritative Teaching, a Christian text, states that 'the worst vices' are 'ignorance and indifference'.[46] Ignorance is living without an awareness of the Oneness. Indifference is retreating from life. Gnosis is the opposite of ignorance and indifference. It is communion and compassion. Communion is knowing the essential Oneness of the Mystery. Compassion is loving the many appearances of the Mystery. The mystical marriage is living in communion and with compassion. Gnosis is being the One loving all.

In the Cosmos But Not of It

The *psychic* and *pneumatic* initiations combine to teach us how to be 'in the cosmos but not of it'. To help us understand what this means the ancients likened life to a play.[47] A modern version of this analogy would be watching a film. Our present problem is that we completely identify with the hero of the movie. That's great in the enjoyable bits, but when things get exciting we are really terrified. We actually believe we are going to get horribly done in by the bad guys. The *pneumatic* initiation leads to the reassuring revelation that we are not actually in the film at all. Yet to simply be a disinterested witness of life is as crazy and unsatisfying as sitting in a cinema constantly reminding oneself that the film is fantasy. That defeats the whole point of the film. In the same way, withdrawal into detachment defeats the whole point of life.

There is a third possibility, however, which is a marriage of the two understandings. We abandon ourselves to the drama of the film, yet retain an implicit awareness that it is only a movie. This is, of course, exactly what we do when we go to the cinema, and it enables us to enjoy the film, even the scary bits. Small children often can't watch frightening films, because they believe them to be real. In the same way the spiritually immature are so completely swept up with the drama of life that they are full of fear. But the realization of Gnosis enables us to be 'in the film but not of it', and so appreciate it unreservedly.

Free from fear, we are able to enjoy the extraordinary show we have laid on for ourselves without souring our pleasure with constant anxiety. We can take the risks that living demands, because we know that whilst our *eidolon* struts its stuff on the stage of the world, winning and losing, suffering and celebrating, laughing and crying, we are the witness who watches.

There is one important respect in which the cinema analogy breaks down, however. To sit in a cinema is, in itself, not particularly pleasurable, but to commune with Consciousness is to bathe in the bliss of our being. To experience the rich variety of experiences offered by life is a wonder, but to be conscious of the Mystery of God is to have found the source of all joy. Plotinus explains:

> 'Consciousness has two powers. First to know its own contents.
> Second to know that which transcends it. The first way of seeing
> belongs to Consciousness when it is sane. But the second is
> Consciousness in love, transported and drunk with nectar. Satisfied
> and fulfilled, it dissolves in contentment. Better to be drunk than too
> solemn for such delights.'[48]

Love

It is easy with a book such as this one, full of old myths and philosophical concepts, to get a picture of Gnosis as a heady, abstract theory about of life. But the spiritually awake are heady with intoxication, not conceptualization. They are drunk with love, not sober with intellectual understanding. The purpose of philosophy is to open us to the possibility of ecstasy. The followers of the Christian sage Montanus were said to possess an 'infinite number of books', but called ecstasy the only true Christianity.[49]

Previously we saw that the Gnostics imagined the motivation behind the Mystery coming into manifestation to be the desire for self-knowledge. This can sound somewhat dry, but it is only one way of picturing something which is completely beyond understanding. Valentinus imagines the motivation behind manifestation to be love:

> 'Since the Father was creative, it seemed good to him to create and
> produce what was most beautiful and most perfect in himself. For he
> was all love and love is not love if there is nothing to be loved.'[50]

The nature of the Mystery is love, but this remains only a latent potential unless there is something to love. So the Mystery objectifies itself to give itself something beautiful to love and in so doing becomes love.

We are the Mystery wanting to love and be loved. Everyone is searching for love, whether they know it or not. There is nothing better than love. It feels good because it is the Good. Love is what happens when we connect deeply with another sentient being because love is the way we experience the mysterious paradox of being the One appearing to be many. Love is the Mystery aware of the Mystery, so when we plumb the depths of our being we fall in love with ourselves. Plotinus enthuses:

> 'Beauty evokes wonderment, delicious longing and trembling with delight, so when you see that you yourself are beautiful within, what do you feel? What is the Dionysiac exultation that thrills through your being? The surging upwards of your psyche? These are the emotions of someone enchanted by the spell of love.'[51]

Gnosis is not a theory, it is 'that love passion of vision known only to a lover come to rest in that he loves' as Plotinus puts it.[52] It is being content in the state of simple happiness that is naturally ours when we are free from ignorant fear and selfish craving. It is discovering we are more than we ever imagined or ever could imagine. It is a reality shift. It is the world turned inside-out.

Faith

Ironically, Gnosis is knowing we don't know. As we progressively free ourselves from the conceptual matrix we have mistaken for reality, we become certain about less and less until we find ourselves living in the Mystery. It is an extraordinary twist that the great Gnostic injunction 'Know your Self' most famously finds its fulfilment in Socrates, whom the Oracle of Delphi declares the wisest man alive, because 'He knows that he knows nothing.'[53]

Gnosis is knowing nothing and loving everything. Paul teaches:

> 'Make no mistake about it, if there is anyone among you who fancies himself wise, he must become a fool again to gain true wisdom.[54] If anyone thinks he knows, he knows nothing yet in the true sense of *knowing*.'[55]

If we want to experience what Paul calls 'the peace of God which surpasses all understanding' and what Plotinus calls 'the Presence beyond all understanding', then we must be willing to go beyond understanding.[56]

We create conceptual models of reality because we are scared of life and want to know what is going on so that we can protect ourselves. But Gnosis is understanding that we are utterly safe, because essentially we exist outside the human predicament altogether. When we are aware of this, we can let go of our conceptual reality and live in the Mystery, allowing life to continually surprise us with its infinite innovations.

We start out on the spiritual quest because we don't know who we are and what life is. Having filled our heads with all sorts of fancy ideas, as the realization of Gnosis deepens it dawns on us that we knew the answer in the first place. We began searching for meaning because life didn't make sense and we were right. Life doesn't make sense. It's an absolute Mystery.

Yet as we progress on our journey something changes. We begin our search because we are terrified by the fact that we don't know what is going on. Through the process of awakening we discover something wonderful – the source from which life originates and towards which it is evolving is more perfect, more beautiful, more loving, than words can possibly communicate. Life is essentially Good.

This can sound like glib positivity, but it is not. Gnosticism is not about avoiding the fact of suffering and retreating into wishful thinking. It is expressing our natural compassion by doing all we can to ameliorate the terrible suffering we encounter, yet at the same time knowing that, despite appearances, all is well. It is understanding that everything arises from and is returning to the Good. It is trusting that ultimately, therefore, good will come from bad, and choosing to play an active part in that process.

We can't understand the Mystery of Life, but we can come to trust it, and this transforms everything. Ironically, Gnosis turns out to be synonymous with faith. But by 'faith' Gnostics don't mean blind belief in historical events, as Literalists do, they mean complete confidence in the life process. For Philo faith is 'the queen of the virtues'.[57] Basilides eulogizes: 'Faith is the best quality.'[58] Simon Magus teaches: 'Gnosis and faith give the soul which chooses them permanent peace.'[59] The mystical marriage is living with Gnosis of the eternal Mystery and unshakeable faith in the fundamental goodness of the unfolding drama of the temporal world.

We start the spiritual quest because we experience life as a terrifying mystery which we want to understand. This is Hell. We end by trusting in the goodness of life, which we know is a Mystery beyond comprehension. This is Heaven.

The *Treatise on the Resurrection* boldly asserts: 'Nothing within the account of the Truth is truly difficult.'[60] Considering the complicated mythology and sophisticated philosophy we have been exploring, we could be forgiven for finding this statement ironically amusing. Yet, despite the apparent complexities, the essence of the Christian gospel of Gnosis could not be more simple. It is so simple and so obvious, in fact, that it can take years of philosophical exploration before we finally understand that the 'good news' it brings us is all we really need to know: *Everything is OK.*

SUMMARY

❖ Gnosis is simultaneously being aware of the two poles of our syzygistic nature. Our present problem is that we are aware of appearing to be a person, but not of essentially being the Mystery. The purpose of the Christian Way is to bring us to an awareness of the Mystery.

❖ Gnostic ethics, taught in the *psychic* stage of initiation, do not limit our actions with a set of moral injunctions, but encourage us to uncover our essential goodness, so that we are free to act spontaneously from our authentic nature.

❖ Gnostic philosophy, taught in the *pneumatic* stage of initiation, does not limit our understanding with a set of doctrines, but teaches us to transcend thought altogether and be Consciousness, which is the ground and source of all experience.

❖ Gnosis is neither being lost in appearances nor renouncing them. It is being 'in the cosmos but not of it'. It is not about retreating from the world, but participating in the process of collectively creating Heaven on Earth.

❖ The *psychic* initiation teaches us to reach out to others with compassion and the *pneumatic* initiation teaches us to reach inside and commune with our shared essence. The mystical marriage is living with compassion and in communion. Gnosis is being the One loving all.

❖ We can't understand the Mystery of Life, but we can come to trust it, and this transforms everything. Ironically, Gnosis turns out to be synonymous with faith.

From our exploration of the secret teachings of the original Christians it is clear that Christianity was not always the safe, pre-packaged, off-the-shelf religion it has become. The Christian Way was once travelled by philosophical adventurers who proclaimed life to be an opportunity for self-discovery, for spiritual creativity, for living our own myths. Christianity may have ended up a power-crazed Literalist religion spreading guilt and fear, but it began as a movement of mystical enthusiasts with a beautiful vision of the meaning and mystery of life. Does it serve any purpose to resurrect their vision?

The original Christians taught that although we have our eternal being outside the dramas of history, we are also a temporary part of the evolving cosmos. Can rearticulating their secret teachings, after all this time, play some positive role in this evolution? This book has involved us in studying the distant past and intuiting the eternal now which lies beyond time altogether. Let's finally turn our attention to the future that we are presently creating, and explore the current state of play in the ongoing struggle to unite Heaven and Earth.

chapter twelve

THE NEW IMPROVED
Testament

'The most beautiful thing we can experience is the mysterious. It is the source
of all true art and all science. He to whom this emotion is a stranger, who can
no longer pause to wonder and stand rapt in awe, is as good as dead: his eyes
are closed.'

Albert Einstein[1]

Religion is the Devil's greatest achievement. In the guise of religion he has
pulled off his most audacious coup. He has flagrantly masqueraded as God.
He has had us bow down and worship him. He has had us commit every
type of evil in the name of holiness. He has passed off his bigotry as God's
opinions. He has had us segregate humanity into the 'ins' and the 'outs',
believers and non-believers, the saved and the damned. He has convinced
us that God likes us but not them. And convinced them that God likes
them but not us. And then, in a stroke of dark brilliance, he warns his
faithful flock of sheep: 'Be sure you do not pay heed to anyone but me, for
the Devil is a wily wolf and he will surely trick you.'

The original Christians exposed the Devil-in-disguise when, as part
of their general critique of moribund Jewish Literalism, they portrayed

Jehovah as the arrogant Demiurge. Not that the Devil was overly perturbed. He just did what he always does – he put into effect a takeover operation of the new spiritual tradition these radicals had founded, turning Christianity into the most authoritarian and barbaric religion of all time.

How does the Devil do it? It's a confidence trick. In a world seething with insecurity he offers certainty. He convinces his disciples that they (and they alone) know how it is. Blinded by opinion, they no longer see the reality of the Mystery. They commit the only true blasphemy by conflating the relative with the Absolute. Inflated with feelings of specialness, they willingly enlist into the Devil's *élite* corps of martyrs and murderers, ready to die and kill for concepts and catchphrases. All for a promised pay day cunningly put off until the afterlife.

Certainty divides us. Doubt unites us. We all have different ways of seeing life, which is not surprising since we each have a unique experience of it. We agree and disagree, and that makes life interesting. But there is one thing that, if we are completely honest, we can all agree about – we can't find concepts big enough to express the enormity of life. It is beyond understanding. It is bigger than we can think.

Let's put this in perspective. If we live to be 80 years old that gives us 4,000 weeks to work life out. And we live in an infinite universe. And every inch is an enigma. As the Pagan philosopher Metrodorus says so eloquently, 'In reality none of us know anything. Not even whether we know anything or not.'[2] That is, apart from the Devil's people. They know for sure. Theodotus writes:

> 'Those that are most asleep think they are most awake, being under the power of very vivid and fixed dream visions, so that those who are most ignorant think they know most.'[3]

When we talk of the 'Devil' we are, of course, not expecting to be taken literally. We are talking about a mythical character. But sometimes mythic language is the most powerful with which to make a point. Christ is the uniter and the Devil is his evil brother the divider. It is easy to spot when the divider is at work, because people see themselves as separate from each other and end up suffering needlessly. Selfishness and hypocrisy thrive. Conflicts erupt about irrelevant nonsense. The Good becomes conflated with what is good for 'us'. Blame is projected onto 'them'.

It is just as easy to see when the Christ is at work. Wherever the unifier goes he leaves a legacy of love and understanding. People help each other spontaneously because it is their nature to be good. Selfless compassion works its miracles. Cries for vengeance turn to humble forgiveness. The cycle of suffering created by the 'an eye for an eye' mentality is broken. People recognize that we are all One.

We hope this book may contribute in some way to fulfilling Paul's vision of God's 'secret plan' – that we all be made one with Christ through love.[4] Our criticisms of Literalist religion, like those of Gnostics before us, are not intended to instigate yet more conflict, but to clarify what is standing in the way of unity. Divisions cannot be overcome with wishy-washy wishful thinking. We must become conscious of their causes. If spirituality is to advance beyond the stage of conflicting regional religions, we must be willing to face the truth. History shows us that Literalist religion, like nationalism, unites people only by dividing them from others. It may claim to represent the uniter, but actually it is the work of the divider.

We have attempted to elucidate the secret teachings of the original Christians because we feel that something valuable was lost when the Devil annexed Christianity. Something which, despite constant persecution, has refused to die. Something which is resurfacing in our culture right now. Something which may be the future.

Yes. This is a book with an agenda. We have not written a dispassionate survey of a quirky period in the history of ideas. That would be an absurd thing to do. Why, faced with the awesome mystery of existence and the inevitability of death, would we choose to waste years of our short lives investigating something unless we felt it to be important and that it might *help*? No. This book is not an academic exercise. It is written with a purpose. And that purpose is to change history.

In the future the past will be different. That much is for sure. Our picture of the past constantly changes along with our picture of the present. The stories we tell about where we have come from matter, because they inform our choices about where we want to go. Our reappraisal of the history and meaning of Christianity, the most influential religion in the history of the world, leaves us with a different past and the possibility of a better future.

We feel that we potentially stand at the threshold of a positive new era in the unfolding evolution of consciousness. But the original Christians undoubtedly felt that too – and they could not have been more wrong. To make sure humanity doesn't make the same mistakes again, we must understand what really happened some 2,000 years ago. It's no good dismissing the absolutist claims of the Roman Church that kept us in the Dark Ages for so many centuries if we continue to believe their propaganda, which they have passed off as history. As long as we do that, the spectre of a return to spiritual fascism will always haunt us.

We are not saying we have the *truth* about Christianity. History is always bogus. There can be no absolute and definitive description of the present, let alone the past. Each moment is too rich. The past, like the present, is an absolute that we can only express relatively. But just because any idea can at best be relatively true does not mean that we have to end up with a mush in which every idea is as good as any other. Some ideas are clearly better than others. Ideas can never embody the Absolute Truth, but they can get relatively nearer or further from it.

We feel that our account of the origins and meaning of Christianity takes us nearer to the truth. In our previous book, *The Jesus Mysteries*, we presented overwhelming evidence that the Jesus story was a myth based on Pagan allegories of a dying and resurrecting Godman. In this book we have shown that the original Christians also adapted the Pagan myth of the lost Goddess, which was the partner myth to the Godman story. We have attempted to bring out the allegorical meaning of the whole Christian myth cycle and show its origins in the ancient Gnostic tradition. All of this evidence taken together, we feel, conclusively endorses what we have called 'the Jesus Mysteries Thesis' – that Christianity was originally a Jewish adaptation of the Pagan Mysteries.

By interpreting the Jesus myth as a factual biography Literalist Christianity has created a religion based on history rather than mystery. The great mythologist Joseph Campbell writes:

'Wherever the poetry of myth is interpreted as biography, history, or science, it is killed. The living images become only remote facts of a distant time or sky. Furthermore it is never difficult to demonstrate that as science and history mythology is absurd. When a civilization begins to interpret its mythology in this way, the life goes out of it, temples become museums, and the link between the two perspectives dissolves. Such a blight has certainly descended on the Bible and on a great part of the Christian cult.'[5]

Ironically, rediscovering its Gnostic roots is probably the only hope that Christianity has of long-term survival. But that is not going to happen. Religions come and go, and Christianity looks more and more like a religion whose time has gone. It will merely be a matter of how long and how unpleasant its death throes turn out to be.

But our agenda is not to rescue Christianity by resurrecting Christian Gnosticism. For all its essential profundity, Christian Gnosticism is of another time and an alien culture. After all, few today would choose to represent the concept of transcending identification with the body with the grotesque image of a man being tortured to death. We don't think in these ways anymore. The lives we lead are less routinely brutal, thank God. The dying and resurrecting Godman myth is a great story, but it's yesterday's story.

For the same reason, we also are not suggesting rectifying centuries of patriarchal chauvinism with a return to Goddess worship. Myths are hard to throw off, as Christianity demonstrates, but even harder to success-fully revivify when the life has gone out of them.[6] No. The future will not be a return to archaic myths. The Goddess need not be rescued from captivity as a museum exhibit. The dying and resurrecting Godman can finally be allowed to rest in peace.

We are not promoting the regressive romanticism of getting back to the 'lost ancient wisdom' of the original Christians. But we are suggest-ing we do what they did. They reinvigorated the perennial philosophy of Gnosticism, by successfully reworking it into a form that was accessible to their own day and age. Now is the time for us to do likewise.

Occasionally in the history of the West there have been short periods in which the conditions were right for the Gnosis to be rediscovered, re-interpreted and popularized, with massively positive effects on human culture. The heyday of Classical Athens was such a period. It lasted for a mere 30 years, but it shaped the ancient world. The Florentine Renaissance was another such period. It also lasted for only a few decades, but it sowed the seeds of much of what is best in contemporary society. We are living in such a period of possibility today. The suffocating grip of organized religion is loosening, leaving us disorientated and hungry for meaning. New forms of spirituality are springing up everywhere. Many visionaries have realized the precious opportunity we have to transform our collective understanding of what it is to be alive.

There has never been more fertile ground for the Gnosis to take root. But such conditions do not last long. Classical Athens and the Renaissance were both brutally suppressed by an unforeseen reactionary backlash. This could happen again. When the old certainties crumble, some move on but others cling on – and with fanatical tenacity. Whilst Literalist religion generally is in decline, Fundamentalism, its extreme right wing, is more belligerently vocal than ever, particularly within Christianity and its old adversary Islam. These people are in need of a lot of love and reassurance that life is safe. But in the meantime they are extremely dangerous, make no mistake about it.

Feeling threatened and vulnerable, both Christian and Islamic Fundamentalists are growing edgy and excitable, and could do with a divinely-sanctioned scrap to relieve the tension. There is nothing like holy conflict to galvanize support for religion – and Fundamentalists know it. The great irony is that, if they could but see it, Christian and Islamic Fundamentalists are the same people. Their vision of life and how to live it is driven by the same needs and neuroses. What they hate in the other is a projection of what they hate in themselves. If fate had birthed them in the other culture they would be Fundamentalists of the other persuasion.

The other great irony is that they have both completely misunderstood their spiritual traditions. Like Christianity, Islam was also originally a radical movement of Gnostic free-thinkers (*see* Appendix II: 'Gnostic Islam'). In their degenerate state, as dogmatic religions, Christianity and Islam are irreconcilable enemies, fighting over whose cult is God's favourite. But they once taught the same perennial Gnostic philosophy. They weren't always subsidiaries of Beelzebub, Inc.

OBJECTIVE SCIENCE
AND SUBJECTIVE GNOSIS

If Christianity and Islam could rediscover their common Gnostic roots the world would enter a new era of spiritual tolerance and eclecticism. But this is not going to happen. Fundamentalism is growing. And this is in large part because there is a new cult in town, which has become so popular it is threatening the old established cults, and they are worried. They tried hard to kill it at birth, but it was unstoppable. They cannot begin to compete with its magic. Its devotees promise no end to the power it will eventually bestow upon humanity. This modern sorcery which has bewitched the world is Science.

The visionaries who inspired the birth of modern Science were violently persecuted by the Literalist Christian Church, which has left a bitter aftertaste of antagonism between Science and religion. And rightly so. Science is based on the freedom to question. Religion is based on the duty to believe. But religion and spirituality are not the same thing. Whilst Science is a natural enemy of religion, it is a natural ally of Gnostic spirituality.

Indeed, Science finds its roots in Pagan Gnosticism, as the greatest scientists have acknowledged. Galileo and Copernicus saw themselves as reviving the Pythagorean tradition.[7] Newton regarded his studies of ancient myths as more important than his scientific works and claimed to have made the perennial Gnostic discovery of a common meaning underlying all mythology. In the twentieth century, the great physicist Wolfgang Pauli was passionately interested in the Christian Gnostics.[8] Werner Heisenberg, a winner of the Nobel Prize for Physics, asserted that modern science 'confirmed Pythagoras' beliefs to an inconceivable degree'.[9] Albert Einstein, an icon of Science, writes of his experience of scientific inquiry in words that could be those of the great Gnostic masters:

'The most important function of science is to awaken the cosmic religious feeling and keep it alive. It is very difficult to explain this feeling to anyone who is entirely without it. The individual feels the nothingness of human desires and aims, and the sublimity and marvellous order which reveal themselves both in nature and in the world of thought. He looks upon individual existence as a sort of prison and wants to experience the universe as a single significant whole.'[10]

Despite the fact that cutting-edge scientists present an ever more abstract picture of the universe, amongst the uninitiated, Science is equated with materialism – perhaps the ultimate form of Literalism. Materialism seeks to reduce everything to physics, because matter is all that exists.[11] But the great physicists do not endorse this sort of crass reductionism. In fact it is in physics, which should be the bedrock of materialism, that the worldview of scientific Literalism has fallen apart.[12]

Science is not essentially Literalist, however. It is the legacy of Pagan Gnosticism and at its heart are Gnostic values. Both Science and Gnosticism are based on questioning what is taken for granted. Both refuse to accept anything on blind faith. Both regard conceptual pictures of the world as working models. Like the ancient Gnostics, modern scientists are internationalists who embrace each other's discoveries regardless of nationality or political ideology. In fact 'Gnostic' and 'scientist' mean exactly the same thing: knower.[13]

Science and Gnosticism are complementary ways of exploring the mysteries of existence. Science is concerned with objective knowledge about the cosmos. Gnosticism is concerned with subjective self-knowledge. Science is concerned with the tangible appearances, Gnosticism with the ineffable essence. Science is about solving the relative mysteries of the world of becoming. Gnosticism is about dissolving into the Absolute Mystery of Being. Science is attempting to understand something so complex that it can't be comprehended. Gnosticism is attempting to understand something so simple that it can't be comprehended. Science is a collective venture over time. Gnosis is immediate and can only be attained individually.

Could the future see a return to the ancient understanding of subjective spirituality and objective Science as complementary sides of humanity's exploration of existence? This would require a revolution in the way we understand life – a rejection of Literalism and the rejuvenation of Gnosticism. That may seem unlikely, but the future often hits us from the direction we weren't looking in. Perhaps it is not the birth of the Space Age we are witnessing, but of the Inner Space Age, in which we begin a collective exploration of Consciousness and the great existential mysteries of life and death.

TWENTY-FIRST CENTURY GNOSTICISM

The history of humanity can be understood as a battle between good and bad ideas. Bad ideas are like viruses that can infect whole populations, causing them to behave in the most horrendous ways. The twentieth century probably saw more people die needlessly from bad ideas than from disease epidemics.[14] The only cure is to replace bad ideas with good ideas. If we want to revivify the essence of Gnosticism in a new form for the twenty-first century, this is what we must do. It's as simple as that.

We could start by dumping an entire rogues' gallery of bad ideas concocted by Christian Literalists:

Original sin. That's such a bad idea. Let's never again tell our children they've been born bad and reassure them instead that they are naturally good.

The Bible is the word of God. Ridiculous idea.

There is only one way to God. Obvious nonsense.

The Day of Judgement and the resurrection of the flesh. Spooky ideas.

The world is a bad place and we should hate it. In the face of the wonders all around us that's just ungrateful.

Eternal damnation. Horrible, grotesque, really, really bad idea.

God likes some people more than others. Please! What sort of God is that?

Sex is evil. If you believe this you must be doing it wrong.

God is male. What could that possibly mean? Does God have a penis?

Men are more spiritual than women. This idea must have been thought up by a man who never had a mother.

God has opinions – and only some people know what they are. That's got to be one of the worst ideas ever, because it is regularly used to justify a whole edifice of bad ideas.

Let's imagine jettisoning this sort of pernicious nonsense and replacing it with some simple but profound Gnostic ideas. Let's start with Gnosticism's 'big idea', which is very big indeed. It is this: *All is One.* Can you imagine the massive transformation that would occur in human culture with the spread of this idea? We would have unconditional love for all beings as expressions of a common essence. We would become tolerant, generous, co-operative, altruistic – in short, understanding ourselves to be kindred, we would become kind.

Let's imagine a society where the taboo against stating the obvious is broken and we all openly acknowledge that life is a Mystery and we wouldn't want it any other way. We all know how we kill a relationship with a lover as soon as we start to think we know who they are and put them into a conceptual box. It is the same with life. When we think we know how it is, it goes dead on us. It is the same with our relationship with ourselves. When we think we know who we are, we imprison our ineffable nature in the confines of a limited 'thought' – and the magic goes out of existence.

Let's imagine the Gnostic vision that the purpose of life is about exploring the Mystery becoming a commonly held worldview. Let's imagine the strange notion currently in vogue, that the purpose of life is to accumulate wealth, being regarded as on a par with believing that the Earth is flat. Let's imagine a time when presidents win elections by promising to create the best opportunities for the electorate to expand their awareness, plumb the depths of possibility, reach for new levels of experience, transcend their fear of death and really be *alive*.

Let's imagine a revival of Gnostic 'partnership spirituality' in which men and women value each other's characteristically different perspectives on life. Let's imagine a balanced form of spirituality, honouring both the archetypally male obsession with disembodied, impersonal, universal essence and the archetypally female infatuation with embodied, personal, particular appearances. Let's imagine women in love with men's ability to make the truth conscious by struggling to articulate it and men in love with women's silent sense of having naturally known it all along. Let's imagine liking learning from each other.

Let's imagine being able to laugh at the humour of our predicament. It is a fascinating fact that for most Fundamentalists, spirituality isn't a laughing matter. A good yardstick of how deep someone's spiritual understanding goes is how precious they are about their beliefs and how seriously they take themselves. Gnostics can laugh at themselves and their ideas (because it reminds them how limited all ideas are), and at what is sacred (because either nothing is sacred or everything is). Those who worry that God easily takes offence are confusing God with the Devil, who is a bully and can't bear being ribbed. After all, it was God who came up with a reality based on uniting two irreconcilable principles – and jokes ever since have been variants on that original wisecrack.

Let's imagine no more self-righteous spiritual autocrats who put their own opinions into God's mouth to give them authority, and a return instead to Gnostic guides who encourage us to challenge all the beliefs we have inherited unquestioningly from others. Let's imagine no more hierarchies of professional priests negotiating a spiritual career structure, and a return instead to the natural model for spiritual organization – a group of students around an authentic master. Let's imagine no more spiritual power-trippers who seek to enlarge their congregations, and a return instead to genuine teachers who seek to be redundant, because they want their students to spiritually mature and find their own way, not cling on like lost children.

Let's imagine replacing religious divisions with an all-embracing eclecticism which acknowledges that the Absolute Truth can never be said, but that relative truths can be expressed in various conceptual vocabularies. We are living in amazing times in which the wisdom of the world is available at the local bookshop. Gnosticism's internationalist spirit is just what we need to synthesize a common human spirituality out of the plethora of approaches. In a universe which is slowly evolving towards conscious unity, this moment has been a long time coming and we should embrace it wholeheartedly. But this is not to say that we should carve out some monolithic one-world religion. That would just be a recipe for the destruction of the variety of human culture. Gnosticism is about unity-in-variety. It is Literalists who want to impose one religion on the world, as the Roman Church attempted when it laid waste our Pagan heritage and gave us the Dark Ages. We don't want that again!

Let's imagine a culture which treats spirituality as a completely private matter, like sexuality. Let's imagine as much spiritual variety as possible, with everyone finding their own idiosyncratic path, for, as Theodotus teaches:

'All people, according to their stage of development, possess the Gnosis of God in a way special to themselves.'[15]

Yet let's also imagine this diversity being understood as different approaches to a shared endeavour. All spiritual practices and philosophies fit into the simple initiatory framework of the ancient Mysteries. We are either engaged in exploring the range and depth of experience – the *psychic* or soul initiation – or in becoming conscious of Consciousness which is the ground of all experience – the *pneumatic* or spirit initiation. If these two aspects of the spiritual path are understood as complementary, then everyone, in their completely different ways, can be seen as participating in the same adventure.[16]

Let's imagine no longer seeing spirituality as something otherworldly and esoteric, but as inherent in the natural processes of ordinary human existence – birth, childhood, sex, parenting, ageing, death, joy, suffering, waking, dreaming, sleeping, and so on. Let's stop attempting to add a special spiritual dimension to life and recognize that life *is* the spiritual process,[17] for, as Plotinus assures us:

'This is *it*. This and no other. Not what it chanced to be, but simply what it must be – but without the "must".'[18]

Let's imagine a life-affirming spirituality which sees self-knowledge and true enjoyment as the same thing. Which embraces pleasure, delights in the senses and is committed to joy. Which understands that the universal quest for the Good manifests in each one of us as the desire for good experiences. Which encourages us to have a good time, but not at the expense of others, because we are all One, and others are also Consciousness trying to have a good time. Let's imagine spiritual philosophy being understood as simply a clever way to really be happy. After all, happiness is what everyone is naturally driven to desire. As Sophia herself teaches:

> 'With all the worry with which they work at countless enterprises, mortal men travel by different paths, but all strive to reach one and the same goal. Happiness. This is the goal which, once obtained, leaves nothing more to be desired.'[19]

Let's dare to imagine the world we really want. Why not? It's our collective dream and we can dream it any way we choose. Let's imagine humanity waking up at last from its nonchalant numbness, overcome with awe at the inexplicable miracle *that we are*. Let's imagine living our lives as a celebration of the Great Mystery in which 'we live and move and have our being'.[20] Let's imagine a world in which we embrace the great Gnostic injunction to 'love one another', not because we should, but, as Paul says, 'because we are parts of each other'.[21] Let's imagine fulfilling the great ambition which motivates evolution. Let's imagine Heaven on Earth.

BLUEPRINT FOR
Reality

In his version of the Christian myth cycle, before beginning the story of the fall and redemption of Sophia, Ptolemy describes the arising of the *aeons* or archetypes that make up the *pleroma* and form the blueprint for reality. In his system there are eight principal *aeons* which give rise to two minor subsets of 10 *aeons* and 12 *aeons*, making 30 *aeons* in all. Here we will explore the significance of the eight principal *aeons* which, for Ptolemy, are the fundamental archetypes which structure all that exists.

The eight principal *aeons* arise in pairs as four fundamental syzygies. Each syzygy consists of a 'male' *aeon*, representing the *ousia* or essence of the syzygy, and a 'female' *aeon*, representing the *hypostasis* or appearance of the syzygy.[1] The 'marriage' of the male and female aspects of the first syzygy throws up a synthesis which is, in turn, a syzygy. The new pair combine to create a new synthesis and so on, in an expanding dialectical process. This model of origination is found in ancient Egyptian and Babylonian myths, in which the fundamental archetypes are represented by eight primal deities which emerge in four male–female pairs.[2]

Four Fundamental Syzygies	
Deep	Silence
Consciousness	Truth
Logos	Life
Human	Community

These four archetypal syzygies structure existence by manifesting as the four levels of reality and the levels of our human identity.[3]

Syzygies	Levels of Reality	Levels of Human Identity
Deep–Silence	Mystery	Mystery
Consciousness–Truth	Archetypes	Consciousness
Logos–Life	Psychic Heavens	Psyche
Human–Community	Physical Cosmos	Body

Ptolemy represents the paradoxical dazzling darkness of pure Consciousness with the syzygy Deep–Silence. The Deep is the essence of the syzygy, representing the potentiality of the One. The Silence is the appearance of the syzygy, representing the void of the Nothing. In the modern world, with computerization, we have found that from just 1 and 0 we can create a virtual reality. The original Christians teach that from the 1 and 0 comes this actual reality. In Ptolemy's myth, the process of manifestation begins when the Deep (male/1) deposits a seed in the womb of the Silence (female/0), which gives birth to the syzygy Consciousness–Truth, beginning the generation of the archetypes.[4]

The Levels of Human Identity

The easiest way to understand the process of archetypal emanation is by exploring how it manifests as the levels of human identity.

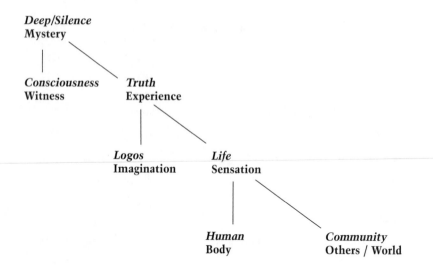

**The Fundamental Syzygies
as Expressed by the Levels of Human Identity**

1. In the primal Deep–Silence the One appears to itself as Nothing. We experience this on the human level in the state we call 'deep sleep' in which pure subjectivity is 'experienced' as absence of experience.

2. The arising of the syzygy Consciousness–Truth from the Deep–Silence happens archetypally 'in the beginning'. It manifests on the human level in each of us every morning when we 'wake up' as the syzygy Consciousness–psyche. In the 'depths' of our being something mysteriously stirs to break the 'silence' of the unitive state of 'deep sleep' and we inexplicably find ourselves no longer unconscious but a witness of experience.

3. We experience Truth dividing into the syzygy *Logos*–Life as the two fundamental qualities of our experience: abstract imagination and concrete sensation, our private inner world and our shared external world.

4. *Logos* orders Life by dividing it into the syzygy Human–Community. We experience this as the division of the physical world into our personal body and everything else – 'me' and 'others'.

The basic teachings of the Gnostic myth of origination, which we explored in Chapter 7, 'Consciousness Conceives the Cosmos', are inherent in the structure of the four fundamental syzygies. Using these concepts, the myth of origination could be told in a condensed form like this:

> The Mystery (Deep–Silence) wants self-knowledge, so it wakes up (Consciousness) and conceives of itself (Truth), imagining (*Logos*) a conceptual matrix (Life) within which it identifies itself separately with each individual appearance (Human), which lives amongst other manifestations of the Mystery (Community).

Subject and Object

Ptolemy treats the Mystery as a syzygy. But he also calls it simply 'the Primal Parent' and describes it as being beyond all duality, because the Mystery can only be considered as *appearing* to be a syzygy from the standpoint of duality, which it actually transcends. The syzygy Consciousness–Truth really represents the arising of duality. This syzygy is the archetype of syzygy itself.

The process of emanation is implicit in the concept of a syzygy. The interrelated opposites which form the poles of a syzygy – *ousia* and *hypostasis* – can be understood as 'subject and object'. The process of emanation is the syzygy 'subject–object' ricocheting down through the levels in a process of generation which creates the archetypal blueprint for our nature and the reality we inhabit.

Let's examine this process in our own experience.

1. The Mystery is beyond duality, but can be conceptualized as the paradoxical syzygy One and Nothing – subjectivity without an object.
2. The Mystery becomes conscious when it partially objectifies itself, creating the syzygy subject–object. This expresses itself on the human level as the syzygy witness (subject) and experience (object).
3. Our experience in turn divides into the syzygy imagination (subjective experience) and sensation (objective experience); our private inner world of thoughts and feelings and our public outer world of physicality.
4. Our sensual experience divides into the syzygy body (subject) and world (object); that part of physical reality which we identify with as ourselves and the rest that we regard as other.

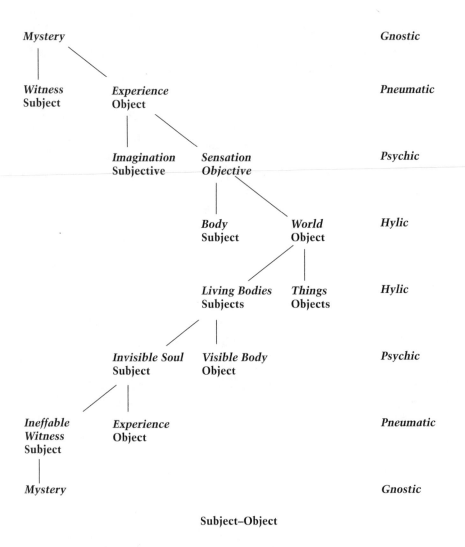

Mystery			*Gnostic*
Witness Subject	*Experience* Object		*Pneumatic*
	Imagination Subjective	*Sensation* Objective	*Psychic*
	Body Subject	*World* Object	*Hylic*
	Living Bodies Subjects	*Things* Objects	*Hylic*
	Invisible Soul Subject	*Visible Body* Object	*Psychic*
Ineffable *Witness* Subject	*Experience* Object		*Pneumatic*
Mystery			*Gnostic*

Subject–Object

Here the primary process of emanation stops. Why? Because the last primary archetype, Community, is the octave of the first archetype, the Deep. The easiest way to understand this is by looking at how it manifests in our own experience. The fourth archetypal level of emanation manifests as the physical world. The world appears to have its own objective existence, regardless of us as a subject. The essential absolute subjectivity of the first syzygy finally manifests as the apparent absolute objectivity of the physical cosmos. Having apparently turned into its opposite, the only way to go is back. Now begins the process whereby the apparent object –

the human body in the physical world – awakens to its essential nature as absolute subjectivity.

There is something else that is extraordinary about the physical level of reality. Behind the objectivity of the physical cosmos we intuit hidden subjectivity. When we look into someone else's eyes, we intuit (but cannot see) Consciousness looking back at us. Everything else we experience is an appearance – a fleeting, relative reality. But when we connect with Consciousness through another body we confront the Mystery. On the physical level of reality, which embodies the fourth archetypal syzygy Human–Community, absolute subjectivity meets absolute subjectivity by appearing to itself in separate forms. When the Mystery has emanated so far that it meets itself in other forms, the process of discriminating subject and object leads back to the Mystery.

1. Our experience of the world divides into the syzygy other sentient bodies (subjects) and inanimate things (objects).

2. Our experience of sentient bodies is that, like us, they are a syzygy of an invisible psyche (subject) and a visible body (object). Sentient bodies have an inner life. That's how we distinguish them from inanimate things.

3. Sentient bodies are, like us, Consciousness (subject) witnessing experience (object).

4. The being of others is utterly ineffable. We cannot *experience* the witness within others any more than we can *experience* the witness within ourselves. It is the absolute Mystery.

The Ladder to Heaven

We can understand the Christian path of self-knowledge as the process of returning up the ladder of the four archetypal syzygies. This is simultaneously an inner and an outer journey of transformation. Inwardly we expand our understanding of ourselves and outwardly we expand our understanding of others, until finally we embrace all of the levels of existence.

As uninitiated *hylics* we are aware of ourselves and others only as bodies in the physical cosmos, which gives rise to the *eidolon* or ego – the 'I am the body' idea. We see others in terms of our own selfish ends and as competitors trying to use us for their selfish ends.

As *psychic* initiates we come to understand that the body and the physical cosmos are just our 'outer' world. We start to explore the inner world of ideas and imagination. We begin to see ourselves as an embodied soul, not just a body that happens to be conscious. We no longer see others only as bodies. We see fellow souls who are on an adventure of awakening – whether they know it or not. We empathize with others because we realize that they are feeling, thinking, experiencing beings, just like we are.

As *pneumatic* initiates we become aware that the inner and outer worlds comprise the totality of our experience and that our subjective essence is not to be found objectified as an experience. We are neither the body nor the soul. We are the ineffable witness which experiences both. We become aware of ourselves and others as impersonal Consciousness witnessing the unfolding of manifestation. We know ourselves to be the same essence as others, but dressed up in a different guise.

Finally, the realization of Gnosis is the healing of the primal syzygy which has ricocheted down through the levels, manifesting as all the subsequent syzygies. Realized Gnostics know that the knower and the known are one. They find that they are the Mystery of God manifesting as all that is. There is no self and other. No subject and object. All is One. With the realization of Gnosis, we find ourselves no longer separate from others, or indeed from anything, but at One in the Mystery with all that is. We dissolve into mystical communion. We are in love with all beings.

GNOSTIC
Islam

Religions begin with a group of radical Gnostic mystics and end up as authoritarian institutions dominated by Literalists. It happened to Christianity. And it happened to Christianity's greatest rival, Islam. Islam was inspired by the mystical visionary Mohammad in the seventh century. Like Christianity, within a few hundred years it had degenerated into an authoritarian institution. Islamic dogmatists imposed a strictly Literalist interpretation of Islamic scripture and declared: 'The gates of independent thinking have been closed.'[1]

The winners write history to serve their own agenda. Christian Literalists created the account of the origins of Christianity which brands Christian Gnostics as heretics. The Muslim authorities, likewise, justified their power with an appropriate history and condemned Islamic Gnostics as heretics. Islamic Gnostics, however, do not see themselves as practising a distorted form of Islam any more than Christian Gnostics thought of themselves as practising a distorted form of Christianity.

Islamic Gnostics, such as the Ismaili Shiites and Sufi Sunnis, teach that they represent the true Islamic tradition of Mohammad and the original Muslims.[2] As we have found with Christianity, rather than simply accepting the propaganda of the religious authorities, we would do better to trust the so-called heretics' account of the origin and meaning of their spiritual tradition. The picture they paint of the Islam of the original Muslims is in essence the same as the Christianity of the original Christians.

The similarities between the original Christians and the original Muslims are not coincidental. The eminent historian Adolf von Harnack defined Islam as 'a transformation on Arab soil of a Jewish religion that had itself been transformed by Gnostic Judaeo-Christianity'.[3] Mohammad was part of the Middle-Eastern Gnostic tradition. His teachings particularly show the influence of the Ebionite school of Christianity and Manichaeism.[4] He developed his notion of what it is to be a prophet specifically from Mani.[5]

According to the Ismailis, as well as exoteric or 'outer' teachings, Mohammad imparted to his closest students secret esoteric or 'inner' teachings.[6] The master's secret teachings were passed down through a line of enlightened masters called Imans, starting with Mohammad's son-in-law Ali ibn Abi Talib, each of which embodied 'the Light of Mohammad'.[7] In the Sunni tradition, Sufis likewise claim to be the inheritors of Mohammad's secret teachings.

Islamic Gnostics teach that esoteric doctrines are encoded in the Qur'an, but whether they are understood or not depends on the state of being of the reader. They emphasize the practice of ta'wil – understanding teachings on many levels simultaneously.[8] They relate a saying of Mohammad:

'The Qur'an has an outer and inner meaning and the inner meaning has in turn an inner meaning, and so on up to seven inner meanings.'[9]

The deeper meaning of Islam is the perennial Gnostic philosophy. Allah, whose name signifies 'Being and Nothingness',[10] is called the 'Mystery of Mysteries' and 'He who cannot be reached by the boldness of thoughts'.[11] Just as Christian Gnostics picture God as a dazzling darkness, so Muslim Gnostics talk of Allah as a 'black light' or as the 'luminous night'.[12] This Absolute Mystery manifests as a masculine principle and feminine principle. For the Ismaeli, as for the original Christians, the mystical reunion of the two is the supreme image symbolizing Gnosis.[13]

The Ka'aba in Mecca, the most sacred site for Muslims, was once a shrine to the Goddess and originally the Qur'an sanctioned the traditional worship of God in feminine form. But later these so-called 'Satanic Verses' were removed and the story created that Satan had deceived

Mohammad into including them.[14] Islamic Gnostics continued the 'Sophia' tradition of the Pagan and Christian Gnostics, however, even treating Mohammad's daughter Fatima as an image of Sophia.[15]

Ibn Arabi, a Sufi known as 'the Great Master', relates having a vision of Sophia while performing the ritual sevenfold circumambulation of the Ka'aba.[16] He believed that women were a potent incarnation of Sophia because they inspired in men a love that was ultimately directed towards God.[17] Like the libertine Christians, he venerated sex as a spiritual practice which could help human beings participate in the cosmic sexuality through which the Mystery knows itself.[18] Like a true eclectic Gnostic, he even did a Persian translation of a Sanskrit scripture on Tantric Yoga![19]

Literalist Islam, like Literalist Christianity, is associated with the oppression of women. But, just as the original Christians were radical egalitarians, in Mohammad's lifetime there was equality of the sexes in the Muslim community. Women were amongst Mohammad's closest followers and their emancipation was important to him. The Qur'an forbade the killing of girl children, or regretting that they were not boys, and gave women legal rights of divorce and inheritance.[20]

In the same way that Christian Gnostics took Pagan texts and Christianized them, Islamic Gnostics adapted Christian Gnostic scriptures to fit a Muslim context.[21] Like Christian Gnostic texts, the Qur'an gives a docetic account of the death of Jesus in which only the appearance of Jesus dies, proclaiming:

> 'They did not kill him. They did not crucify him. They were taken in by an appearance.'[22]

Like the original Christians, Islamic Gnostics treat Christ as an image of the Consciousness of God, our shared essential identity. The famous Sufi poet Rumi teaches that if we could free ourselves from identification with the body, 'we would all be Christ'.[23] Like the original Christians, Islamic Gnostics regard Jesus' virgin birth as an allegory representing initiation,[24] with the Virgin Mary representing the psyche,[25] and her visit from the angel Gabriel representing the beginning of the initiation process.[26]

Islamic Gnostics regarded Jesus as such an important figure that some of them even amended the Muslim profession of faith to 'There is no God but Allah and *Jesus* is his prophet', which was deliberately provocative, in true Gnostic style.[27] Jesus was the hero figure of the great Sufi master al-Hallaj who, in imitation of Jesus, publicly proclaimed: 'I am God.'

For Gnostics this is simply a statement of the ultimate truth, but for Literalists it is the ultimate way to annoy a jealous deity. The Jesus myth represents Jesus as being executed at the request of the Jewish Literalist authorities for his blasphemy. In a tragic case of life imitating art, the Islamic Literalists crucified al-Hallaj.[28]

Like the Christian Gnostics, the Islamic Gnostics were international-ists who embraced wisdom wherever they could find it, regardless of religious, cultural or political boundaries. They honoured the Pagan philosophers and translated their works into Arabic.[29] Ibn Arabi was so immersed in Pagan Gnosticism that he was known as 'the Son of Plato'.[30] Suhrawardi, who was honoured as 'the Master of Illumination', taught that all the sages of the ancient world had preached one doctrine which had reached him through his teachers al-Bistami and al-Hallaj.[31] He portrayed the Pagan sages Pythagoras and Empedocles as Sufis, clearly equating Islam and Paganism in the same way that the original Christians equated Christianity and Paganism.[32] Suhrawardi attempted to create a universal philosophical system which united all spiritual traditions into one – for which noble endeavour the Islamic Literalists had him put to death.[33]

Islamic Gnostics adopted Pagan and Christian images, such as the Cross of Light.[34] They encoded traditional Gnostic ideas into their own myths – for example, the ladder of seven steps leading to the *ogdoad* and the heavenly *pleroma* became Mohammad's mythical journey of seven steps to heaven.[35] Like Pagan and Christian Gnostics, the Islamic Gnostics also portrayed this world as the underworld of the spiritually dead. Rumi writes:

'The mind sees things inside-out. What it takes to be life is really death, and what it takes to be death is really life.'[36]

Like Pagan and Christian Gnostics, the original Muslims taught that God created creation so that he could come to know himself.[37] Mohammad has Allah proclaim:

'I am a hidden treasure; I wanted to be known. I created the cosmos so that I might be known.'[38]

The Qur'an teaches that God created humanity as an image of himself, so that he could contemplate himself as in a mirror. We are God in search of himself. 'He who knows himself knows God' was a common Sufi saying.[39] Teaching the perennial paradox that we are all individual expressions of the Oneness of God, which is the essence of Pagan, Christian and Islamic Gnosticism, Rumi has Allah tell us:

'I am your tongue and eyes.
I am all your senses.
I am your happiness and anger.
You are my property,
but I belong to you.
Sometimes I say, "You are you."
Other times I say, "You are Me."
Whichever way –
I am the Sun which illuminates it.'[40]

NOTES

ABBREVIATIONS

AH   Irenaeus, *Adverses Haereses*

AV   Tertullian, *Adversus Valentinianos*

BG   Papyrus Berolinensis 8502 in Robinson, J. M., *The Nag Hammadi Library*, HarperCollins paperback edition, 1978

DK   Diels, H., and Kranz, W., *Die Fragment der Vorsokratiker*, sixth revised edition by Kranz, W., Berlin, 1951

DL   Diogenes Laertius, *Lives of the Eminent Philosophers*

DP   Tertullian, *De Praescriptione Haereticorum*

Enn.   Plotinus, *The Six Enneads*, trans. Stephen Mackenna and B. S. Page

Exc. Theod.   *Excerpta ex Theodoto*

G   Mandaean quotations from *Ginza: Der Schatz oder das Grosse Buch der Mandaer*, Göttingen, 1925, quoted in Jonas, H. (1958), 52

HE   Eusebius, *Historia Ecclesiastica*

NHC   Nag Hammadi Codex, Robinson, J. M., *The Nag Hammadi Library*, HarperCollins paperback edition, 1978

Pan.   Epiphanius, *Panarion*

Ref.   Hippolytus, *Refutationis Omnium Haeresium*

Strom.   Clement of Alexandria, *Stromata*

TJM   Freke, T., and Gandy, P., *The Jesus Mysteries: Was the 'Original Jesus' a Pagan God?* Page numbers refer to the hardback editions, UK (1999) and US (2000).

CHAPTER 1: THE GOSPEL OF GNOSIS

1. *The Gospel of Thomas*, NHC, 2.2.17, in Robinson, J. M. (1978), 128. The Church Father Hippolytus records this as part of the oath of secrecy for those being initiated into the 'Gnosis of the Father', Hippolytus, *Ref.*, 5.24, *see* Pagels, E. (1975), 58. It also occurs in the *First Letter of Clement*, *see* Louth, A., (1968), 37, and *The Acts of Peter*, 3.39, *see* Davidson, J. (1995), 306. Paul also uses this in *1 Corinthians* 2.9. The Old Testament source for this saying is *Isaiah* 64:4. The Pagan Mysteries were often referred to as *arreta* or *aporreta*, literally 'unspeakable' or 'unsayable', not simply because it was forbidden by oath to describe what happened, but more mystically that these things cannot be put into words.

2. *The Second Treatise of the Great Seth*, NHC, 7.2.60, in Robinson, op. cit., 367

3. Origen instructed his pupils that perfect piety required a knowledge of Pagan philosophy, which he calls 'a fine meal prepared for sophisticated palates'. In comparison he claims that Christians 'cook for the masses'. Likewise, Clement of Alexandria wrote that Greek philosophy purged the soul and prepared it beforehand for the reception of faith, on which the Truth built up the edifice of Gnosis. *See* discussion in *TJM*, 90.

4. Clement of Alexandria, *Strom.*, 1.12 and 7.61

5. Sophia receives a bewildering variety of titles in the Gnostic texts: Barbelo, Achamoth, Mother, Truth, Life, Justice, Holy Spirit, Virgin Spirit and even masculine titles like Lord.

6. *1 Corinthians* 2.6. There is great scholarly debate about Paul's letters, with only 7 of the 13 letters of the New Testament accepted as, mostly, authentic. Although we do not quote from texts dismissed as complete forgeries, such as the 'Pastoral Letters' *1* and *2 Timothy* and *Titus*, we have quoted material from other disputed letters which we think expresses Gnostic, if not definitely Pauline, thoughts.

7. Irenaeus, *AH*, 3.12.7, cf 1.13.2, and *see* Pagels, op. cit., 23. Baptism was also performed in the name of the Goddess of Wisdom. Kurt Rudolph gives two baptismal formulae used by the Gnostics; *see* Rudolph, K. (1987), 243.

8. In his secret celebration of the mass, Marcus the Gnostic taught that the wine symbolized the blood of the Mother. *See* Pagels, E. (1979), 73, for the many epithets of the 'Mother of the All'.

9. Irenaeus, op. cit., 1.13.2

10. *The Acts of Thomas*, 50. *See* Rudolph, op. cit., 241.

11. As Mead writes, 'But when we find that [the Gnostics] treated the Gospel-legends also not as history, but as allegory, and not only as allegory, but as symbolic of the drama of initiation, the matter becomes of deep interest for the theosophical student.' Mead, G. R. S. (1906), 370.

12. Hippolytus, *Ref.*, 7.27.7. *See also* Rudolph, op. cit., 152.

13. *The Gospel of Thomas*, NHC, 2.2.1, in Robinson, J. M. (1978), 127

14. Hoeller, S. A. (1989), xviii. After quoting this translator's remarks Hoeller states: 'It is time that a Gnostic interprets the Gnostic scriptures.' As Mead writes, 'It is of course quite natural that orthodox scribes should blunder when transcribing Gnostic documents, owing to their ignorance of the subject and the strangeness of their ideas.' Mead, G. R. S., *The Gnostic Crucifixion* (1907), 20.

CHAPTER 2: THE ORIGINAL CHRISTIANS

1. Quoted by Clement of Alexandria, *Strom.*, 6.52.3–4. There is a useful collection of the extant fragments of Valentinus in Layton, B. (1987), 229ff.

2. Vivekananda, *Collected Works*, vol. V, 348. Our thanks to David for sending us this. Vivekananda (1863–1902) is famous for his announcement at the World Congress of Faiths in Chicago in 1893 that 'All religions are one.' He had a profound influence on Blavatsky's Theosophical Society and several schools of Vedanta were founded in America as a result of his visit.

3. As part of the thesis we advanced in *TJM* we argued that the gospel story is a myth and there had never been an historical Jesus. As we stated, this theory is not new. As Van Voorst writes, 'Some readers may be surprised or shocked that many books and essays – by my count, over one hundred – in the past two hundred years have fervently denied the very existence of Jesus.' (Van Voorst, R. E. (2000), 6.) Lord Bolingbroke proposed the idea at the end of the eighteenth century. In the late 1790s Constantin

François Volney argued that Jesus was a solar myth derived from Krishna. Charles François Dupuis traced the myth back to Egypt (Dupuis, C. F., *Origine de tous les cultes, ou la religion universelle* (1795–1812)). In 1840 Bruno Bauer contended that Jesus was an invention of Mark. Other 'Christ-Mythers' include Karl Marx, Allard Pierson, A. Loman, W. C. van Manen, Thomas Whittaker, Pierre Couchoud, John M. Robertson (*Pagan Christs*, 1903), William Benjamin Smith, Arthur Drews (*The Christ Myth*, 1910), Albert Kalthoff, Peter Jensen, G. A. Wells and Earl Doherty. The history of the theory is discussed in S. J. Case, *The Historicity of Jesus* (1912); Arthur Drews, *Die Leugnung der Geschichtlichkeit Jesu in Vergangenheit und Gegenwart* (1926); Maurice Goguel, *Jesus the Nazarene: Myth or History?* (1926); Herbert G. Wood, *Did Christ Really Live?* (1938).

4. *See* 'The First Christians?', *TJM*, 184.

5. Jung, C. G. (1953), 86

6. *See especially* Huxley, A. (1946). Huxley states that the phrase was coined by Leibniz, (intro., 1); however, Agostino Stueco used it in 1536 and other researchers have traced it back to the Neoplatonists. Copenhaver, B. P. (1992), xlviiii.

7. The Greek term *gnostikos* was used by Plato as a rare philosophical term meaning 'leading to knowledge' or 'capable of knowledge'. Plutarch used it in this sense: 'Human souls have a faculty that is *gnostikos* of visible things.' (Layton, op. cit., 8.) As will become clear, this book extends the conventional use of the term 'Gnostic' to include the classical esoteric tradition on which Jewish and Christian Gnosticism is so obviously and heavily dependent. At the head of this classical tradition stands Pythagoras, closely followed by his disciple Parmenides, who brought these teachings to Athens in the middle of the fifth century BCE and had a profound effect on the young Socrates (Plato, *Parmenides*, b–d). In his initiatory poem written *c*.480 BCE, Parmenides describes how he was led 'on the renowned way of the Goddess, who leads *the man who knows* through every town' (Kirk and Raven (1957), 266). As Kingsley notes, 'In ancient Greek this was the standard way of referring to the initiate.' (Kingsley, P. (1999), 69.) Only by uniting Jewish and Christian Gnosticism with its Pagan predecessor can any sense be made of the elaborate Gnostic mythology of the Nag Hammadi library. By a reverse process much new information can also be gleaned about what took place in the Pagan Mysteries.

8. For *Arifs*, *see* Nicholson, R. A. (1926), 24.

9. The fact that Christianity has split into over 20,000 denominations worldwide is evidence of this tendency.

10. Both the Church Fathers and Pagan critics such as Plotinus and Celsus accused the Gnostics of deriving their doctrines from Greek philosophy. This charge was not taken seriously until the discovery of the Gnostic gospels. At the first conference of specialists in Platonism and scholars of Gnosticism held in 1992 in New York, J. P. Kenney described the Nag Hammadi texts as reading like 'a riot in Plato's cave' (*see* 'The Platonism of the Tripartite Tractate', NHC, 1.5, in Wallis, R. T. (1992), 204). Nock likewise described Gnosticism as 'Platonism run wild'. (Nock, A. D. (1972), 949)

11. Philo paints the Therapeutae and Essenes as the Jewish equivalents of the active and contemplative division found in the many earlier Pagan schools. The community

founded by Pythagoras recognized two orders of followers – those who came to hear the teachings and those who committed themselves and their worldly goods to the community. The Stoics and Cynics were likewise regarded as two wings of one school of philosophy.

12. Plato, *Phaedo*, 109

13. For more information on Jewish integration into Pagan society *see* http://www.jesusmysteries.demon.co.uk/judaism.html.

14. Philo, *De Sept.* 3.4, quoted in Kingsland, W. (1937), 106

15. This tradition continued into the Middle Ages. The *Zohar*, written by Moses de Leon *c.*1305 CE, claimed to draw on the secret teachings of Simeon ben Yohai, a rabbi of Galilee in the second century CE, which were in turn said to have been drawn from the hidden wisdom of Moses. *See* Campbell, J. (1949), 267. Scholem's work leaves no doubt that the medieval flowering of Kabbalah in the south of France in the thirteenth century was inspired by Jewish Gnostic traditions that had somehow survived from the first centuries. *See especially* Scholem, G. (1987).

16. Hermippus, *c.*220 BCE, was the first Jewish scholar to claim that Pythagoras acquired his wisdom from the Jews (Josephus, *Against Apion*, 1.16). This was later repeated by Aristobulus, *c.*150 BCE, who added that Socrates and Plato also borrowed their ideas from the laws of Moses (Clement, *Strom.*, 1.72.4). Eupolemus, *c.*170 BCE, claimed that Moses taught the alphabet first to the Jews, from whom the Phoenicians received it and from them in turn the Greeks (Eusebius, *Praeparatio Evangelica*, 9.26.1; *see* Gruen (1998), 153). According to Artapanus, Moses acquired the name Mousaios (a Greek teacher of Orpheus according to legend) from the Greeks themselves (Eusebius, *Praeparatio Evangelica*, 9.9.27, 3–4). As many scholars have demonstrated, none of these extravagant claims made by Alexandrian Jewish scholars have any basis in reality.

17. *See* 'Adapting the Past' in *TJM*, 196. Philo Judaeus (25 BCE–50 CE) is the finest example of the syncretism of Judaism and Platonism and repeats the claims of his predecessors that everything good, true and beautiful amongst the Greeks had in fact been derived from Moses by Plato. *See* Martin, L. H. (1987), 105ff.

18. Josephus, *Antiquities of the Jews*, 15.371

19. Josephus, *The Jewish War*, 2.8.10. Elsewhere Josephus tells us that he once spent a year living amongst the Essenes.

20. Clement of Alexandria, op. cit., 1.15.72 and 2.19.100

21. 'The contemplative life' was a term used in the Pagan world to describe the life lived in Pythagorean communities. Parmenides was said to have been converted to the 'contemplative life' by a fellow Pythagorean (DL, 9.21–3; *see* Kirk and Raven (1957), 264). Philo, *On the Contemplative Life*, 2.21

22. 'The Way' was a phrase used by Essenes, Cynics and Christians to describe their faith. *See* Ellegard, A. (1999), 167, and Epictetus, *The Teachings of Epictetus*, 209.

23. The editor of the Loeb edition of Eusebius' *History* states: 'Nowadays it seems needless to argue that the theory has no foundation whatever.' *See* Philo of Alexandria, *Book IX*, 107. The editor of the Penguin edition states categorically that this theory is wrong; *see* Eusebius (1965), 406. See also *TJM*, 184ff.

24. Philo wrote about the Therapeutae *c.*10 CE, 20 years before the supposed date of the crucifixion.

25. Many modern scholars have speculated about a link between the early Christians and the Essenes and Therapeutae. Hoeller examines the similarities between the Essenes and Gnosticism (Hoeller, S. A. (1989), 42ff); Ringgren calls the Essenes a 'preparation for Gnosticism, a pre- or proto-Gnosticism' (Ringgren, H. (1995), 119–20).

26. Philo, op. cit., 28

27. Epiphanius, *Pan.*, 26.1.4. *See* Layton, B. (1987), 203.

28. At the heart of the Pagan Mysteries was a dramatization of the descent and return of the soul and so it is no surprise that Jewish philosophers seized on *Genesis* and *Exodus* as the starting-point for the allegorization of their sacred texts. Whether the Pentateuch was meant to be an allegory from its first conception is not known, but the failure of historians to find historical evidence for most of the events portrayed in it suggests that it might have been. Whatever its origin, the allegorization of the *Exodus* enabled Hellenistic Jewish scholars to prove, at least to their own satisfaction, that the Pagan Mysteries had in fact been inspired by Mosaic traditions. This would later provide justification for the staggering degree of syncretism found in Philo.

29. Plato's *Timaeus*, the most cryptic and mystical of all Plato's dialogues, was composed from Pythagorean texts bought from a Pythagorean of southern Italy called Timaeus. The influence of this text on Gnostic speculation was profound. As Layton writes, 'The formation of the gnostic myth ultimately drew on Platonist interpretations of the myth of creation in Plato's *Timaeus*, as combined with the *Book of Genesis*.' Layton, op. cit., 7–8

30. Philo, *On the Creation of the World*. *See* Layton, op. cit., 16.

31. *See Joshua*, Chapter 1. A pre-Christian cult of Joshua/Jesus could have been around for many centuries before the supposed birth of Christianity. As Drews wrote in 1910, 'Many signs speak in favour of the fact that Joshua or Jesus was the name under which the expected Messiah was honoured in certain sects.' He cites *Ezra* 3:2, in which it is the high priest Joshua who leads the Jews back into their old homes after the Babylonian captivity (*c.*458 BCE), just as the older Joshua brought back the Israelites into the Promised Land. In *Zechariah* 3, Joshua is invested as high priest by the 'Angel of the Lord' and is later crowned as Messiah (*Zechariah* 6:9–15). *See* Drews, A. (1910), 57f. Justin Martyr claimed that both the Old Testament and Babylonian Joshuas revealed 'in parable the mystery of Christ' (*Dialogue with Trypho*, 65). The fact that many of the false prophets so heavily criticized by Josephus were attempting to perform miracles first performed by Joshua, such as dividing the Jordan or bringing down the walls of the Roman garrison as Joshua had brought down the walls of Jericho, is also significant.

32. Joshua/Jesus makes his first appearance in *Exodus* 17:8.

33. Hoeller, op. cit., 52

34. *Hebrews* 11:24–7

35. Hippolytus relates the Peratic Gnostic exegesis of the *Exodus* myth: 'Those who are ignorant ... are Egyptians. And this, they assert, is the departure from Egypt, (that is,)

from the body.' Hippolytus, *Ref.*, 5.11. For Jung's psychological interpretation of this, *see* Jung, C. (1957), 199, *also* 14, para 257.

36. *1 Corinthians* 10:1–6. In *1 Corinthians* 10:6 Paul states: 'These things were our examples [*typos*]...'

37. The Naasene Gnostics as described by Hippolytus, op. cit., 5.1–2ff. *See* Mead, G. R. S. (1906), 199, 496. Hippolytus refers to the three churches of the Gnostics, the 'angelic, the psychic and the earthly, and their names are the chosen, the called and the captive'. These terms clearly derive from the myth of *Exodus*.

38. *The Tripartite Tractate* explains that 'Humankind came to be in three essential types' which it calls 'the spiritual', 'the psychic' and 'the material', *see* Robinson, J. M. (1978), 94. Mani likewise preached that there were three paths which divided human souls. The way of the elect led to the Gardens of Paradise, the way of the listeners, guardians of the religion and sustainers of the elect led to the world and its horrors, and the third way of the sinners led to Hell. *See* Stoyanov, Y. (2000), 113. Clement regarded those Christians who have yet to reach Gnosis as being of three different types, defined by their relationship to God, as the slave, the faithful slave and the friend, *see* Clement, *Strom.*, 3. The Gnostic Theodotus describes the effect of scripture on these three types: 'When the Scripture is read, one is helped to faith, another to morality, and a third is freed from superstition by the Gnosis of things.' *Exc. Theod.*, 28. *See* Foerster, W. (1972), 222–33. Elsewhere, Clement writes: 'Now, since there are three states of the soul – ignorance, opinion, knowledge – those who are in ignorance are the Gentiles, those in knowledge, the true Church, and those in opinion, the Heretics.' Clement, op. cit., 7.16. Augustine writes: 'The third grade of soul is the highest, and is called mind, where intelligence has its throne. "Now this part of the soul of the world," Varro says, "is called 'God' and in us is called 'Genius'." ' Augustine, *City of God*, 7.23

39. *See* Mead, op. cit., 186.

40. Justin Martyr, *Dialogue with Trypho*, Chapter 113, entitled 'Joshua was a Figure of Christ'. Justin refers to the Old Testament Joshua 38 times in an effort to convince the Jew Trypho that the Hebrew scriptures are full of references to Jesus.

41. *Numbers* 21:8. *See* Justin Martyr, *First Apology*, Chapter 60, entitled 'Plato's Doctrine of the Cross'. In the venerable tradition of Jewish allegations of Greek plagiarism, Justin claims that Plato borrowed his idea of the 'Son of God' crucified in the cosmos (*Timaeus*, 34) from Moses.

42. *John* 3:14

43. *Joshua* 3:13

44. Ibid., 4:20. After the crossing of the Jordan Joshua orders that 12 stones be set up, one for each of the 12 tribes, at a place called Gilgal – Hebrew for 'wheel' or 'circle'. We suspect that in the later Jesus myth Gilgal was interpreted as the zodiac and the Jordan as the Milky Way. Sallust tells us that Attis being born by the river Gallus symbolizes 'the Galaxy, or milky circle, from which a passive body descends to the Earth' (Sallust, *On the Gods and the World*, 4). In mystical Judaism reincarnation is still called *gilgul*. Jesus' appearance in Galilee (which derives from the same root), where he selects the 12 disciples, echoes these early exploits of the Old Testament Jesus. *See* Drews, A. (1910), 240.

45. Eupolemus credits Abraham with the discovery of astrology, which he taught to both the Phoenicians and the Egyptian priests in Heliopolis. Eusebius, *Praeparatio Evangelica*, 9.17.3 and 9.17.8. *See* Gruen (1998), 148.

46. *Matthew* 2:2–16, cf the myth of the birth of Zeus. Kronos devours all the children of Rhea because of a prophecy that he would be overthrown by one of them. Rhea is smuggled away to a secret cave where she gives birth to Zeus, who later supplants his father.

47. Qur'an, sura 19, 'Maryam: Mary'. *See* Pelikan, J. (1996), 97.

48. *Matthew* 2:15

49. *See* Doherty, E., 'The Gospels as Midrash and Symbolism', (1999), 225ff.

50. *See* ibid., 240ff.

51. The Essene *Damascus Document*, 5.2–4. *See* Hoeller, S. A. (1989), 50.

52. Hoeller, 40. The writers of the Dead Sea Scrolls regarded the 'Teacher of Righteousness' as a new Joshua and his teachings as the 'Second Torah'. *See* Allegro, J. , *The Dead Sea Scrolls and the Christian Myth*, 170.

53. *Ephesians* 3:3–6

54. *See TJM*, 16ff.

55. Or Demeter and Dionysus. The Goddess was often represented in two aspects, as in the Sumerian myth of Inanna, who descends to the underworld kingdom of her twin sister Erishkegal, and in the Greek Mysteries as Demeter, the Goddess of the Earth, and her daughter Persephone, the Goddess of the Underworld. In Egypt the Goddess Nut is represented in two aspects. In her heavenly aspect she arches over the world and is speckled with stars. In her underworld aspect every night she swallows the sun, which passes through her body to be born again the next morning from her vulva.

56. Schaup, S. (1997), 3. In Sumer it was Innana and her son-lover Dumuzi, who were succeeded by the Assyrian-Babylonian Ishtar and Tammuz. In Asia Minor the principal Goddess was Cybele, who was worshipped at Rome as the Great Mother in conjunction with her son-lover Attis. The Great Goddess of the Phoenicians, Philistines and Moabites was Astarte or Asherah, who became Aphrodite in the Greek world.

57. *TJM*, 4

58. Philo, *On the Contemplative Life*, 11–12

59. Qumran, where the Essene library of the Dead Sea Scrolls was discovered in 1947, is only a few miles from the place where Joshua crossed the Jordan like a second Moses crossing the Red Sea. *See* Hoeller, op. cit., 29.

60. *Matthew* 1:1–18 and *Luke* 3:23–38

61. As Jung points out, the 'King' is a ubiquitous symbol of the self (quoted in Segal, R. A. (1992), 69). It is an obvious image of the self-ruled sage.

62. Plotinus, *Enn.*, 5.3.3–4

63. *Romans* 8:9 and *see 1 Corinthians* 2:11, 2:14, 3:16.

64. *Colossians* 1:24

65. The 'enthronement' of the initiate was a ritual carried out in the Pagan Mysteries, *see* Harrison, J. (1922), 514. The Christian Dion Chrysostom tells us that in the Mysteries the initiate is seated as if enthroned whilst his instructors dance around

him. Aristophanes parodies this ritual in his comedy *Clouds*, 254–5: '*Socrates*: You want to know the truth about the gods, what they really are? *Strepsiades*: By God I do, if it's possible. *Soc*: And to enter into communion with the Clouds, who are our deities? *Streps*: I'd like to very much. *Soc*: Then sit yourself upon the sacred sofa. *Streps*: I'm ready. *Soc*: Very well. Now take hold of this wreath. *Streps*: A wreath? Good heavens, Socrates, you're not going to sacrifice me? *Soc*: Oh no. We perform this ceremony for everyone we initiate.' Plato alludes to the same ritual in *Euthydemus*, 277d.

66. *See* discussion in Doherty, E. (1999), 160.

67. *Pistis Sophia*, 1.59

68. Paul alludes to (but does not quote) several sayings that are later attributed to Jesus in the gospels. Stanton observes: 'Paul fails to refer to a saying of Jesus at the very point where he might well have clinched his argument by doing so.' Stanton, G. (1995), 130

69. Most scholars agree that the gospels were written between *c*.70 CE and 100 CE, which makes Paul's epistles, written *c*.50 CE, the earliest Christian texts we possess. However, Paul tells us very little that could relate to an historical Jesus, apart from that fact that he was born of a woman, baptized, died and resurrected – all of which Pagans could equally claim of Osiris-Dionysius, without intending to imply that he had been an historical figure. Paul makes no mention of the cleansing of the Temple (which according to *Mark* and *Luke* was responsible for the decision of the chief priests and scribes to kill Jesus), there is no conflict with the authorities, no agony in Gethsemane, no trial, no thieves crucified with Jesus, no weeping women, no word about the place or the time and no mention of Judas or Pilate, no mention of Mary or Joseph, the Sermon on the Mount or any miracles performed by Jesus. G. A. Wells quotes the words of several New Testament scholars who refer to the 'scantiness of Paul's Jesus tradition' as 'surprising', 'shocking' and a 'matter of serious concern'. Stanton remarks that 'Paul's failure to refer more frequently and at greater length to the actions and teaching of Jesus is baffling' (op. cit., 131). As Wells also notes, Paul's complete silence on the historical Jesus 'remains a problem only for those who insist that there was a historical Jesus to be silent about' (*Did Jesus Exist?*, 21). In fact, Paul tells us quite specifically that he never met an historical Jesus but a being of light whom appeared to him in a vision. As we note in *TJM*, 167, in his *Letter to the Colossians* Paul describes himself as having been assigned by God the task of delivering his message 'in full'; of announcing 'the secret hidden for long ages and through many generations' which is now being disclosed to those chosen by God. And what is this great secret? Is it, as we might expect from an orthodox apostle, the 'good news' that Jesus had literally come and walked the Earth, worked miracles, died for our sins and returned from the dead? No. Paul writes: 'The secret is this: Christ in you.' *Colossians* 1:25–8

70. *Hebrews* 8:4

71. *Colossians* 1:25–8

72. *Romans* 6:4-6, *Ephesians* 4:22, *Colossians* 3:9

73. Rudolph considers that these Gnostic texts date to the beginning of the second century and in parts to the first. *See* Rudolph, K. (1987), 307. *The Epistle of Barnabbas* and *The Shepherd of Hermas* are also both believed to date from the first century, although like the Gnostic texts they were also excluded from the canon of the New Testament.

74. *See TJM*, 144ff.

75. Despite the widespread assertion that the gospels originated *c*.70 CE–110 CE, the only 'evidence' to back this up are some vague allusions in Papias and Polycarp, whose testimony has in turn been through the 'Holy Forgery Mill' of Irenaeus and Eusebius. We suggest that the texts we now call the gospels are in fact late second-century constructs. It is profoundly suspicious that Justin Martyr, writing in the middle of the second century in Rome, never mentions *Matthew, Mark, Luke* or *John* in his entire extant works and yet just a generation later in the same part of the world Irenaeus states that there are only four gospels and the canon is closed. Celsus, writing *c*.170 CE, knows nothing about *Matthew, Mark, Luke* or *John* but refers to gospels of Helen, Mariamme, Salome and a host of other women, and the texts known to Plotinus in Rome at the beginning of the third century are Gnostic works, copies of which have now been found in Nag Hammadi. Nor does 'hard' archaeological evidence support a first-century date for the gospels. In 1992 Carsten Thiede's *The Earliest Gospel Manuscript?* claimed that the three fragments stored for a long time in Magdalene College, Oxford, date from the middle of the first century. However, the eminent papyrologist Graham Stanton has clearly demonstrated that the fragments are written in the 'Biblical Uncial' handwriting which only emerged in the late second century (Stanton, op. cit., 13). In addition, these tiny fragments can tell us nothing about the texts they came from and for whole texts we must wait until the fourth century – a suspicious fact in itself.

76. According to Clement of Alexandria, there were originally three gospels attributed to Mark – the one in the New Testament, a second *Secret Gospel of Mark*, of which we have fragments, and a third oral gospel too profound to be written down, but passed on from master to master. *See The Secret Gospel of Mark* in Barnstone, W. (1984), 341. Professor Wilhelm Wrede (1859–1906) of Breslau University was the first to show that the supposedly 'primitive' *Gospel of Mark* had undergone extensive theological rewriting and editing. In 1919 Karl Ludwig Schmidt demonstrated that the gospel had been composed from previously existing fragments and that the connecting links between these were Mark's own invention.

77. *See* Wells, G. A. (1996), 95. The realization that Matthew and Luke copied *Mark* led to the discovery that they both also used another text which scholars have identified as Q. S. L. Davies (1983) demonstrates that both Q and *Thomas* are related works which depend heavily on Wisdom sayings.

78. *See* 'Gospel Truth?', *TJM*, 139ff.

79. *Joseph and Aseneth*, the story of the conversion of an Egyptian girl to Judaism written in the second or first century BCE, is considered by Momigliano to be the oldest Greek novel in existence. *See* Momigliano, A. (1971), 117. It was extremely popular with Christians in late antiquity.

80. *See* 'The Cruci-Fiction' in Price, R. M. (2000), 213ff. Price draws attention to the affinity of the gospel story to the genre of the ancient romance novel. Favourite themes common to both include lovers separated by tragic events (cf the Gnostic myth of Sophia and Jesus, their tragic separation and ultimate reunion), empty tombs and heroes surviving crucifixion. Bickerman writes about Hellenistic Jewish litera- ture and its passion for 'modernizing' biblical stories: 'Because pure fiction did not exist at this date, in order to express new ideas an author had to remodel an existing factual narrative.' Bickerman (1988), 206

81. Despite the best efforts of biblical archaeologists to prove that the Exodus took place during the reign of Rameses (*Genesis* 47:11), there is no evidence that this has any basis in historical fact. As Rohl states, 'The link between Rameses II and the Israelite bondage was an illusion without any real archaeological foundation.' Rohl, D. M. (1995), 115, 138

82. *Luke* tells us that Jesus was born at the time of the census of Quirinius, which schol- ars date to 6 CE. Unfortunately for the supposed inerrancy of the gospels, *Matthew* 2:1 tells us that Jesus' birth was during the reign of King Herod, who died 10 years earlier in 4 BCE.

83. According to Josephus and Philo, Pilate was particularly detested by the Jews (*see* Brandon, S. G. F. (1969), 292). Pilate was prefect for 10 years from 26 until 36, when he was sent back to Rome to answer for a massacre. He was so hated that he is the only prefect from the years 6 to 41 to be mentioned by name by Josephus and Philo. He violated Jewish religious taboos many times and was the first Roman to defile the Jerusalem Temple. Josephus writes, 'Pilate, during the night, secretly and undercov- er, conveyed to Jerusalem the images of Caesar known as *sigma*. When day dawned this caused great excitement among the Jews: for those who were near were amazed at the sight, which meant that their laws had been trampled on – they do not permit any graven image to be set up in the city.' Josephus (1959), 126

84. According to Plato's pupil Heraclides of Pontus, Pythagoras was the originator of the word 'philosopher'. *See* Cicero, *Discussions at Tusculum*, 5.3.7.

85. As Kingsley notes, 'Every single figure Parmenides encounters in his poem is female, and he is taught by a goddess. The universe he describes is a feminine one and if this man's poem represents the starting point for Western logic, then something very strange has happened for logic to end up the way it has.' (Kingsley, P. (1999), 56.) In *Timaeus*, Solon the Egyptian priest tells Socrates that 'the Goddess' was the founder of both Greek and Egyptian civilizations and expresses his 'gratitude to the Goddess to whom it has fallen to bring up and educate both your country and ours'. (Plato, *Timaeus*, 23)

86. Philo calls Sophia 'the Way' and the royal road which leads to God. *Deus Imm.* 142–4, *Somn.* 1.66; *Quaest in Genesis* 2.12; 4.46. There is a useful discussion, 'Sophia and Philo', in Scott, M. (1992), 58ff.

87. It is often assumed that the Hebrews were fiercely opposed to Goddess worship, but archaeologists have unearthed many inscriptions dedicated 'To Jehovah and his Asherah' (Armstrong, K. (1993), 58–9). Manasseh and Amon, early kings of Israel, worshipped an effigy of Asherah in the Temple (ibid., 64; *see especially* Scott, op. cit.,

37ff, 'Sophia in the Context of Ancient Near Eastern Goddesses'). *Ezekiel* 8.14 makes clear that the cult of Tammuz and Innana was celebrated in Jerusalem itself (*see also* Jaroslav, P. (1985), 902). The Old Testament is full of references to Israel defecting to the cults of her neighbours, for example *Numbers* 25.3.5 (in which the Lord tells Moses to have the ringleaders of the cult publicly crucified), *Deuteronomy* 23.18, *I Kings* 15.12, *Psalms* 28, 105, 106, *Jeremiah* 16.5, *Hosiah* 4.14, *Amos* 7.9 and *Wisdom* 12.3, 14.5.

88. A vestige of the cult of Ishtar and Marduk survives in the Old Testament *Book of Esther* as the story of Esther and Mordecai (*Esther* 8:2).

89. Jews stationed at Elephantine in Egypt in the fifth century BCE worshipped Jehovah and his goddess Anat Jahu. *See* Hoeller, S. A. (1989), 66.

90. The Wisdom texts of the Old Testament and the Apocrypha include *Proverbs*, *The Song of Songs*, *The Wisdom of Jesus ben Sirach*, *Ecclesiastes*, *Baruch* and *The Wisdom of Solomon*. Due to the number of references in the New Testament and Gnostic gospels, the Jewish Wisdom tradition was clearly of major importance to early Christianity. Wisdom (feminine in both Hebrew and Greek) is represented as present with God at the creation (*Proverbs* 8:22–31), but according to Baruch she is also said to have appeared on Earth and lived among men (*Baruch* 3:37). She is the guide of Israel (*The Wisdom of Solomon* 7:22–30) and, more significantly given the Gnostic exegesis of this key text, she is said to have led the Israelites during the Exodus (*The Wisdom of Solomon* 10). She sits by the throne of God (*The Wisdom of Solomon* 9.4), (cf the Orphic Goddess Justice, who sits by the throne of Zeus). Wisdom is loved by God (*The Wisdom of Solomon* 8.3) and the whole history of salvation is under her control (*The Wisdom of Solomon* 7:10–19). She is a redeemer who grants immortality (*The Wisdom of Solomon* 6:18, 8:17); *see* Rudolph, K. (1987), 281ff, *also* Matthews, C. (1992), 97ff. As several scholars have noted, the Jewish figure of Wisdom manifests many of the attributes ascribed to Isis in the cults of Alexandria. *See especially* Kloppenborg, *HTR* 75 (1982), 57–84. Resemblances to the Egyptian Goddess Maat have also been detailed; *see* Scott, op. cit., 67ff. This is not surprising given the Egyptian influence on *Proverbs*, the *locus classicus* of Jewish sapiential literature. *See* Pritchard, J. B. (ed.) (1955), 421–4.

91. *The Wisdom of Solomon* 8:4 and 7:14

92. Ibid., 6:12–16

93. The opening chapters of *The Wisdom of Solomon* depict the fate of the 'Just Man', Wisdom's ideal representative, whose suffering and death show his perfect obedience, which leads to his exaltation after death. *See* discussion in Wells, G. A., (1975), 38.

94. *Deuteronomy* 34.9

95. *Colossians* 2:3. *See also* 1 *Corinthians* 1:24, where Paul calls Christ 'the power of God and the Sophia of God'. As George Wells notes, 'The influence of Jewish Wisdom literature on Paul is undeniable ... statements about Wisdom in this literature are made of Jesus in the Pauline letters.' *See* Wells, G. A. (1999), 97, and (1975), 38.

96. *The Wisdom of Solomon* 2:20; *see* Wells, G. A. (1999), 99.

97. Irenaeus, *AH*, 1.30.12. Layton, B. (1987), 179

98. Wells, G. A. (1999), 102

99. *See* 269.173ff. In *Luke* 13:34 it is Wisdom who says, 'I will send them prophets and messengers.' Luke's retention of Wisdom suggests that he has remained faithful to *Q*, his source for this saying. *Matthew* 23:37, however, places these words in Jesus' mouth, even though the imagery of a hen gathering her chicks under her wings betrays the saying's origin. Price considers whether the sayings of *Q* were originally all attributed to Wisdom who is later 'shoved aside'. *See* Price, R. M. (2000), 163. Doherty concurs with this, *see* Doherty, E. (1999), 169, and 91, where he notes that sayings attributed to Wisdom are ascribed by Paul to God's Son who 'has absorbed both the Logos and personified Wisdom'. Regarding *The Gospel of Thomas*, which shares nearly a third of its sayings with *The Gospel of Q*, Davies observes: 'Jesus speaks as a wise man does, in the form of sayings of the wise, but he is not simply a wise man; he sometimes speaks as Wisdom herself. An intimate of God, agent in creation, Revealer of mysteries, the light within which the Image of God is hidden – all these are characteristics of Jesus as Wisdom in the Gospel of Thomas. In sum, the Christology (Jesusology) of the Gospel of Thomas is a naive but thoroughgoing Sophiology.' *See* 'Christology and Sophiology' in Davies, S. L. (1983).

100. In the bedrock layer of *Q* there is no sign of Jesus at all and the material is of a strikingly non-Jewish character. Many commentators consider it to be of Hellenistic Cynic origin. *See* Doherty, op. cit., 162.

101. *Luke* 11:49

102. Philo, *Fug.* 19. Likewise in the Gnostic literature Wisdom is repeatedly called 'Mother'. In the *Untitled Text* 2.16 the Mother establishes her 'First-born Son'. *See also Untitled Text* 2.12, *Teachings of Silvanus* 91,115. Irenaeus tells us that the Mother was also called by the Gnostics 'Ogdoad, Sophia, Terra, Jerusalem, Holy Spirit, and, with a masculine reference, Lord. Her place of habitation is an intermediate one, above the *demiurge* indeed, but below and outside of the Pleroma.' *See* Irenaeus, *AH*, 1.5.3, *also Clementine Recognitions*, where the creative power of God is called 'Wisdom, the Mother of all things', 2.12.

103. For the *Logos* as guide *see Op. Mund.* 118–19, *Fug.* 199–200, *Mut. Nom.* 113, 128. *See also* Scott, M. (1992), 92.

104. Philo, *Fug.* 109; *see also* 'Yaweh and the Feminine' in Martin, L. H. (1987), 108.

105. *See* 'The Hymn of Jesus' (the 'Round Dance') in *The Acts of John.*

106. Bultmann considered the original to be a hymn to a Gnostic redeemer (*see* Bultmann, R. (1971) 25–31, 61–6) also that the Wisdom sayings which underlie the Prologue originated in a Gnostic context (23, note 1). *See* Scott, op. cit., 88, *also The Original New Testament*, 479.

107. *See especially* Ringgren, H. (1947): 'Everything said of the Logos in the prologue of John is said of the heavenly figure of Wisdom in late Jewish literature.' *See also* Grant, R. M. (1966), 167. The impressive parallels are listed by Dodd, C. H. P. (1970), 274–7. See also Ashton, J., *NTS* 32 (1986) 161–86: 'The Logos of the Prologue is none other than Sophia.' *See* Scott, op. cit., 113.

108. Philo's Sophia is, as Engelsmann notes, 'a far cry from the Sophia of Proverbs who stands in the streets of Israel calling out to men to forsake the whore and to dine at her own table'. *See* Engelsmann, J. C. (1972), 102. Nonetheless, for Philo, Sophia is

still the embodiment of the unlimited knowledge of God. *See Migr. Abr.* 40–1, *Leg. All.*, 1.77–8.

109. The New Testament scholar F. C. Baur (1792–1860) was the first to notice that much of the New Testament only made sense once one realized that there was a major conflict between two rival Christianities, one Jewish in orientation and led by Peter, the other Gentile and led by Paul. *See* Price, R. M. (2000), 23.

110. The Church Father Irenaeus called Simon 'the father of all heretics' (*AH*, 3.1). Justin Martyr wrote his *Second Apology* solely for the purpose of repudiating his fellow countryman: 'And I despised the wicked and deceitful doctrine of Simon of my own nation. And if you give this book your authority, we will expose him before all, that, if possible, they may be converted. For this end alone did we compose this treatise.' (*Second Apology*, 15.) Shortly after Justin wrote this, *The Book of Acts* was forged, in part to attack Simon; *see* Acts 8:9. Justin clearly did not know this work or he would have quoted it. Its appearance a generation later in the hands of Irenaeus is profoundly suspicious.

111. *See* Welburn, A. (1994), 155. Hence it was natural that when the Romans made Palestine a province of the empire they located their administrative centre in Samaria.

112. The Jews considered the Samaritans to have betrayed the Covenant after they refused to take part in Ezra's reforms and rebuilding of the Second Temple, *c.*450 BCE. The Samaritans worshipped God on Mount Gerizim and revered the Torah of Moses but none of the succeeding books of the Old Testament.

113. Justin Martyr, *First Apology*, Chapter 26: 'And almost all the Samaritans, and a few even of other nations, worship him, and acknowledge him as the first god.' *See* Mead, G. R. S. (1906), 164.

114. Hippolytus, *Ref.*, 6.20. *See* Rudolph, K. (1987), 296.

115. Regarding the correspondences between the Essenes' *Community Rule* and the Zoroastrian *Avesta*, Burgmann writes, 'There are so many parallels that this Iranian-Zoroastrian writing, which is very much older, must have served as the foundation for the Qumran text.' (*See* Welburn, A. (1994), 51.) Zoroastrian influence on Gnosticism, particularly its 'dualistic' doctrines, has been repeatedly argued for by scholars. This influence may well have been via Platonism, however, as Colotes, 280–250 BCE, alleged that Plato had borrowed from Zoroaster (Proclus, *In Rpubl.* 2.109). Aristoxenus likewise claimed that Pythagoras had been a pupil of the Chaldaean Zaratas (fr. 13 Wehrli). (*See* Momigliano, A. (1971), 143.)

116. Faustus reappears in history as the name of the Manichean Gnostic who came to debate with the ex-Manichean Augustine (*see Contra Faustus*, http://www.webcom.com/~gnosis/library/polem.htm). The Faust legend lived on in the work of Marlowe and particularly Goethe (1749–1832). In his quest for the 'Eternal Feminine' (the Sophia of the Gnostics), Goethe's Faust travels to ancient Greece to find Helen of Troy, the same Helen who is said to have travelled with Simon Magus. The reappearance of Helen in Goethe's alchemical epic is testimony to the persistence of the Gnostic spirit in Europe.

117. The Church Fathers claimed that Simon considered himself a Christ. The coy statement in *Acts* 8:9 that Simon claimed he was 'some great one' indicates that he was in fact hailed as a 'Christ' (*see* Hippolytus, Book 10; Tertullian, *Against all Heresies*, Chapter 1; etc). Simon, in his 'Great Annunciation', claimed to be an incarnation of the 'Great Unlimited Power' or 'Standing One' and was considered a god by his disciples. Schmithals discerns behind the 'Standing One' a reference to the Christ. *See* Welburn, op. cit., 159.

118. Ibid., 155ff

119. Irenaeus, *AH*, Chapter 23: 'Simon of Samaria, from whom all sorts of heresies derive their origin, formed his sect out of the following materials: Having redeemed from slavery at Tyre, a city of Phoenicia, a certain woman named Helena, he was in the habit of carrying her about with him, declaring that this woman was the first conception of his mind, the mother of all.' *See also* Hippolytus, *Ref.*, 6.14. In the *Clementine Homilies*, we are told that 'Simon goes about in the company of Helen and, even until now, stirs up the crowds. He says that he has brought down this Helen from the highest heavens to the world; she is the Queen, since she is all-maternal Being and Wisdom (Sophia).' Quoted in Grant, R. (1961), 27.

120. Irenaeus, op. cit.,1.29. *See* Mead, G. R. S. (1906), 583.

121. For Barbelo, *see especially Allogenes*, *The Apocryphon of John*, *Melchizedek*, *Marsanes*, *The Three Steles of Seth* and *Pistis Sophia*. In *Trimorphic Protennoia* Barbelo says of herself: 'I am the Image of the Invisible Spirit, and it is through me that the All took shape, and (I am) the Mother (as well as) the Light which she appointed as Virgin ... the incomprehensible Womb, the unrestrainable and immeasurable Voice.' NHC, 13.1.38.

122. Hippolytus, op. cit., 6.14.1

123. This was especially the teaching of the Alexandrian Platonist Carpocrates and his son Epiphanes. Irenaeus tells us that the Carpocratians thought that souls should have every enjoyment of life, so that when they depart they are deficient in nothing and that freedom must be gained by a complete demonstration of it whilst on Earth. Irenaeus, op. cit., 1.25.4. *See also* Rudolph, K. (1987), 256, and Clement of Alexandria, who calls Epiphanes the founder of the school (*Strom.*, 3.5.2). A female follower called Marcellina brought Epiphanes' teachings to Rome, where the sect of the 'Marcellians' was flourishing c.130 CE; *see* Rudolph, op. cit., 299.

124. Pagels, E. (1979), 62. Elsewhere Basilides writes: 'Those who confess Jesus as the crucified one are still enslaved to the God of the Jews. He who denies it has been freed and knows the plan of the unbegotten Father.' Barnstone, W. (1984), 626ff

125. Cerdo, quoted in Irenaeus, op. cit., 1.27.1

126. The Paulicians can be traced historically to the mid-seventh century. They may in turn derive from the Massalian Gnostics of fourth-century Syria. *See* Stoyanov, Y. (2000), 128–9.

127. *See especially* Stoyanov, op. cit, 289ff, for a detailed examination of the Paulicians, Manichaeans, Massalians and other 'heretical' groups, and their part in the emergence of the Bogomils in the Balkans and Bulgaria and the Cathars in southern France and Italy. Arthur Evans famously called the Bogomils the first Protestants in western Europe, bearers of what he called 'Gnostic Puritanism'.

128. Jerome, quoted by both Godwin, J. (1981), 85, and Lacarrière, J. (1989), 100, but unsourced.

129. Clement of Alexandra, op. cit., 7.17. Valentinus said that Jesus used metaphors in public and his complete teachings were passed on to his disciples in private, and that this was the real meaning of *Luke* 8:9–10: 'The knowledge about the secrets of the Kingdom of Heaven has been given to you, but to the rest it comes by means of parables so that they may look but not see and listen but not understand.' (Irenaeus, *AH*, 1:3:1.) This secret tradition provides the key that is essential for a complete understanding of Jesus' message, as one of his followers stated: 'The scriptures are ambiguous and the truth cannot be extracted from them by those who are ignorant of tradition.' (Ibid., 3:2:1.) The Valentinians claimed that the secret teachings are meaningful only to those who are spiritually mature (pneumatically initiated) because 'their value can be judged only on a spiritual basis' (*1 Corinthians* 2:14). Paul and the other apostles revealed these teachings only to those who were 'spiritually mature' (ibid., 2:6).

130. Martin, L. H. (1987), 138

131. *See* list in Layton, B. (1987), 267. The Valentinian movement was divided into two wings, the Italic school founded by Ptolemy and Heracleon, and the Oriental school founded by Theodotus and Marcus.

132. Pagels suggests that ecclesiastical Christians might have preferred to exclude Paul's letters 'but it was too late, he was already a chief apostle and stood in high regard'; *see* Pagels, E. (1975), 161. Towards the end of the second century the Literalists therefore took another approach. *The Acts of the Apostles*, the Pastoral Letters, *2 Thessalonians*, *3 Corinthians* and other documents were forged to refute specific Gnostic/Pauline doctrines in the apostle's own name. *See* Lüdemann, G. (1995), 201.

133. *See* 'The Genuine Paul?' in *TJM*, 160ff.

134. *1 Corinthians* 2:14. The Gnostic Theodotus tells us that Paul taught in 'two ways at once' in order to reach both psychic and pneumatic Christians (Clement, *Exc. Theod.*, 23.3–4). *See* Pagels, op. cit., for a full exegesis of these different levels of teaching in Paul.

135. *2 Corinthians* 11:6

136. *Colossians* 1:28

137. In *Acts* 9:3 Saul sets out to Damascus armed with letters of authority from the high priest in order to persecute followers of 'the Way'. It is unlikely that Paul was headed for Damascus in Syria, as this was a Roman province over which Jerusalem had no authority. Qumran, however, with its community of fiercely anti-Jerusalem Jews, might well have been Paul's destination (*see* Baigent, M., and Leigh, R., (1991), 144ff. The Essenes referred to their faith as 'the Way' and the Dead Sea Scrolls also refer to the 'Mystery' that has been hidden for a long time and is now revealed to the elect, a sentiment expressed by Paul in *1 Corinthians* 2:7, *Romans* 16:25 and *Ephesians* 3:3–9. *See* Ringgren, H. (1995), 62ff, and Allegro, J. (1956), 145.

138. The *Damascus Document* found amongst the Dead Sea Scrolls tells of how the 'Teacher of Righteousness' took the 'righteous remnant' (the Essenes) into the wilderness where they entered into a 'new covenant in the land of Damascus' (6.19; 19.33).

139. Josephus tells us that the Essenes regarded 'fate [*heimarmene*] as the mistress of all things' (*Antiquities*, 13:174). In *Galatians* 4:3 Paul refers to 'bondage under the elemental rulers of the cosmos', *ta stoiceia tou kosmou, stoicheia tou kosmou*, a phrase equivalent to the astrological meaning of *heimarmene*. *See* Martin, op. cit., 106–7.

140. *Ephesians* 6:12: 'For we wrestle not against flesh and blood, but against principalities [*arche*], against powers, against the rulers [*kosmokrator*] of the darkness of this world [*aion*], against spiritual wickedness in high places.'

141. *Galatians* 5:1, 2:4, 5:13; *1 Corinthians* 7:21; *2 Corinthians* 3:17. *See* Martin, L. H. (1987), 123.

142. *Philippians* 2:8 and 2:10–11

143. *Romans* 3:30

144. *Galatians* 3:6–11; *see also* 3:13–14.

145. *Ephesians* 2:14–16

146. *See* Layton, B. (1987), 321. The Greek *khrestos* was pronounced like *khristos*.

147. Several Gnostic groups are known to have referred to Jesus not as Christ, but as Crestus, 'the Good' (Mead, G. R. S. (1906), 249). According to Suetonius (*Life of Claudius*, 25), in a text assumed to refer to Christians causing trouble in Rome in the middle of the first century, these Jews are said to be followers of Crestus. An inscription found in a Syrian Marcionite church dated 318 CE reads: 'The Lord and Saviour Jesus the Good' – Chrestos, not Christos. In the earliest New Testament we possess, the Codex Sinaticus (late fourth century) three passages – *Acts* 11:26, 26:28, *1 Peter* 4:16 – use the name 'Chrestian' for Christian. Profoundly influenced by Plato as they were, the Gnostics probably chose this name as Plato had used it as the highest definition of God. A trace of this is left in the gospels where Jesus echoes the words of Pythagoras, who was called 'wise' and responded: 'Why do you call me wise? No one is wise but God.' In the gospels Jesus responds to being called 'good' with: 'Why callest thou me good? There is none good but one, that is, God.' (*Matthew* 19:17.) This novel twist must have delighted readers of the Gnostic texts.

148. *2 Corinthians* 11:4

149. *Galatians* 5:12

150. *See* discussion in Lüdemann, G. (1995), 56ff, of the Pseudo-Clementine polemic against Paul. Paul is regarded as 'the enemy' and a new gospel had to be sent out to correct his 'heresies' (*Pseudo-Clement Hom.*, 2.17.4). According to Epiphanius, *The Ascension of James* (a hero of the Ebionite Gnostics) told how Paul had originally been Greek but had gone over to Judaism because he wanted to marry the high priest's daughter. When she turned him down he wrote against the Jews and ridiculed their law (Lüdemann, op. cit., 62). *See TJM*, 161ff.

151. *Colossians* 4:10–12. Paul writes, 'Of the Jewish Christians, these are the only ones that work with me,' and names Mark, Aristachus, Barnabas and Jesus Justus. Paul recruits Gentiles but is attacked by Jews in Antioch (*Acts* 13:45ff, Iconium 14:1ff, Thessalonica 17:1ff and Macedonia 18:4ff). Only in Ephesus is he attacked solely by angry Pagans (19:19).

152. Epiphanius, *c.*375 CE, describes Ebionism as still existing in Syria two centuries before the birth of Islam. Several scholars have suggested that Ebionism was developed and

amplified in Islam. Von Harnack defined Islam as 'a transformation on Arab soil of a Jewish religion that had itself been transformed by Gnostic Judaeo-Christianity' (von Harnack, A., *Dogmengeschichte*, II.537, quoted in Corbin, H. (1983), 66).

153. Irenaeus calls the Ebionites 'Gnostics' (*AH*, 1.26). Eusebius records that it was already too late for Melito to rehabilitate the Jerusalem Christians as they had all 'become' Ebionite heretics (*HE*, 4.26.14). We suggest they always had been (see Lüdemann, op. cit., 31, 247, note 111; *TJM*, 172ff). According to Klijn there were three Jewish/Christian gospels circulating in the second century – *The Gospel of the Ebionites* (east of the Jordan), *The Gospel according to the Nazarenes* (Beroia in Syria) and *The Gospel of the Hebrews* (Egypt). *See* Robinson, J. M. (1978), and Boardman, J., Griffin, J., Murray, O., (1986), 10. For the remains of *The Gospel of the Ebionites*, *see* Barnstone, W. (1984), 336ff.

154. *Galatians* 1:19

155. 'Brother' appears throughout Paul's letters, clearly a common designation Christians gave to each other. Mark's gospel gives Jesus four brothers and more than 500 'brothers' are mentioned in *1 Corinthians* 15:6.

156. James is 'said to be the Lord's brother only in a purely spiritual sense' (NHC, 5.3.24.10–30, in Robinson, J. M. (1978), 260).

157. *See* Wells, G. A., (1975), 124ff. As Wells notes, 'There is nothing in Paul's letters to support the view that the Cephas he mentions had the career and connection with Jesus alleged of Peter in the gospels.' The recently discovered *Letter of the Apostles* lists Peter and Cephas as separate apostles (see 'The curious differentiation of Cephas and Peter' in Metzger, B. M. (1987), 181, note 43; *also TJM*, 153). It is odd that the gospels refer 156 times to Peter, who starts life as Simon but is later renamed Peter by Jesus (*Mark* 3:16). The identification of Cephas with Peter is based on only *one* reference in *John* 1:42. Here Peter is renamed Cephas and then *never* referred to in this way again! Paul mentions a Cephas five times, but *never* identifies him as Peter. Only once, in *Galatians* 7–9, does Paul mention a Peter; however, a close look at this passage leaves one with the question as to why the same man is called by two different names in the same sentence.

158. Irenaeus, *AH*, 1.31.1. *See* Rudolph, K. (1987), 139.

159. *On the Origin of the World* calls the serpent 'the wisest of all creatures' (NHC, 2.5.118.25). Other Gnostics asserted that Sophia became the snake and 'thus introduced Gnosis into humankind' (Irenaeus, op. cit., 1.30.7).

160. Marcion, *Antitheses*, quoted in Lacarrière, J. (1989), 96.

161. 'They keep asking us how it is that when they confess the same things and hold the same doctrine, we call them heretics!' Irenaeus, op. cit., 3.16.1

162. Epiphanius and the Messalian Gnostics, *see* Lacarrière, op. cit., 110.

163. The Greek poets, the Mysteries of Eleusis and Samothrace and the mythology of the Jews expressed one philosophy. Hippolytus, *Ref.*, 5.3, and *see* Mead, G. R. S. (1906), 200.

164. Hippolytus tells us that the Naassene Gnostics 'constantly attend the mysteries called those of the "Great Mother", supposing especially that they behold by means of the ceremonies performed there the entire mystery'; op. cit., 5.4.

165. The Naassenes referred to the Son as 'many-named ... Assyrians style thee thrice-longed-for Adonis, and the whole of Egypt Osiris ... Greeks denominate Wisdom; Samothracians, venerable Adam; Haemonians, Corybas; and Phrygians Papa ... multiform Attis ... Pan ... Bacchus ... shepherd of brilliant stars.' Hippolytus, op. cit., 5.4. *See also* Mead, op. cit., 203.

166. Hippolytus, op. cit., 5.1: 'The Sethians ... purloining their theories from the wise men among the Greeks, they have patched together their own system out of shreds of opinion taken from Musaeus, and Linus, and Orpheus.' According to Hippolytus (ibid., 5.2), the Naassenes equated the Christ with the sacred marriage performed at Eleusis: 'This is the Christ who, he says, in all that have been generated, is the portrayed Son of Man from the unportrayable Logos. This, he says, is the great and unspeakable mystery of the Eleusinian rites, Hye, Cye.' (*See also* Mead, op. cit., 216.) The cries 'Hye, Cye' went up at the end of the Eleusinian Mysteries when two vessels were poured out, one to the east and one to the west, whilst the initiates cried out to the heavens: 'Rain,' and to the Earth: 'Conceive.'

167. Hadrian writing to the Consul Servianus. At this time, c.130 CE, several of the most renowned Gnostics – Valentinus, Basilides and Carpocrates – were teaching in Alexandria. *See* Lacarrière, op. cit., 59.

168. Irenaeus, *AH*, 1.25.6

169. Hippolytus, op. cit., 4.51. This criticism of the Gnostics is uncannily similar to that of the Pagan critic Plotinus, who writes: 'All this terminology is piled up only to conceal their debt to the ancient Greek philosophers...' (*Enn.*, 2.9.6.) Scholarship has been incredibly slow in taking these early testimonies seriously.

170. The Nag Hammadi library demonstrates the wide catchment area of beliefs that make up early Christianity. For those who see Gnosticism as a radical form of Platonism, there are fragments of the works of Plato. For those who see parallels with Hermeticism, there are fragments of the Hermetica. For those who trace Gnosticism to Iranian origins, there is the apocalypse of 'Zostrianos' = Zarathustra/Zoroaster. For those who see its origin in Judaism, there are traditions ascribed to Seth, Melchizedek and Adam. As Price notes, 'Gnosticism was not just a "many-headed heresy", as the Church Fathers called it; it was a doctrine with many roots as well.' Price, R. M. (2000), 32–3.

171. Plotinus, op. cit., Book 2, tractate 9, usually entitled 'Against the Gnostics'. Plotinus does not mention his opponents by name, or refer to them as Gnostics, but their identity as 'Christians and other sectaries' is confirmed by Porphyry. Plotinus charges his opponents with 'abandoning the ancient philosophy' in favour of revelations by Zostrianos, Allogenes and others, works that have now been rediscovered at Nag Hammadi (Wallis, R. T. (1992), 112). What is extraordinary is that although in Rome at the time of Plotinus, c.250, there were many Gnostic sects, including Sethians, Barbelognostics, Ophites, Archontics, Valentinians and others (the fact that Plotinus, Porphyry and others wrote against them demonstrates that they represented a real threat to 'The True Doctrine'), Literalist Christianity as we now know it (i.e. the literal story without its accompanying Gnosis) is not mentioned. As one scholar notes, 'There is in my view no certain reference to non-Gnostic Christianity in the *Enneads*.' *See* Wallis, op. cit., 475.

172. Plotinus, op. cit., 2.9.10

173. Ammonius Saccus, *fl. c.*200 CE, was a Pagan philosopher of Alexandria. Although he taught both Origen and Plotinus, little is known about him and he apparently wrote no books.

174. *The Gospel of Philip*, NHC, 2.3.53, in Robinson, J. M. (1978), 142

175. Since the isolation of Q it has become clear that one of the major influences on early Christianity was Cynic/Stoic philosophy, which had spread to the eastern Mediterranean at an early date. Although the founder of Stoicism, Zeno of Citium in Cyprus (350–260 BCE), lived and taught at Athens all his life, he was a Semite who never lost his accent and was nicknamed 'the Phoenician' (Athenagoras, *Deispnos*, 13.2, and Cicero, *Fin.*, 4.20.56). His father travelled between Tyre, Sidon and Athens, from where he brought back a number of 'Socratic books' which attracted his son to Athens (DL, 7.31–2). In Athens Zeno sought out that person 'most like Socrates' and was directed to Crates of Thebes, the successor of Diogenes (ibid., 7.3). Whilst still a Cynic, Zeno wrote his *Politeia*, or 'Republic', a radically egalitarian and anti-authoritarian description of the ideal *Politeia*. Zeno dismissed the current political system as useless. In his ideal society there would be no gymnasia, law courts, coinage, temples or images of the gods. The institution of marriage would be abolished in favour of open relationships in which men would feel paternal affection for all children. There would be no distinction in the dress of men and women, indeed clothes would be purely functional and could be abandoned without inhibitions. Homosexuality would be acceptable. Given the subjection of the East after Alexander, it is not surprising that Cynicism and Stoicism proved most attractive to the masses. The Cynics formulated a doctrine which especially appealed to those who felt themselves simple and oppressed, which has been well described by Gomperz as 'the philosophy of the proletariat of the Greek world'. *See* Arnold, E. V. (1911), 49, and Erskine's excellent study: *The Helleistic Stoa:Political Thought and Action*, Cornell University Press, 1990. Nor is it surprising that scholars have isolated as the bedrock of Q a collection of Stoic/Cynic sayings attributed to Jesus. *See especially* Downing, Francis Gerald, *Cynics and Christian Origins*, T & T Clark, 1992.

176. Epiphanes' Utopia is clearly a restating of Zeno's *Politeia*. *See* Rudolph, K. (1987), 269, for Epiphanes' *On Righteousness* and Lacarrière, J. (1989), 73–6, for Epiphanes' *On Justice*.

177. Quoted in Lacarrière, op. cit., 75. Also anticipated is the Communist maxim 'From each according to their ability, to each according to their needs'. *Pistis Sophia* (3.124) states: 'For from every one to whom more is entrusted, of him will more be demanded, and to whom much is handed over, of him much is required.'

178. Beginning with Plato's *Republic*, followed by Antisthenes, who wrote a *Politeia*, now lost (*see* Arnold, op. cit., 66), which formed the basis for the *Politeia* of Zeno. Crates the Cynic put forward a playful ideal *polis* – the *Pera*, the philosopher's bag, which symbolized his self-sufficiency, *autarkeia* (DL, 6.85; *see* Erskine, A. (1990), 29). When the Platonic tradition was revived in the Renaissance it sparked a host of utopias by Giordano Bruno, Campanella and most famously Thomas More, whose *Utopia* is dedicated to the visionary Pico della Mirandola, protégé of Marsilio Ficino.

179. The followers of Pythagoras established religious communities dedicated to the 'Orphic Life' in southern Italy in the sixth century BCE. Men and women were admitted as equals, all possessions were shared in common, neophytes took a five-year vow of silence. The Pythagoreans rose at dawn to worship the rising sun, spent the day in philosophical study and religious observances, and at a communal evening meal there were readings from sacred scriptures. They were strict vegetarians, wore white and practised celibacy. These practices are distinctly reminiscent of the practices of the mediaeval monasteries, but this similarity is not accidental. Anthony, the founder of the first Christian monastery, was himself a Pythagorean and modelled his monastic community on the Pythagorean communities of Croton in southern Italy. *See* Lietzmann, H. (1961), Book 4, 136ff.

180. *See* Price, R. M. (2000), 114.

181. The 32 references to the Kingdom of Heaven in the gospels refer to it as 'Kingdom of the Skies' (*ouranos*). However, when Paul refers to the Kingdom of Heaven in *Philippians* 3:20, he refers to it not as a *basileia* (from *basileus*, 'king'), but as a *politeuma*, a commonwealth or republic ruled by its citizens. This is much more in keeping with the Gnostic vision of themselves as the 'kingless ones'.

182. *On the Origin of the World*, NHC, 2.5.124, and *see* Rudolph, op. cit., 206.

183. Tertullian, *DP*, 41, and *see* Pagels, E. (1979), 66.

184. The Gnostics were in principle anti-cult. Irenaeus writes of the Valentinians: 'They reject all practices, and maintain that the mystery of the unspeakable and invisible power ought not to be performed ... nor that of the unthinkable and immaterial beings through sensible and corporeal things. Perfect salvation is the cognition itself of the ineffable greatness: for since through ignorance came about defect and passion, the whole system springing from ignorance is dissolved by knowledge.' (Irenaeus, *AH*, 1.21.4; *see also* Martin, L. H. (1987), 142, and Wallis, R. T. (1992), 254.) As Lacarrière notes, 'For the counter-nature the Gnostics preached, the counter-life they attempted to lead on all possible levels, implied in turn a system, or an anti-system, which ran out of steam precisely because of its own refusal to "exist" and to set itself up as an institution.' (Lacarrière, op. cit., 72)

185. Epiphanes, *On Righteousness*, quoted in Lacarrière, op. cit., 75. Amongst Valentinians women were equal to men and acted as prophets, teachers, travelling evangelists, healers and priestesses.

186. As Kingsley notes, 'One of the – by classical standards – most extraordinary features of ancient Pythagoreanism was the equal status of women side by side with men.' *See* Kingsley, P. (1995), 162.

187. Philo, *On the Contemplative Life*, 68

188. As Hoffmann observes, 'One cannot but be impressed by the number of women-founded sects known to Celsus.' *See* Hoffmann, J. (1987), 42.

189. Irenaeus admits that Marcus had attracted 'many foolish women', including the wife of one of his deacons, but claims that this was because Marcus was a diabolically clever seducer. However, his later admission that the Marcosians worshipped the feminine element of the divine being, 'She who is before all things', and encouraged women to prophesy and act as priests must surely be the real reason. Irenaeus, op. cit., 1.13.5, 1.13.1–2, and Hippolytus, *Ref.*, 6.35. *See* Pagels, op. cit., 80.

190. 'The very women of these heretics, how wanton they are! For they are bold enough to teach, to dispute, to enact exorcisms, to undertake cures – it may be even to baptize.' Tertullian, *DP*, 41

191. *1 Corinthians 9:5*

192. *See The Acts of Paul and Thecla*, Barnstone, W. (1984), 445. The tradition of Paul's companion Thecla, who baptizes and preaches, was part of a well-established oral tradition in Syria. Thecla's story is one of many in the Apocryphal *Acts* which portray women giving up riches and sexual activity to follow the Apostles. Like her Athenian antecedent Hipparchia, Thecla was said to be an aristocratic woman who left family, fiancé and fortune to follow Paul.

193. *Romans 16:3, 7, 15*. Paul tells us that Prisca and her husband risked their lives to save his. He praises Junia as a prominent apostle who had been imprisoned for her labour. Mary and Persis are commended for their hard work, *Romans 16:6, 12*. Euodia and Syntyche are called his fellow-workers in the gospel, *Philippians 4:2–3*.

194. Hippolytus, op. cit., 6.20. *See* Rudolph, K. (1987), 296.

195. Hippolytus, 10.15. These early Gnostics were again following in the tradition of the Cynics. When the Cynic philosopher Crates (fourth century BCE) won the love of the aristocrat Hipparchia, she abandoned all her property and went from house to house with Crates dressed in the same Cynic cloak (DL, 7.96–7; Arnold, E. V. (1911), 65). Hipparchia flaunted Athenian custom by going to dinners with her husband and was proud of her education, time she would otherwise have wasted at the loom (DL, 6.97–8; Baldry, H. C. (1965),106–7).

196. The work of the alchemist Zosimos (*fl. c.*300 CE), abounds in Gnostic concepts and images. Jung called Zosimos 'the connecting link between alchemy and Gnosticism', *see* Jung, C. G. (1957), 437. In later medieval alchemy, the alchemists' *soror mystica* continued to remain essential for the success of 'the Work'. *See* Jung, C. G. (1983), 134.

197. Montanus, *fl. c.*170 CE, claimed to be an incarnation of the Paraclete (a claim also made by Mani a few years later) and called ecstasy the only true Christianity. Despite their taste for ecstatic worship the Montanists were also said to possess an 'infinite number of books' (Hippolytus, op. cit., 8.12. Armstrong, K. (1993), 124). Sadly, everything we know about the Montanist movement comes from patristic polemical sources. Their own writings were burned by imperial edict in 398 CE. *See* Scott, M. (1992), 252, *also* Lane-Fox, R. (1986), 409.

198. Lacarrière calls this deconditioning 'the very heart of Gnostic doctrine'. Lacarrière, J. (1989), 97f

199. As Jonas notes, the seemingly contrary paths of the ascetic and the libertine derive from a shared philosophy. The ascetic believes that the possession of Gnosis obliges him to avoid contamination by the world, whilst the latter considers that Gnosis gives him the privilege of absolute freedom. *See* Jonas, H. (1958), 46, 275.

200. Epiphanes, *On Justice*, quoted in Lacarrière, op. cit., 75

201. The mystical marriage was at the heart of both the Pagan Mystery schools and Gnosticism. The 'Bridal Chamber' is referred to in *The Gospel of Thomas, The Authoritative Teaching, Teachings of Silvanus, The Second Treatise of the Great*

Seth, *Dialogue of the Saviour*, *Tripartite Tractate* and over 25 times in *The Gospel of Philip*. References are also found in the gospels, *Mark* 2:19 and more significantly in *John* 2:1–11, where Jesus is said to have 'manifested his Glory' at the wedding at Cana. *John* 3:39 describes John the Baptist as the 'bridegroom's friend'. Paul calls *Genesis* 2:24, 'The two shall be one flesh', a 'great mystery' for Christians.

202. *See* Wallis, R. T. (1992), 262. Augustine tells us about the Adamites who pray, listen to sermons and celebrate the Eucharist naked and 'because of this their church is paradise'. (*See* Lacarrière, op. cit., 86.) In *The Gospel of Thomas* the disciples ask Jesus, 'When will you appear to us, and when will we see you?' Jesus replies, 'When you strip without being ashamed, and you take your clothes and put them under your feet like little children and trample them, then you will see the son of the living one and you will not be afraid.' (*The Gospel of Thomas*, 37)

203. Epiphanius, *Pan.*, 26.17.4ff. Epiphanius immediately reported the Gnostics he found in Egypt to the bishop and 80 people were expelled from the city (ibid., 9; *see also* Lacarrière, op. cit., 86).

204. Lacarrière, op. cit., 70. *See* Jung. C. G., *Aion*, *CW*, 9.2.313, *also* Segal, R. A. (1992), 72.

205. The Carpocratians were in fact teaching the Pagan doctrine of reincarnation with its associated teachings about karma. *See* Hippolytus, *Ref.*, 7.20. They stated that this was the true meaning of Jesus' words in *Matthew* 5:25, 'You won't get out till you pay the last farthing.' Irenaeus writes that a soul 'must pass from body to body, until he has experience of every kind of action which can be practised in this world, and when nothing is longer wanting to him, then his liberated soul should soar upwards to God' (Irenaeus, *AH*, 1.25.4). *See* Mead, G. R. S. (1906), 229.

206. *Romans* 3:8

207. As Heraclitus writes, 'For God all things are fair and good and just, but men have taken some things as unjust and others as just.' Heraclitus, LXVIII in Kahn's numbering; Kahn, C. H. (1979), 61

208. Lacarrière, J. (1989), 109

CHAPTER 3: CHURCH OF THE ANTI-CHRIST

1. Augustine, *Retractions*, 1.13.3

2. Freke, T., and Gandy, P., *The Complete Guide to World Mysticism*, Piatkus Books, 1997

3. The criticisms of the Gnostics by Irenaeus, and especially by the Roman lawyer Tertullian, display the typical Roman distaste for ecstasy, woman's participation and 'cultish' behaviour generally. This was the complete antithesis of the sober dignity, piety and patriarchy of Roman religious practice and was regarded as *superstitio* – literally 'over-enthusiastic' religion. For example, when the Cult of the Great Mother was imported into Rome at the beginning of the second century, the high priest had to be a man, not a woman as was usual. The practice of castration in honour of Attis was also banned. When the Bacchic Mysteries were put down in 186 BCE, the hysteria whipped up against them was that they were orgiastic, oriental and led by women. The violent purge against them set the trend for attacking imported Mystery cults, *collegia*, burial societies and other groups for centuries after.

4. *See* 'Taking Things Literally', *TJM*, 211ff. The Pythagoreans allegorized the works of Homer in the sixth century BCE. This technique was then taken over by Hellenistic Jews. It is used extensively by Philo, often in the most contrived fashion, to read Platonic philosophy into the Hebrew scriptures.

5. Jesus' prophecies in *Matthew* 16:28 and *Luke* 21:12–36 that some of his audience would live to see the Apocalypse were, if taken literally, clearly mistaken. *See TJM*, 143–4.

6. *See* for example, Tertullian, *Apology*, 50. Although Tertullian wished to 'obtain from God complete forgiveness' by martyrdom, he somehow managed to avoid this fate.

7. *See* 'Glorious Gore', *TJM*, 225ff.

8. According to Irenaeus the Carpocratians considered themselves, and the other disciples such as Paul and Peter, as 'in no way inferior to Jesus himself'. Irenaeus, *AH*, 1.25.2, quoted in Hanratty, G. (1997), 27.

9. *Luke* 6:40

10. Augustine announced the triumph of Literalist Fundamentalism, writing, 'Nothing is to be accepted except on the authority of scripture, since greater is that authority than all powers of the human mind.' (Quoted in Fidler, D. (1993), 180.) He also declared: 'I would not believe the Gospel if the authority of the Catholic Church did not compel me.' (Ibid., 320)

11. The Bishop of Newark writes about his disillusionment with Literalism: 'I look at the authority of the Scriptures as one who has been both nurtured by and then disillusioned with the literal Bible. My devotion to the Bible was so intense that it led me into a study that finally obliterated any possibility that the Bible could be related to on a literal basis... A literal Bible presents me with far more problems than assets. It offers me a God I cannot respect, much less worship ... Those who insist on biblical literalism thus become unwitting accomplices in bringing about the death of the Christianity they so deeply love.' John Shelby Spong, quoted in Leedom, T. C. (1993), 116.

12. Barnstone observes that: 'We can say categorically that the Bible, with the absence of sacred texts from the entire inter Testamental period, with its acceptance of a small and repetitious canon for the New Testament, with the exclusion of all later Christian Apocrypha, and the total rejection of Gnostic scriptures, has given us a highly censored and distorted version of ancient religious literature. The impression is given that somehow Christianity sprang self-generated like a divine entity, with no past, into its historical setting.' (Barnstone, W. (1984), xviii.) Mack observes about the canon: 'What is striking is the severe reduction of a large spirited literature to a very small set of gospels and letters.' (*See* Mack, B. L. (1993), 228.)

13. This belief has been undermined by the discovery that *Mark* was the source used by both Luke and Matthew, and perhaps even by John, whose supposed independence of *Mark* is challenged.

14. The names Matthew, Mark, Luke and John never appear in Justin Martyr's extant work, written in the mid-second century. However, a generation later, Irenaeus brings forward these four gospels as authoritative: 'It is not possible that the Gospels can be either more or fewer in number than they are, for there are four zones of the world and four principal winds.' (Quoted in Stevenson, J. (1957), 117.) As Lüdemann

notes, Irenaeus' 'artificial arguments' at least demonstrate that the idea was a novelty which needed defending (Lüdemann, G. (1995), 196). Likewise Justin has never heard of *Acts* (or Paul, the hero of most of that book, whom he likewise never mentions), which turns up in Irenaeus for the first time *c.*175 CE. It is widely accepted that it was Marcion's set of authoritative writings that spurred the Roman Literalists to establish their own canon. (*See* Price, R. M. (2000), 80.)

15. *See* 'A Church of Bishops', *TJM*, 213ff.

16. Of the 13 letters of Paul in the New Testament, seven are accepted as being largely authentic. Of the remaining six, the Pastoral Letters – *1 Timothy*, *2 Timothy* and *Titus* – are widely held to be forgeries. Their sudden appearance in the late second century in the hands of Irenaeus makes perfect sense, as they turn Paul into a hostile opponent of Gnosticism. Suspiciously, Irenaeus' massive work against heretics, *Unmasking and Refutation of the Gnosis, Falsely So-Called*, leans explicitly on a quotation from *1 Timothy* 6:20. See Lüdemann, op. cit., 135.

17. As Doherty observes: 'In fact, the apologists as a group profess a faith which is nothing so much as a *Logos* religion. It is in essence Platonism carried to its fullest religious implications and wedded with Jewish theology and ethics.' *See* 'The Apologists as Platonic Philosophers', Doherty, E. (1999), 276ff.

18. Athenagoras of Athens is concerned only with the Son of God as the *Logos* and never once mentions the historical Jesus in 37 chapters of his *Plea for the Christians. See* Doherty, op. cit., 279.

19. Ibid., 286

20. Minucius Felix, *Octavius*, Chapter 9, quoted ibid., 287

21. Ibid., 289

22. Theophilus, *Autolycus*, 1.9.13, quoted ibid., 278

23. And yet, apart from the oft-repeated 'crucified under Pontius Pilate', Justin gives us the barest details of Jesus' life. Ibid., 284

24. Justin Martyr, *First Apology*, 20: '...on some points we teach the same things as the poets and philosophers whom you honour, and on other points are fuller and more divine in our teaching.' In *Dialogue with Trypho*, 2, Justin describes his rejection by both Pythagorean and Platonic schools before setting up on his own.

25. Tatian, *Apology*, 21. See Doherty, op. cit., 282. Tatian later abandoned his master's Literalism and became a Gnostic, as did the Church Father Tertullian.

26. Despite the attempts of Christian apologists to belittle the significance of the Gnostics, it is clear that in the majority of Mediterranean countries Gnosticism was the original Christianity. As Gibbon wrote in *The Decline and Fall of the Roman Empire*, the Gnostics 'covered Asia and Egypt, established themselves in Rome, and sometimes penetrated into the provinces of the West'. Gibbon writes with characteristic wit: 'For the most part they arose in the 2nd century, flourished during the 3rd, and were suppressed in the 4th or 5th by the prevalence of more fashionable controversies.' (Gibbon, E. (1796), 458)

27. The finding of the Nag Hammadi library, buried *c.*350 CE, supports this evidence.

28. Lieu, S. N. C. (1985), 39

29. Quoted in Lacarrière, J. (1989), 100.

30. Bardesanes was born in 135 CE in Syria. He converted the local ruler to Gnostic Christianity and between 202 and 217 there existed a Gnostic Christian state in Syria. It was subsequently destroyed by the Roman emperor Caracalla. *See* Hoeller, S. A. (1989), 81.

31. Robert Price provides a useful discussion of the extent of Gnosticism in the East in Price, R. M. (2000), 24ff.

32. *The Living Gospel of Mani* opens with words that deliberately echo those of Paul: 'I, Mani, the Apostle of Jesus...' In Mani's work a constant battle is fought between the 'New Man' and the 'Old Man', terms which are clearly borrowed from Paul, *see* Lieu, op. cit., 18.

33. Although Manicheism had spread across the Western world by the fourth century CE (Augustine, for example, was a Manichean for nine years before his conversion to Literalist Christianity in 386 CE), it suffered harsh persecution under Theodosius at the end of the fourth century. By the sixth century it was anathematized, its leaders were beheaded and their followers murdered or exiled, *see* Lieu, op. cit., viii. In the East, however, Manicheism spread eastward along the Silk Road and became the state religion of the Uigur Empire (eastern Iran) in 762. Manichean apostles appeared at the Chinese imperial court in 694 and according to Portuguese reports the religion was still surviving in southern China in the seventeenth century. Our knowledge of Manicheism has been revolutionized by the discovery in Turkestan in 1902 and Egypt in 1930 of a vast number of previously unknown Manichean texts in Coptic, Iranian, Turkish and Chinese.

34. Lieu, op. cit., 108

35. Hollroyd, S. (1994), 54

36. *See* 'No Orthodoxy', *TJM*, 219ff.

37. Mithraism first appears on European soil at Tarsus in the middle of the second century BCE. According to Plutarch, Romans were first initiated into the cult by followers brought back from the campaign waged against Mithradates (note name) by the Roman General Pompey in *c.*64 BC (Plutarch, *Life of Pompey*, 24). After Commodus (emperor 180–192 CE) was initiated into the cult there was an explosion in the building of Mithraic sanctuaries across the empire. *See* Cumont, F. (1903), 83. The cult of Jesus followed a similar trajectory from persecuted minority cult to imperial patronage over a similar time-scale.

38. *See TJM*, 246ff. In the mind of Theodosius, Christianity and citizenship were coterminous and anyone who denied Christ automatically made himself an outlaw of Roman society. As Campbell observes, 'In the reign of Constantine, Christianity was accorded equal status with the pagan religion of the empire, but half a century later in the reign of Theodosius (379–395) it was declared to be the only religion allowed, and with that the period that has since been known as the Dark Ages was inaugurated by imperial decree.' *See* Campbell, J. (1964), 389, and Lieu, S. N. C. (1985), 112.

39. Tertullian writes: 'The devil, whose business is to pervert the truth, mimics the exact circumstances of the Divine Sacraments. He baptizes his believers and promises forgiveness of sins from the Sacred Fount, and thereby initiates them into the religion of Mithras. Thus he celebrates the oblation of bread, and brings in the symbol of the

resurrection. Let us therefore acknowledge the craftiness of the devil, who copies certain things of those that be Divine.' (Quoted in Kingsland, W. (1937), 99, and King, C. W. (1887), 123.) Justin Martyr accuses the Mithraists of mimicking the Eucharist even down to the commemoration 'This is my body ... This is my blood ... Do this in commemoration of me.' (Justin Martyr, *First Apology*, 1.66)

40. The phrases 'Mysteries that make men freeze with awe' and 'This is known to initiates' are repeated in many of the Greek sermons written in the fourth and fifth centuries, *see* Campbell, J. (1955), 367. With Paganism out of the way, Christianity no longer had to hide its debt to the Mysteries.

41. Christian initiates were led naked to baptism and afterwards they put on white garments and a sign of the cross was made on their foreheads with oil. The procession then returned to the Basilica with each initiate carrying a candle and in the Alexandrian liturgy also wearing a crown. As d'Alviella states: 'It is precisely the Eleusinian procession where the Mystics dressed in white, wearing a crown on their heads and carrying a torch in their hands, pass by singing hymns on their way to the sanctuary.' (D'Alviella, G. (1981), 114.) The descriptions of this procession by the Christians Chrysostom, Cyril and Dionysius the Areopagite could be placed next to those of Pagan authors like Claudius, Themistius and Plutarch.

42. *Matthew* 23:9. *See also* Cumont, op. cit., 179.

43. *See* Gruber and Kersten (1985), 230. The Mithras cult had six other sacraments which correspond completely with those of the Catholic Church.

44. At Ephesus there was the Temple of Artemis, the Great Mother Goddess of Asia Minor, the largest temple ever built by the Greeks and one of the seven wonders of the world. It is no surprise that Theodosius II summoned the council to the city where, only a few years earlier, the Pagan 'Mother of God' had previously been worshipped (*see* Campbell, J. (1964), 410, and Matthews, C. (1992), 193). Soon after the council, legends began to be created that Mary and John retired to Ephesus after the crucifixion (*see* Pelikan, J. (1996), 207).

45. The title 'Queen of Heaven' can be traced back to the Armana tablets and the reign of Akhenaten, *see* Gray, J., 'The Queen of Heaven', *IDB* III, 975, *also* Scott, M. (1992), 46.

46. Augustine, *On Female Dress*, 1.1, quoted in Armstrong, K. (1993), 145.

47. Ibid.

48. Once again it is the forged Pastoral Letters which are instrumental in turning Paul into a misogynist. *See 1 Timothy* 2:11: 'Let the woman learn in silence with all subjection' and *1 Timothy* 2:12: 'But I suffer not a woman to teach, nor to usurp authority over the man, but to be in silence.'

49. Scott writes: 'The whole area of relationship between the Fourth Gospel, Women, Sophia and Gnosticism certainly merits serious attention in the near future.' Scott, op. cit., 252. We hope that *Jesus and the Goddess* has answered this call.

50. The identity of the 'Beloved Disciple' of 'John's' gospel has long been a mystery. *John* 21:20-4 asserts that the gospel was written by the Beloved Disciple on eye-witness testimony, but this person's identity is never revealed.

51. The majority of biblical scholars today agree that 'John' did not write the gospel that bears his name. The only basis for the attribution of this gospel to John is the childhood memory of Irenaeus. Irenaeus, *AH*, 2.22.5

52. *See* Irenaeus, op. cit., 3.3.4, for the Church Father's amusing/pathetic attempts to slander Cerinthus.

53. *See* especially the website of Ramon K. Justino at http://www.beloveddisciple.org. Justino makes a powerful case for the reattribution of this gospel to Mary Magdalene. When this is done the role of the Beloved Disciple within the gospel begins to make perfect sense. It is natural that she rests her head on Jesus' breast at the Last Supper (*John* 13:23-6). She is the voice of the Paraclete (16:7), because for the Gnostics the Mother is the Holy Spirit. As the gospel now stands, Jesus' handing over of John into the safe-keeping of his mother (19:26-7) makes no sense, especially as this is Jesus' final act, after which he knew 'that all things were now accomplished' (19:28). But in Gnostic myth (*see especially A Valentinian Exposition*), the return of Sophia (Mary) to her Mother is the specific goal of Jesus' redemptive mission. *See also* Price, R. M. (2000), 58. Thomas W. Butler also argues that Mary was both the Beloved Disciple and the voice behind the fourth gospel (Butler (1998)). The tampering with the text of *John* has introduced many inconsistencies and contradictions, the most glaring of which can be found in *John* 20:1-11. In verse 1 Mary arrives at the tomb to find it empty. In verse 2 she runs away from the tomb to fetch Peter and the 'other disciple' John. In verse 3 Peter and the 'other disciple' run to the tomb but Mary stays behind. In verse 11 Mary Magdalene is abruptly back at the tomb with no explanation of how she got there.

54. *See The Gospel of Philip*, NHC, 2.3.63.25-35 (where Mary Magdalene is mentioned in a context that specifically equates her with Sophia) and 2.3.59.6-11. In *The Gospel of Mary*, Peter acknowledges that 'the Saviour loved you more than the rest of women' (10:5) and asks her for the 'hidden wisdom' which the saviour had revealed to her. *See also The Gospel of Mary*, NHC, BG, 1.1-8. In *Pistis Sophia* Mary asks 39 of the 42 questions addressed to the resurrected Jesus (Mead, G. R. S. (1921), xxxii).

55. Scott, M. (1992), 239-40

56. The Gnostics are repeatedly classified as 'radical dualists', but this discourse has been so tainted with apologetic that it amounts to little more than a 'war of labels'. *See* Lacarrière, J. (1989), 99, and Stoyanov, Y. (2000), 287ff.

57. Tertullian, *Apology*, 50

58. See *TJM*, 249ff. Gibbon's original intention in *The Decline and Fall of the Roman Empire* was to end with the destruction of Rome by Alaric the Goth and his horde of 'barbarians' in 410 CE. However, on discovering that Alaric was a Christian, the 'barbarians' were bands of Christian monks and it was Pagans who were hunted down and killed whilst Christians remained safe in their churches, Gibbon changed his plan. Instead he continued his work until the fall of the Holy Roman Empire at the Reformation.

59. All the great themes of mysticism elaborated by Origen were continued in the work of the Cappadocians, Basil (329-79), his brother Gregory (335-95) and Gregory of Nazianzum (329-91). Gregory of Nyssa coined the paradoxical phrase 'dazzling

darkness' for God, writing that every concept of God becomes a false idol which cannot reveal God himself (Gregory of Nyssa, *Against Eunomius*, 3). Basil of Caesarea made the same distinction as Philo between God's essence, *ousia*, and his activity, *energias*, in the world. 'We know our God only by his *energias* but we do not undertake to approach his *ousia*.' (Basil, *Epistle*, 234.1.) As Armstong notes, this would be the keynote of all future theology in the Eastern Church. *See* Armstrong, K. (1993), 135.

60. Evagrius (d. 399) and Diodochus (early fifth century) were both Eastern 'Hesychast' mystics whose writings continued the Gnostic tradition of Clement and Origen. Just as Clement called the Christian 'the true Gnostic' (Clement, *Strom.*, 7.1), Evagrius writes that the secrets of the scriptures can only be revealed 'thanks to the Gnosis' (*Selecta in Psalmos* commentary on verse 16, *Psalm 138*). More categorically, he asserts: 'It is Gnosis that heals the mind.' *See* Bouyer, L. (1990), 219.

61. '...which our holy fathers have preserved in a silence ... to safeguard the sacred character of the Mystery. The uninitiated are not permitted to behold these things, their meaning is not to be divulged by writing it down.' Basil of Caesarea, *On the Holy Spirit*, 28.66. These sentiments can be exactly paralleled by Pagans writing about their Mysteries.

62. *Selecta in Psalmos*, op. cit. Like Aristotle, who noted that initiates attend the Mysteries not to learn something, *mathein*, but to experience something, *pathein*, so Basil of Caesarea distinguished between the public teaching of the Church and the deeper meaning of biblical truth which could only be apprehended through religious experience and expressed in symbolical form. *See* Armstrong, op. cit., 133-4.

63. *See* ibid, 255. Devotion to Mary found its supreme expression in the Byzantine liturgy. Eastern Mariology was to exert a decisive influence on the West in the medieval period, *see* Pelikan, J. (1996), 105. It is also significant that the great basilica built in the new Christian city of Constantinople was named 'Hagia Sophia'.

64. *Acts* 17:34

65. In 529 Justinian closed the ancient school of philosophy in Athens whose last great master had been Proclus (412-485), an ardent disciple of Plotinus. Four years later four mystical treatises appeared under the name Denys the Areopagite (*see* Armstrong, op. cit., 147). According to Dodds, Dionysius' dependence on Proclus is well established. Dionysius reproduces with 'a minimum of Christian disguise the whole structure of Athenian Neoplatonism' and 'transfers to Christ and the Holy Ghost the epithets with which Proclus had adorned his henads' (*see* discussion in Proclus (1963), xxviff). The apparent fraud was a total success – not only did the works escape the ban of heresy that they certainly merited, but they became accepted as an authority second only to Augustine and were the inspiration for nearly all later Christian mysticism. Dionysius' work had a profound influence on Erigena, Albertus Magnus, Thomas Aquinas, Dante, Nicholas of Cusa, Meister Eckhart, Pico della Mirandola, Marsilio Ficino, Edward Spenser, Coleridge etc. (*see* Proclus, op. cit., xxxff). However, in the light of the Jesus Mysteries Thesis, it is worth considering whether these works in some form may indeed be the thoughts of a first-century Christian Gnostic. They were dismissed as later forgeries after the Protestant

Reformation, when scholars first became aware that many ancient writings were in fact forgeries. However, these scholars had the agenda of getting back to what they saw as 'authentic' Christianity and removing what they believed to be later Pagan accretions. The decidedly Pagan/Gnostic works of Dionysus were, therefore, rejected as spurious – and indeed they may be. But books by the Jewish writer Philo were dismissed as forgeries at this time and have since been reinterpreted as genuine. Maybe the works of Dionysius need to be also reconsidered?

66. Adolf von Harnack wrote that for Dionysius 'the historical Christ is a symbol of the universal purifying and sanctifying activity of the Logos and little more' (quoted in Pseudo-Dionysius (1987), 20).

67. Dionysius, *The Divine Names*, 1.597c. 296.58. There is a useful résumé of this in Armstrong, op. cit., 147.

68. Ibid., 1.592b, 296.52

69. Dionysius, *The Letters*, 1,105c–d

70. *See* Pseudo-Dionysius, op. cit., 33ff, '...the book that saved the thought of the Middle Ages' (Ker, W. P. (1923), 107). Both Alfred the Great and Queen Elizabeth I made translations of it. Chaucer and Sir Thomas More wrote imitations of it. Its influence is to be found in the oldest English poetry of pre-Conquest times and is marked in Chaucer, Gower, Spenser and many other later poets. In Italy, Dante makes Thomas Aquinas point out the spirit of Boethius in Paradise. His *Divine Comedy* is in fact a great elaboration of the Neoplatonic concept of the ascent of the soul to God, ending with a reference to Boethius' 'the love that moves the sun and other stars' (*Paradiso*, 33.145).

71. As Watts observes, 'Was Boethius a Christian, and if so why does the *Consolation* lack all reference to the faith that should have been his greatest consolation in the hours of imprisonment and pending death?' (Watts, V. E., intro. to Boethius, *The Consolation of Philosophy*, 14)

72. *See* Rudolph, K. (1987), 374. *See* Stoyanov, Y. (2000), 39 and 338 for the survival of the Gnosis from antiquity to the Cathar heresy. As Toynbee writes, 'The substantial identity of the Paulician, the Bogomil and the Cathar faith is not in doubt. The common features are too similar and too numerous to be explained away as fortuitous, and it is clear that we are in the presence of a single religion masquerading under different names in different places.' Toynbee, A. (1939), 624

73. The Paulicians praised Paul as 'the Apostle', professed a docetic Christianity and worshipped Mary not as the mother of Christ but as the Heavenly Jerusalem, *see* Stoyanov, op. cit., 105. The Bogomils are thought to have arisen from a sect of Paulicians from Asia Minor who in *c*.872 were compulsorily settled in Macedonia. Despite intense persecution, the Bogomils retained a powerbase in Serbia and Bosnia until the fifteenth century. *See* Rudolph, op. cit., 375.

74. The Catholic Church became obsessed with the figure of the *Antipape des Heretiques Albigeois*, said to reside in the Balkans. Rome eradicated 'Gnostic heresy' in France and Italy, but Bosnia became known as the irredeemable land of heresy. Pope Urban V (1362–70) called it 'the cesspool of heresy of all parts of the world'. *See* Stoyanov, op. cit., 190–1.

75. Patriarch Germanus (1220–40) warned the citizens of Constantinople against the 'dark mysteries' of the 'satanic Bogomil heresy' (ibid., 184). A school of Gnosticism is said to still secretly survive in Bulgaria, *see* Hollroyd, S. (1994), 82, and Hoeller, S. A. (1989), 92.

76. Cosmas the Priest, *Against the Bogomils*, quoted in Lacarrière, J. (1989), 113.

77. The word 'Cathar' derives from the Greek for 'purity'. As a synonym for initiates it can be traced back to the Orphic *Gold Leaves* *c.*400 BCE, where souls who are absolutely pure, *katharai*, are said to escape reincarnation and go directly to the fields of Persephone to become gods. (*Gold Leaves*, A2–3, lines 6–7. *See also* Zuntz, G. (1971), 337–8.) The Manichaeans also called themselves 'The Pure Ones' (Stoyanov, Y. (2000), 116). The earliest certain indication of medieval Cathars is the disclosure in 1143 of a heretical community in Cologne. The Cologne sectarians claimed that they had numerous adherents 'throughout the world, particularly among the clergy and the monks' and that their religion had persisted in secrecy 'from the time of the martyrs'. *See* Stoyanov, Y. (1994), 155–6.

78. Bogomil ideas had penetrated into Italy and France by the middle of the eleventh century (*see* Stoyanov (1994), 193, for the close resemblance between the Slavonic rituals and the Cathar ritual of Lyons). Between 1150 and 1300 Catharism was the dominant religion of southern France and northern Italy (where Cathars were known as Patarenes).

79. In the Platonic tradition, 'Friends of God' became a synonym for initiates (*see* Plato, *Timaeus*, 24, and Plotinus, *Enn.*, 2.9.9). Theo of Smyrna (*Mathematica*, 18) declared 'friendship with divinity' as the highest level of initiation. The Cynic Crates stated: 'For everything belongs to God, friends have everything in common, and the wise are friends of God.' *See* Price, R. M. (2000), 152, *also Exodus* 33:11: 'And the LORD spake unto Moses face to face, as a man speaketh unto his friend.'

80. *See* Stoyanov (1994), 155–6.

81. Raynaldus, *Annales*, in Maitland, S. R. (1832), 392–4. *See also* Raynaldus, *On the Accusations against the Albigensians*, http://www.fordham.edu/halsall/source/heresy1.html. According to Raynaldus, the Cathars were vegetarian celibates who believed in reincarnation. Like Simon and Marcion they considered the God of Jesus and the New Testament to be benevolent but the Old Testament God to be a tyrant.

82. Mead, G. R. S. (1906), 499

83. Raynaldus, op. cit.

84. Ellerbe, H. E. (1995), 72–3

85. Ibid., 77

86. Ibid.

87. Lea, H. C. (1888), 75. *See* Mead, op. cit., 74ff. The destruction of the Gnostic Cathars culminated on 16 March 1244 when 200 Cathar 'Perfects' were burned to death in the fall of Montségur, the last stronghold of Catharism. Gerald Durell famously called this the 'Thermopylae of the Gnostic soul'.

88. *See* Stoyanov (1994), 192.

89. Birks, W., and Gilbert, R. A., (1987), 71

90. *See* Ellerbe, op. cit., 83.

91. 'The people of this faith viewed the Catholic church as the antichrist or the devil...'
See Nicole Brogan, *The Cathars*, at http://www.millersv.edu/~english/homepage/
duncan/medfem/cathars.html, *also* Raynaldus, *On the Accusations against the
Albigensians*: 'They said that almost all the Church of Rome was a den of thieves;
and that it was the harlot of which we read in the Apocalypse.' http://www.fordham.
edu/halsall/source/heresy1.html

92. *See* Meister Eckhart, *Selected Writings*, Penguin, 1994, xxii. Eckhart (1260–1327)
called Plato 'the great priest' and his inspiration came from the Neoplatonism of
Erigena and Dionysius. *See* Inge, W. R. (1899), 78. In 1329 a Papal Bull condemned his
writings, but Eckhart had the good sense to die two years earlier.

93. John Tauler (1300–1361), Henry Suso (1295–1365) and John Ruysbroeck (1293–1381)
were the leading spirits in the great informal society of the Friends of God. Formed
in Strasbourg, the Friends later spread through the Rhenish province and beyond to
Switzerland and Bavaria. In 1350 the *Theologia Germanica* was written in Frankfurt
by an anonymous 'Friend'. In his youth Martin Luther was deeply inspired by the
Theologia Germanica and organized its first publication in 1518. Some commenta-
tors have seen the Movement of the Free Spirit as the forerunner of the Reformation,
see Underhill, E. (1993), 464–5. In Württemberg, a Protestant enclave in southern
Germany, the Swabian Fathers, who called themselves 'Free Spirits', anticipated the
Romantic philosophy that later flourished in the work of Goethe, Novalis, Holderlin,
Schelling and Hegel. One of the most radical of the Swabian priests, Gottfried
Arnold, wrote *c.*1700: 'It would have been far more beneficial for us and for mankind
if those heresies, which were condemned in the Councils and Symbols of the Church,
had prevailed and thus prevented the victory of the orthodox system of belief.' *See*
Hanratty, G. (1997), 89. It is a sentiment that Hegel will repeat almost verbatim in a
letter to Schelling, who has just written a thesis on the second-century Gnostic
Marcion. *See* ibid., 103.

94. Contemporary document of the 'Brethren and sisters of the fellowship of the Free
Spirit and of Voluntary Poverty' cited by Jung in *Aion*, *CW*, 9.II.139. The 'New Age'
of the 'Free Spirit' declared by Joachim of Fiora (d. 1202) was the inspiration for
numerous heretical movements – the Concorrici, Waldenses, Poor Men of Lyons,
Beghards, Beguines Brothers of the Free Spirit, etc. *See* Hanratty, op. cit., 47ff.

95. Cohn argued that the extremist Christian sects of seventeenth-century England were
a revival of the fourteenth-century heresy of the Free Spirit. Cohn, N., *The Pursuit of
the Millennium, Revolutionary Millenarians and Mystical Anarchists of the Middle
Ages*, London, 1957. *See* Armstrong, K. (1993), 367.

96. Dante is a key figure in the transmission of the 'Hidden Tradition'. His teacher in
alchemy ('the Art by which men become immortal') was Brunetto Latini, *see
Purgatorio*, 15.85. *The Divine Comedy* signals its inspiration at the outset in the
figure of Vergil, Dante's Pagan guide through the underworld. Just as the Roman poet
had encoded many Orphic/Pythagorean teachings in his work, reformulating the
Greek esoteric tradition for a Roman audience, so Dante translated the esoteric traditions he had inherited into an epic allegory acceptable to his contemporaries.
Whilst Dante's underworld journey owes much to Book 6 of the *Aeneid*, his journey

through Hell, Purgatory and Heaven also drew heavily on Sufism, and particularly on Ibn al-'Arabi's account of the *mi'raj*, the heavenly ascent of Muhammad (*see* Merkur, D. (1993), 242). This was the Classical period of Islamic civilization and men like Dante were profoundly influenced by the Arabic philosophers such as Averoes and Avicenna. The Moors of Spain reintroduced Neoplatonism, alchemy, Gnosticism and a host of other long-lost traditions to the West.

97. After the fall of Constantinople in 1453 many scholars fled to the West with the ancient contents of the Byzantine libraries. Amongst these were Gemistus Pletho (1355?–1452), who announced to astonished Florentines that with the rebirth of Platonism the religious deception of Moses, Jesus and Mohammad was at an end. One of his listeners was the wealthy Cosimo Medici. For over seven centuries no Florentine had spoken Greek, but in a few short years the complete works of Plato, Plotinus, Iamblichus and Porphyry, the Greek playwrights and historians, the Chaldaean Oracles and the Hermetica were assembled and translated by scholars working at the court of Cosimo Medici. A 'New Platonic Academy' was begun by Marsilio Ficino and the 'New Learning', as the revived Pagan knowledge was called, became the chief inspiration of the Florentine Renaissance (*see especially* Cronin, V. (1967), 110). In 1509 Raphael painted *The School of Athens*, which famously depicted Leonardo as Plato presiding over the reborn Academy. Other famous persons identified in the work include Plato, Aristotle, Socrates, Pythagoras, Euclid, Alcibiades, Diogenes, Ptolemy, Zoroaster and, of course, Raphael himself.

98. The Wisdom tradition of Sophia exerted a profound influence on the alchemical theosophy of Boehme (1575–1624), for whom she was the mirror of God's will. 'There is nothing in Heaven or Earth which did not, at the beginning, become manifest in this mirror.' See Matthews, C. (1992), 268ff. 'Lady Alchemy' became a synonym for the Sophianic tradition. Boehme exerted a profound influence on Henry More, Isaac Newton, William Blake and William Law.

99. Johann Wolfgang von Goethe was the flower of the German Romantic movement. His inspiration lay in the works of Eckhart, the Friends of God and the revival of Pagan learning engendered by the Italian Renaissance. His masterwork, *Faust*, is a Gnostic fantasy that represented for Jung the ultimate expression of the alchemical quest.

100. The theologian Christian Baur was the first to argue that Hegel's system was a modern version of early Gnosticism, and particularly of the system of Valentinus. *See especially* Hanratty, op. cit., 81ff, 'The Gnostic Synthesis of G W F Hegel'.

101. Quoted in Hoeller, S. A., (1982), 16. *See* Matthews, op. cit., 321.

102. *See* Jung, C. G., op. cit., 9.14.1.347, *also* Segal, R. A. (1992), 34.

103. Jung, quoted in Segal, 246.

104. *Sermo I, see* ibid., 181ff.

105. It was written in 1916 and circulated privately to friends, including Hermann Hesse, who wrote *Daimian* under its influence. At Jung's request it was excluded from his *Collected Works*.

106. Jung in the *Face to Face* interview, quoted in Segal, op. cit., 52.

107. Jung, C. G., *Psychology and Alchemy*, CW, 12.1.12–13. *See* Jung (1953), 12.

108. The Inquisition, which had been formed specifically to repress the Cathars, was licensed by the Church to torture heretics in 1252 (Stoyanov, Y. (1994), 187, and Ellerbe, H. E. (1995), 83ff) and subsequently went on to have a grisly future in Spain and the Spanish territories in the New World. In 1570 it was established in Peru and Mexico and natives who did not convert to Christianity were burned like any other heretics (see Ellerbe, op. cit., 88). In Goa in India the Inquisition murdered 4,000 people during the sixteenth and seventeenth centuries. It continued to operate in some parts of the world until the middle of the nineteenth century.

109. See Potter, H. (1993). Potter demonstrates that the Anglican Church embraced abolition of the death penalty 'only at the eleventh hour'. Slavery is endorsed in the Old Testament. Leviticus 25:44 states that Israelites may buy slaves from the nations that surround them. It is also endorsed by the forged Pastoral Letter 1Timothy, which counsels acceptance of slavery by both slave and master (5:1). William Wilberforce noted that the Church clergy obstructed the anti-slavery cause while Nonconformists and 'godless' reformers were his staunchest allies. See Trevelyan, G. M. (1944), also Wells on 'Social Ethics' (1999), 232ff, and 'The Inquisition and Slavery' in Ellerbe, op. cit., 76ff.

110. Bernhardt, R., Christianity without Absolutes, SCM, 1994, 9

111. In 1999 the Church of England stopped publishing church attendance figures due to their precipitous decline. In the same year Archbishop Carey declared that the Church would be extinct 'within a generation'.

112. Although now applied loosely to all theological conservatism, the term was originally applied specifically to a group of American Protestants who, in 1910, published a series of tracts, The Fundamentals, setting out the conservative theological position. Their aim was to oppose 'liberal' theology of the time. The essential feature of all Fundamentalism is its unshakeable dogmatism. See Gilbert, R. A. (1993), 12.

113. Tertullian, DP, 43. Likewise Irenaeus castigates knowledge, scientia, and claims that only 'Holy Writ' should be the study of 'sound, safe cautious reason'. (Irenaeus, AH, 2.26.2; 2.27.1. See Rudolph, K. (1987), 373.) Augustine perfectly articulates the triumph of dogmatism over reason: 'Nothing is to be accepted except on the authority of scripture, since greater is that authority than all powers of the human mind.' With the triumph of this kind of Christianity the curtain came down on the Western scientific tradition and the Dark Ages began. See TJM, 304.

114. 2 Corinthians 3:6

115. Genesis 7

116. Ibid., 38:9

117. Exodus 7–11

118. Ibid., 12, 17:8–16, 21:20–1 and 32:27–9

119. 1 Samuel 5:8,9

120. Leviticus 27:28. An example is in Judges 11:30–9.

121. Deuteronomy 7:2, 20:16

122. Numbers 15:32–6, 16:49

123. Ibid., 21:3,6, 21:35, 31:9,17,18

124. The followers of Mani also composed a treatise like the *Antitheses,* a juxtaposition of Old and New Testament texts designed to prove that the 'Just God' of the Old is not the 'Good God' of the New. Mani's understanding of the role of Jesus strongly resembles that of Marcion (*see* Lieu, S. N. C. (1985), 39). Interestingly, the forged letter of 'Paul' to Timothy warns: 'O Timothy, keep that which is committed to thy trust, avoiding profane and vain babblings, and contradictions [*antithesis*] of gnosis, falsely so called.' (*I Timothy* 6:20. *See* Lacarrière, J. (1989), 100.)

125. *Leviticus* 15:19–24

126. Ibid., 25:44

127. Ibid., 10:10

128. *Exodus* 35:2

129. *Deuteronomy* 21:18–20

130. *Hebrews* 8:13

131. Other options include: a Cynic-like sage in the works of Mack, Crossman, Downing and others; a liberal Pharisee or a loosely orthodox Hasid in the work of Falk and Vermes; a magician in the work of Morton Smith; a magic mushroom in the work of Allegro. Further Jesuses on offer include priestly zealot, proto-feminist, exorcist, healer, prophet, demi-god, etc., etc. (*see* Price, R. M. (2000), 14). The very number of Jesuses who can be constructed out of 'the available evidence' is testimony to how scanty and ambivalent this evidence really is.

132. On 26 March 1997, 39 members of the Heaven's Gate cult were found dead. They had been told that if they 'shed their containers' (their bodies), they could board a UFO travelling behind comet Hale Bopp. For seats on the next shuttle go to: http://www.heavensgatetoo.com.

133. Schweitzer, A. (1910), quoted in Price, op. cit., 12.

134. 'Now all these heresies have their own peculiar Jesus; but he is seen differently according as the place is different towards which, he says, each soul is borne and hastens. (Now each soul) supposes that (the Jesus seen from its particular place) is alone that (Jesus) who is its own peculiar kinsman and fellow-citizen. And on first beholding (this Jesus, that soul) recognizes Him as its own peculiar brother, but the rest as bastards.' Hippolytus, *Ref.,* 8.3 (translator's brackets)

135. There is a useful discussion of docetism (the Gnostic doctrine of Jesus as a symbolic visionary figure) and its relevance 'to the contemporary discussion of the historical Jesus' in Price, op. cit., 16ff.

136. *The Gospel of Philip,* NHC, 2.3.58

137. *The Acts of John* 88–9. *See* Merkur, D. (1993), 130.

138. *The Acts of Peter* 20–1

139. From *The Acts of Peter,* quoted in Merkur, op. cit., 130.

140. Pagels, E. (1975), 5–7

141. *Acts* 9:3, 22:6

142. *The Apocryphon of John,* NHC, 2.1,3.1,4.1. *See* Robinson, J. M. (1978), 105, *also* Merkur, op. cit., 133.

143. *The Gospel of Philip,* NHC, 2.3.58. *See also The Acts of John* 97–102, the discussion of docetism in Rudolph, K. (1987), 158, and the teachings of Basilides in Barnstone, W. (1984), 627.

144. Hippolytus, *Ref.*, 8.3

145. It was not until the second century CE that long hair became fashionable after its adoption by Hadrian in imitation of Greek philosophers.

146. *1 Corinthians* 2:14–15

147. A miracle he performed for a Syrian king, who used the portrait to cure his leprosy and defeat his enemies in battle.

CHAPTER 4: KNOW YOUR SELF

1. Oxy. 654, 9–21 and cf NHC, 2.32:19–33:5; Grenfell, B. P., and Hunt, A. S., *New Sayings of Jesus and Fragment of a Lost Gospel from Oxyrhynchus*, London, 1904.

2. According to Plato, it was the Delphic command, 'Gnothi seauton,' which set Socrates on his quest for true knowledge. Plato, *Apology*, 22e–23c

3. For Plato the Delphic proverb meant the knowledge of the divine spirit, *nous*, in man. For later Jewish Gnostics self-knowledge became synonymous with the Gnosis itself. 'Whoever has not known himself has known nothing, but he who has known himself has at the same time already achieved Gnosis about the depth of all things.' *The Gospel of Philip*, NHC, I, 2.3.67. *See* Rudolph, K. (1987), 113. Philo seeks to find a Jewish equivalent of the Delphic injunction in the words of Moses, but the best he can come up with is 'Give heed to yourself' in *Exodus* 34:12. *See* Migr., 8.

4. The tripartite nature of the human being was a fundamental tenet of Platonism (*The Republic*, 434d–41c, *Timaeus*, 89, etc). In accordance with this doctrine Plato divided his ideal *Republic* into three classes according to which aspect was most marked in each individual. That this doctrine derived from Pythagorean sources is confirmed by Burkert, who observes: 'The Platonic and Pythagorean material is seen as a unity, and Aristotle's reports lead in a different direction.' Burkert, W. (1972), 74

5. Plotinus, *Enn.*, 5. 3.1–10

6. *The Gospel of Thomas*, 29. NHC, 2.2.29. The priority of the psyche to the body is an axiom of Platonism. 'Whereas God made the psyche in origin and excellence prior to and older than the body, to be the ruler and mistress, of whom the body was to be the subject.' *Timaeus* 34b–c. '...psyche is prior to body, body secondary and derivative, psyche governing in the real order of things and body being subject to governance.' *Laws*, 896c–e

7. Plato, *Timaeus*, 36e: 'Now when the Creator had framed the soul according to his will, he formed within her the corporeal universe, and brought the two together, and united them centre to centre. The soul, interfused everywhere from the centre to the circumference of heaven, of which also she is the external envelopment, herself turning in herself, began a divine beginning of never ceasing and rational life enduring throughout all time. The body of heaven is visible, but the soul is invisible, and partakes of reason and harmony, and being made by the best of intellectual and everlasting natures, is the best of things created.' Plato is here describing the creation of the world soul, or universal psyche, of which every individual soul is an expression created after the same fashion.

8. Plotinus, op. cit., 3.9.2. Plotinus attributes this observation to Plato.

9. The Gnostics suggest we reverse the picture of ourselves as a body which moves about in the world and instead see ourselves as a still point of consciousness around which the world moves. Consciousness, at the centre of the circle, is what Plotinus calls our 'stationary essence', around which everything we experience turns. (Plotinus, op. cit., 4.2.1) All that exists for us exists in relation to this 'still point of the turning world', as the poet T. S. Eliot describes it, drawing on the same perennial image nearly two millennia later. (T. S. Eliot, 'Burnt Norton', *Four Quartets*, 1935, 2)

10. Porphyry, *Letter to Marcella*, 1.8, quoted in Gregory, J. (1987), 201. Porphyry is alluding to Plato, *Timaeus*, 27, and *Phaedrus*, 247c–d: 'The region of which I speak is the abode of that reality with which true knowledge is concerned. A reality without colour or shape, but utterly real, apprehensible only by Consciousness, which is the pilot of the psyche.'

11. *The Gospel of Thomas*, 17, NHC, 2.2.17

12. Philo asks why Adam, who assigned the names to all the creatures, was unable to name himself. He answers: 'The mind (*nous*) which is in each of us is capable of apprehending other objects, but is incapable of knowing itself... It is likely then, that Adam, that is the Mind (*nous*), though he names and apprehends other things, gives no name to himself, since he is ignorant of himself and his own nature.' Philo, *Allegorical Interpretations*, 1:91–2 (translator's brackets)

13. Clement of Alexandria, *Paedagogus*, 3.1. See Martin, L. H. (1987), 141.

14. In the Gnostic text *Allogenes* we read: 'If you seek with a perfect seeking, then you shall know the Good that is in you; then you will know yourself as well, [as] one who derives from the God who truly pre-exists.' NHC, 11.3.56, in Robinson, J. M. (1978), 495. The Teachings of Silvanus instructs: 'But before everything [else], know your birth. Know yourself.' NHC, 7.4.92, quoted ibid., 385. *See also Corpus Hermeticum*, 1.21: 'He who has understood himself advances toward God.'

15. Plotinus, *Enn.*, 6.8.18

16. Armstrong, K. (1993), 123

17. Plotinus, op. cit., 3.3.7

18. Dionysius, *On the Divine Names*, 644a, and *see* Plotinus, op. cit., 1.7.1.

19. Hippolytus, *Ref.*, 4.51, and *see* 6.12, *also* Welburn, A. (1994), 170.

20. Ibid., 8.8. Hippolytus likewise traces Monoimos' system to its origin in Pythagorean 'sacred geometry'.

21. Plotinus, op. cit., 6.9.8

22. Monoimos the Arab, quoted in Hippolytus, op. cit., 8.5. *See* discussion in Jung, C. G. (1960), 109.

23. Plotinus, op. cit., 6.7.15

24. Dionysius, *The Mystical Theology*, 1.997b: '...the pure, absolute and immutable mysteries of theology are veiled in the dazzling darkness of the secret silence.' *See* Pseudo-Dionysius (1987), 135ff.

25. 'No reality without polarity,' as Jung puts it succinctly. Jung, C. G. (1959), 276

26. Plotinus, *Enn.*, 6.5.5

27. *Colossians* 2:2

28. *Hippolytus*, op. cit., 8.12. *See* Philip, J. A. (1966), 124, and Metzger, B. M. (1987), 99.

29. Plotinus, op. cit., 6.6.15
30. Ibid., 1.1.12
31. *Pistis Sophia*, 1.39.6: 'I have become like a peculiar demon, which dwells in matter, in whom is no light.'
32. Mead, G. R. S. (1919), 35. Basilides also calls it the 'appended psyche'.
33. Plotinus, op. cit., 6.4.14
34. As with the majority of Gnostic doctrines this division of humanity into three types has its origin in Pagan philosophy. Its earliest appearance is a simple Pythagorean parable. 'Life, [Pythagoras] said, is like a festival; just as some come to the festival to compete, some to ply their trade, but the best people come as spectators, so in life the slavish men go hunting for fame or gain, the philosopher for the truth.' (DL, 8.8. *See* Kirk, G. S., and Raven, J. E. (1957), 228, and Dillon, J. (1990), 72.) Plato writes: 'The just man does not allow the several elements in his soul to usurp one another's functions; he is indeed one who sets his house in order, by self-mastery and discipline coming to be at peace with himself, and bringing into tune those three parts, like the terms in the proportion of a musical scale, the highest and lowest notes, and the mean between them, with all the intermediate intervals. Only when he has linked these three parts together into a well-tempered harmony and has made himself one man instead of many will he be ready to go about whatever he may have to do.' (*The Republic*, 433d.) Platonic psychology had a profound effect on later politics, as Plato's ideal state, outlined in *The Republic*, is modelled on the individual man. To the three parts of the soul correspond three classes of citizens – the rulers, whose virtue is wisdom; the guardians, on whom courage is incumbent; the labourers and tradesmen who owe the state soberness and obedience (*see* Arnold, E. V. (1911), 58). Philo adopted this schema, referring to three types of men: the Earth-born, Heaven-born and God-born. 'But the men of God ... have risen wholly above the sphere of sense-perception and have been translated into the world of the intelligible and dwell there registered as freemen of the commonwealth of Ideas [*ideon politeia*] which are imperishable and incorporeal.' (*On the Giants*, 60–1.) Plotinus also develops this schema at length. (Plotinus, op. cit., 5.9. *See also* 'The theory of three classes of men in Plotinus and Philo' in Dillon, op. cit.) As Dillon observes, the closest analogy to the scheme of Philo and Plotinus is to be found in the well-known triadic distinction found in many Gnostic systems between 'corporeal' or 'material' [*sarkikoi, choikoi, hylikoi*, 'psychic' [*psychikoi*], and 'spiritual' [*pneumatikoi*] men. *See* Irenaeus, *AH*, 1.6f; Hippolytus, *Ref.*, X9–10; and, most clearly, Clement's *Exc. Theod.*, preserved in Book 7 of the *Stromateis*, which are notes of an account of Valentinianism 'according to the oriental teaching' as opposed to the Italian school: 'From Adam three natures are begotten. The first was the irrational [*alogos*], which was Cain's, the second the rational and just, which was Abel's, the third the spiritual [*pneumatike*], which was Seth's.' (Dillon, op. cit., 72.) The Valentinian division of mankind into the *Pneumatikoi*, the *Psychikoi* and the *Hylikoi* (or *Somatikoi*) was also accepted by Mani (*see* Lieu, S. N. C. (1985), 51). *The Teachings of Silvanus* states: 'Understand that you have come into being from three races: from the earth, from the formed, and from the created. The body has come into being from the earth with an earthly

substance, but the formed, for the sake of the soul, has come into being from the thought of the Divine. The created, however, is the mind, which has come into being in conformity with the image of God.' (NHC, 7.4.92, in Robinson, J. M. (1978), 385.) In *The Book of Thomas the Contender* these three types are described as 'blind people', 'beginners' and 'perfect ones' (NHC, 2.7.138.35–139.28). *See also* Rudolph, K. (1987), 208.

35. Ptolemy, quoted in Irenaeus, op. cit., 1.3.1. *See* Layton, B. (1987), 286.

36. *1 Corinthians* 2:14

37. Twenty-five uses in the gospels and epistles with parallels in the Dead Sea Scrolls. *See* Welburn, A. (1994), 187.

38. Pseudo-Dionysius (1987), 72

39. Jonas, H. (1958), 61

40. Clement of Alexandria, *Strom.*, 6.26, and *see* 7.55 and 6.109.

41. 'Disengage' comes from Plotinus (*Enn.* 1.2.5).

42. *The Gospel of Thomas* opens with the promise: 'Whoever discovers the interpretation of these sayings will not taste death.'

43. *Zostrianos*, NHC, 8.75.23. *See* Welburn, op. cit., 171.

44. *See* Layton, op. cit., 294, for Layton's commentary on Irenaeus, *AH*, 1.6.2.

45. Quoted in Freke and Gandy, *Hermetica*, 29. *Asclepius* 13, *see* Copenhaver, B. P. (1992), 74.

46. Armstrong, K. (1993), 117

47. 'This is the Good, the aim of those who have Gnosis: to become God.' Hermes Trismegistus, *Poimandres*, trans. Willis Barnstone (1984), 573

48. *John* 17:22–3

49. *The Gospel of Thomas* illustrates the paradoxical twists on the Gnostic path: 'Jesus said, "Those who seek should not stop seeking until they find. When they find, they will be disturbed. When they are disturbed, they will marvel, and will reign over all." (And after they have reigned they will rest.)' *The Gospel of Thomas*, 2 (translator's brackets)

50. The Gnostic sage Basilides explains that pneumatic Christians are moral simply 'by nature' and quotes Paul's *Letter to the Romans* 2:2–16 in support. Pagels, E. (1975), 19.

51. *Treatise on the Resurrection*, NHC, 1.4.45. *See* Layton, B. (1987), 321.

52. *1 Corinthians* 12:27 and *see Ephesians* 5:30.

53. *Ephesians* 4:4

54. 'You are my mind; bring me forth! ...give me the perfect thing that cannot be grasped!' *A Prayer of the Apostle Paul*, NHC, 1.1.5. Later in the *Prayer* Paul asks to be granted 'what no angel-eye has seen, and no archon-ear has heard, and what has not entered into the human heart'. Cf *1 Corinthians* 2:9. In *The Gospel of Mary*, BG, 10, Jesus tells Mary: 'Blessed are you because you are not shaken when you see me. For where the mind [*nous*] is, there is the treasure.'

55. Dionysius, *The Ecclesiastical Hierarchy*, 372a. *See* Pseudo-Dionysius (1987), 195, and Merkur, D. (1993), 243.

56. For the derivation of the Christian *Logos* doctrine from Paganism *see* 'The Logos', *TJM*, 82ff.

57. *John* 1:9

58. *Corpus Hermeticum*, 1. *The Poimandres*, trans. Nock and Festugière. Welburn, A. (1994), 195

59. Quoted in Inge, W. R. (1899), 87. According to Hippolytus, Marcus the Gnostic received the following revelation from the Pythagorean *tetraktys*, which appeared to him as a woman and said: 'When first the self-existent Father, He who is inconceivable and without substance, He who is neither male nor female, willed that His own ineffability should become realized in something spoken, and that His invisibility should become realized in form, He opened His mouth, and sent forth similar to Himself a *Logos*. And this (*Logos*) stood by Him, and showed unto Him who he was, viz., that he himself had been manifested as a (realization in) form of the Invisible One.' Hippolytus, *Ref.*, 6.37 (translator's brackets)

60. Hippolytus, quoted in Mead, G. R. S. (1906), 381.

61. *John* 14:6

62. Paul teaches: 'The Son is the image of the invisible God.' (*Colossians* 1:15.) Origen writes: 'The Lord and Saviour is the image of the invisible God.' (*In Lucem homila*, 8, quoted in Jung, *Aion*, CW, 9.2, para 70.) *The Gospel of John* states: 'No one has ever seen the Father, but God's only Son, who is nearest to the essence of the Father, has made him known.' (*John* 1:18)

63. For *anastasis* as 'awakening', *see* Rudolph, K. (1987), 190.

64. As Hans Jonas notes, 'In Gnostic thought the world takes the place of the traditional underworld and is itself already the realm of the dead.' (Jonas, H. (1958), 68.) Again, the Gnostics were taking up a theme that had already been fully elaborated in Pagan mythology and philosophy. *See* Burkert, W. (1972), 134, note 80: 'Empedocles has no underworld, for him earthly existence is Hades.' Plato writes: 'I should not be surprised, you know, if Euripides was right when he said, "Who knows, if life be death, and death be life?" [Euripides, *Polyidus*, fr. 7.] And perhaps we are actually dead, for I once heard one of our wise men say that we are now dead, and that our body is a tomb.' Plato, *Gorgias*, 493a

65. Plato, *Cratylus*, 400c, confirms that the 'wise men' referred to in *Gorgias*, 493, are in fact Orphics.

66. Olympiodorus, *Commentary on the Gorgias*, quoted in Porphyry, *On the Cave of the Nymphs*, 69.

67. Plotinus, *Enn.*, 1.8, quoted in Taylor, T., *Oracles and Mysteries* (1995), 60. The theme that this world was the Underworld was widely held, but rarely explicitly stated, by philosophers and poets in the ancient world. Taylor supplies passages from Empedocles, Heraclitus, Plato, Philolaus and Clement of Alexandria that testify to the importance of this theme in the Pagan Mysteries.

68. 'I am the Pronoia of the pure light; I am the thinking of the virginal Spirit, who raised you up to the honoured place. Arise and remember that it is you who hearkened, and follow your root, which is I, the merciful one, and guard yourself against the angels of poverty and the demons of chaos and all those who ensnare you, and beware of the deep sleep and the enclosure of the inside of Hades.' *The Apocryphon of John*, NHC, 2.1.31, in Robinson, J. M. (1978), 122. *See also* Layton, B. (1987), 141.

69. 'Yet you are sleeping, dreaming dreams. Wake up and return.' *The Concept of our Great Power*, NHC, 6.4.40, in Robinson, op. cit., 314

70. *Ephesians*, 5:14. *Ephesians* has preserved what Rudolph calls the 'gnostic call', *see* Rudolph, op. cit., 120.

71. *Romans* 8:9–10

72. *Thomas*, 113

73. *Corinthians*, 2:17

CHAPTER 5: THE LOST GODDESS

1. *The Thunder: Perfect Mind*, NHC, 6.2.13 and 16, in Robinson, J. M. (1978), 297, 299. The introduction to this text in the NHC makes clear that the two parts of the title are unrelated. We have consequently omitted *Thunder*, as it appears nowhere in the text.

2. Plotinus, *Enn.*, 6.7.36. The Pagan philosopher Heliodorus tells us that initiates received 'preliminary instruction in the form of myths'. Heliodorus, *An Ethiopian Story*, 9.9

3. The philosopher Sallustius writes: '…myths are divine … for they are used by poets agitated by divinity, by the best of philosophers, and by such as disclose initiatory rites.' (*On the Gods and the World*, 3. See Taylor, T. (1994), 5.) In defence of the primacy of myth over its literal meaning, Sallustius makes an analogy with the primacy of psyche over body: 'In myths too, the energies of the gods are imitated; for the world may very properly be called a myth, since bodies, and the corporeal possessions which it contains are apparent, but souls and intellects are occult and invisible.' (Ibid., 4. See Taylor, op. cit., 6.)

4. Fidler writes: 'The teachings of the mystery religions were characteristically embodied in allegory, myth, and symbolic imagery, both as "teaching stories" and as basic paradigms of human experience. Certain philosophical schools, especially the Stoics and Platonists, drew upon traditional myths to illustrate insights which transcend merely logical description. Moreover, they held that the interpretation of the traditional myths, like the pursuit of philosophy itself, constituted, at its core, a process of initiation.' (Fidler, D. (1993), 6.) For the path of philosophy likened to the path of initiation, *see* Plato, *Symposium*, 210a, and Plutarch, *Isis and Osiris*, 382d, two examples of this ancient and widespread analogy. Macrobius writes: 'The Mysteries are concealed in myths so that the few may know the real secret, through interpreting them wisely, while the rest are able to happily venerate the Mystery, defended by these allegories against banality.' (Macrobius, *Commentary on Cicero's Somnium Scipionis*, 1.2.17f, quoted in Burkert, W. (1987), 79.) Likewise Sallustius writes: 'To inform all men of the truth concerning the gods, produces contempt in the unwise, from their incapacity of learning, and negligence in the studious; but concealing truth in fables, prevents the contempt of the former, and compels the latter to philosophize.' Sallustius, op. cit., 3; *see* Taylor, op. cit., 6.

5. 'Even the gods, if it is permissible to say it, are created by poetry.' Ovid, *Ex Ponto*, 4.8.55. *See* Feeney, D. C. (1991), 224.

6. *The Gospel of Philip*, NHC, 2.3.72

7. Jung readily admitted that he discovered the concept of the archetypes in the religious and philosophical teachings of the Hellenistic world, particularly in Philo Judaeus and the Gnostic sources quoted by Irenaeus. *See* Jung, C. G., *The Archetypes and the Collective Unconscious*, CW, 9.1.45, and the discussion in Hoeller, S. A. (1989), 3.

8. *See* Merkur, D. (1993), 66. Jung refers to the archetype as 'a kind of readiness to produce over and over again the same or similar mythical ideas'. *See* Jung, CW, 7, 106–9.

9. Plato insists repeatedly that the separation of psyche and body, 'dying', is the goal of all true philosophy, so that pure truth may be apprehended by the psyche in its pure state. Purification, *katharsis*, is achieved through *philosophia* – see for example: 'True philosophers make dying their profession.' *Phaedo*, 67e and 64a

10. Jung, C. G., (1983), 120

11. Jung, C. G., *Symbols of Transformation*, CW, 5.26–9, dating from 1912

12. Gnostic texts with a special emphasis on Sophia include *Pistis Sophia*, *Sophia of Jesus Christ*, *The Exegesis on the Soul*, *The Gospel according to Mary*, *Thought of Norea* and *Thunder: Perfect Mind*.

13. The twofold position of Sophia led in Valentinianism to the conception of a higher ('incorruptible') and a lower fallen Sophia called 'little Sophia' or 'Sophia of death' (NHC, 2.3.60, 12–15, and *see* Clement, *Exc. Theod.*, 33.3–4). Kurt Rudolph notes about the paradoxical statements made by the female figure in *Thunder: Perfect Mind*, NHC, 6.2: 'Behind her is evidently concealed Sophia, but also the soul, both in their two manners of existence: as perfect divine and redeeming power, and as fallen phenomenon exposed to deficiency.' (*See* discussion in Rudolph, K. (1987), 80–1.) Plotinus elaborates the same mythos but illustrates it with the Pagan goddess Aphrodite: 'There the soul is Aphrodite of the heavens; here, turned harlot, Aphrodite of the public ways: yet the soul is always an Aphrodite. This is the intention of the myth which tells of Aphrodite's birth and Eros born with her.' (Plotinus, *Enn.*, 6.9.9.) This last observation is very close to the Gnostic understanding that the soul is feminine and has a womb which can give birth to the Word.

14. As Tertullian writes: 'Sophia has the surnames of Earth and of Mother – "Mother-Earth" of course – and (what may excite your laughter still more heartily) even Holy Spirit.' Tertullian, *AV*, 21

15. Jonas, H. (1958), 186, from *chokmah*, Hebrew for 'wisdom'.

16. Sophia belongs 'to the oldest and most important elements of the structure of Gnosis'. Rudolph, op. cit., 83.

17. The text refers to Homer simply as 'the poet'. *The Exegesis on the Soul*, NHC, 2.6.136, in Robinson, J. M. (1978), 197.

18. As Patricia Cox Miller observes: 'Gnostic texts ... speak a poetry of the body that has few rivals in late antiquity. Expressed primarily in metaphors of desiring, lovemaking and giving birth, Gnostic theological language has sensuous qualities that are striking.' Wallis, R. T. (1992), 223–8

19. *The Exegesis on the Soul*, NHC, 2.6. Harlot, *prunikos*, was one of the titles of Sophia and in the Simonian Gnosis the Holy Spirit is incarnated in a harlot of Tyre named Helen.

20. Sophia has a womb because she gives birth to thoughts and actions. Philo writes: 'God alone can open the wombs of the souls, sow virtues in them, make them pregnant and cause them to give birth to the Good.' Philo, *Leg all.*, 3.180. *See* Jonas, op. cit., 278.

21. The beautiful *Naassene Psalm* is quoted in Hippolytus, *Ref.*, 5.5, who attributes it to the 'Phrygians' (= Naassenes), a sect of Gnostics who existed under the reign of Hadrian (110–140 CE). *See* Barnstone, W. (1984), 635. Unlike *The Exegesis on the Soul*, with which it has many similarities, it refers explicitly to Jesus, who declares: 'Behold, Father, she [the lost soul, Sophia] wanders the Earth pursued by evil. Far from thy Breath she is going astray. She is trying to flee bitter Chaos, and does not know how she is to escape. Send me forth, o Father, therefore, and I, bearing the seal, shall descend and wander all Aeons through, all mysteries reveal. I shall manifest the forms of the gods and teach them the secrets of the holy way which I call Gnosis...'

22. The text explains Jesus' words: 'If one does not hate his soul he cannot follow me.' (cf *Luke* 14:26.) It goes on to state that '...the beginning of salvation is repentance.'

23. *The Exegesis on the Soul*, NHC, 2.6.131–2

24. Plotinus, *Enn.*, 3.8.8

25. *The Teachings of Silvanus*, NHC, 7.4.94. When we experience the mystical marriage we become aware of ourselves as *being*. We are at rest, the still centre of the turning world of appearances. *The Authoritative Teaching* explains that in the mystical marriage the Goddess 'reclined in the bridal chamber and came to rest in him who is at rest' NHC, 6.3.36. *See* Merkur, D. (1993), 152. *The Gospel of Philip* teaches: 'The children of the bridal chamber have just one name, which is "rest".' NHC, 2.3.72.

26. *The Exegesis on the Soul*, NHC, 2.6.134, in Robinson, op. cit., 196

27. Ibid. Describing the Gnostic ascent, Epiphanius writes: 'When [the soul] has become imbued with knowledge she ascends to Heaven and gives a defence before each power and thus mounts beyond them to the upper Mother and Father of the All whence she came down into this world.' *Pan.*, 40.2

28. *The Gospel of Philip*, NHC, 2.3.82

29. *Romans* 7:4–6 and *see 2 Corinthians* 11:2.

30. *Romans* 7:4

31. *2 Corinthians* 3:18

32. *The Gospel of Philip*, NHC, 2.3.67, in Robinson, J. M. (1978), 150

33. Jonas, H. (1958),105

34. *The Golden Verses of Pythagoras*, quoted in Davidson, J. (1995), 998.

35. *Jeremiah* 3:1–4

36. *Ezekiel* 16:23–6

37. *The Exegesis on the Soul*, NHC, 2.6.130, in Robinson, op. cit., 194

38. '...the prophet said (*Genesis* 2:24) concerning the first man and the first woman, "They will become a single flesh." ' This is a topic of recurring interest in the New Testament, *see Matthew* 19:5,19:6, *Mark* 10:8, *1Corinthians* 6:16. Paul commenting on *Genesis* refers to it as a 'Great Mystery' for Christians, *see Ephesians* 5:32.

39. *The Exegesis on the Soul*, NHC, 2.6.133, and *see* Esther de Boer's commentary on *The Gospel of Mary*, BG, 7.1–19.5: 'The soul has landed on earth because part of God, namely Wisdom, turned her back on her male partner... Wisdom has committed adultery and that is how all wretchedness began... Christ was sent to earth to show the way back, to reunite each soul with its male element.' de Boer, E. (1996), 91

40. Philo, quoted in Matthews, C. (1992), 103, referring to the Wisdom and Folly of *Proverbs* 4:11 and 5:5. Folly is likened to a prostitute, see *Proverbs* 7.4 and 7:10–13, whereas Wisdom is likened to an invitation to a wedding feast as in Gnostic literature and the gospel story of the marriage at Cana.

41. *The Exegesis on the Soul*, NHC, 2.6.136, quoting *The Odyssey*, 4.260–1. Esoteric exegesis of Homer was a feature of the Pythagorean school as early as the sixth century BCE, when the texts were redacted by the Orphic poet Onomacritus. *The Iliad* and *The Odyssey* represent respectively the descent and return of the soul. The heroes of *The Iliad* leave their homes to fight a war in a foreign land under the patronage of Apollo, the sun god, whereas the patron deity of *The Odyssey* is Hermes, the messenger of the gods and guide of souls in the Underworld. Whilst *The Iliad* moves in a male world of war and conquest, in *The Odyssey* we move in a feminine universe in which Odysseus encounters one strong woman after another – Circe, Calypso, Nausica, etc. – before finally returning home to his wife Penelope, who sits weaving and unweaving the hero's fate. Porphyry writes: 'Odysseus in Homer's *Odyssey* is a symbol of the man who passes through the temporal cycle and is thus restored to that company who live beyond the waves of the sea of time.' *The Cave of the Nymphs*, 2.34. *See* Gregory, J. (1987), 211.

42. Robert Segal writes in *The Gnostic Jung*: 'About this distinction between the soul and its image, its *eidolon*, which makes contact with matter, there is still another story. Helen is said to have eloped with Paris and to have been the cause of the war between Greeks and Trojans. But it is not true that Helen was ever in Troy: she remained in Egypt and the Greeks and Trojans fought only about her idol, a "doll" which resembled her. The Pythagoreans say that this refers to the soul, which does not become incarnate in the body proper, but makes contact with it through its *eidolon*, its lower part, properly speaking its image reflected in a mirror or in water, but here meant to indicate the subtle or astral body. It was after the pattern of these stories that the oldest Gnostics known to us, Simon Magus of Samaria and his followers, told that the tragic fate of divine Wisdom, raped by hostile powers and at last saved from dispersion, was symbolized by the myth of Helen of Troy and her *eidolon*. And this, I think, throws an unexpected light upon Gnostic origins.' Segal, R. A. (1992), 254

43. In Euripides' lost work *Helen*, the real Helen is blown ashore in Egypt whilst the Trojan War is fought about her image. *See* Plato, *Phaedrus and Letters vii and viii*, 44, note 2.

44. Significantly, *Helen* is the only Classical Athenian drama to be set in Egypt.

45. Plato quotes Stesichorus, a Sicilian poet *c.*650 BCE, as saying: 'The Greeks fought about the shadow of Helen at Troy in ignorance of the truth.' *The Republic*, 586c, and *Phaedrus*, 243f

46. 'Having redeemed from slavery at Tyre, a city of Phoenicia, a certain woman named Helena, he was in the habit of carrying her about with him, declaring that this woman was the first conception of his mind, the mother of all, by whom, in the beginning, he conceived in his mind [the thought] of forming angels and archangels. ...As to himself, they had no knowledge of him whatever; but his Ennoea was detained by those powers and angels who had been produced by her. She suffered all kinds of contumely from them, so that she could not return upwards to her father, but was even shut up in a human body, and for ages passed in succession from one female body to another, as from vessel to vessel. She was, for example, in that Helen on whose account the Trojan war was undertaken; for whose sake also Stesichorus was struck blind, because he had cursed her in his verses, but afterwards, repenting and writing what are called palinodes, in which he sang her praise, he was restored to sight. Thus she, passing from body to body, and suffering insults in every one of them, at last became a common prostitute; and she it was that was meant by the lost sheep. [*Matthew* 18:12]' Irenaeus, *AH*, 1.23.2, Hippolytus, *Ref.*, 6.14

47. So much of the information we have about Simon is legendary that it is possible that Simon was not an historical figure at all. He could have been the hero of a Samaritan Christ myth in which the Godman Simon (the Sun?) rescued the Wisdom Goddess Helen (Selene – the Moon?) (*see* Jonas, H. (1958), 108), just as the Jewish Godman Jesus rescued the Wisdom Goddess Sophia/Mary in the more familiar version. As Jonas notes: 'Selene (Moon) is merely the exoteric name of the figure, her true name is Epinoia, Ennoia, Sophia and Holy Spirit.' Ibid., 109

48. '...also a Samaritan by birth... He affirms that the primary Power continues unknown to all, but that he himself is the person who has been sent forth from the presence of the invisible beings as a saviour, for the deliverance of men. The world was made by angels, whom, like Simon, he maintains to have been produced by Ennoea.' Irenaeus, op. cit, 1.23.5

49. Plato, *Phaedo*, 79c–d

50. Plotinus, *Enn.*, 6.9.9

51. Ibid., 3.5.8: 'Aphrodite [= the *habra*, delicate] indicating the beauty and gleam and innocence and delicate grace of the Soul.'

52. Ibid., 6.9.9

53. Ibid., 1.2.4

54. Ibid., 6.7.34

55. The myth of Eros and Psyche was preserved into the Christian era in two sources, Ovid's *Metamorphoses* and Lucius Apuleius' *Golden Ass*. There is a useful discussion, 'The Myth of Eros and Psyche in Plotinus and Gnosticism', by Patricia Cox Miller in Wallis, R. T. (1992), 223–8.

56. Eros was the patron deity of the Orphics, Pythagoreans, Plato and Socrates. As W. K. C. Guthrie notes in his 'Outline of the Orphic Theogony', Eros was also known as *Phanes*, 'Light', *Protognos*, 'First-born', and also Dionysos (Guthrie (1952), 80). Eros had his own cult at Phlya in the south-western part of the Peloponnesus where the Mysteries of Andana were celebrated. In age and venerability they were second only to those of Eleusis. At Phlya there was a *Telesterion* – an initiation hall, a bridal

chamber and a cult of Demeter, Persephone and Eros (*see* Pausanius, *Description of Greece* II, 4.1.5–7 and 26.8, *also* Meyer, M. W. (1987), 49ff, and Harrison, J. (1922), 594, 643–4). The Mysteries of Eros evidently impacted directly on the Gnostics, for according to the evidence of Hippolytus, the Sethian Gnostic school system was nothing other than the tenets of the Orphic Mysteries which were celebrated at Phlya, long before the Eleusinian (Hippolytus, *Ref.*, 5.15, and *see* Mead, G. R. S. (1906), 116). This might explain the Gnostic obsession with the bridal chamber, to which there are over 25 references in *The Gospel of Philip* alone.

57. *On the Origin of the World*, NHC, 2.5.109, in Robinson, J. M. (1978), 178

58. Graves' alternative title for *The Golden Ass* (*see* Lucius Apeuleius, The Golden *Ass*, intro). There is a useful discussion of the multi-layering of meanings in 'The Golden Ass in a Labyrinthine World' in Martin, L. H. (1987), 18ff.

59. Proclus writes about the dual aspect of Persephone: 'Hence, according to the rumour of theologists, who delivered to us the most holy Eleusinian initiations, Persephone abides on high in those dwellings of her mother which she prepared for her in inaccessible places, exempt from the sensible world. But she likewise dwells beneath with Pluto, administering terrestrial concerns.' Proclus in *Theol. Plat.*, 371, quoted in Taylor, T., *Oracles and Mysteries* (1995), 92

60. Sallustius writes about the soul 'falling from the celestial regions', followed by its reascent to the gods, as the reason for the celebration of the Mysteries at the equinoxes – the Lesser Mysteries (or Dionysia) in spring and the Greater Mysteries (or City Dionysia), dramatized at Eleusis, in the autumn. Writing about the rape of Persephone enacted at Eleusis, Sallustius writes: '...this rape alludes to the descent of souls.' (*On the Gods and the World*, Chapter 4.) Thomas Taylor, in his introduction to *Hymns and Initiations* (Prometheus Trust, vol. V, 1996), elaborates: '... the rape of Persephone, which was exhibited in these mysteries, signifies, as we are informed by Sallustius, the descent of souls. And the descent of souls into the realms of generation is said, by Plato in the tenth book of his *Republic*, to take place at midnight, indicating by this the union of the soul with the darkness of a corporeal nature. This too, I suppose, is what Clemens Alexandrinus means when he says, "that the mysteries were especially performed by night, thus signifying that the compression [i.e. confinement] of the soul by the body was effected at night." ' Hippolytus comments on the descent and ascent as the Mystery revealed to those 'admitted to the highest grade of the Eleusinian rites' and states that the Naassene Gnostics had plagiarized their doctrine from this source (*Ref.*, 5.3). Even without this explicit statement it is clear that the Gnostic myth of the descent of Sophia is dependent on the Pagan Mysteries.

61. Olympiodorus, *Commentary on the Phaedo*, quoted in Taylor, T., *Oracles and Mysteries* (1995), 82.

62. '...and other arcane rites which Eleusis the Attic sanctuary conceals in profound silence.' Quoted ibid., 89.

63. Lucius Apuleius, *The Golden Ass*, 286, and *see* Taylor's commentary, op. cit., 90.

64. Hippolytus, op. cit., 5.3

65. Plato, *Cratylus*, 404c-d. In *Phaedo* Plato hints at the true meaning and purpose behind the myth of the descent into the Underworld: 'Some, in order to see again those whom they loved, have undertaken the journey to Hades [e.g. Orpheus] and therefore with what greater joy must we then start out for Hades in order to obtain Wisdom [Sophia] and be with her.' *Phaedo*, 68a, see Campbell, J. (1955), 68.

66. 'The Ode to Sophia' in *The Acts of Judas Thomas*, see Mead, G. R. S. (1906), 419.

67. In some versions of this myth, Persephone is gathering narcissus flowers when she is abducted by Hades. (*See* 'On the Eleusinian Mysteries' in Taylor, T., *Oracles and Mysteries* (1995), 100.) This is an allusion to the myth of Narcissus, which contains the same basic mythologem as the Persephone myth. Narcissus becomes so enamoured with his own refection in a lake that he falls in and drowns. Plotinus explains that the story of this 'dupe', as he calls him, is an allegory for how Consciousness identifies with its *eidolon* or image and 'drowns' in the world (*Enn.*, 1.6.8).

68. Kerenyi, C. (1967), 38

69. In *Laws*, 870e, Plato states that the doctrine of 'karma' was taught by the priests of the Mysteries: 'They will also state a truth firmly believed by many who have learned it from the lips of those who occupy themselves with these matters at the Mysteries, that vengeance is taken on such crimes beyond the grave, and when the sinner has returned to our own world once more, he must infallibly pay nature's penalty – must be done by as he did.'

70. Porphyry, *On Images*. On Delos Demeter was honoured side by side with Isis, who, as Kerenyi notes, was a Goddess who, like Demeter, 'grieved and wandered'. *See* Kerenyi, op. cit., 32-3

71. Epiphanius, *Ancoratus*, quoted in Jung, C. G. (1957), 20.

72. It is impossible to ignore the similarities between the Egyptian quarternity: Isis and Nepthys (known as 'the Two Goddesses' in Egypt), Osiris and Set (personifications of life and death), and the leading characters of the Eleusinian drama: Demeter and Persephone (also known simply as 'the Two Goddesses'), Dionysus and Hades. Diodorus of Sicily, first century BCE, clearly states that the initiatory rites of Demeter in Eleusis were transferred from Egypt (Diodorus Siculus, 1.29.2). Later he states: 'The rite of Osiris is the same as that of Dionysus and that of Isis very similar to that of Demeter, the names alone having been interchanged, and the punishments in Hades of the unrighteous, the Fields of the Righteous and the fantastic conceptions, current among the many – all these were introduced by Orpheus in imitation of the Egyptian funeral customs.' (1.96.4-5)

73. *See also* the story of Cinderella (whose name, 'Little Spark', was an image used by the Gnostics for the soul), who must descend into the kitchen as a servant but whose ultimate fate is to marry the prince.

74. *The Tripartite Tractate*, NHC, 1.5.122

75. *Matthew* 1:1-18

76. Significantly, considering the theme of adultery and prostitution in the Gnostic Sophia myth, each of these women played a crucial role in the royal line of Israel by her adultery. In *Genesis* 38:14 Tamar sits by the wayside as a prostitute to secure the seed of her father-in-law. In *Joshua* 2:1 Rahab the prostitute hides in her brothel

the spies who precipitate the fall of Jericho. Ruth the Moabite widow returns to Bethlehem, where she has sex with Boaz on the threshing floor. Baathsheba ensured by her adultery that her son Solomon became king, *2 Samuel* 19:9. *See also* the Gnostic *Protoevangelium of James*, which describes Jesus' mother as a *kadesha*, or temple prostitute, a name deriving from Qadesh, the Queen of Heaven of Sinai. (*Numbers* 20:11)

77. *Joshua* 2:1–3, 6:17, 6:23
78. *John* 13:23
79. *The Gospel of Philip*, NHC, 2.3.63–4
80. *Luke* 7:38
81. 'It was the greatest disgrace for a woman to unbind her hair in the presence of men.' Scott, M. (1992), 210. *See also* Haskins, S. (1993), 18.
82. In *Sophia and the Johannine Jesus* Scott observes that women appear at the key christological moments throughout *The Gospel of John*. 'A woman is present at the beginning of his ministry (2.1–11, the marriage at Cana; it is to a woman that the Messiah first reveals his true identity (4:26); it is a woman who first makes the true confession of Jesus as the Christ (11:27); it is a woman who anticipates the sign of true discipleship in the anointing of Jesus' feet (12:1–8); the women are found to be faithful to the end at the cross (19:25–7); and finally it is to a woman that the Risen Christ first makes himself known (20:1–18).' Scott, op. cit., 174–5
83. *The Gospel of Philip* (NHC, 2.3.59), likewise, describes Sophia as 'barren and without child'.
84. *See* 'Baptism' in *TJM*, 34ff, for the parallels between John the Baptist and Jesus.
85. Origen decodes this part of the allegory: 'John is the voice but Jesus is the Word.' Origen, *Commentary on the Gospel of John*, 6.30
86. *John* 8:3 in KJV but tagged onto the end of *The Gospel of John* in others. Regarding its disappearance from some texts, Augustine believed that men had removed the passage out of fear of the consequences of such teachings!
87. *John* 4:14
88. Philo describes Rebecca, the mother of Jacob, as the recipient of Sophia through her drawing at the well: 'Now, it says, Rebecca went down to the spring to fill the water jug and (then) came up. For from where is a mind, thirsting for meaning [*phronesis*], likely to be filled but from the Wisdom of God, the spring that never fails. Descending to this, she ascends after awhile, akin to an eager disciple. Therefore, on seeing that she has drawn understanding from Wisdom, the divine spring, the one who is eager to learn, runs up and, encountering her, begs her to satisfy his thirst for learning. And she, having been taught the most important lesson, immediately – unselfishly and generously – holds out the stream of Wisdom and bids (him) drink deep, while calling him "lord" of the house. Now this is the most decisive (proof) that only the sage is a free man and ruler, even though he might have ten thousand masters of his body.' Philo, *Cain's Exile*, 136, 138 (translator's brackets). *See also* Philo, *Fug.*, 195, and *Poster C*, 136, *Quaest. in Gen.*, 4.98, and Scott, op. cit., 188.
89. *Luke* 10:42

90. *John* 12:3. *Matthew* 26:13 sees the anointing as a highly significant act and makes Jesus say: 'Verily I say unto you, Wheresoever this gospel shall be preached in the whole world, there shall also this, that this woman hath done, be told for a memorial of her.' Unfortunately, with the deletion of the Sophia myth from Literalist Christianity the real significance of this act in the Jesus story has been lost.

91. *Mark* 16:9, *Luke* 8:2 and *see* Marcion, *Gospel of the Lord*, 5.2. The Dance of the Seven Veils performed by Salome, the lover of John the Baptist, must be an allusion to this same doctrine.

92. The Mysteries dramatized the descent and reascent of the soul during incarnation. Lights symbolized the planets and stars were imagined as a celestial ladder connecting Earth and Heaven. Origen reveals the Mithraic doctrine about the planets and the stars 'and the soul's passage through these. The symbol is this. There is a ladder with seven gates and at its top an eighth gate.' Celsus implies that this is not new to Mithraism. He calls it an 'ancient system that there are seven heavens and that the way of the soul is through the planets'. The Christians that Celsus criticized in the second century were clearly teaching the same doctrines as Mithraism. He says, 'That [the Christians'] system is based on very old teachings may be seen from similar beliefs in the old Persian mysteries associated with the cult of Mithras.' *See* Hoffmann, J. (1987), 95.

93. Albinus the Platonist tells us that the planets are gods, there are seven of them, and in the eighth place is the 'power from above' which 'encompasses the others'. Following the *Timaeus*, he goes on to say that the Demiurge assigned the creation of men to gods inferior to himself, for if he had made men himself they would have been immortal. These lower gods made men out of the elements; the Demiurge sent down souls for them. The body, made by the lower gods, is the seat of the affections, such as sensory perception and the emotions of pleasure, grief, fear and anger, only the soul, the gift of the Demiurge, is immortal. (Albinus *Esiagoge*, 14, 170, 36; 16, 172.4, 8, in Hermann, ed., *Platonis Dialogi*. 115.) Each of these ideas can be set side by side with its counterpart in the Christian Gnostic texts of the NHC.

94. The Gnostic Theodotus writes: 'He whom the Mother generates is led into death and into the world, but he whom Christ regenerates is transferred to life into the *ogdoad*.' (Quoted in Campbell, J. (1955), 392.) Cyril of Alexandria describes the consecration as the '*mysterion Christi* which is symbolized by the *ogdoad*', demonstrating that the *ogdoad* was still part of Christian Literalist theological speculation in the fourth century CE (ibid., 390). There is a useful diagram of the Gnostic cosmos modelled after the Ophite diagrams in Rudolph, K. (1987), 68.

95. The distant ancestor of this motif would appear to be the Sumerian ziggurat, a pyramid of seven steps topped by a temple in which there was a sumptuous bed. On one day of the year a Sumerian priestess would be visited by the God. *See* 'The Sacred Marriage', Chapter 12 in Frazer, J. (1922), 142.

96. Mary is the first witness of the resurrection in all four gospels. *Mark* 16:9: 'Now when Jesus was risen early the first day of the week, he appeared first to Mary Magdalene.' *See also Matthew* 28:1, *Luke* 24:10, *John* 20:18.

97. *The Dialogue of the Saviour*, NHC, 3.5.139. *Pistis Sophia* also portrays Mary as the most spiritual of all the disciples, *see* Mead, G. R. S. (1906), 467.

98. *The Gospel according to Mary*, 9.10

99. *See* 'Bread and Wine' in *TJM*, 48ff.

100. *John* 15.1

101. Matthews, C. (1992), 203

102. *The Book of the Great Logos* portrays Jesus commanding his disciples to go to Galilee and find a man or woman in whom the greater part of evil is dead and to take two jars of wine from them to the place where He is, and also two vine branches. When they have done so, Jesus creates a place of offering, placing one wine jar on the right and one on the left, and strews certain berries and spices round the vessels. He then makes the disciples clothe themselves in white linen robes. *See* Mead, op. cit., 524. The scene thus described is identical to representations of the Mysteries of Dionysus found on ancient Greek vases – red-figured vases of the sixth–fifth century with the crowned Dionysus set up on a wooden post before two wine jars and loaves of bread. *See* the vases illustrated in *TJM* plate section.

103. The Naasene Gnostics, according to Hippolytus, *Ref.*, 5.3.

104. Lietzmann relates the numerous connections between the wine miracles of Jesus and Dionysus and writes: 'No explanation is needed to show how this very day came to be adopted for commemorating the marriage at Cana when Jesus performed the miracle which used to be performed by Dionysus.' Lietzmann, H. (1961), vol. III, 320ff.

105. A recurring theme in the New Testament, *see Matthew* 9:15, 25:5, 25:6, 25:10, *Mark* 2:19, 2:20, *Luke* 5:34, 5:35, *John* 2:9, 3:29, *Revelations* 18:23.

106. *John* 3:29

107. *Matthew* 25:1–13

108. Ibid., 22:1–14

109. From the *Interrogationes maiores Mariae*, quoted by Epiphanius, *Pan.*, 26.8. *See* Segal, R. A. (1992), 73.

CHAPTER 6: THE ASCENT FROM THE CAVE

1. Jung, C. G., 'A Psychological Approach to the Doctrine of the Trinity', *The Psychology of Religion East and West*, CW, 2.233. See Hoeller, S. A. (1989), 130.

2. Quoted in Irenaeus, *AH*, 3.2.1. The Valentinians taught that the secret teachings are meaningful only to those who are spiritually mature. If a person was unready they would seem like nonsense 'because their value can be judged only on a spiritual basis' (*1 Corinthians* 2:14). According to the Valentinian tradition, Paul and the other apostles revealed these teachings only to those who were 'spiritually mature' (*1 Corinthians* 2:6).

3. See 'Psychic and Pneumatic Teachings', *TJM*, 168ff, and Pagels, E. (1975), 5–7. According to Theodotus Paul recognized that 'each one knows the Lord in his own way and not all know him alike'. So on the one hand he preached the saviour 'according to the flesh' as one 'who was born and suffered'. This 'kerygmatic gospel' of

'Christ crucified' he taught to *psychic* Christians 'because this they were capable of knowing' (*1 Corinthians* 2:2). But to *pneumatic* Christians he proclaimed Christ *pneumatically* or 'according to the spirit' (*see* Pagels, 5, quoting *Romans* 1:3 and *1 Corinthians* 2:2). Each level of initiate would take from his teachings what they were wise enough to be able to hear (*see 1 Corinthians* 2:14–15). The Gnostics taught that only those who had been initiated into the secret oral teachings of the Inner Mysteries were capable of understanding the deeper meaning of Paul's letters. Elaine Pagels writes: 'The Valentinians claim that most Christians make the mistake of reading the scriptures only literally. They themselves, through their initiation into Gnosis, learned to read Paul's letters (as they read all the scriptures) on the symbolic level, as they say Paul intended. Only this pneumatic reading yields "the truth" instead of its mere outward "image".' (Ibid., 7)

4. The term *mathetes*, translated in the New Testament as 'disciple', is a Pythagorean term used in the Greek world to describe the pupils of philosophers (*see* Aristophanes, *Clouds*, 140; Plato, *Protagoras*, 315a; *Apology*, 33a; *The Republic*, 618c). In *The Republic* (525a) Plato uses it specifically to describe 'the study of unity ... that will guide and convert the soul to the contemplation of true being'. Diodorus of Sicily uses it specifically to describe 'a pupil of the philosopher Pythagoras' (12.20.1).

5. Josephus was in command of Galilee during the Jewish revolt and lists in his writings what appear to be all the region's main towns and villages, but makes no mention of Nazareth (*see* Wilson, I. (1984), 66–7). As Wells has noted, Paul says nothing about Nazareth and never calls Jesus a Nazarene (Wells, G. A., (1975), 157). The name 'Nazorean' or 'Nazarene' occurs in *Matthew* 2:23, which cites an unknown prophecy, 'He shall be called a Nazarene,' which is not found in the Old Testament. Grant has shown that the word cannot mean 'from Nazareth' (Welburn, A. (1994), 282) and it is now widely held to refer to the sect of the Nazarenes. *The Gospel of Philip* explains 'The Nazarene' as 'He who reveals what is hidden' (NHC, 2.3.56, in Robinson, J. M. (1978), 144). The Nazarenes were still found scattered throughout Syria and the Decapolis in the late fourth century. Mead writes: 'These Nazarenes knew nothing of the Nazareth legend, which was subsequently developed by the "in order that it might be fulfilled" school of historicizers.' Mead, G. R. S. (1906), 126–9

6. Dower, E. S. (1960), ix. *See* Welburn, op. cit., 282.

7. *Colossians* 1:24 and *Galatians* 2:20

8. *Romans* 6:7

9. *See* 'The Sacred Spectacle at Eleusis', *TJM*, 18ff.

10. The passion is enacted with such realism in Mexico and the Philippines that the actor playing Christ is often seriously injured and sometimes killed. The Oberammergau passion play in Germany is less violent and consequently has a better safety record. In *The Golden Bough* Frazer sets out the parallels between customs still performed in Italy and Sicily in the nineteenth century and the ancient rites of Adonis. Frazer, J. (1922), Chapter 33

11. *Galatians* 3:1

12. It is hard to believe that if this Christian community in Asia Minor had really been at the crucifixion in Jerusalem Paul would feel free to call such important witnesses 'stupid Galatians' (literally *anoetos*, 'without *nous*') or criticize them in clearly Gnostic terminology for looking to a 'material' (*sarkic* = *hylic*) rather than 'spiritual' (*pneumatic*) understanding of this event.

13. Paul uses the term *prographo*, meaning, amongst other things, 'to set forth' in writing.

14. *See* 'The Mystery Play' in Robertson, J. M. (1903), 47ff.

15. Hoffmann, J. (1987), 71

16. *Galatians* 6:17

17. An epitaph from Philippi in Macedonia reads: 'Revived, thou livest in the flowery meadows of the Elysian fields, where thou art welcomed into the troop of satyrs by the Mystae of Bacchus, marked with the sacred seal.' (Quoted in Turcan, R. (1992), 315–16.) Initiates dedicated to the Mother received her 'seal' (*sphragitis*), burned into them with red-hot needles, and at their burial this was covered with a gold plate. According to legend Pythagoras was said to possess a 'Golden Thigh'. Several myths record the favourite of the Great Mother being wounded in the thigh, sometimes on their way into the Underworld. As Burkert notes, only one who bears this sign can enter the Underworld (*see* Burkert, W. (1972), 160). Significantly, Odysseus is recognized by his nurse Eurycleia by a scar on his thigh which he received from a wild boar (*The Odyssey*, 19.377–454). Perhaps this motif refers to Dionysus, who was born from the thigh of Zeus, a wound that was imitated by initiates to show that they had in their turn given birth to Dionysus.

18. Clement describes the revelation of Christianity in the exact language of the Pagan Mysteries: 'O truly sacred Mysteries! O pure light, in the blaze of the torches I have a vision of heaven and of God. I become holy by initiation. The Lord reveals the Mysteries. He marks the worshipper with His seal. If thou wilt, be thyself also initiated, and thou shalt dance with angels around the unbegotten and imperishable and only true God.' Clement of Alexandria, *Exhortation to the Greeks*, 12

19. *Romans* 6:3–4

20. *The Gospel of Philip*, NHC, 2.3.64.25

21. *Galatians* 4:19 and 3:27–8

22. Sallustius, *On the Gods and the World*, 4. *See* Taylor, T. (1994), 8.

23. Kerenyi reproduces a Greek vase from the fifth century BCE depicting Dionysus (lifted up on a stake) flanked by two Maenads carrying torches, one points upwards and one downwards, symbolic of the Mystery school teachings on the *anodos* and *cathodos*, the way up and the way down of the soul, into and out of incarnation (Kerenyi, C. (1976), figure 85). Another illustration shows a Thracian Maenad tattooed with a ladder on the right arm and insteps (Lindsay, J. (1970), 198). *See* Cumont, F. (1922), 154, for the ladder of Mithras made of seven metals representing the sun, moon and planets.

24. The triumph of astrology over Graeco-Roman thought is illustrated by its spectacular growth in Rome. As Barton notes, astrology was marginal to elite politics until the Late Republic (Barton (1994), 33), when suddenly it became fashionable for every demagogue to employ his own astrologer. Sulla was advised by 'Chaldaeans', as were

Pompey, Crassus, Julius and Augustus (Plutarch, *Sulla*, 37.1, Cicero *De Divinatione*, 2.47.99). Octavian began early, consulting the astrologer Theogenes in 44 BCE (Suetonius, *Augustus*, 94.12). Astral lore became fashionable in Augustan poetry to the extent that Bouché-Leclercq called it *'une manie littéraire'* (Bouché-Leclercq (1899), 552). Tiberius is said to have neglected the gods because he believed only in fatalism (Suetonius, *Tiberius*, 69). Vespasian was inspired to move on Rome due to the favourable positions of the planets (Tacitus, *Histories*, 2.78). By the end of the first century CE Pliny wrote that: 'There is no one who is not eager to learn his destiny or who does not believe that the truest account of it is to be gained from watching the skies.' (Pliny, *Natural History*, 30.1.1–2.) A century later in the time of the Severi, as Cumont observed, 'Anyone who should have denied the influence of the planets upon the events of this world would have been considered more preposterous than he who would admit it today.' (Cumont (1911) 168.) It is not at all surprising therefore, that the Gnostic gospels also demonstrate an obsession with astrological lore.

25. Cicero, *On the Nature of the Gods*, 2.55

26. Cicero continues: 'I cannot understand the regularity of the stars, the harmony of time and motion in their various orbits through all eternity, except as the expression of reason, mind and purpose in the planets themselves, which we must therefore reckon in the number of the gods.'

27. *John* 10:31–6, referring to *Psalms* 82:6.

28. Hippolytus, *Ref.*, 9.5. See Kahn, C. H. (1979), 71. In the Hermetica this saying is attributed to Osiris. Given the initiatory nature of Heraclitus' teachings (Diogenes writes of Heraclitus teaching: 'It is a hard road to follow, filled with darkness and gloom; but if an initiate leads you on the way, it becomes brighter that the radiance of the sun', quoted Kahn, 95), Heraclitus may in fact have derived it from an undeclared source which the Hermetica is keen to correct.

29. *See* Faulkner, R. O., 'The King and the Star-Religion in the Pyramid Texts', *JNES* 25 (1966), 153–61.

30. Plato, *Timaeus*, 41

31. Plotinus, *Enn.*, 3.5.5

32. 'I am a star wandering about with you, shining forth out of the deep.' From the so-called *Mithras Liturgy. See* Kingsley, P. (1999), 147.

33. *The Gospel of Truth*, NHC, 1.3.32 and 12.2. *See* Matthews, C. (1992), 150.

34. *Matthew* 5:14

35. Bousset writes: 'The Gnostics believed that human beings ... carry within them from the beginning a higher element (the *spinther*) deriving from the world of light, which enables them to rise above the world of the Seven into the upper world of light, where dwell the unknown Father and the heavenly Mother.' (Bousset, W. (1907), 321. *See* Segal, R. A. (1992), 89, note 139.) Hippolytus tells us that in the doctrine of the Sethians, the darkness held 'the brightness and the spark of light in thrall' (*Ref.*, 5.19.7) and that this 'very small spark' was finely mingled in the dark waters below. Simon Magus taught that in milk and semen there is a very small spark which 'increases and becomes a power boundless and immutable'. (Quoted ibid., 6.17.7. *See*

Segal, op. cit., 90.) As Jung has demonstrated, the alchemical quest for the liberation of gold from dross is a continuation of the Gnostic quest for the recovery of the divine sparks lost in matter (Jung, C. G. (1957), 48).

36. Hippolytus, op. cit., 5.4. In Egyptian myth Osiris was the shepherd (hence the crook held by every pharaoh in imitation of Osiris) who guides souls (each of which is a star in Egyptian mythology) back to the Fields of the Righteous (the star-fields of the constellations) after death.

37. *Luke* 2:7. *See* Wilson, I. (1984), 52. A very early tradition locates Jesus' birth in a cave and it was over a cave that the emperor Constantine built Bethlehem's Church of the Nativity. Jesus is born into a cave and laid out in a cave after his death. The cave represents both womb and tomb, which conveys the Gnostic teachings that to be born as a human being is to die as a spiritual god (hence Heraclitus' saying about mortals/immortals above). Later Christian mythographers transferred the same imagery to the idea that Jesus was born at an inn. They explain that the cosmos is called the 'inn' in which one 'lodges' and 'to keep the inn' is a metaphor for 'being in the world' or 'in the body'. *See* Jonas, H. (1958), 55.

38. *See* Barnstone, W. (1984), 390, *also* Aristophanes, who refers to Dionysus as the 'light-bringing star of the nocturnal Mysteries' (*Frogs*, quoted in Kerenyi, C. (1976), 79). Coins from Crete (where the decipherment of 'Linear B' texts show a cult of Dionysus in existence *c.*1200 years BCE) show a star in the centre of the labyrinth (ibid., 105–6).

39. According to Orphic myths, Dionysus was born in a cave where he was immediately enthroned as King of the World. *See* Burkert, W. (1977), 297, quoting the *Orphic Rhapsodies*. Mithras was likewise born into a cave and underground Mithraic sanctuaries were made as an image of the 'World Cave'.

40. Taylor, T., *Oracles and Mysteries* (1995), 101

41. The Neoplatonic interpretation of Empedocles' *Katharmoi* is that the 'covered-over cave' which Empedocles describes fallen souls as descending into is not a literal cave but a symbol of the world we live in. Porphyry compares Empedocles' cave to that of Plato's *Republic* in defence of his fundamental thesis that in both cases the cave is a symbol of this world. *See* Kingsley, P. (1995), 36–8.

42. 'Behold men as if living in a subterranean cavern, and in a den-like habitation, whose entrance is open to the admission of the light throughout the cave. Now, my dear Glaucon, I went on, this simile must be connected throughout with what proceeded it. The visible realm corresponds to the prison, and the light of the fire in the prison to the power of the sun.' Plato, *The Republic*, 517b

43. Porphyry, *On the Cave of the Nymphs*, 29

44. 'Everywhere [Plato] expresses contempt for all that is of sense, blames the commerce of the psyche with the body as an enchainment, an entombment, and upholds as a great truth the saying of the Mysteries that the psyche is here a prisoner. In the Cavern of Plato and in the Cave of Empedocles, I discern this universe, where the breaking of the fetters and the ascent from the depths are figures of the wayfaring toward the Realm of Consciousness.' Plotinus, *Enn.*, 4.8.1

45. Ibid., 4.8.3

46. Ibid., 2.9.6

47. 'All this terminology is piled up to conceal their debt to the ancient Greek philoso-phy.' (Ibid.) Plotinus' criticisms, however, only serve to illustrate just how similar Pagan and Christian Gnosticism were. He describes the Gnostics both as 'friends' who had been so badly contaminated by the new teaching before they met him that they could not get over it even after they had been taught the true doctrine by him (2.9.10) and as apostates who had abandoned the honourable tradition of Platonic philosophy and tried to set up a new school. He did not expect them to come back to the right road, but he desired to enlighten the rest of his pupils that whatever was worthy in Gnostic teaching had been taken from Plato and that what had been added to it was far from true. *See* Evangelious's 'Plotinus' Anti-Gnostic Polemic and Porphyry's *Against the Christians*' in Wallis, R. T. (1992), 111–28.

48. 'Let us reverence inexorable and venerable Justice, who is said by Orpheus, our instructor in the most holy initiations, to be seated by the throne of God, and to inspect all the actions of men.' Demosthenes, *Aristogeiton* II (quoted in Willoughby, H. R. (1929), 105). Parmenides gives us more information on this figure: '...and in the midst of [the spheres] is the Goddess who steers all, for she it is that begins all the works of hateful birth and begetting, sending female to mix with male and male in turn with female.' (Kirk, G. S., and Raven, J. E. (1957), 283.) The Goddess 'sends the souls, now from the visible into the invisible, now back again' (Burkert, W. (1972), 284). Plotinus refers to the same figure as 'Adrasteia, the Inevitable Retribution' who is responsible for the karmic laws whereby souls are punished by being 'done by as they did' – '...for in very truth this ordinance is an Adrasteia, justice itself and a wonderful wisdom.' (Plotinus, op. cit., 3.2.13.) The Gnostics have clearly derived their mythology from this same Orphic/Pythagorean stream. In *Pistis Sophia* we are told how souls are led to 'the Virgin of Light, the Judge' who tests whether the soul has found the Mysteries. If not: 'The Virgin of Light sealeth that soul and handeth it over to one of her receivers, and will have it carried into a body, which is the record of the sins which it hath committed.' (*Pistis Sophia*, 3.113. *See* Mead, G. R. S. (1921), 245–6, *also* (1906), 498.) A Mandaean text relates: 'I went and found Truth as she stands at the outer rim of the worlds.' (*G*, 390, in Jonas, H. (1958), 91)

49. Kirk and Raven, op. cit., 283

50. In Gnostic texts the mother is called 'She of the Left-hand', *sinistra*. Mead (1906), 334.

51. *Matthew* 25:31–3. The judgement of the dead in an afterlife court goes back to ancient Egypt, but their division into those on the right and the left can be seen evolving as these beliefs steadily entered the West. In *The Republic*, Book 10, 614b–d, Plato discourses on the Orphic teachings of the fate of the soul after death. About the afterlife judgement he writes '...after every judgement they bade the righteous journey to the right and upward through the heavens with tokens attached to them of the judgement passed upon them, and the unjust to take the road to the left and downward, they too wearing behind signs of all that had befallen them...' In the Sethian Gnostic scheme described by Irenaeus, *AH*, 1.30.14, souls on the right ascend to the light of the divine world, souls on the left return to Earth/Hades. There is a

discussion of 'right' and 'left' in Gnostic doctrine in Perkins, P. (1993), 57. The motifs found in Pythagorean and Orphic teaching are also found in Virgil's *Aeneid*, Book 6. Finally, in *Matthew*, Jesus places 'the sheep at his right hand, but the goats at the left'. The two paths motif is also alluded to when Jesus is portrayed as crucified between two thieves. One ascends with him to Heaven and one descends to Hell.

52. Cicero illustrates the initiate's view of the Underworld myth in the first century BCE (Cicero was initiated at Eleusis in 79 BCE, *see* Magnien, V. (1938), 25): '...all of this is false as everyone knows.' (*Pro Cluentio* 171. *See* Bernstein (1993), 115.) In *Tusculan Disputations* he states, significantly, that: 'Ignorance of philosophy has produced the belief in hell and its terrors.' (*Tusc. Disp*, 1.16.36.) Elsewhere he implies that these beliefs were a human invention that had long since lost their currency (*Catalina*, 3.8). In *Tusculan Disputations*, 1.46.111, he acknowledges that the gullible crowd is convinced of the reality of the Underworld, whereas the learned few have no need of such a myth. Similar sentiments were expressed by the Augustan poets Vergil and Ovid, who, like Cicero, were not sceptics but initiates. Their reticence in stating directly that this world is the Underworld suggests that this was a secret doctrine of the Mysteries. Unfortunately, despite Cicero's inability to find 'any old woman so silly as to believe the old stories of the horrors of the world below' in the first century BC (Cicero, *de Natura Deorum*, 2.2.5, *see* Arnold (1911), 223, 264–5), their numbers had clearly multiplied three centuries later when Celsus ridiculed Christians for concocting 'an absolutely offensive doctrine of everlasting punishment and rewards, exceeding anything the philosophers (who have never denied the punishment of the unrighteous or the reward of the blessed) could have imagined'. (NB Celsus carefully avoids attributing these to an afterlife.) *See* Hoffmann, J. (1987), 70.

53. Eisler (1931) records numerous grave inscriptions containing the well-known Pythagorean symbol of the letter 'Y' (26–7, 76, 148, 150). To the Pythagoreans this was a symbol of the two paths open to man in both life and in death. In life the left-hand path leads to dissolution and the right to virtue, likewise after death the left-hand path leads to reincarnation and the right-hand path to the Elysian Fields. We also have a seemingly strange piece of ancient graffiti carved behind a pillar in Rome some time between 193 and 235 CE. It sketches a man with a donkey's head crucified on a cross and has been interpreted as a Pagan insult towards Christianity, but it is far more likely that it is a Dionysian representation of the crucifixion of the lower 'animal' nature, which, as we demonstrated in *TJM*, was symbolized by a donkey. In the top right of this graffito is scratched the Pythagorean symbol of the 'Y'. *See* King, C. W. (1887), 279, cf Wilson, I. (1984), flyleaf. *See TJM*, 52.

54. *The Sophia of Jesus Christ*, NHC, 3.4.117, in Robinson, J. M. (1978), 242

55. Thomas Taylor writes: 'As soon as the soul gravitates towards the body she experiences matter flowing into her essence. Plato in *Phaedo* says that the soul is drawn into the body staggering with recent intoxication. Oblivion, the companion of intoxication, silently creeps into the recesses of the soul. A defect of memory is the origin of opinion. But those who discover most have drunk least of oblivion.' (Taylor, notes on Porphyry's *Cave of the Nymphs*, 63.) The Orphic *Gold Leaves* (fourth century BCE) discovered in southern Italy gives instructions to the deceased on how to escape the

'sorrowful wheel' of reincarnation by avoiding the spring of Lethe (forgetting) and drinking only of the spring of Mnemosyne (memory) before journeying 'to the right' and into the 'starry heavens'. (See Guthrie, W. K. C. (1952), 172–4.) Virgil (first century BCE) tells us how: '…souls who are destined to live in the body a second time, at Lethe's wave drink the waters which abolish care and give enduring release from memory.' (Virgil, *Aeneid*, 6, 699–720.) 'God calls all of them forth in long procession to Lethe River, and this he does so that when they again visit the Sky's Vault they may be without memory, and a wish to re-enter bodily life may dawn.' (Ibid., 748–51.) In Gnostic terms, incarnation is seen as the ultimate bad hangover, waking up in a strange place not knowing how you got there. The descent of souls into incarnation is viewed as a continuous parade of drunken amnesiacs.

56. There is a useful discussion of the Gnostic metaphors of 'Numbness, Sleep, Intoxication' in Jonas, op. cit., 68.

57. Mead, G. R. S. (1906), 334

58. Campbell, J. (1955), 392

59. Mead, op. cit., 499. A trace of this teaching is preserved in *The Gospel of Matthew* (12:42), where Jesus hints that it is not himself but the mysterious 'Queen of the South who will judge this generation'. As Jesus goes on to talk of Solomon, it is clear that this figure is meant to be seen as Wisdom, *see* Matthews, C. (1992), 42.

60. Plotinus, *Enn.*, 2.9.9

61. In the last book of *The Republic* Plato describes the nature of the cosmos, and how 'the spindle turns on the knees of Necessity' (a title of the Goddess Justice according to Parmenides, *see* Kirk, G. S., and Raven, J. E. (1957), 284) Close to Justice are seated the Three Fates, Lachesis, Clotho and Atropos, who spin, weave and cut the thread of each soul's fate.

62. Celsus confirms the early appearance of this tradition (*see* Hoffmann, J. (1987), 57). Similarly, in *The Odyssey*, Penelope remains at home weaving and unweaving a tapestry on which is woven the fate of Odysseus.

63. Plato, *Laws*, 870e, and *see Meno* 81b–d : '…the soul of man is immortal. At one time it comes to an end – that which is called death – and at another is born again, but is never finally exterminated. On these grounds a man must live all his days as righteously as possible. Thus the soul, since it is immortal and has been born many times, and has seen all things both here and in the other world, has learned everything that is.'

64. Plotinus, op. cit., 3.2.13, and *see Corpus Hermeticum Asclepius*, 28: '…one pays the penalty precisely in proportion to one's wrongdoing.' *See also* Copenhaver, B. P. (1992), 84.

65. *Matthew* 7:1–5

66. Plato, *Cratylus*, 400c. The Manichaeans regarded the cosmos as a hospital for light and a prison for darkness. *See* Lieu, S. N. C. (1985), 14.

67. *Luke* 12:58. Irenaeus gives us the exegesis of this passage according to Carpocrates, that a soul 'must pass from body to body, until he has experience of every kind of action which can be practised in this world, and when nothing is longer wanting to him, then his liberated soul should soar upwards to God'. Irenaeus, *AH*, 2.25.4

68. *Pistis Sophia*, 3.113. See Mead, G. R. S. (1921), 245–6.

69. Mead, G. R. S. (1906), 516f. *See Pistis Sophia*, 6.144 and 4.131, which intriguingly states that the 'cup of the water of forgetfulness becomes body outside the soul ... which is what is called the counterfeiting spirit'. The 'body outside the soul' equates to the circumference of the circle where the shadow of the spirit, the *eidolon*, appears as a separate body in a world of separated bodies.

70. Cross, F. L. (1958), 733. The nativity of John is celebrated on 24 June in the West and 25 June in the East.

71. Porphyry, *On the Cave of the Nymphs*, 11, and Macrobius, *Commentary on Cicero's Somnium Scipionis*, 12. See Porphyry (1991), 45, 61. In astrology Cancer is ruled by the Moon, the mistress of life, Capricorn by Saturn, the master of death.

72. *See TJM*, 36.

73. Mead, G. R. S. (1906), 522. *See also TJM*, 156.

74. *Matthew* 3:11

75. Ibid.

76. *John* 3:3

77. *Matthew* 3:12, *Luke* 3:17

78. In Greek vase paintings initiates are pictured veiled and seated with a winnowing fan being waved above their heads. Harrison, J. (1922), 547

79. *John* 3:30

80. *Mark* 6:7, *Matthew* 10:1, *Luke* 6:13, *John* 6:67, and *see Joshua* 4:20.

81. Plato, *Laws*, 745d–e

82. The importance of the pole and zodiac to the ancient Egyptians is demonstrated by the two so-called 'air shafts' found in the King's Chamber of the Great Pyramid. They are inclined to within one degree of accuracy on the celestial pole to the north and the constellation of Orion in the south. Lamy gives a more likely explanation of these peculiar shafts as 'two ways offered to each individual, that of final liberation to the north or reincarnation on the wheel in the south' (Lamy, L. (1981), 28). In the Pyramid Texts the distant realm to which the Pharaoh always goes is the sky. ('He climbs to the sky among the imperishable stars.' Ibid., quoting a Pyramid Text.) The stars of the circumpolar region were considered eternal, for unlike the zodiacal band, they never descended below the horizon, i.e. they never come into reincarnation. *See* Highbarger, E. L. (1940), 10.

83. Cumont, F. (1903), 152–3. As Cumont notes, the sacred masks 'were interpreted by Pagan theologians as an allusion to the signs of the zodiac, and even to the doctrine of metempsychosis'.

84. *The Acts of John*, 97–102. During the hymn the disciples say: 'The number Twelve paces the round aloft – Amen.' The Gnostic *Book of Jehu* also contains an allusion to the round dance (*see* Campbell, J. (1955), 171).

85. An Orphic text written c.fourth century BCE in southern Italy records the hope of the deceased to have 'flown out of the sorrowful weary wheel' (quoted in Guthrie, W. K. C. (1952), 173).

86. *Corpus Hermeticum*, Book 16, 12–18

87. *Exc. Theod*, 55, quoted in Foerster (1972), 222–33

88. Plotinus, *Enn.*, 2.3.1

89. Guthrie, K. S. (1987), 145

90. 'This is what those who are initiated by Orpheus to Dionysus and Kore pray that they may attain: "To cease from the wheel and breathe again from ill."' Proclus, *Commentary on Timaeus*, 330. *See* Willoughby, H. R. (1929), 99.

91. *Exc. Theod.*, 74.2. *See* Martin, L. H. (1987), 136.

92. *The Book of Thomas the Contender*, NHC, 2.7.138, in Robinson, J. M. (1978), 201

93. See introduction to *The Gospel of Thomas*, ibid., 124. Pagels is right to suggest that the opening lines of both *The Gospel of Thomas* and *Thomas the Contender* can be read as if 'you, the reader, are Jesus' twin brother'. This is an axiom of Gnostic teaching. *See* Pagels, E. (1979), 47.

94. *Matthew* 13:55: 'Is not this the carpenter's son? is not his mother called Mary? and his brethren, James, and Joses, and Simon, and Judas?'

95. Judas betrays his master when, like Peter, he clashes with Mary Magdalene, representing the conflict between the ego and the awakening psyche.

96. There are a suspiciously large number of Simons in the New Testament: Simon, Jesus' brother; Simon Peter the apostle; Simon called Zelotes or the Kanaites; Simon, father of Judas who betrayed Jesus; Simon Magus; Simon the tanner; Simon the Pharisee; Simon of Cyrene who carried the cross of Christ; Simon, son of Cleophas, the cousin of Jesus; and finally Simon the leper.

97. In *Pistis Sophia*, 2.72, Mary tells Jesus: 'I am afraid of Peter because he threatened me and hateth our sex.' In *The Gospel of Mary* Peter and Andrew represent orthodox positions and deny women the authority to teach. Through its portrayal of Mary Magdalene as the saviour's beloved who possessed knowledge and teaching superior to that of the public apostolic tradition, the gospel attacks this position head on. *See* the introduction to *The Gospel of Mary* in Robinson, op. cit., 524. The confrontation between Mary and Peter is also found in *The Gospel of Thomas* and *The Gospel of the Egyptians*.

98. *John* 13:38

99. Ibid., 20:11

100. *The Gospel of Mary*, BG, I.17. Peter asks: 'Did he really speak with a woman without our knowledge and not openly? Are we to turn about and all listen to her?' In her exegesis of *The Gospel of Mary*, de Boer makes the following interesting observations: 'The Gospel makes clear that the four elements, Earth Water Air and Fire, indicated by the names Darkness, Desire, Ignorance and Wrath respectively, are what bind the soul to the material realm. Each seeks to discourage the soul from ascending to its Rest and are its adversaries.' Later the text makes Levi say: 'Peter, you have always been hot-tempered. Now I see you arguing with the woman *like these adversaries.*' As de Boer notes, this clearly equates Peter with the ignorant elements, and, as we know from other sources, Mary is a synonym for Sophia/the soul (de Boer, E. (1996), 92–5). This insight helps us to understand much of *The Gospel of John* where it is primarily women who both recognize Jesus and behave like true disciples – his mother at Cana, the Samaritan woman at the well, Martha and Mary, Mary anointing Jesus, the woman who touches the hem of his garment, the women at the foot of the cross and the women at the tomb. By contrast, the male disciples are often shown

as confused, critical or cowardly. Peter denies him (*John* 18:17), Judas betrays him (*John* 12:4), Thomas doubts him (*John* 20:25), many disciples leave him (*John* 6:66) and those that remain understand the significance of his teachings only after his death (*John* 2:22 and 12:16).

101. Wells, G. A. (1999), 262, quoting Caragounis' summary of Matthew's depiction of Peter.

102. *Matthew* 16:23

103. Commenting on the evidence for the Gnostics' allegorical approach to the gospels in *The Gospel of John*, the Reverend W. R. Inge writes: 'The fourth Gospel is steeped in symbolism of this kind. The eight miracles which St. John selects are obviously chosen for their symbolic value; indeed, he seems to regard them mainly as acted parables. His favourite word for miracles is *semeion*, signs or symbols.' Inge (1899), 58

104. The Jesus story often divides the witnesses of Jesus' miracles into three categories. Those who reject him, despite the miracle he has performed, represent *hylics*. Those who believe because of the miracle represent *psychics*. Those who believe before witnessing the miracle represent *pneumatics*. Scott (who discerns so many allusions to Sophia in John's gospel that he uses the composite name Jesus-Sophia) observes that throughout *The Gospel of John* it is women who 'demonstrate the Johannine principle of true faith' in that 'their response is to the *word* of Jesus-Sophia rather than to the sign' (Scott, M. (1992), 202). In contrast, the disciples 'often play no active role at all, being mere bystanders whose only response is to believe because of what they have seen' (ibid., 182).

105. *Exodus* 16:15, *Matthew* 14:16–21, *Mark* 8:1–9

106. *John* 11:16

107. *See* 'Jesus the Daemon', *TJM*, 117ff, *also The Book of Thomas the Contender*, which opens with the words addressed by Jesus to his twin 'Brother Thomas'. *The Book of Thomas the Contender*, NHC, 2.7.138, in Robinson, J. M. (1978), 201

108. Mack, B. L. (1988), 215f, and *see* discussion in Doherty, E. (1999), 238.

109. Scott, op. cit., 167. As Scott notes, 'Once again Sophia's influence can be traced behind a major feature of the Fourth Gospel's presentation of Jesus Christ. Jesus Sophia performs his *semeia* in parallel to those attributed to Sophia [in *The Wisdom of Solomon* 11–19] culminating like hers in the delivery and salvation of the people.'

110. In *The Gospel of Mark* we hear that Jesus 'kept speaking to them in allegories, according as they could hear, and he said nothing to them without allegories, but privately to his own students he always gave the key' (*Mark* 4:11–12). In *The Gospel of John* 16:12,25, Jesus promises his disciples more explicit teachings when they are ready to receive them: 'I have yet many things to say unto you, but you cannot bear them now. These things I have spoken to you in allegories: the hour is coming when I shall no more speak in allegories, but shall tell you plainly of the Father.' But, as Kingsland notes, none of these 'Mysteries' are in fact explained by Jesus in the canonical gospels. Instead we must turn to the Gnostic texts, where we find the teachings of the resurrected Jesus. *See* Kingsland, W. (1937), 25–6.

111. In Bultmann's famous phrase: 'Jesus as the Revealer of God reveals nothing but that he is the Revealer.' Bultmann, R. (1955), 2.66. *See* Scott, op. cit., 145.

112. According to *Acts* 1:3, the resurrected Jesus spends 40 days among his disciples before ascending to heaven, 'speaking of the things pertaining to the kingdom of God', but we are not told what they are. The time between the resurrection and the ascension was one day according to *Luke*, 10 days according to *John*, and 40 days in *Acts*. As both *Luke* and *Acts* are said to have been written by the same author, this discrepancy is puzzling.

113. *John* 15:15-17, abridged

114. *Galatians* 5:14. *See also Romans* 13:8: 'Owe no man anything, but to love one another: for he that loves another has fulfilled the law.'

115. *1 Corinthians* 13:1-3

116. Plotinus, *Enn.*, 6.8.15

117. *1 John* 4.7

118. Basilides, quoted in Clement of Alexandria, *Strom.*, 4.12. *See* Layton, B. (1987), 435.

119. *Matthew* 5:38-45: 'You have heard the saying "You shall love your neighbour and hate your enemy." But I say to you, love your enemies and pray for those who persecute you. Then you will become children of your Father in Heaven. For he makes the sun shine on the evil and the good alike; and sends the rains to unjust men as well as just men. You have heard the saying "An eye for an eye and a tooth for a tooth." But I say to you, don't resist evil with evil. If someone strikes you on your right cheek, turn the other one to him as well; and if someone wants to sue you for your coat, let him also have your cloak; and if someone forces you to walk a mile with him, walk with him for two miles; and don't ignore someone who want to borrow from you, but if you are asked for something, then give it away.'

120. *The Gospel of Thomas*, 95, NHC, 2.2.95: 'If you have money, don't lend it at interest. Rather give it to someone from whom you won't get it back.'

121. *Galatians* 4:4-5

122. *Mark* 7:8

123. *Matthew* 21:31

124. *Luke* 11:52. One of two uses of 'Gnosis' that remain in the gospels, both in *Luke*.

125. *John* 8:44

126. Ibid., 4:20-4

127. *Luke* 22.66

128. *See TJM*, 53ff. In Lucius Apuleius' tale of initiation, Lucius is transformed into a donkey through his own foolishness and endures many adventures, representing stages of initiation. At his final initiation into the Mysteries of Isis he is transformed back into a human being. This story is symbolic of the initiate being overcome by his lower nature and then, through initiation into the Mysteries, rediscovering his true identity. Isis tells Lucius that the donkey is the most hateful to her of all beasts because it is sacred to Set, who in Egyptian mythology is the murderer of Osiris. *See* Lucius Apuleius, *The Golden Ass*, 13.

129. As Price notes, Mark's gospel has a circular structure which ends with the women fleeing from the tomb after a young man tells them Jesus will rejoin his disciples in

Galilee. Mark wants the readers to look next at the only place there is left to look: the beginning. There we find the episode of Jesus' calling the disciples at the lakeside and their mysteriously immediate response to drop what they are doing and follow him. (*See* Price, R. M. (2000), 35.) This literary device draws attention to the fact that 'Galilee' itself means 'circuit, district' or 'a wheel, rolling'. Arthur Drews connects this with the wandering of the sun through the 12 signs of the zodiac (Drews, A. (1910), 240).

130. 'This mother they call also the eighth, wisdom, land, Jerusalem, holy spirit and Lord in the masculine gender. She occupies the place of the midpoint, and until the end, she is above the craftsman but below or outside the fullness [*pleroma*].' (Irenaeus, *AH*, 1.5.3.) Thus Jesus rescues Mary/Sophia from Galilee 'the wheel' = the zodiac, and takes her up to Jerusalem (the Mother) and hands her over at the foot of the cross – the *stauros* that in Gnostic myth divides Heaven from Earth, the *pleroma* from the *kenoma*.

131. Porphyry begins his esoteric exegesis of the 'Cave of the Nymphs' in the thirteenth book of Homer's *Odyssey* with the line: 'High at the head a branching olive grows.' (Quoted in Gregory, J. (1987), 210.) In Pagan mythology olives were sacred to the Goddess of Wisdom. In Gnostic mythology, before his crucifixion, Jesus preaches on the Mount of Olives.

132. *The Apocalypse of Peter*, NHC, 7.3.81, in Robinson, J. M. (1978), 377

133. *The Paraphrase of Shem*, NHC, 7.1.39; ibid., 357

134. Basilides taught that 'because he was Mind, Jesus did not suffer' but Simon of Cyrene suffered in his stead, while Jesus laughed 'because he could not be held and was invisible to all'. *See* Barnstone, W. (1984), 628, quoting Hippolytus, *Ref.*, 7.20–7, on Basilides, *also Matthew* 27:32 and *Mark* 15:24.

135. Walker, B. (1983), 30

136. *See* depiction at Dendera in Egypt – Mariette, *Denderah*, vol. IV, plate 56 – *also* Jung, C. G., *CW*, 9.2, para 129–30.194.78. Set and Horus are sometimes pictured as having one body and two heads.

137. Euripides, *The Bacchae*, 1,098–1,103. In Euripides' drama King Pentheus functions as a surrogate for Dionysus. First he is dressed up in the clothes of the God, in *imitatio dei*, before being lifted up on a tree – the fate that we know was actually suffered by the God in other myths. Although this idea of the surrogate is missing from Literalist Christianity, it is the favourite interpretation of the Gnostics about the crucifixion. In *The Second Treatise of the Great Seth* it is Simon who is crucified as a 'similitude' of Jesus, whilst the real Christ, who cannot suffer, is elsewhere (*The Second Treatise of the Great Seth*, NHC, 7.2.56, in Robinson, op. cit., 365). This finally makes sense of the story recorded in *Matthew* (27:32), where Simon of Cyrene is dragooned into carrying Jesus' cross.

138. Lieu, S. N. C. (1985), 128

139. *Matthew* 27:3

140. *The Apocryphon of James*, NHC, 1.2.6, in Robinson, op. cit., 32, and Merkur, D. (1993), 138

141. *See* discussion in Angus for the relevant passages in Plato, Themistius, Apuleius, Proclus, etc. (Angus, S. (1925), 96ff.) In Greek the words for 'death' and 'initiation' are similar and were a familiar pun. 'To die is to be initiated,' says Plato. Initiation was considered a death from which believers arose through rebirth. Lucius Apuleius, for example, was known as 'a man resurrected from the dead' after his initiation in the Mysteries of Isis. (Apuleius, *The Golden Ass*, 11.18. Martin, L. H. (1987), 78. *See* 'Spiritual Rebirth' in *TJM*, 59ff.)

142. *Matthew* 16:24-6

143. *Galatians* 5:24

144. Plato, *Phaedo*, 67e

145. *1 Corinthians* 15:3

146. Valentinus quoted in Clement of Alexandria, *Strom.*, 4.89.2-3. *See* Layton, B. (1987), 241, and Rudolph, K. (1987), 319.

147. Hippolytus, *Ref.*, 7.26-8

148. *The Gospel of Philip*, NHC, 2.3.68.26-9, in Robinson, J. M. (1978), 151

149. *Hebrews* 4:12

150. *The Acts of John*, 36. *See* Barnstone, W. (1984), 420.

151. *See* Campbell, J. (1964), 372ff. Campbell gives the relevant chapters from *The Acts of John* and comments on docetism.

152. *The Gospel of Truth*, NHC, 1.3.29-30. *See* Segal, R. A. (1992), 245, and Merkur, D. (1993), 139.

153. Plotinus, *Enn.*, 1.4.7

154. *Pistis Sophia*, 2.33

155. Welburn, A. (1994), 315

156. Rudolph, K. (1987), 297

157. *The Treatise on the Resurrection*, NHC, 1.4.45-6, referring to *Romans* 6:3-7. The text refers to Paul simply as 'the apostle'.

158. Valentinus, quoted in. Clement, *Strom.*, 4.89.2-3. *See* Rudolph, op. cit., 319.

159. *The Gospel of Philip*, NHC, 2.3.63, in Robinson, J. M. (1978), 148. *See* discussion in Merkur, op. cit., 138.

160. *Galatians* 6:14

161. *The Treatise on the Resurrection*, NHC, 1.4.48

162. *John* 16:33

163. 'Jesus cried out with a loud voice and gave up the ghost. And the veil of the temple was torn in two, from top to bottom.' *Mark* 15:37-8

164. Josephus, *The Jewish War*, 5.5.4. There is an interesting discussion of 'The Heavenly Veil Torn: Mark's Cosmic "Inclusio"' by David Ulansey, *Journal of Biblical Literature* 110, 1 (Spring 1991), 123-5, and *see* http://www.well.com/user/davidu/veil.html. Ulansey argues that '... there was a connection in the mind of the author of the Gospel of Mark between the tearing of the heavens at the baptism of Jesus (Mk 1:10) and the tearing of the temple veil at the death of Jesus (Mk 15:38).' This is further evidence (*see* note above) for the circular nature of *The Gospel of Mark*.

165. The greatest festival in Classical Athens was the Panatneaea, the depiction of which takes up the entire inner frieze (the Elgin Marbles) of the Parthenon. At this festival

a new *peplos* – veil or robe – was woven for Athena, the virgin Goddess of Wisdom. As Mead writes, this was a symbol of the Mysteries and signified the Veil of the Universe, studded with stars (Mead, G. R. S., *Thrice-Great Hermes* (1964), vol. I, 42). According to *The Hymns of Orpheus, peplos* was one of the names of heaven. *See* Matthews, C. (1992), 71.

166. Porphyry records this as an Orphic myth; *On the Cave of the Nymphs,* 38.

167. *On the Origin of the World,* NHC, 2.5.98

168. Matthews, op. cit., 71

169. 'Now the unseen and mental light was made an image of the Word of God interpreting its origin. And it is the star beyond the heavens, the source of the sensible stars.' Philo, *Creation,* 31a

170. *The Treatise on the Resurrection* explains that ordinary human existence is spiritual death but the resurrection is spiritual enlightenment (*The Treatise on the Resurrection,* NHC, 2.4.48–9, in Robinson, J. M. (1978), 52ff, and *see* Pagels, E. (1979), 42). The purpose of initiation was to awaken the psyche from this death-like state and this is the true doctrine which lies behind Empedocles' claim to be able to resurrect a man from the dead. With the triumph of Literalist Christianity this became completely misunderstood as the bringing back to life of people who had actually died. Guthrie traces most Christian doctrines on the afterlife to the Orphics with the one exception that the Orphics would have found the doctrine of the resurrection of the body 'repulsive'. Guthrie, W. K. C. (1952), 269

171. Tertullian, quoted in Mead, G. R. S. (1919), 95

172. Ibid., 97

173. *The Treatise on the Resurrection,* NHC, 1.4.49, in Robinson, op. cit., 56

174. Ibid.

CHAPTER 7: CONSCIOUSNESS CONCEIVES THE COSMOS

1. Hippolytus, *Ref.,* 6.18.47, and *see* Mead, G. R. S. (1906), 173–4

2. According to Theodotus, Gnosis is knowledge of: 'Who were we? Where were we? Into what place have we been cast? Where are we going? From what have we been saved? What is birth? What is rebirth?' *See* Hanratty, G. (1997), 24, quoting *Exc. Theod.*

3. For example, there are six differing accounts of the Valentinian system in the heresiological literature. *See* Rudolph, K. (1987), 320.

4. The Gnostics freely adapted inherited teachings, a fact which appalled Literalists like Irenaeus: 'They all generate something new each day; for no one is considered initiated or mature among them unless he develops some enormous fiction!' (Irenaeus, *AH,* 1.18.) The Gnostics' creativity is a sign of the vitality of this new movement. As Burkert notes in another context, 'Only dead dogma is preserved without change, doctrine taken seriously is always being revised in the continuous process of reinterpretation.' (Burkert, W. (1972), 135)

5. The Pagan sage Thales writes: 'God is the consciousness of the cosmos.' (Quoted in Aetius, 1.7.11. *See* Kirk, G. S., and Raven, J. E. (1957), 94.) Empedocles taught that

God 'is holy unspeakable consciousness' (quoted in Ammonius, *de interpretatione*, 249. *See* Kirk and Raven, op. cit., 350.) This theme fascinated the philosophers of the ancient world. Cicero writes: 'Then came Pythagoras, who held that mind was present and active throughout the whole universe and that our own minds were a part of it.' (Cicero, *On the Nature of the Gods*, 1:27.) Plato writes: 'No son of man will ever come to a settled fear of God until he has grasped the two truths we are now affirming, the soul's dateless anteriority to all things generable, her immortality and sovereignty over the world of bodies, and moreover that presence among the heavenly bodies of a mind of all things of which we have spoken so often already.' (Plato, *Laws*, 967d.) Empedocles, Xenophanes and Anaxagoras uttered similar sentiments and even Aristotle identified God with mind. (Aristotle fr. 49, *see* Cartledge, P. (1993), 164.) *See also* the introduction to our *Hermetica*: 'At the heart of Hermes' teachings is one simple idea – God is a Big Mind. Everything which exists is a thought in the Mind of God. This book is a thought in the Mind of God. Your body is a thought in the Mind of God. These ideas which are being discussed are thoughts in the Mind of God.' (Freke, T., and Gandy, P. (1997), 21.) Regarding the cosmos as the Mind of God, Plato further suggests that the archetypal Ideas are the thoughts of God (*The Republic*, 10.597b; *see also Timaeus*, 52c, which suggests that God and the Ideas are really One). To interpret the Ideas in this way was common by the time of Philo, who says explicitly that God created the Ideal world to serve as a pattern for the phenomenal creation and that the Ideas are the thoughts of God. (Philo, *De Optifico Mundi*, 16. *See* Cherniss, H. (1977), 271.)

6. *The Apocryphon of John* (also known as *The Secret Book of John*), NHC, 2.1.106
7. Ptolemy, quoted in Irenaeus, op. cit, 1.1.1. *See* Layton, B. (1987), 281
8. Plotinus, *Enn.*, 3.8.9
9. Ibid., 3.8.10
10. *The Apocryphon of John*, NHC, 2.1.2
11. Dionysius, *The Divine Names*, 7.3. *See* Armstrong, K. (1993), 149.
12. Ibid., 1. *See* Pseudo-Dionysius (1987), 51.
13. Gregory, J. (1987), 38
14. Ibid.
15. Ibid., 35
16. The Egyptians honoured their supreme God Atum as 'the undifferentiated One'. *See* 'Glossary of Gods' in Hornung, E. (1982), 275.
17. *The Tripartite Tractate*, NHC, 1.5.54. As J. P. Kenney observes, 'The most striking feature of the *Tripartite Tractate's* strict monotheism is its rigorous negative theology.' (*See* Wallis, R. T. (1992), 189.)
18. Plotinus, *Enn.*, 6.9.3. *See* Wallis, op. cit., 451.
19. Quoted in Inge, W. R. (1899), 110. Dean Inge observes that Augustine repeats this verbatim.
20. Basilides, quoted in Mead, G. R. S. (1906), 267. Augustine, who in his youth was 'fired by the works of Plotinus', writes of a vision in the very words of Plotinus: 'My mind withdrew its thoughts from experience, extracting itself from the contradictory throng of sensuous images ... and thus with the flash of one hurried glance, it attained

to the vision of That which Is.' Augustine, *Confessions*, 1.7.17. *See* Underhill, E. (1993), 331.

21. Plotinus, op. cit., 5.5.6. *See* Wallis, op. cit., 232.

22. Ibid., 5.3.14

23. Dionysius, *The Mystical Theology*, 1048b. *See* Pseudo-Dionysius (1987), 141.

24. Barnstone, W. (1984), 629. There is a useful summary of Basilides' system in Barnstone, 626–34.

25. Valentinus writes about the creation of the universe by the Father: 'Now because he was able to bring forth, it seemed good to him one day, since he contained within himself whatever is most beautiful and most perfect to bring this to birth. For he was all love, but love is not love if there is no object that is loved.' Hippolytus, *Ref.*, 6.29, and *see* Irenaeus, *AH*, 1.1.1. *See also* 'The First Unfolding of the Procession' in Wallis, op. cit., 298, which notes that: 'The Valentinian vocabulary of procession is found again, whole and entire, in Plotinus.'

26. Actually, as is characteristic of Christian writers, Simon treats the Mystery as a male 'Father' figure, but we have made his quote gender neutral here so as not confuse things unnecessarily. There is an extensive, albeit polemical, summary of Simon's system in Hippolytus, op. cit., 6.4–15. *See The Great Annunciation of Simon the Magus* in Welburn, A. (1994), 181.

27. Although it is obvious why the natural analogy to draw on to represent the concept of syzygy is male and female, we must be clear that the syzygy 'man–woman' is a distant echo of the archetypal primal syzygy and to crudely equate the two is to completely misunderstand the subtlety of Gnostic thought. The primal syzygy is the archetype of every complementary–opposite such as man and woman, day and night, life and death, and so on. All such syzygies are images of the archetypal primal syzygy, but they are not identical to the primal syzygy or each other. It is the differences which make them conceptually distinct and which gives manifestation its rich variation.

28. As *The Gospel of Philip* states: 'Light and darkness, life and death, right and left, are brothers of one another. They are inseparable. Because of this neither are the good good, nor the evil evil, nor is life life, nor death death.' *The Gospel of Philip*, NHC, 2.3.53, in Robinson, J. M. (1978), 142

29. *Zostrianos*, NHC, 8.1.82–3. *See* Wallis, R. T. (1992), 466.

30. *The Wisdom of Solomon* (also known as *The Sophia of Solomon*.), 7.25–6. *See* discussion in Armstrong, K. (1993), 82.

31. An Egyptian hymn from *c.*1500 BCE reads: 'Three are all the gods, Amon, Ra, Ptah; there are none like them. Hidden in his name as Amon, he is Ra, his body is Ptah. He is manifested in Amon, with Ra and Ptah, the three united.' Murray, M. A. (1949), 46

32. Plotinus, *Enn.*, 5.5.8. 'This is the explanation of Plato's Trinity, in the passage where he names as the Primals the Beings gathered about the King of All, and establishes a Secondary containing the Secondaries, and a Third containing the Tertiaries.' This famous passage from Plato's *Second Letter*, 312d–e, was used by post-Renaissance Platonists as justification for a *rapprochement* between Platonism and Christianity, and by the deist Founding Fathers of America as an argument for rejecting

Trinitarianism as Paganism in disguise. *See* Walker, D. P. (1972), 85ff, and Smith, J. Z. (1990), 15ff.

33. 'We need not, then, go seeking any other Principle; this – the One and the Good – is our First, next to it follows Consciousness, the Primal Thinker, and upon this follows psyche. Such is the order of nature. The Realm of Consciousness allows no more than these and no less.' (Plotinus, op. cit., 2.9.1.) 'One must not posit more existents there than these nor make superfluous distinctions in such realities.' (Ibid., 2.9.2, and *see* Wallis, op. cit., 397.) These passages are directed specifically at the Gnostics, whom Plotinus criticizes elsewhere for 'piling up' their 'terminology' unnecessarily.

34. Rudolph, K. (1987), 319. *The Gospel of Philip* makes it clear that the Holy Spirit was regarded as female by the Gnostics. It wryly observes: 'Some said: "Mary conceived by the Holy Spirit." They are in error. They do not know what they are saying. When did a woman ever conceive by a woman?' *The Gospel of Philip*, NHC, 2.3.55.25, in Robinson, J. M. (1978), 143

35. When Plotinus talks of 'the One', he makes this clear by using male, female and neutral gender terms interchangeably. Gregory, J. (1987), 33

36. Some Gnostics concluded that as *Genesis* places the creation of humanity as 'male and female' (*Genesis* 1:27) after the statement 'Let us make man [Adam] in our image' (*Genesis* 1:26), the God in whose image we are made must also be both masculine and feminine. (*See* 'God the Father/God the Mother' in Pagels, E. (1979), Chapter 3.) Both Marcus and Theodotus argued that God was masculo-feminine (ibid., 78). *The Testimony of Truth* (in a meditation on *Genesis*), having previously described the divine source as a 'bisexual Power', goes on to say that 'what came into being from that Power – that is, humanity, being one – is discovered to be two: a male-female being that bears the female within it.' (NHC, 9.3.68. *See also* Pagels, op. cit., 77.)

37. Quoted in Hippolytus, *Ref.*, 6.37. *See* Mead, G. R. S. (1906), 36. The androgyny of God goes back to ancient Egypt. Akhenaten, for example, called his God Aten 'mother-father' and represented himself graphically in a similar way, *see* Hornung, E. (1982), 171. In Egyptian mythology Isis and Osiris are both brother and sister and man and wife, a mythology which legitimized the Egyptian practice of brothers and sisters marrying. Zeus and Hera were likewise brother and sister and man and wife. The Stoic philosopher Chrysippus interpreted Zeus as God and Hera as matter and their union as the commencement of creation. This, he said, was the only way 'we could understand the beginnings of the universe [i.e. the division of the original divine unity into two antithetical forces], or the poets when they speak of Hera as wife and sister of Zeus' (Chrysippus, in Cicero, *De natura deorum*, 1.15.40). In a response clearly directed at Literalists who were shocked by this mythology, Chrysippus pointed out that it was absurd to criticize cosmic processes as if they were breaches of social decency.

38. Quoted in Hippolytus, op. cit., 6.12.

39. *Trimorphic Protennoia*, NHC, 13.1.45, in Robinson, op. cit., 519. The androgyny of the divine is a recurrent theme in Gnosticism. *The Gospel of the Egyptians* refers to 'the androgynous Father' (NHC, 4.2.42). *The Exegesis on the Soul* refers to the

androgynous soul: 'As long as she was alone with the father, she was virgin and in form androgynous.' (NHC, 2.6.127.) Taking over a Pagan myth, *On the Origin of the World* describes the appearance of the androgynous Eros (NHC, 2.5.109). The theme is also explored in *Eugnostos the Blessed, The Sophia of Jesus Christ, The Hypostasis of the Archons, The Apocalypse of Adam* and *The Apocryphon of John.*

40. In this, the earliest Christian Gnostic schema of all, the *Great Announcement of Simon Magus*, recorded in Hippolytus (op. cit., 6.18.47), the Great Unlimited Power contains Thought as a potential, of which it becomes aware, thus objectivizing thought as a separately existing entity ('appearing to himself from himself he became two, he brought forth himself from himself'). (*See* Wallis, R. T. (1992), 452–3.) The Gnostics developed philosophical ideas which reach back to the Presocratics. As the great classicist F. M. Cornford noted, 'The abstract formula which is common to the early cosmogonies is as follows: 1. There is an undifferentiated unity. 2. From this unity two opposite powers are separated out to form the world order. 3. The two opposite powers unite again to generate life.' (Quoted in Guthrie, K. S. (1987), 22.) Cornford goes on to demonstrate how this universal pattern not only underlies the cosmogonies of Greek myth, but also those of the early Ionian scientific tradition.

41. *The Untitled Text*, Chapter 1 in the Bruce Codex

42. Anaxagoras, quoted in *Simplicius Phys.*, 164.24. *See* Kirk, G. S., and Raven, J. E. (1957), 372, and Arnold, E. V. (1911), 40. Plato describes how 'One day Socrates discovered with pleasure the words of Anaxagoras: "It is mind that orders the world and is the cause of all things. " ' Plato, *Phaedo*, 97c. *See* Arnold, op. cit., 44.

43. The word 'cosmos' shares the same Greek root as 'cosmetic' and was coined by the Pythagoreans to convey their belief that the universe is not only ordered but 'adorned' with order.

44. Consciousness arises with the objectification of psyche. Psyche is the objectified appearances in the process of awakening to their subjective essence. Consciousness results from the One becoming two. Psyche is the impulse to reconcile the two as One.

45. Plotinus, *Enn.*, 2.9.1

46. *The Gospel of Thomas*, NHC, 2.2.50, in Robinson, J. M. (1978), 132

47. The Trinity can be understood as representing consciousness in three fundamental states. The Mystery is Consciousness without an object, and so, paradoxically, unconscious. Consciousness is Consciousness with an object. It is conscious that it is Consciousness and so has Gnosis of its self-nature. Psyche is Consciousness objectified as many self-images with which Consciousness separately identifies. In this state, therefore, Consciousness is unaware of its true ineffable self-nature and so is in a state of ignorance and on a journey of awakening.

48. 'We must in my opinion begin by distinguishing between that which always is and never becomes [and] that which is always becoming but never is.' Plato, *Timaeus*, 27

49. Consciousness is the eternal *NOW*. It defines time by delineating the past and future, yet is itself beyond time. As perfect Consciousness we exist outside time, perfect and permanent. As a psyche-body we exist within time, evolving and temporary.

50. Plato, op. cit., 37. The followers of Marcus taught that the Demiurge created 'times, epochs, and great numbers of years under the delusion that he could represent the

infinity [of the *pleroma*]' (Irenaeus, *AH*, 1.17.2). Jonas writes: 'This, of course, is a parody of the famous passage in the *Timaeus...*' (Jonas, H. (1958), 194)

51. The primal syzygy can be understood simply as unity and duality. From the point of view of the becoming, the Mystery appears as the One to which it seeks to return – the Good which is its goal. The becoming is a movement between two poles. Unity is the Absolute. Duality is the relative. Unity is Good. Duality is good and bad. Unity is Gnosis. Duality is the journey from ignorance to Gnosis. Between the two poles of the duality appear infinite relative points which form the multiplicity.

52. Plotinus, op. cit., 2.3.16

53. Mead, G. R. S. (1906), 262

54. Plato, *Phaedo*, 69a–d. As Taylor writes: 'Instruction in the means of returning to the principles from which they originally fell ... was the ultimate design of the Mysteries.' Taylor, T., *Oracles and Mysteries* (1995), 64

55. *The Three Steles of Seth*, NHC, 7.5.127, in Robinson, op. cit., 401. *See* Layton, B. (1987), 158, cf Heraclitus CIII in Kahn's numbering, Kahn, C. H. (1979), 75. T. S. Eliot uses this aphorism of Heraclitus as the opening quotation of the *Four Quartets*.

56. That the Jewish Merkabah mystics of the first few centuries called themselves 'descenders in the chariot' whilst Jewish Gnostics called the first principle *Bythus*, 'the Deep', perhaps signifies their origination in similar circles, especially as other systems current in the first centuries, Mithraism and Hermeticism, for example, regarded the journey of the soul as a celestial ascent.

57. *The Gospel of Philip*, NHC, 2.3.68, in Robinson, op. cit., 150. *See* Layton, op. cit., 342.

58. Porphyry, *Ad Marcell*, 10. Porphyry continues: '...gathering in from the body all your members which have been dispersed and scattered into multiplicity from the unity which once abounded in the greatness of its power.' As Jonas notes: 'Dispersal and gathering, ontological categories of total reality, are at the same time action-patterns of each soul's potential experience, and unification within *is* union with the One. Thus emerges the Neoplatonic scheme of the inner ascent from the Many to the One that is ethical on the first rungs of the ladder, then theoretical, and at the culminating stage mystical.' Jonas, op. cit., 61

59. Hollroyd, S. (1994), 73

60. Ibid., 74

61. *Pistis Sophia*, 85. *See* Mead, G. R. S. (1921), 159.

62. Plotinus, *Enn.*, 1.5.7

63. Plotinus says, 'Let him journey back to his origin There. Let him put hope in no material or mechanical means but close his physical eyes and activate his spiritual vision. When you become one and see all things as pure light, when you see that you have become this, then you have become sight. You can trust what you are then, you have already ascended and need no one to show you. Concentrate your gaze and see the enormous Beauty.' Ibid., quoted in Wallis, R. T. (1992), 403.

64. Ibid., 3.5.9. *See* Wallis, op. cit., 228. As *The Apocryphon of John* explains, the so-called 'beginning' is 'beyond time and eternity'. (*The Apocryphon of John*, NHC, 2.1.3, in Robinson, J. M. (1978), 106. *See* Layton, op. cit., 29.) It is conceptually prior, not temporally.

65. Kirk, G. S., and Raven, J. E. (1957), 235
66. *The Gospel of Thomas*, NHC, 2.2.18
67. Ibid., 2.2.19

CHAPTER 8: THE FATHER'S SECRET PLAN

1. *Ephesians* 1:9–10
2. The myth explored in this chapter is variously described as 'the Valentinian Speculation' or 'Ptolemy's system' and is reported at length, but in a garbled and hostile fashion, in Irenaeus, *AH*, 1.1.1–1.8.5. Bentley Layton has composed a useful synthesis of the fragments of Ptolemy found in Irenaeus and elsewhere, *see* 'Ptolemy's Version of the Gnostic Myth' in Layton, B. (1987), 276ff.
3. The *aeons* perform a similar function to Plato's 'Ideas'. Both are the archetypes on which the physical cosmos is modelled. The Ideas were vital to Plato (Cherniss calls the doctrine 'the centre of gravity of all the Platonic writings', Cherniss, H. (1945), 4), and the *aeons* may, like many other Gnostic doctrines, be inspired by Platonism. However, we might also speculate that both go back to a Pythagorean/Egyptian source from which they have since diverged and that the Gnostic version preserves 'un-Platonized' material.
4. Gnostic mythology breaks new ground by creating overtly philosophical myths from traditional Pagan mythological motifs. Mythology had always encoded philosophical ideas, but with the Christian myth cycle this is made explicit. This is found in the earliest strata of Gnostic Christianity. Simon Magus, for example, called his consort Helen the *ennoia*, or thought, of God. In Ptolemy's myth the '30 silent and unrecognizable *aeons*' that make up the *pleroma* include intellect, truth, life, union, pleasure, faith, love, etc., etc. This tendency to mythologize, anthropomorphize and hypostasize philosophical terms has led to Gnosticism being called 'mythological Platonism'. It would perhaps be fairer to call Platonism 'de-mythologized Pythagoreanism' and to regard Christian Gnosticism as a continuation of this earlier pre-Platonic body of Orphic/Pythagorean/Mystery teachings.
5. *Pleroma* means 'fullness' and *kenoma* means 'emptiness'. Here we get the characteristic Gnostic inversion of our common-sense notion of things. The cosmos of appearances that we take to be real is called the 'emptiness' because, although it is full of appearances, it is empty of essential reality. Invisible Consciousness, that we think of as empty, is called the 'fullness' because it is reality overflowing with possible expressions of itself. *Kenoma* also means 'deficiency' or 'incompleteness', because the cosmos of appearances is a deficient image of the archetypal perfection of the *pleroma* or 'completeness'. In Gnostic thought the whole phenomenal universe was seen as an 'image' or 'deficiency'. See Mead, G. R. S. (1906), 313. The Christian myth cycle narrates the story of how and why the *kenoma* comes to be manifested as an imperfect copy of the archetypal perfection of the *pleroma*. The influence of Plato's *Timaeus* is clear. The *pleroma* and *kenoma* are equivalent to the Platonic realms of being and becoming: 'The one apprehensible by intelligence and with the aid of reasoning, the other the object of opinion and irrational sensation,

coming to be and ceasing to be, but never fully real.' (*Timaeus*, 27–8.) There are 13 references to the *pleroma* in Paul's letters. *See Galatians* 4:4; *Romans* 11:36, 13:10; *Colossians* 1:19, 2:9, 3:11, etc.

6. '...the only being that had Gnosis of the Father was the Only-Begotten ... to all the others this was invisible and incomprehensible.' Irenaeus, op. cit., 1.2.1. *See* Layton, op. cit., 283.

7. Ibid., 1.2.3. *See* Layton, op. cit., 284. *The Gospel of Truth* (NHC, 1.3.17) comments on this part of the creation drama: 'The *pleroma* searched for the One from whom they had emanated. But the *pleroma* was inside of Him – the inconceivable uncontained, who is superior to all thought. Ignorance of the Father caused agitation and fear. And the agitation grew dense like a fog so that it was impossible to see. Thus Error became strong.'

8. *Exc. Theod.*, 31.3f. *See* Jonas, H. (1958), 183.

9. *The Gospel of Truth*, NHC, 1.3.16–17, in Robinson, J. M. (1978), 40

10. Irenaeus, op. cit., 1.2.3: 'Her passion was a desire to know the Father, for she craved to grasp His greatness. Unable to realize her hope, because she aimed at the impossible, she fell into extreme agonies because of the unfathomable depth of the Father's unsearchable nature and her love for Him. Always yearning for Him, she would have been annihilated in His sweetness and dissolved into His infinite being, had she not been restricted by that power, *Horos* (the Limit, Finiteness), who exiled her from the *Pleroma*.' The story continues with Sophia's 'longing for the bliss of the Ideal World' giving birth to 'the soul of the whole universe ... earth arose from her despair, water from the agitation caused by her sorrow, air from the materialization of her fear, while fire, causing death and destruction, was inherent in all these elements...' Finally, in a psychological insight which Giles Quispel calls 'breathtaking', Sophia finds herself imprisoned in the material realm, which is, we are told, the product of her own disordered emotions. *See* Victor White, 'Some Notes on Gnosticism' in Segal, R. A. (1992), 211–12, referring to Irenaeus, 1.4 and 1.11, Quispel trans.

11. In *The Acts of John* this is called the Cross of Light, in other sources it is called *horos*, 'limit', *stauros*, 'stake' or 'cross', the midst, middle or *nonad*, the intermediary space between the *kenoma* and *pleroma*.

12. The Gnostics pointed out the story of the woman 'who had had a flow of blood for 12 years' but was cured when she touched the hem of Jesus and was cured as an allegory of the suffering Sophia. Her passions flowed out (creating the *kenoma*) until she was limited by *horos* (the hem of Jesus). *Mark* 5:25, and *see* Irenaeus, *AH*, 2.12.

13. Irenaeus, 1.17.2

14. Ibid., 1.5.1. Layton, B. (1987), 290

15. Although these words are often attributed to Jesus we have been unable to source this exact saying, although there are parallels in *The Gospel of John*.

16. Mead writes about *The Ode to Sophia* in *The Acts of Judas Thomas*: 'In this marriage the cosmic Sophia was received back into the Light-world and united with her heavenly spouse. This was to take place at the Great Consummation; but, mystically, it was ever taking place for those who had united themselves with their Higher Selves. As in the consummation of the universe the World-soul was reunited with the

World-mind, so in the perfectioning of the individual the soul was made one with the Self within.' Mead, G. R. S. (1906), 420ff.

17. The myth cycle relates the journey of the Goddess, or female principle of psyche/soul, through three states, represented by her three forms: Sophia, Achamoth and Holy Spirit. Sophia, meaning 'wisdom', is the archetypal possibility of Gnosis or Self-knowledge. She manifests as Achamoth, who represents the fallen state of the psyche, lost in illusory conceptual knowledge. After the purifying experience of undergoing many human lifetimes she emerges as the triumphant figure Holy Spirit, with whom the archetypal possibility of Gnosis is finally actualized. Then the Goddess is united with her syzygy Christ, representing psyche's essential nature as Consciousness.

18. In the Valentinian Speculation the Only-Begotten alone, having issued from him directly, can know the Fore-Father. To all the other *aeons* he remains invisible and incomprehensible. The Only-Begotten alone enjoyed contemplation of the Father. *See* Jonas, H. (1958), 181.

19. We can understand the essence of Ptolemy's myth as follows. The first two *aeons* to arise from the Mystery are the syzygy Consciousness and Truth. This represents the archetypal potentiality for self-knowledge – the possibility of consciousness of truth. The first syzygy Consciousness–Truth is actualized in the mystical marriage of the last syzygy Christ–Purified Consciousness, which represents the communion of Consciousness and redeemed psyche. This is the completion of the journey of self-knowledge – the Mystery is conscious of itself. The actualization of the possibility of self-knowledge starts when ignorance (Achamoth) is projected out of the archetypal cosmos as an appearance, which simultaneously precipitates the arising of the Christ archetype. At that moment the latent possibility of Consciousness is realized, because Consciousness has an object. Without an image to be conscious of, the Mystery remains as the dazzling darkness of unconscious Consciousness. No appearance, no Consciousness. No Achamoth, no Christ. No ignorance, no Gnosis. The archetype Consciousness is *perfectly* actualized in the Christ when the archetype Truth is *imperfectly* actualized as Achamoth. She is the appearance of ignorance, the conceptual substitute for Truth. *The Gospel of Truth* likewise describes 'the imagined form which is a substitute for Truth' (NHC, 1.3.16–17, in Robinson, J. M. (1978), 40). *On the Origin of the World* describes the *kenoma* as 'an appearance which has arisen from Truth' (NHC 2.5.103). *See* Shlain, L. (1999), 75. When we all realize Gnosis and Achamoth is transformed into Purified Consciousness, the archetype of Truth will finally be perfectly actualized. Then Jesus and the Goddess – Consciousness and perfected psyche – will celebrate the mystical marriage which heals the primal division. Through the multiplicity the Mystery will have become aware of its primal unity. Through ignorance it will have grown to Gnosis. Through manifestation it will have realized its ineffable essence.

20. In *The Tripartite Tractate* the Father withholds Gnosis from the *aeons* so that they will be perfected through the process of searching. Without this they would have come to believe that they had achieved Gnosis by their own power and become arrogant. Had the Father revealed himself all at once the *aeons* would have perished (*The*

Tripartite Tractate, NHC, 1.5.61). *The Tripartite Tractate* goes on to state that the creation of the lower world was good, the result of great love for the Father and according to the will of the Father. (NHC, 1.5.75–6, in Robinson, op. cit., 72. *See* discussion in Wallis, R. T. (1992), 288. *The Gospel of Truth* teaches: 'Oblivion did not come into existence close to the Father, but it did come into existence because of him.' (NHC, 1.3.18, quoted in Jonas, op. cit., 182.)

21. John Findlay describes his youthful interest in 'Theosophical-gnosticism' before he became a noted scholar of Neoplatonism: 'I accept the view of Plotinus and Proclus of an absolute Unity at the centre of Being, which has, however, to go forth from itself as part of fully reverting to itself in a living and significant manner...' Wallis, op. cit., 7

22. *Ephesians* 1:9–10

CHAPTER 9: THE IMAGE OF CHRIST

1. *Ephesians* 4:13
2. Irenaeus, *AH*, 1.2.2
3. Plato asserts: 'All the evils that afflict the psyche derive from trying to discover the true character of the One.' Plato, *Second Letter*, 313a. *See* Bouyer, L. (1990), 202.
4. Ptolemy, quoted in Irenaeus, op. cit., 1.6.1. *See* Layton, B. (1987), 293.
5. *Colossians* 3:11, *Romans* 11:36, *Colossians* 2:9, *Ephesians* 1:10. *See* Layton, op. cit., 287, and Irenaeus, op. cit., 1.3.4.
6. *Colossians* 1:17–19
7. *Ephesians* 3:19
8. Ibid., 4:13
9. *Matthew* 3:17, *Luke* 3:22
10. *Matthew* 3:16, *Mark* 1:10, *Luke* 3:22, *John* 1:32. And *see* Irenaeus, op. cit., 1.7.2: '...it was into him at baptism that the saviour, who comes from the *pleroma* and derives from all the *aeons*, descended in the form of a dove.' The dove was an ancient image of the Goddess and was sacred to Aphrodite/Ishstar/Astarte. In addition, Irenaeus tells us that in Greek, where every letter equals a number, dove equals 801 and symbolizes the Alpha (1) + Omega (800). Thus the dove is a symbol of the All, the fullness or the *pleroma* (1.14.6). In Hebrew *jonah* or *jonas* means 'dove' and the fact that Simon Peter is surnamed Barjonas may also be significant, especially if Simon Magus were the protagonist of the earliest gospel story, upon whom the dove descended, thereby making him *Barjonas*, the son of the dove. In this context, the story of Jonah (referred to many times in the gospels) who was in the body of the whale (really a serpent) for three days, may go back to ancient myths in which the dove and the serpent were respectively the Goddess and the Godman. Hence Jesus' command to be as wise as serpents and harmless as doves (*Matthew* 10:16) is an injunction to manifest both the male and female aspects of our syzygistic nature.
11. Mead, G. R. S. (1906), 354
12. *See* Matthews, C. (1992), 53.
13. Irenaeus, *AH*, 1.30.12, and *see* Mead, op. cit., 191.

14. *1 Corinthians* 1:24

15. Plato, *The Republic*, 7.517b

16. *On the Origin of the World*, NHC, 2.5.98, in Robinson, J. M. (1978), 172. *See also The Hypostasis of the Archons*, NHC, 2.4.94. Kurt Rudolph traces this idea to Philo, *see* Rudolph, K. (1987), 72.

17. '...until the soul is able to endure the contemplation of essence and the brightest region of being.' Plato, op. cit., 518c

18. Ibid., 7.517a

19. *Matthew* 13:55, *Mark* 6:3

20. *The Gospel of Philip*, NHC, 2.3.73, in Robinson, op. cit., 153

21. *Isaiah* 45:21, 46:9. 'Thinking himself to be completely alone the Demiurge arrogantly announces: "I am God and there is no other God than me." ' (Irenaeus, op. cit., 1.5.4. Layton, B. (1987), 292.) *The Apocryphon of John* comments wryly: 'By announcing this he indicated to the angels that another God does exist; for if there were no other one, of whom would he be jealous?' (NHC, 2.1.11.) (*See* Pagels, E. (1979), 56, which quotes similar sentiments from *The Hypostasis of the Archons*.) Paul refers to the Unknown God in *Acts* 17:22-3.

22. *Matthew* 1:1-18, *Luke* 3:23-8

23. Ptolemy, quoted in Irenaeus, *AH*, 1.5.2, Layton, op. cit., 291

24. Irenaeus, op. cit., 1.25.6. *See* Rudolph, op. cit., 226.

25. *Colossians* 2:15

26. Ibid., 2:20

27. Ptolemy, op. cit., 1.2.4. Layton notes that the term used for the separation of Achamoth from her passions, *apo-stauizein*, is related to the words 'crucify', *staurizein*, and 'cross', *stauros*. See Layton, op. cit., 284.

28. Justin Martyr, *First Apology*, 60, referring to Plato, *Timaeus*, 36. Plato is describing the two 'Great Circles' of the zodiac and the celestial equator. The obliquity of the zodiac (23° to the plane of the equator) means that it intersects with the celestial equator to form an 'X'. This cross defines the four nodes of the equinoxes and solstices, and in Plato's schema it is on this cross that the world soul, or Second God, is suspended. Justin Martyr shows himself clearly aware of this Platonic doctrine, referring to the 'discussion concerning the Son of God in the *Timaeus* of Plato, where he says, "He placed him crosswise in the universe."' In a vain attempt to defend Christianity against charges of plagiarism Justin insists that Plato 'borrowed' this idea from Moses. (*See* 'Plato's Doctrine of the Cross' in Justin Martyr, *First Apology*, 60.) As Eisler notes, 'It is at bottom the same cosmic symbolism which is also responsible for the dating of the crucifixion on 25th March, when the sun passes the big X formed by the ecliptic and the equator, and for the fixing of Jesus' birthday on 25th December, the *dies natalis solis invicti*.' (Eisler, R. (1931), 302)

29. In *The Book of the Logos* Jesus teaches: 'Save all my Limbs, which since the foundation of the world have been scattered abroad, and gather them all together and receive them into the Light.' (Quoted in Mead, G. R. S. (1906), 539.) In *The Acts of John*, Jesus teaches that 'the multitude that is about the cross' represent the 'Limbs of Him' that have yet to be 'gathered together' (quoted in Mead, 426). In Egypt Osiris was dismembered at the

hands of his evil brother Set. In the Orphic myth Dionysus is dismembered by the Titans. Robert Segal decodes the Orphic myth: 'The young god Dionysus was set upon a throne as soon as he had been born in a cave on the isle of Crete. But the Titans gave him a mirror to distract his attention, and while the child gazed in the mirror and was fascinated by his own image, the Titans tore the child into pieces and devoured him. Only the heart of the god was saved. This means that Dionysus, when he saw his *eidolon*, his reflection in the mirror, in a sense was duplicated and vanished into the mirror and so was dispersed in the universe. According to the Orphic sages, this means the world soul is divided and dispersed through matter. But the world spirit remains undivided and pure from every contact with matter.' See Segal, R. A. (1992), 254.

30. Ptolemy calls the Son *monogenes* (quoted in Irenaeus, op. cit., 1.2.1). *See* Layton, op. cit., 283. Although usually translated 'only-begotten', a more accurate translation would be 'begotten-alone', because Consciousness does not arise from duality but is the child of the Oneness.

31. *John 19:23–4, Matthew 27:35, Luke 23:34*

32. *Luke 23:34*

33. *The Hymn of the Pearl* is found in *The Acts of the Apostle Thomas*, otherwise known as *The Song of the Apostle Thomas in the Land of the Indians*. It is thought that it may be the work of Bardesanes. (*See* Barnstone, W. (1984), 308ff.) As Corbin notes, all of the Gnostic themes articulated in the *Pearl* reappear in the work of the great Sufi master Suhrawardi. (Corbin, H. (1971), 23)

34. *The Acts of John*, 97–102. *See* Barnstone, op. cit., 418ff. Mead decodes the symbolism in *The Gnostic Crucifixion* (1907).

35. Ibid.

36. Ibid. *See* Barnstone, op. cit., 418ff, and Hollroyd, S. (1994), 70.

37. Jonas, H. (1958), 186. As Jonas explains, in Valentinian symbolism, the horizontal bar is the limit between the upper and the lower world over which Christos stretches himself out to reach the lower Sophia, while the vertical bar divides the right and the left areas of the lower world.

38. The keys used to lift the heavy latches on the doors of Egyptian temples were also deliberately made to resemble the ankh. Such practical uses of the ankh had symbolic meaning to the Egyptians, encoding Gnostic teachings that were later adopted by the original Christians. Just as the ankh is the key to the door of the temple, so the Christian Cross of Light is metaphorically the key to our salvation and, as Jesus says in *The Acts of John*, the 'doorway' back to the 'Father'. Robertson, J. M. (1903), 14

39. Ptolemy, quoted in Irenaeus, *AH*, 1.3.2. *See* Layton, B. (1987), 287, and Lieu, S. N. C. (1985), 127.

40. *John 19:25–7*

41. As Scott notes, 'The words spoken to the mother of Jesus and the Beloved Disciple are part of the completion of the earthly ministry of Jesus, after which he is able to hand over his spirit and die.' (Scott, M. (1992), 217.) We suggest that this *is* the ministry of Jesus. Having united the two Marys, Jesus calls out, 'I am thirsty,' is given wine to drink and then announces, 'It is finished,' and dies. These events refer back

to the first miracle performed by Jesus at the marriage at Cana where Jesus' mother points out that the wedding guests are thirsty, prompting Jesus to miraculously turn water into wine. Mother Mary does not then appear again until she is portrayed at the cross receiving Mary Magdalene as her child, thus framing the beginning and end of the Jesus story.

42. *See The Second Treatise of the Great Seth*, NHC, 7.2.57, in Robinson, J. M. (1978), 366.

43. *The Gospel of Philip*, NHC, 2.3.69–70. As Welburn notes, this is an 'analogy to the progress of the Christ-initiate to the goal, the Bride Chamber' (Welburn, A. (1994), 312, note 125).

44. Matthews, C. (1992), 116

45. *Daath*, from *yada*, 'to know'. For the sexual connotations, *see Genesis* 4:1: Adam *knew* his wife Eve. *See* discussion in Armstrong, K. (1993), 59.

46. *On the Origin of the World*, NHC, 2.5.103. In *The Hypostasis of the Archons* the Demiurge is called Samael, which the text tells us means 'God of the Blind'. An allusion to the blind Demiurge is found in the gospel story of the blind beggar Bartimaeus in *Mark* 10:46. His name Bartimaeus – son of Timaeus – clearly signals the allusion to the Demiurge of Plato's *Timaeus*. However, the placing of this miraculous healing in the gospel story also contains other allusions. Jesus cures Bartimaeus immediately after he 'comes down from Jericho'. Jericho means 'moon' in Hebrew and signals that Jesus has descended into the sublunary realm of the Demiurge. In addition, Jericho was the first city conquered by Joshua/Jesus upon entering the Promised Land of Canaan in *1 Kings* 16:34.

CHAPTER 10: THE GOD OF THE BLIND

1. Boethius (1969), 141

2. This doesn't quite work, of course, because these first two *aeons* both represent the primal syzygy Deep–Silence and Consciousness is the third of the eight *aeons* of the *pleroma*, not the second. This inconsistency suggests that Ptolemy is trying, in this case unsuccessfully, to integrate two separate metaphysical systems, one based on the seven heavenly bodies, with the starry heavens as the *ogdoad*, the home of the Goddess (a Babylonian system?), the other based on the eight primal emanations in four male–female syzygies (an Egyptian system?)

3. Hoeller, S. A. (1989), 149

4. In Ptolemy's myth when the Demiurge creates the cosmos, he creates the Devil and his wicked angels from the 'Mother's grief'. Other texts describe the Devil as having been created from Achamoth's 'perplexity' (Jonas, H. (1958), 193). Ptolemy's *Letter to Flora* paints the most positive of the Gnostic portraits of the Demiurge. The 'maker of this universe' is not the 'perfect God himself' but is nonetheless responsible for the administration of justice, as he occupies the 'middle point' between Good and evil. *See* Barnstone, W. (1984), 621ff.

5. Irenaeus records the teaching that the Mother Achamoth bore the Christ, but 'not without a kind of shadow' (*AH*, 1.11.1). From what follows it appears that the

Demiurge is formed from this shadow. Other Gnostic sources make explicit what is only hinted at here – that Christ and the Devil are twins. *See* Jung's discussion of 'The Shadow' in Jung, C. G. (1959), 8ff.

6. Jung writes: 'From various hints dropped by Hippolytus, it is clear beyond doubt that many of the Gnostics were nothing other than psychologists.' Ibid., 222

7. Ptolemy, quoted in Irenaeus, op. cit., 1.5.3. *See* Layton, B. (1987), 291.

8. It has become spiritually fashionable in recent decades to talk about 'creating our own reality'. The Christian myth cycle explains the way in which this both is and isn't true. Just as the Demiurge is the apparent creator of the cosmos, so the ego is an apparent autonomous agent which creates the particular conceptual matrix which structures our experience. In this sense we all create our own conceptual realities. But, as Ptolemy explains, although the Demiurge thinks he is creating the cosmos as he wishes it to be, he is actually 'creating images of the archetypes in the *pleroma* of which he knows nothing' (quoted in Irenaeus, ibid). Like the Demiurge, we also unconsciously create our cosmos based on universal archetypes. We are each dreaming our own dream. Yet all dreams coincide so that we find ourselves inhabiting basically the same cosmos (or close enough for us to interact with each other to some extent at least!) This is because actually it is the Consciousness of God (Christ) which is dreaming a universal dream (Achamoth) of which, as separate individuals, we are a part. This manifests on the human level as universal Consciousness dreaming its dream through our particular psyche, which includes our ego, which plays out the fantasy of being a separate person with autonomous will.

9. As Plato says, 'Man is a puppet of the Deity, and this is the finest thing about him. All of us then, men and women alike, must fall in with our role and spend life in making our play as perfect as possible.' Plato, *Laws*, 803c

10. As Jesus says in *The Gospel of Thomas*, 'Become passers-by.' (NHC, 2.2.42, in Robinson, J. M. (1978), 131)

11. Monoimos, quoted in Hippolytus, *Ref.*, 8.5. *See* Jung, C. G. (1959), 222.

12. Plotinus, *Enn.*, 1.2.4

13. Philo, *Leg all.*, 1.49, and cf 3.32f. *See* Jonas, H. (1958), 279.

14. *Galatians* 2:20

15. *John* 14:10

16. 'We men are found to be governed by Nature equally, and by Fortune differently, and by our Free-will each as he pleases.' Mead, G. R. S. (1906), 399, and there is a useful summary of what is known of Bardesanes, 392ff.

17. Ibid., 403

18. Plotinus, op. cit., 2.3.11

19. *See* Gaus, A. (1991), 15.

20. Plotinus, op. cit., 2.9.9

21. Pseudo-Dionysius, *The Divine Names*, 680. *See* Pseudo-Dionysius (1987), 68.

22. *Matthew* 19:17. For Plato the One is synonymous with the Good and the Beautiful.

23. Gregory, J. (1987), 40

24. *See* 'Outline of Orphic Cosmology' in Guthrie, W. K. C. (1952), 69ff, *also* Graves, R. (1955), vol. I, 30.

25. *See TJM*, Chapter 4, note 137.

26. *The Gospel of Philip*, NHC, 2.3.53. Layton, B. (1987), 330.

27. Jung refers to *The Letters of Clement* as 'a collection of Gnostic-Christian writings' dating from about 150 CE. He writes: 'The unknown author understands good and evil as the right and left hand of God, and views the whole of creation in terms of syzygies, or pairs of opposites. In much the same way the follower of Bardesanes, Marinaus, sees good as "light" and pertaining to the right hand and evil as "dark" and pertaining to the left hand.' He also notes that in Irenaeus, *AH*, 1.30.3, Sophia *Prounikos* – Sophia the whore – is called *Sinistra*, the left. *See* Jung, C. G. (1959), 54. A *midrash* on *The Song of Solomon* 2:6 states: 'God's left hand dashes to pieces; his right hand is glorious to save.' Quoted in Jung, 59.

28. Quoted in Foerster W. (1974), 2.169. *See also* Hanratty, G. (1997), 32.

29. Epiphanius reports that the Ebionites believed in a double sonship: 'Two, they maintain, were begotten by God, one of them Christ, the other the Devil.' Epiphanius, *Pan*, 16. The Bogomils maintained that Satanael was the older brother and Christ the younger. *See* Jung, op. cit., 147.

30. Plotinus, *Enn.*, 3.2.17

31. *See* DK, 90a 1.1 and 90a 1.3. Antiphon was a Sophist of the classical period and the author of the *Dissoi Logoi*, or 'Double Accounts', written in nine sections, 'On Good and Bad', 'On Fine and Foul', 'On Just and Unjust', etc. Section I opens: 'Double accounts are offered in Greece by those who philosophize about the good and the bad.' The pursuit of dialectical philosophy leads to the conclusion that the opposites are closer to each other than those things which are merely different, i.e. black and white have more in common than chalk and cheese. The German poet and philosopher Novalis, drawing on his own deep reading of Pythagorean philosophy, put it most succinctly when he wrote: 'Contrasts are inverse analogies.' (Novalis (1989), 85.) The Sophists earned a dubious reputation because they offered to teach students how to prove that black was white and to make the weaker argument seem the strong. They consequently undermined all conventional polarities such as Greek and barbarian, wisdom and folly, etc. Barnes describes the *Dissoi Logoi* as 'the most interesting and the most dangerous of the Sophistic relativisms' (Barnes, J. (1982), 522).

32. Boethius, *The Consolations of Philosophy*, 4.7, and *see* 142.

33. Ibid., 2.8, and *see* 76.

CHAPTER 11: THE MYSTICAL MARRIAGE

1. *The Gospel of Truth*, NHC, 1.3.25, in Robinson, J. M. (1978), 43–4. *See* Jonas, H. (1958), 60, and *The Gospel of Truth*, 1.3.30, Robinson, 45, *also* Hoeller, S. A. (1989), 221.

2. Gnosis is 'a union of union and non-union', to borrow a wonderful phrase from Hegel, quoted in Hanratty, G. (1997), 111. Hegel summarizes the dialectical process as 'unity, separated opposites, reunion'.

3. T. S. Eliot, *Four Quartets: Dry Salvages*, 5

4. *The Gospel of Thomas*, NHC, 2.2.22, in Robinson, op. cit., 129 (abridged)

5. Plotinus, *Enn.*, 4.8.4

6. *See* introduction to *Laws* in Plato, *Collected Dialogues*, 1,226.

7. Plotinus, op. cit., 5.1.1

8. Whereas Gnostics teach that we are intrinsically good, Christian Literalists teach that we are inherently bad. This monstrous dogma of 'original sin' derives from a literal interpretation of the Jewish myth of *Genesis*. In this myth, as punishment for Eve's sin of persuading Adam to eat the forbidden fruit of the Tree of Good and Evil, the first human beings are thrown out of Paradise and subjected to death. As the 'children of Eve', Literalists claim, we are all born in sin. Jewish and Christian Gnostics, however, understand this myth allegorically. For Philo, Eve symbolizes the senses which lure Adam, representing consciousness, into identification with the body. (Philo, *Opifico Mundi*, 165. See Wallis, R. T. (1992), 281). The myth doesn't teach that we are all inherently sinful, but that we have 'fallen' from our original nature, which is all good. By identifying with the body, symbolized by eating the fruit of the Tree of Good and Evil, we leave the Paradise of oneness and enter the world of duality – good and evil.

9. Ptolemy, quoted in Irenaeus, *AH*, 1.6.2–4, abridged. *See* Layton, B. (1987), 294.

10. Ibid.

11. *The Gospel of Philip*, NHC, 2.3.82–3. *See* Welburn, A. (1994), 311.

12. In the most used early manuscript of *The Gospel of Luke* there is a saying now excluded from the New Testament. Coming across someone working on the Sabbath, and therefore breaking a traditional taboo of Jewish Literalism, Jesus remarks: 'Man! If you know what you are doing, you are blessed. If you don't know what you are doing, you are cursed and a transgressor of the law.' (Early passage in *Luke* 6:4 found in the Codex Bezae and quoted in Stanton, G. (1995), 45.) This is a fascinating teaching story. Jesus does not tell the man, as might be expected, that if he is ignorant of Jewish law his actions are forgivable, but that if he knows the law he is guilty of deliberately breaking it. Rather he tells him that he is 'blessed' if he has consciously chosen to break the taboo and cursed if he is just acting unconsciously.

13. Irenaeus, op. cit., 1.25.4, referring to the followers of Carpocrates. *See* Pagels, E. (1975), 45.

14. *Romans* 14:14

15. *Ephesians* 5:20

16. Clement of Alexandria, *Strom.*, 7.35, quoted in Kingsland, W. (1937), 204

17. Ibid., 4.22

18. *Romans* 13:10

19. Ibid., 7:4–6

20. Clement, op. cit., 7.33

21. 'Basilides himself says, we suppose one part of the declared will of God to be the loving of all things because all things bear a relation to the Whole, and another "not to lust after anything," and a third "not to hate anything." ' Ibid., 4.12. *See* Layton, B. (1987), 435.

22. Irenaeus, *AH*, 1.1.36

23. *Romans* 8:5

24. *1 Corinthians* 2:15

25. Plotinus, *Enn.*, 6.9.4. *See* Gregory, J. (1987), 38.

26. According to Nicomachus' *Life of Pythagoras*, Pythagoras restricted the application of the word 'wisdom' (*sophia*) to the 'knowledge of being'. *See* O'Meara, D. J. (1989), 15.

27. Clement of Alexandria, *Strom.*, 2.47. *See* Bouyer, L. (1990), 144.

28. Plotinus, op. cit., 5.9.11

29. 'Reasoning is for the psyche when it is perplexed.' Ibid., 4.3.18

30. As Kingsley notes: '...once someone became a Pythagorean, it started to become a matter of learning less and less.' Kingsley, P. (1999), 213

31. *Hebrews* 4:12

32. 'Disengagement means simply that the psyche withdraws to its own place.' Plotinus, op. cit., 1.2.5. As Plato teaches, this entails 'discriminating that which always is' from 'that which is always becoming' (*Timaeus*, 27). Kingsley traces the word *hesychia* to the Pythagoreans (Kingsley, op. cit., 183). Ancient reports state that Parmenides was 'converted to the contemplative life' or 'led to stillness' (*hesychia*) by a Pythagorean. This information allows us to connect Pythagoras, Parmenides, Philo's Therapeutae, the Gnostics and the Greek Hesychasts to one evolving mystical tradition. For Clement of Alexandria the peak point of contemplation, *theoria*, is found in what he calls *theoria epoptiche*, leading to *epopteia*, which is the 'knowledge of being itself', *to onti episteme* (Clement, op. cit., 2.47).

33. Ibid. *See* Pseudo-Dionysius, *The Mystical Theology*, CW, 37, 1,001a.

34. Quoted in Gregory, op. cit., 167

35. Plotinus, *Enn.*, 5.5.8

36. *See* introduction to *Allogenes* in Layton, B. (1987), 141. Allogenes begins by seeking conceptual knowledge of the Unknowable Mystery, but the Goddess explains to him that this is impossible because the Primal Principle is ineffable.

37. *Allogenes*, NHC, 11.3.60–1, in Robinson, J. M. (1978), 497. *See* discussion in Wallis, R. T. (1992), 448.

38. In the Christian myth cycle, when Christ reveals Gnosis to the *aeons* he likewise tells them that their essence and origin is 'uncontainable and incomprehensible', Irenaeus, *AH*, 1.2.1.

39. *Allogenes*, op. cit., 11.3.59, slightly adapted.

40. Plotinus, op. cit., 6.7.35. *See* Gregory, J. (1987), 174.

41. Pagan philosophers articulated two views about incarnation – either it is seen as a punishment or an opportunity to co-operate in manifesting the divine. Both views are present in Plato. *Phaedrus* suggests incarnation is due to some sort of moral failure, the soul having fallen from the heavenly retinue of the gods and plunged into a life of misery in the body. *Timaeus* suggests that a soul has a constructive mission in the world – to vivify, organize and perfect it (*see* Wallis, op. cit., 256). *Cratylus* expresses both views simultaneously, stating that the soul has the body as a tomb 'in order that it might be saved' (Plato, *Cratylus*, 400c, and *see* Wallis, op. cit., 116, 263). Likewise, Plotinus emphasizes the positive view but allows for moral failure and a fall (O'Meara, D. J. (1989), 38). Iamblichus also regards the descent of the soul into matter as both a fall but also as the opportunity to participate in creation.

42. Marsanes, NHC, 10.1.5, in Robinson, op. cit., 463. *See* Wallis, op. cit., 263.

43. As Plato teaches, we strive 'to become like God, so far as this is possible'. Plato *Theaetetus*, 176b

44. 'There are two ways of life, the contemplative and the active. The chief object of the contemplative life is knowledge of the truth, while that of the active life consists in doing those things indicated by reason. The contemplative life holds the place of honour, the active life is a consequence of it and is an absolute necessity.' (Albinus, *Didask*, 2.) Augustine writes: 'The study of wisdom consists in action and contemplation, so that one part of it may be called active, and the other contemplative – the active part having reference to the conduct of life, that is, to the regulation of morals, and the contemplative part to the investigation into the causes of nature and into pure truth. Socrates is said to have excelled in the active part of that study, while Pythagoras gave more attention to its contemplative part, on which he brought to bear all the force of his great intellect.' (Augustine, *The City of God*, 8.4)

45. *Exc. Theod.* 37

46. *The Authoritative Teaching*, NHC, 6.3.31, in Robinson, op. cit., 308. *See* Rudolph, K. (1987), 263.

47. Plotinus likens life to a drama in which '...the actor alters his make up and enters into a new role. The actor is not really killed. Dying is changing a body like an actor changes costumes. Leaving a body is like the exit of an actor from the stage when he has no more lines to say. Death in all its guises, the reduction of cities to rubble, all must be to us the same as changing scenes in a play. Everything is a twist of the plot. Costume on and off. Grief and lament acted out. For in all the succession of lives we live, it is never the Soul within who grieves and suffers, but the outer shadow who acts out the plot on this world stage.' (Plotinus, *Enn.*, 3.2.15, abridged, and *see* 3.2.17.) Lucian the satirist develops the theme: 'Life is a vast sort of pageant organized by Chance, who provides the people taking part in it with various different costumes. She picks out one man at random and dresses him up as a king, puts a crown on his head and provides him with a bodyguard. She dresses another as a slave, makes up another to look beautiful, and another to look ridiculously ugly. The great thing is, I imagine, that the show should have plenty of variety. Then, instead of letting everyone wear the same costume throughout the performance, she often changes things round half-way through. She makes Croesus switch from being a king to being a slave and a prisoner, and after letting Maeandrius be a slave for a while, she makes him put on the costume that Polycrates has been wearing, and try being a tyrant for a bit. When the show's over, everyone returns his costume, strips off the body that goes with it, and becomes just like he was before, quite indistinguishable from anyone else. I expect you've often seen the same thing on the stage, where an actor has to be prepared to play Creon or Priam or Agamemnon, according to the programme. But when the play's finished, each actor removes his gold-embroidered boots, and comes down to earth, where he goes about like a perfectly ordinary person who's rather short of cash.' (Lucian, *Menippus in the Underworld* in *Satirical Sketches* (1961), 106–7)

48. Plotinus, op. cit., 6.7.35

49. Hippolytus, *Ref.*, 8.12. 277.124. *See* Metzger, B. M. (1987), 99.

50. Quoted ibid., 6.24. *See* Mead, G. R. S. (1906), 336.

51. Plotinus, op. cit., 1.6.5., abridged.

52. Ibid., 6.9.4

53. Plato, *Apology*, 23b. Socrates relates this story about the oracle whilst on trial for his life. He tells the jury about his quest to know himself: 'This investigation has led to my having many enemies of the worst and most dangerous kind, and has given occasion also to many calumnies, and I am called wise, for my hearers always imagine that I myself possess the wisdom which I find wanting in others: but the truth is, O men of Athens, that God only is wise; and in this oracle he means to say that the wisdom of men is little or nothing; he is not speaking of Socrates, he is only using my name as an illustration, as if he said, He, O men, is the wisest, who, like Socrates, knows that his wisdom is in truth worth nothing. And so I go my way, obedient to the god, and make inquisition into the wisdom of anyone, whether citizen or stranger, who appears to be wise; and if he is not wise, then in vindication of the oracle I show him that he is not wise; and this occupation quite absorbs me, and I have no time to give either to any public matter of interest or to any concern of my own, but I am in utter poverty by reason of my devotion to the god.'

54. *1 Corinthians* 3:18

55. Ibid., 8:2

56. Paul, *Philippians* 4:7; Plotinus, quoted in Armstrong, K. (1993), 123

57. Philo, *Mut nom.*, 155. *See* Jonas, H. (1958), 280.

58. Quoted in Clement of Alexandria, *Strom.*, 2.4. Whilst discussing Basilides' thoughts on faith, Clement writes: 'Hence it is thought that the first cause of the universe can be apprehended by faith alone.' Quoted in Layton, B. (1987), 29.

59. Quoted in Clement, op. cit.

60. *The Treatise on the Resurrection*, NHC, 1.4.45, in Robinson, J. M. (1978), 54. *See* Layton, op. cit., 321.

CHAPTER 12: THE NEW IMPROVED TESTAMENT

1. We found this quote on a postcard so we can't reference it properly – but it's so beautiful we used it anyway. If any reader knows the source, please let us know.

2. Metrodorus of Chios (*fl.*440 BCE), *Concerning Nature*, DK, 71 B 1. Metrodorus' near-contemporary, the Sophist Protagoras, wrote in *On the Gods*: 'About the gods I cannot say either that they are or that they are not, nor how they are constituted in shape; for there is much that prevents knowledge, the unclarity of the subject and the shortness of human life.' Such honest doubt has never been popular and as a consequence of this book Protagoras, along with numerous other Athenian intellectuals like Socrates, was put on trial in a purge that effectively put an end to the Athenian Enlightenment. His book was publicly burned in Athens and this single sentence survives (quoted in Burkert. W. (1985), 313).

3. *Exc. Theod.*, 35. *See* Foerster. W. (1972), 222–33.

4. *Ephesians* 1:9–10

5. Campbell, J. (1949), 249

6. Understandably angry at being disenfranchised for the last 2,000 years, some women have, as compensation, developed the fantasy of a prehistoric period when the Goddess dominated the show and all was peace and light, which they urge us to return to. Although this is a very popular view right now, we feel the evidence does not bear it out. It seems to us that there has never been a feminine monotheism, precisely because the feminine archetype, which we have been badly missing during the dark ages of Christian Literalism, is the spirit of partnership and co-operation. The idea that there is one God and he is a man is simply stupid. But replacing him with her is just as daft. It really is time to get gender completely out of spirituality as an issue.

7. The theories of Copernicus and Galileo were widely known to be a revival of Pythagorean science. Copernicus acknowledges this himself in *De revolutionibus orbium coelestium*, where he says the heliocentric theories of the fifth century BCE Pythagoreans Philolaus, Heraclides and Ecphantus (as recorded in Aetius, III, 13, 1–3), gave him the courage to consider the idea seriously. *See* Guthrie, W. K. C. (1962), 327.

8. Wolfgang Pauli and his friends Niels Bohr and Werner Heisenberg are the founding fathers of our modern world picture and our atomic age. Pauli was passionately interested in everything religious and Gnostic. When, on 15 November 1953, the discovery of the first book of the Nag Hammadi Gnostic library, the so-called 'Jung Codex', was made public, he was among the audience. *See* Segal, R. A. (1992), 251.

9. Quoted in Berendt, *The Third Ear* (1988), 84

10. Quoted in Cranston, S. (1977), 294. Elsewhere Einstein writes: 'How can an educated person stay away from the Greeks? I have always been far more interested in them than in science... I maintain that cosmic religious feeling is the strongest and noblest incitement to scientific research.' *The New Yorker*, 22 November 1947, article on Einstein by Nicolo Tucci, quoted ibid, 202.

11. Since quantum physics, the idea that it is possible to study an objective world of matter has looked ridiculous. The modern philosopher Ken Wilber critiques the Literalist approach to science in its own terms, writing: 'Science approaches the empirical world with a massive conceptual apparatus containing everything from tensor calculus to imaginary numbers to extensive intersubjective linguistic signs to differential equations – virtually all of which are *nonempirical* found *only* in interior spaces – and then it astonishingly claims it is simply "reporting" what it "finds" out there in the "given" world – when, in fact, all that is given is coloured patches.' (Wilber, K. (1998), 146.) Of course more exists than we can measure and touch. This idea, for instance, has neither weight, nor place, nor any tangible qualities. Even if someone knows what every neurone in your brain is doing, that won't give them access to a single one of your thoughts. Literalist science, then, is as daft as Literalist religion.

12. At the beginning of the last century the philosophy of the Pythagoreans and Presocratics (who postulated the idea that the substance of God and the cosmos was Mind, of which the human mind was a part), was confidently dismissed as the 'first bungling attempts' to arrive at a distinction between mind and matter. *See,* for example, Millerd, C., *On the Interpretation of Empedocles* (1908), 1–2, 79–81. But

with the birth of quantum physics, the distinction between mind and matter, the observer and the observed, has given way in the face of the Heisenberg 'uncertainty principle'. According to this principle it is not possible to measure both the position and momentum of a particle at the same time. In effect, the 'unobserved observer' so beloved of classical physics has been replaced by the 'quantum participator'. *See* Penrose, R., *The Emperor's New Mind* (1989), 321. Many modern scientists are now consciously aware of the movement 'back' to the Presocratics and are not ashamed to admit it. *See* Kingsley, P. (1995), 9, referring to Capra, F., *The Tao of Physics* (1983), 24–6.

13. From *scientia*, Latin for 'knowledge'.

14. Ideas, like genes, spread and reproduce via human minds and the word 'meme' has been coined to reflect the analogy between these two processes. A complex of ideas, such as a religion, can be called a 'memeplex'. In order to become dominant, a memeplex must contain certain features. For example, it must lay upon its members the obligation to proselytize. It must set itself up as 'true' and 'orthodox' and denounce other competing ideas as 'false' or 'heretical'. It must offer rewards to those who adopt it and threaten punishments to those who refuse. For the idea of Christianity as a memeplex *see* http://www.christianitymeme.org/. The website posts the following axioms on its homepage: '1. Christianity is a meme – a mind virus that lives in the minds of people and is spread through proselytization and other means. 2. Christianity is a meme about God, but it has no other connection to God. 3. The Christianity Meme has been shaped purely by natural selection – the law of survival of the fittest – as it has played out in human minds. It is a sophisticated product of cultural evolution. 4. Being a "true Christian" infected by the Christianity Meme will subject you to its agenda through its adaptations that allow it to control human behaviour. 5. As a consequence, the more Christian you are, the more you are prone to certain kinds of immoral behaviour. The Christianity Meme is not bound by the moral principles it carries. 6. We seek to expose Christianity for what it is and we advocate a conscious and rational approach to morality in its place.'

15. Theodotus, *Exc. Theod.* 57. *See* Foerster, W., *Gnosis: A Selection of Gnostic Texts* (Clarendon Press, 1972), 222–33.

16. To create a common context for the variety of approaches to spirituality would require a new way of speaking about the mysteries of life and death that doesn't carry unnecessary baggage from the past. Jung writes: 'Once metaphysical ideas have lost their capacity to recall and evoke the original experience they have not only become useless but prove to be actual impediments on the road to wider development.' (Jung, C. G., *CW*, 9.2.65. *See also* Jung, C. G. (1959), 34). We need to abandon worn-out spiritual jargon, or at least refusing to use it without stopping to question whether we really know what we are talking about. As Jung says, we need to 'take these thought-forms, that have become historically fixed, and melt them down again and pour them into moulds of immediate experience' (*CW*, 2.148, quoted in Hoeller, S. A. (1989), 230).

17. In the Pagan philosopher Lucian's *Menippus in the Underworld*, the hero (a philosopher from Judaea!), undergoes the initiatory Underworld journey. After his studies of

philosophy and various adventures, he gives some salutary advice that would make an excellent closing passage for a Gnostic 'New *Improved* Testament': 'The best way to live is to be an ordinary human being. So give up all this metaphysical nonsense. Stop worrying about first principles and final causes, and forget all those clever arguments – they don't mean a thing. Just live in the present moment and get along as best you can, trying to see the funny side of things and taking nothing very seriously.' (Lucian, (1961), 109–10)

18. Plotinus, *Enn.*, 6.8.9
19. Boethius, *The Consolation of Philosophy*, 79
20. *Acts* 17:28. Paul quotes the words of Aratus, a Stoic philosopher who had lived in Tarsus two centuries earlier.
21. *Ephesians* 4.25

APPENDIX I: BLUEPRINT FOR REALITY

1. Layton notes with regard to the system of Ptolemy: 'It was a philosophical cliché that the material constituent of an entity was "female" while its form (or Ideal form) was "male".' Layton, B. (1987), 284, note 1.2.3.b
2. In the city dedicated to Hermes the *ogdoad* received cult and for this reason Hermopolis was known as 'eight-city'. As Hornung notes, the *ogdoad* and related ideas about creation by four pairs of primeval deities may go back to the time of the Old Kingdom c.2500 BCE (Hornung, E. (1982), 221). In Egyptian myth the Mystery is conceived of as the male–female syzygy Amun and Amanet, whose names both mean 'the Hidden One' (ibid., 274). For the Babylonian creation myth of new gods emerging in pairs (*see* Armstrong, K. (1993), 14ff).
3. It was one of Plato's unwritten secret teachings which was adopted by later Platonists and Gnostics generally that the underlying structure of reality is an essential trinity with a hidden or different fourth aspect. Hence the famous opening lines of Plato's *Timaeus*: 'One, two, three, but where my dear Timaeus is the fourth....' *See* Wallis, R. T. (1992), 452 for the Platonic and Gnostic speculation on the Pythagorean Tetraktys, which is the key to these various schemes. Irenaeus tells us that the first four of Ptolemy's system are 'the equivalent to the first, primal *tetraktys* of Pythagorean philosophy. They call it the root of the *pleroma*.' (Irenaeus, *AH*, 1.1.1. *See* Layton, op. cit., 281.) The trinity can be seen as Mystery, consciousness and psyche, with the existence of physicality as an appearance within psyche being regarded as the fourth. Conversely, the trinity can be seen from the other direction as physicality, psyche and consciousness, with the hidden fourth being the Mystery which is expressed by them all.
4. The parallels between sex and cosmogenesis are explicit in Ptolemy's system. 'The deep (*bythos*) took thought to emit a source of the *pleroma*. And it deposited this emanation that it had thought to emit, like sperm, in the womb of the silence (*sige*) that coexisted with it. And the latter received this sperm, conceived, and brought forth intellect.' (Ptolemy, quoted in Irenaeus, op. cit., 1.1.1. *See* Layton, B. (1987), 281.) These doctrines are to be found in the earliest strata of Pythagorean speculation

about the creation of the cosmos from the two principles of the atom and the void or the male principles of Limit and the female principle of Unlimit. Raven writes: 'This biological conception fits the notion of the world as a living and breathing creature, which like other living things, would grow from a seed to its full form. The early Pythagoreans may have initiated the cosmogonical process by a similar device, the male principle of Limit being represented as implanting in the midst of the surrounding Unlimited that seed which, by progressive growth, developed into the visible universe.' Just as the sperm is deposited in the womb, so also in cosmogony, the first unit, which represents the principle of Limit, is implanted in the midst of the surrounding Unlimited; and just as the child, immediately after birth, inhales the breath outside, so the first unit, immediately after it is generated, proceeds to draw in the void from the surrounding Unlimited. (Kirk, G. S., and Raven, J. E. (1957), 313.) Cornford quotes from Theo the application of the Tetractys to 'things that grow', 'the seed is analogous to the unit and point, growth in length to 2 and the line, growth in breadth to 3 and the surface, growth in thickness to 4 and the solid'. (Raven, J. E. (1948), 48, and Kirk and Raven, op. cit., 251.) The Christian Gnostics again seem to have preserved intact these early Pythagorean speculations.

APPENDIX II: GNOSTIC ISLAM

1. *See* discussion in Armstrong, K. (1993), 297.
2. *See* 'Islamic Gnosis' in Merkur, D. (1993), 199ff, and Corbin, H. (1983) for his study of Ismaili Gnosis. Douglas-Klotz writes: 'The origins of Sufism are shrouded in mystery. By some accounts, a circle of mystics formed around Mohammad while he and his community were in exile in Medina (about 623 CE). According to some scholars, certain of these mystics were already members of or influenced by pre-existing circles of Christian mystical ascetics living in Arabia and Syria.' (Douglas-Klotz, N. (1995), xxix)
3. Adolf von Harnack, *Dogmengeschichte*, II.537, quoted in Corbin, op. cit., 56.
4. Ibid., 65–6. Historians and theologians who have dealt with the Christianity of the Ebionites have suggested that it was extended and amplified in Islam.
5. Mani (216–276) was raised among the Elkasites, a Jewish Christian baptismal sect in Mesopotamia. Corbin writes: '...we never cease to observe the importance of Manichaean ideas in the growth of Islamic Gnosis.' *See* Merkur, op. cit., 189.
6. Armstrong, op. cit., 206. Isma'ili philosophy had its basis in an esoteric method of Quranic exegesis. As Merkur notes, 'The inner meaning of the Quran, so revealed, proves to be Gnostic.' (Merkur, op. cit., 205–6)
7. Armstrong, op. cit., 206
8. Matthews, C. (1992), 180
9. Corbin, H. (1971), 122. As Corbin notes, this was affirmed from the earliest days of Islam.
10. 'The word *Allah* is not a proprietary name of the divinity invented by Muslims but a continuation of the same root/word of power that had existed for at least six thousand years in the Middle East, beginning with the Old Canaanite *Elat* and extending

through the Hebrew *Elohim* and the Aramaic *Alaha*. All of these words indicate a name pointing to the reality of Cosmic Unity and Oneness, the ultimate force behind being and nothingness, which includes the most mysterious concept: Holy Absence, the "No" (LA) that balances the "Yes" (AL).' Douglas-Klotz, op. cit., 15

11. Corbin, H. (1983), 173. As Corbin notes, all of the negative designations of God used by the Gnostics – the Unnameable God of Carpocrates, the Ineffable and the Abyss of Valentinus, the Unengendered One of Basilides – have their equivalents in Ismaili terminology.

12. Corbin, H. (1971), 110ff

13. Corbin, H. (1983), 47

14. Al-Lat, Al-'Uzza and Manat were considered by the Meccans to be the three 'daughters of God'. The association of sacred site, black stone and 'Triple Goddess' has numerous parallels throughout the Pagan world. For the story of how the Triple Goddess was dispossessed of her authority by the creation of the so-called Satanic Verses, *see* Armstrong, K. (1993), 172–3, 192, and Merkur, D. (1993), 191. Matthews records how the Goddess Al-'Uzza was worshipped in the form of a black stone and it was this that was taken by Mohammad and enshrined in the Ka'aba, *see* Matthews, op. cit., 184. She remarks: 'It is ironic that the religion which has least exoteric veneration for the Divine Feminine has, at its heart, the Black Stone once venerated as the Goddess in Arabia.'

15. As Corbin notes, 'The person of Fatima is indeed the basis of a whole Shiite sophiology.' *See* Corbin, H. (1983), 101.

16. Armstrong, op. cit., 270, and *see* Merkur, op. cit., 232ff, and Matthews, op. cit., 187.

17. Armstrong, op. cit., 272

18. Merkur, op. cit., 232

19. Ibid., 225

20. Armstrong, op. cit., 184

21. Corbin, H. (1983), 162. As Corbin writes, '...the spirit which inspires those variants [of Christian apocryphal scriptures] appears so authentically Gnostic that one must suppose that our theosophers [early Shiite circles who formed the beginnings of Ismailism] had some knowledge of texts which we no longer possess.'

22. Qur'an 4:56–7. *See* Corbin, H. (1971), 129.

23. Quoted in Freke, T. (2000), 81. *See* Rumi, *Mathnawi*, vol. I, v.1,599.

24. Corbin, H. (1983), 183

25. Corbin, H. (1971), 76

26. Ibid., 131

27. Armstrong, K. (1993), 260

28. According to tradition, al-Hallaj, when he saw the cross and the nails prepared for him, said, 'Lord forgive them, for if you had revealed to them that which you have revealed to me, they would not have done what they have done, and if you had hidden from me that which you have hidden from them, I should not have suffered this tribulation.' *See* ibid., 264.

29. Merkur, D. (1993), 214

30. Matthews, C. (1992), 187

31. Armstrong, op. cit., 265. Al-Suhrawardi made it his life's work to link what he called the 'Oriental' religion with Islam. He claimed that all the sages of the ancient world had preached a single doctrine, originally revealed to Hermes, transmitted through Plato and Pythagoras in the Greek world and through the Zoroastrian Magi in the Middle East.

32. Kingsley, P. (1995), 388. As Kingsley notes (Chapter 24, 'From Empedocles to the Sufis'), the connections between Sufism and the classical esoteric tradition, including Hermeticism and alchemy, 'have proved a major source of embarrassment for those interested in maintaining the purely Islamic nature of Sufism and denying its links with previous, non-Arab traditions, but their historical nature can be, and since the start of this century has been, established'. We would go further and assert that Sufism is a development of authentic Islam, which was itself originally a school of Gnosticism.

33. Armstrong, op. cit., 266

34. The Cross of Light 'which separates the things on high that *are* from the things below that *become*' features in the Gnostic *Acts of John*, 88–9. It later became a favourite Manichaean theme and recurs explicitly in Shiite Ismailian Gnosis. *See* Corbin, H. (1983), 60.

35. Armstrong, op. cit., 250. The legend of Mohammad's Night Journey from Arabia to the Temple Mount in Jerusalem where he makes a perilous ascent up a ladder (*miraj*) through the seven heavens betrays obvious similarities with Gnostic and Mithraic doctrines. As Matthews writes, 'The sevenfold circumambulation, or *tawaf*, of the Ka'aba may be a remembrance of the sevenfold ascent of the ziggurat or holy mountain upon which the Black Stone may once have been prominent. This would make the original Arabic Goddess "Queen of the Eighth" in truth.' (Matthews, op. cit., 185)

36. Quoted in Freke, T. (2000), 87. *See* Rumi, *Mathnawi*, vol. V, v.1,763–4.

37. This was part of an early tradition or *hadith*. Armstrong, K. (1993), 175

38. Qur'an 2:32. *See* Armstrong, op. cit., 264.

39. Corbin, H. (1971), 9. This fundamental Sufi saying was based on a saying in the Qur'an.

40. Quoted in Freke, op. cit., 119. *See* Rumi, op. cit., vol. I, v.1,937–40.

THE CAST LIST

Alexander Gnostic mentioned by Clement of Alexandria. Said to have been a follower of Prodicus, who led a Gnostic sect called 'the Sons of the first God'. Alexander, in his book *On the Pythagorean Symbols*, claimed that Pythagoras was a pupil of 'Nazaratus the Assyrian'.

Ambrose A wealthy Valentinian Gnostic who paid for the copying of the texts of his teacher Origen.

Ammonius Saccus *fl. c.*200 CE. Pagan philosopher of Alexandria. Teacher of Origen and Plotinus. Little is known about him and he wrote no books.

Anaxagoras 503–428 BCE. Greek philosopher from Asia Minor who moved to Athens and became tutor and adviser to its leading politician, Pericles. He was eventually banished in the purge of Athens' leading intellectuals which also led to the murder of Socrates.

Antiphon *fl.* 430 BCE. Sophist and radical egalitarian who challenged the Athenian status quo by declaring that for every statement there were 'two accounts'. His dialectical philosophy thus undermined all conventions based on polarization – Greek and barbarian, slave and free, good and bad, etc.

Apelles Disciple of Marcion who probably studied Gnosticism in Alexandria and derived his philosophy from the Greek philosophers, according to Hippolytus. He founded a community in Rome and wrote two books which have not survived – *Syllogisms*, in which he is said to have proved the untruth of the Books of Moses, and the *Revelations* of the prophetess Philumene.

Apuleius 125–190 CE. Pagan author and initiate. Born in Africa, he studied philosophy in Carthage, Athens and Rome. Famous for *The Golden Ass*, otherwise known as *The Metamorphoses of Lucius Apuleius*, an allegorical tale of his initiation into the Mysteries.

Aristophanes 445–385 BCE. Greek initiate of the Mysteries and writer of comedies. He was indicted for revealing too much of the Mystery school doctrines in his plays.

Augustine 354–430 CE. Follower of the Manichaean Gnostics for eight years. In 386 he became a Neoplatonist and four years later a Literalist Christian. In 395 he was appointed the Bishop of Hippo in Africa.

Axionicus Valentinian Gnostic of the 'Oriental' school mentioned along with Bardesanes by Hippolytus. Axionicus asserted that Jesus was purely spiritual and that it was Sophia who descended on Mary as the Holy Spirit.

Barbelo, Barbeloites, Barbelo Gnostics Gnostic devotees of the *aeon*/Goddess Barbelo who was the first emanation of the Unknown Father, 'the First Virginal Invisible Spirit'. She appears in the Gnostic texts *Allogenes*, *The Apocryphon of John*, *Melchizedek*, *Marsanes*, *The Three Steles of Seth*, *Trimorphic Protennoia* and *Pistis Sophia*. Various etymologies have been advanced for the name 'Barbelo', including the suggestion that it means 'in four is God', derived from the *tetraktys* of the Pythagoreans.

Bardesanes born *c.*135 CE in Syria. He converted the local ruler to Gnostic Christianity and between 202 and 217 there existed a Gnostic Christian state in Syria. It was subsequently destroyed by the Roman emperor Caracalla.

Barnabas *c*.100 CE. *The Epistle of Barnabas* was one of the best-known texts of the early Church, attributed to the co-worker of Paul. It was barred from the New Testament because it contained too many Gnostic ideas.

Basilides Syrian Gnostic active in Alexandria *c*.117–161 CE. One of the most distinguished of the Gnostics, according to Hegel. Derived his doctrines from Aristotle, according to Hippolytus. A disciple of Menander of Antioch. He received 'secret words' from the apostle Matthias. Reports of his teachings in Irenaeus and Hippolytus disagree. His son Isidore became his successor and the school of Basilides was still in existence in the fourth century.

Boethius 480–524 CE. Neoplatonic philosopher and author of the hugely influential *The Consolations of Philosophy*. *See* Websites.

Bogomils 'Lovers of God'. The Bogomils are thought to have arisen from a sect of Paulicians from Asia Minor, who in *c*.872 were compulsorily settled in Macedonia. Despite intense persecution the Bogomils retained a powerbase in Serbia and Bosnia until the fifteenth century. At the anti-Bogomil council of 1211 the Bogomils were accused of performing 'unholy mysteries like the Hellenic Pagan rites'.

Candidus In 229 CE Origen travelled to Athens to engage in debate with its leading Gnostic teacher Candidus.

Carpocrates *c*.110 CE. Alexandrian Platonist who founded a sect of Gnostic Christians using *The Secret Gospel of Mark* as its initiatory document. The Carpocratians were radical communists who condemned private property as the source of all injustice.

Cathars The word 'Cathar' derives from the Greek for 'purity'. As a synonym for initiates it can be traced back to the Orphic *Gold Leaves* *c*.400 BCE. The Manichaeans also called themselves 'the Pure Ones'. The earliest certain indication of medieval Cathars is the disclosure in 1143 of a heretical community in Cologne. Between 1150 and 1300 Catharism was the dominant religion of southern France and northern Italy (where they were known as Patarenes). The Cathars were vegetarian celibates who believed in reincarnation. Like Simon and Marcion they considered the God of Jesus and the New Testament was benevolent but the Old Testament God was a tyrant. They called the Church of Rome 'a den of thieves ... the harlot of which we read in the Apocalypse.' From 1139 on the Church began calling councils to condemn the Cathars. In 1208 Pope Innocent III offered indulgences and eternal salvation, as well as the lands and property of the heretics, to anyone who would take up the Crusade against the Cathars. The 30-year Crusade decimated Langedoc and on 16 March 1244 200 Cathar 'Perfects' were burned to death in the fall of Montségur, the last stronghold of Catharism. *See* Websites.

Celsus Wrote *The True Doctrine*, a critique of emerging Christianity, *c*.170 CE. Seventy per cent of the work survives in quotation in the work of Origen.

Cerdo Lived in Rome *c*.136–142 CE. Advocated the antithesis of the Old Testament 'Just God' and the 'Good God' of Jesus, a theme that was taken up by Marcion and Mani.

Cerinthus *fl*.100 CE. Gnostic philosopher trained in 'the Egyptian tradition', according to Hippolytus. Irenaeus goes out of his way to attack Cerinthus, whose followers claimed he was the author of *The Gospel of the Beloved Disciple*, aka *The Gospel of John*. His work shows traces of Ebionism.

Cicero 106–43 BCE. Roman lawyer and politician of the late Republic. Initiated at Eleusis in 80 BCE, he was instrumental in making Greek philosophy and education fashionable in Rome.

Clement of Alexandria 150–215 CE. Born in Athens, became the pupil of Pantaenus of Alexandria in 180 and head of the Catechetical school in 190. Traditionally regarded as a Literalist Christian and even beatified by the Roman Church, but his works actually have far more in common with Gnosticism. Clement calls the Gnostic 'the true Christian'.

Clement of Rome Said by Eusebius to have been the fourth Bishop of Rome *c.*90 CE. His writings suggest that Ebionite Gnosticism was one of the first sects to reach Rome. However, little can be known about Clement, as numerous letters attributed to him were forged in the fourth and fifth centuries.

Constantine 272–337 CE. Roman emperor from 307 until his death. First Roman emperor to become a Christian.

Diodorus 80–20 BCE. A Greek historian of Sicily who wrote a *Universal History* of the time in 40 books.

Diogenes 420–324 BCE. Follower of Antisthenes, the disciple of Socrates, and founder of the Cynic school of philosophy.

Dionysius aka **Pseudo-Dionysius** A co-worker with Paul, according to *Acts* 17:34. In 529 CE Justinian closed the ancient school of philosophy in Athens and a few years later four mystical treatises appeared under the name Dionysius the Areopagite. If the works are forgeries, the fraud was a total success – not only did the works escape the ban of heresy that they certainly merited, but they became accepted as an authority second only to Augustine and were the inspiration for nearly all later Christian mysticism. Dionysius' work had a profound influence on Erigena, Albertus Magnus, Thomas Aquinas, Dante, Nicholas of Cusa, Meister Eckhart, Pico della Mirandola, Marsilio Ficino, Edward Spenser, Coleridge, etc.

Dositheus Dositheus is mentioned along with Simon as a Samaritan heretic. His disciples held that he had not really died. As late as the sixth century there were controversies among the Samaritans as to whether the 'prophet like Moses' was Joshua or Dositheus. The convergent testimony of Epiphanius and an Arabic chronicle of the fourteenth century suggest that the Dositheans might have been adherents of a Semitic baptizing sect and originated as early as the second or first centuries BCE.

Ebionites/Ebionaeans The Ebionites, or 'Poor Ones', were Christian Gnostics based in Jerusalem and led by Peter and James in the first century, who repudiated Paul because 'he was an apostate from the law'. Ebionites wanted Christian Gnosticism to retain its ties with traditional Jewish religion. Because they were based in Jerusalem, later Christian Literalists claimed they were the original disciples of the historical Jesus.

Elkesai 'The hidden power of God', a prophet who appeared in Syria *c.*100 CE. The Elkesaites were a Gnostic Judaeo-Christian Baptist sect. Like the Ebionites, they denounced Paul and the 'Way of the Greeks'. Mani's father was a member of this sect. The Mandeans originated in this same Jewish Baptist sectarian world.

Empedocles 490–430 BCE. Disciple of Pythagoras, priest and miracle worker who wrote an initiatory poem in which he proclaimed himself an 'immortal god' whose teachings could bring men back from the dead.

Epictetus 50–130 CE. A crippled Phrygian slave brought up in the household of Nero. When freed, he became the first century's greatest exponent of Cynic philosophy. Driven out of Rome by Domitian in 90 CE along with all other philosophers. Many of the doctrines of Epictetus can be placed alongside their counterparts in the New Testament, testifying to the closeness of Cynicism and early Christianity.

Epiphanes Author of *On Justice*. Thought to have been the son of Carpocrates, the leader of a Gnostic school in Alexandria at the beginning of the second century CE, and to have died at the young age of 17. Some scholars dispute that there ever was an Epiphanes, claiming this was the name of an Alexandrian god whose festival was called Epiphany.

Epiphanius 315–403 CE. Literalist Christian who became Bishop of Salamis in Greece, although he was born in Judaea. His most important work is the *Panarion*, or *Medicine Chest against All Heresies*. He later joined forces with Jerome in Rome to denounce Origen's works as heretical.

Essenes Jewish sect based at Qumran a few miles from where the Old Testament Joshua crossed the Jordan into the Promised Land. In recent years a cache of Dead Sea Scrolls has been discovered, which scholars believe belonged to the Essenes. The Jewish historian Josephus, who spent a year among the Essenes in his youth, likens them to Pythagoreans. Philo describes them as one wing of a common Jewish movement which included the Therapeutae.

Euripides 484–406 BCE. The last Classical Athenian tragedian, most famous for his great tragedy *The Bacchae*. The play alludes to Mystery school doctrines and is a vital source of information about the cult of Dionysus in Classical Athens.

Eusebius 260–340 CE. Trained at the school in Caesaria established by Origen. Became Bishop of Caesaria in 311. Arrived at the council of Nicaea in 325 a convicted Arian heretic but left it as Constantine's official historian and biographer. Known as the 'Father of Church History', but his work is profoundly unreliable and is widely held to be little more than propaganda for Literalist Christianity.

Firmicus Maternus died *c*.360 CE. Wrote a compendium of astrology whilst still a Pagan, converted to Literalist Christianity late in life and appealed to the Roman emperors to destroy Pagan idols by force.

Flora Roman Christian woman who was the recipient of a letter from the Valentinian Gnostic Ptolemy which is still preserved in the writings of Epiphanius.

Gregory of Nyssa 335–95 CE. One of the Cappadocians' Fathers, along with Basil (329–79 CE) and Gregory of Nazianzum (329–91 CE), whose work continued to develop the Gnostic mystical philosophy of Origen. Gregory of Nyssa coined the paradoxical phrase 'dazzling darkness' for God, writing that every concept of God becomes a false idol which cannot reveal God himself.

Helen of Troy In Homer, Helen of Troy was the cause of the war between the Greeks and Trojans. The Pythagoreans regarded the works of Homer as an initiation allegory in which

Helen represents the human soul and it was after the pattern of these stories that the oldest Gnostics known to us, Simon Magus of Samaria and his followers, told the tragic story of how divine Wisdom (Sophia/Helen) was raped by hostile powers but was finally saved. Simon is said to have rescued Helen in her last incarnation as a whore in the city of Tyre and to have travelled about with her, teaching Gnosis. According to Celsus, the Pagan critic of Christianity, there was a 'Gospel according to Helen' circulating in the late second century.

Heliodorus *fl. c.*230 CE. Priest of Helios in Syria and author of *An Ethiopian Romance*, which encoded secret teachings on the Mysteries.

Heracleon Roman Gnostic and disciple of Valentinus. Only a few quotations from his memoirs survive in the work of Origen and Clement.

Heraclitus *fl. c.*500 BCE. Mystic philosopher of Ephesus in Asia Minor who wrote about the Word of God (*Logos*). Diogenes tells us that his cryptic works can only be understood by an initiate of the Mysteries. Heraclitus was an important influence on the Gnostics.

Hermas *The Shepherd of Hermas* was one of the most widely known early Christian texts, said to have been written *c.*90 CE in Italy. It is a curious mixture of Hermetic, Sibylline and Jewish/Christian apocalypse that contains no definite quotation from either of the Testaments. Not surprisingly, it never made it into the New Testament.

Hermes Trismegistus Patron deity of the Hermetic literature written in Egypt in the second and third centuries CE, a synthesis of the Greek 'Guide of Souls' Hermes and the Egyptian god Thoth, the legendary sage and inventor of writing.

Herodotus 484–430 BCE. Greek historian known as 'the Father of History'. He travelled in Egypt and records that the Mysteries of Dionysus at Eleusis were modelled on those of Osiris in Egypt.

Hesiod Greek poet of the late eighth century BCE. *The Theogeny* describes the origin of the gods of Greek mythology.

Hippolytus 170–236 CE. Literalist Christian and heresy-hunter who called the Gnostic Bishop of Rome Callistus a heretic and set himself up as anti-Pope. *The Refutation of All Heresies*, published *c.*210, traces the Gnostic 'heresies' to their origin in Greek schools of philosophy.

Homer Greek poet(s) of the seventh century BCE, author(s) of *The Odyssey* and *The Iliad*. The Homeric poems were first collected, revised and ordered at the court of Pisistratus in Athens at the end of the sixth century BCE. Three of the four editors of Homer are said to have been Orphics and this is probably where Pythagorean and Mystery school teachings were first smuggled into the text. This exegesis of Homer as an initiatory text was clearly important to the Gnostics, as Homer is often quoted in the Gnostic gospels.

Iamblichus 250–325 CE. Syrian philosopher who became a student of Porphyry. Wrote 10 volumes on Pythagorean philosophy and *The Life of Pythagoras*.

Ignatius of Antioch Said to have been active *c.*120 CE. Supposedly an early Literalist Christian, but interpolations of his letters in later centuries make it almost impossible to know what is genuine.

Irenaeus 130–202 CE. Literalist Christian and vehement opponent of Gnosticism. Born in Asia Minor, became Bishop of Lyons in Gaul in 178. Author of the massive work *Against All Heresies*, a polemic against Gnosticism.

Isidore Said to have been the son of Basilides, although this might mean he was simply his spiritual successor. He is known to be the author of three writings which have not survived: *On the Grown Soul, Ethics* and *Expositions of the Prophet Parchor*.

Jerome 342–420 CE. Biblical scholar and translator of the Bible into Latin. A Literalist Christian who attacked Origen's doctrines of reincarnation and *apocatastasis*, the ultimate salvation of all.

Josephus 38–107 CE. Jewish historian who visited Rome in 64, aged 26. During the campaign in Galilee in 67 he defected to the Romans. His book *The Jewish War* was published in Rome *c.*95. His books were later amended by Christian Literalists to include glowing references to Jesus.

Jung, C. G. 1875–1961. Swiss founder of depth psychology. Jung was profoundly influenced by the classical esoteric tradition, Gnosticism and Hermeticism, and especially its survival in the West as alchemy. The purchase of the first Gnostic codex discovered in Nag Hammadi was made possible by a foundation set up by Jung and in his honour is now known as the Jung Codex.

Justin Martyr 100–165 CE. Born in Samaria, came to Rome *c.*140. Rejected by Platonic and Pythagorean schools, he later converted to Literalist Christianity. Published the first defence of Christianity whilst violently attacking the Jews.

Lucian Gnostic disciple of Marcion.

Lucian 117–180 CE. Pagan philosopher. Born in Syria, educated at Tarsus, became a teacher of literature in France. Specialized in satire about religious and philosophical frauds. Friend of Celsus.

Mandeans From *manda* = Gnosis. A Gnostic sect, the origins of which go back to pre-Christian times but which still survives today in the marshes of Iraq.

Mani Born in Babylon in 216 CE, he founded a Gnostic religion which soon spread across the Roman Empire. Augustine was a Manichaean 'hearer' for nine years. In the Great Persecution of 303 CE it was Manichaean Christianity that was made the first victim of the purge, followed a year later by all Christianity.

Marcellina A female Valentinian and follower of Epiphanes who introduced his teachings to Rome, bringing with her painted icons illuminated with gold representing Jesus, Pythagoras, Plato and Aristotle. The sect of the Marcellians flourished *c.*130 CE.

Marcion Influential Gnostic teacher born in Pontus in Asia Minor, where his father was a bishop. He appeared in Rome *c.*140 CE and by the end of the second century his Church 'filled the whole world'. Hippolytus traced Marcion's teaching to Empedocles. Marcion rejected the Old Testament and parts of the gospels that he regarded as falsified. It is widely accepted that it was Marcion's criticisms that spurred the creation of the first Literalist canon.

Marcus *fl. c.*170 CE. Gnostic teacher from Asia Minor or Egypt. By the late second century his teachings had reached as far as the Rhone valley. His wisdom was received by revelation of the Pythagorean Tetraktys, which appeared to him in female form.

Marcus Aurelius Roman emperor from 161 to 180 CE. Stoic philosopher and author of *Meditations*. His rule marks the high point of the Roman Empire, a period later called the Second Sophistic. This was both a tribute to the triumph of philosophy over Rome and a reference to the First Sophistic, when philosophy triumphed over Athens in the fifth century BCE during the 'Athenian Enlightenment' of the Classical Age.

Menander One of the 'earliest heretics', according to Tertullian.

Monoimos 'The Arab'. Not known to be a member of any particular Gnostic sect. Monoimus declared: 'Man is the universe' and derived his doctrines from 'Geometers and Arithmeticians' (e.g. Pythagoreans), according to Hippolytus.

Montanus A priest of Cybele and her son Attis who fell into a trance and began speaking in tongues. Believing himself to be inspired by the Holy Spirit, he later travelled through Asia Minor, accompanied by two women prophetesses. He regarded ecstasy as the only true Christianity.

Naassene Gnostics Gnostic sect which existed under the reign of Hadrian (110–140 CE). Naassenes derived their name from *Naas*, meaning 'serpent', and believed that every temple (*Naos* in Greek) was secretly dedicated to this divinity. According to the Church Father Hippolytus, the Naassenes 'constantly attend the mysteries called those of the "Great Mother", supposing especially that they behold by means of the ceremonies performed there the entire mystery'.

Origen 185–254 CE. Born in Alexandria, studied Pagan philosophy with Plotinus under Ammonius Saccus. Became a pupil of Clement and castrated himself in accordance with *Matthew* 19:12 (a practice that was also followed by the Pagan followers of the Godman Attis). He established a school in Caesaria in 231. Although often portrayed as a Literalist Christian, his works have far more in common with Gnosticism. He was posthumously condemned as a heretic by the Roman Church in the fifth century.

Parmenides born *c.*515 BCE. Italian Pythagorean who came to Athens in the mid-fifth century BCE, where he taught Socrates and others. Plato's dialogue *Parmenides* shows the philosopher teaching a highly sophisticated system of dialectical philosophy.

Paul of Tarsus Traditionally pictured as a Literalist, but claimed by the Gnostics as the 'Great Apostle' of Gnosticism. It is believed that his mission to Greece lasted from 48 to 53 CE, but many of his letters are now known to have been either forged or doctored and his dates are uncertain. The legend that he was martyred in Rome, like that of Peter, was created to legitimize the authority of the Roman Church and has no basis in fact.

Philo Judaeus 25 BCE–50 CE. An Alexandrian Jew whose works demonstrate the thorough interpenetration of Greek philosophy and Jewish traditions among Hellenized Jews. Philo's thought is dominated by the idea of the *Logos* and many of the doctrines of the Christian Gnostics can be found in his works. In the history of ideas he is an important bridge between the Greek philosophical tradition and later Christian Gnosticism.

Plato 429–348 BCE. Disciple of Socrates and founder of the philosophical school in Athens known as the Academy. His philosophy is indebted to the doctrines of the Mysteries, the mysticism of Pythagoras and the poetry of Orpheus.

Plotinus 204–270 CE. The most influential mystic philosopher after Plato. After 11 years of study in Alexandria with Ammonius Saccus, he came to Rome, where his lectures were attended by the emperor and several senators. Most famous for his vast work *The Enneads*, lecture notes which were organized by his pupil Porphyry. Although Plotinus wrote against the Christian Gnostics, in fact his thought and theirs have much in common.

Porphyry 232–303 CE. Pagan philosopher. Born in Tyre, studied philosophy at Athens, became a Neoplatonist after meeting Plotinus in Rome in 263. Wrote *Against the Christians* in 15 volumes.

Proclus 412–485 CE. Pagan philosopher. Born in Constantinople, studied in Athens. One of the last heads of the Platonic Academy in Athens before its abolition by Justinian in 529 CE.

Protagoras 480–410 CE. First professional philosopher in Athens. Indicted for heresy and put on trial. Escaped and perished at sea.

Ptolemy *fl. c.*140 in Rome. Gnostic teacher, disciple of Valentinus, founder, along with Heracleon, of the Italic school of Valentinus, 'bloom of the school of Valentinus', according to Irenaeus. He was the first exegete of the fourth gospel and his letter to his disciple Flora is still preserved. Ptolemy has been identified with the martyr Ptolemy mentioned by Justin Martyr. If true, this would make him one of the earliest Christian martyrs.

Pythagoras 581–497 BCE. Philosopher of the Greek island of Samos who travelled widely in Egypt, Phoenicia and Babylon, and later founded communities of mystics in the Greek colonies of southern Italy. A Hierophant of the Mysteries of Demeter and Dionysus, a poet who wrote works ascribed to Orpheus, the first in the Greek world to call himself a 'philosopher', a social reformer, educationalist, musician, mathematician and scientist. His influence on Plato and the whole Greek philosophical tradition was profound.

Sallustius *fl.* 360 CE. Neoplatonic philosopher and adviser to the emperor Julian in his attempts to bring about a Pagan revival.

Saturnilus (Saturninus) of Antioch Christian Gnostic who was a contemporary of Basilides.

Seneca 4 BCE–65 CE. Roman philosopher and politician. Became a vegetarian follower of Pythagoras in his youth. Later became tutor to Nero.

Simon Magus The arch-heretic and father of all heresies, according to the Church Fathers, the man from whom 'the Gnosis took its beginnings'. It is possible that Simon, like Jesus, is a mythical Messiah figure. Simon is said also to have called himself 'Christ', to have 'suffered in Judaea' and to have gone about with a redeemed harlot, just as Jesus did.

Socrates The most famous philosopher of antiquity. Plato portrays him as a barefoot sage teaching Pythagorean philosophy in Athens. He was put to death in 399 BCE for heresy.

Tatian According to Hippolytus, Tatian derived his doctrines from 'Valentinus and Marcion'.

Tertullian 160–220 CE. Born in Carthage, became a lawyer in Rome, converted to Literalist Christianity *c.*195, became a Gnostic in 207.

Thales In 570 BCE Thales came to Greece as one of many eastern Greeks from Ionia and Asia Minor whose number included Pythagoras. With them they brought Egyptian and Babylonian knowledge which caused a revolution in both science and mysticism. Thales is said to have studied in Egypt, where he correctly calculated the height of the pyramids and was the first man to predict an eclipse.

Thecla It was part of a well-established oral tradition in Syria that Thecla was a high-born lady from Iconium who at the age of 18 became the companion of Paul and travelled around baptizing and preaching. According to *The Acts of Thecla*, she became a martyr. *See* Websites.

Theodotus Through Clement of Alexandria a book of *Excerpta* have been preserved. Theodotus is said to have belonged to the 'Oriental school' of Valentinus.

Therapeutae. A sect of mystical Jews who lived near Alexandria in Egypt at the beginning of the first century CE. They are described by Philo in his book *On the Contemplative Life* as a Jewish Pythagorean school which also included the Essenes. Some say that Philo himself may have been a member. Although the Church historian Eusebius argued that the Therapeutae were the first Literalist Christians, as Philo wrote about them in 10 CE, 20 years before the supposed date of the crucifixion, this theory has now been thoroughly discredited. Philo writes about the Therapeutae in terms suggesting that they were practising a Jewish version of the Pagan Mysteries. Ironically, Eusebius may well have been right. The Therapeutae are most likely the proto-Christians who created the Jesus story.

Valentinus 100–180 CE. Alexandrian Gnostic poet. Author of *The Gospel of Truth* found at Nag Hammadi. Founded a school in Rome *c.*140. Tertullian described Valentinus as 'of Plato's school' and Hippolytus thought he 'may justly be reckoned a Pythagorean and Platonist, not a Christian'. He was apparently familiar with the work of Philo of Alexandria. Valentinian Christianity spread to all parts of the Roman world – Gaul, Rome, Asia Minor, Syria, Egypt, Carthage and eventually Mesopotamia. Records from the end of the seventh century still talk of Valentinians. The Valentinian school was itself supposedly divided into two schools, the Italic, founded by Ptolemy and Heracleon, and the Oriental, founded by Theodotus and Marcus.

Zeno of Citium in Cyprus 350–260 BCE. The founder of Stoicism. Although he lived and taught at Athens, Zeno was a Semite who was nicknamed 'the Phoenician'. His father travelled between Tyre, Sidon and Athens, from where he brought back a number of 'Socratic books' which attracted his son to Athens. In Athens Zeno sought out 'that person most like Socrates' and was directed to Crates of Thebes, the successor of Diogenes. Since the isolation of Q it has become clear that one of the major influences on early Christianity was Cynic/Stoic philosophy, which had spread to the eastern Mediterranean at an early date.

Zostrianos Eponymous hero of a work which Porphyry names as one of the Gnostic texts in circulation at the time of Plotinus, who charged his opponents with 'abandoning the ancient philosophy' in favour of revelations by Zostrianos, Allogenes and others – works that have now been found at Nag Hammadi. The text *Zostrianos* uses the same philosophical terms, questions and categories as the Neoplatonists, especially Plotinus, but sets them in the form of a revelation to the prophet Zostrianos while he meditated in the desert.

BIBLIOGRAPHY

A

Aldredge-Clanton, J., *In Search of the Christ-Sophia: An Inclusive Christology for Liberating Christians*, Twenty-Third Publications, 1995

Allegro, J., *The Dead Sea Scrolls*, Penguin, 1956

Anderson, G., *The Second Sophistic*, Routledge, 1993

—, *Sage, Saint and Sophist*, Routledge, 1994

Angus, S., *Mystery Religions*, Dover Books, 1925

Aristophanes, *The Frogs*, Penguin Classics, 1964

Armstrong, K., *A History of God*, Mandarin, 1993

Arnold, E. V., *Roman Stoicism*, Routledge & Kegan Paul Ltd, 1911

Ashton, J., 'The Transformation of Wisdom: A Study of the Prologue of John's Gospel', *NTS* 32 (1986), 161–86

Athanaissakis, A. P., *The Homeric Hymns*, Johns Hopkins University Press, 1976

B

Bachofen, Johann Jakob, *Das Mütterrecht*, 1861

Barnes, J., *The Presocratic Philosophers*, vol. I, Routledge & Kegan Paul, revised edition, 1982

Barnstone, W., *The Other Bible*, HarperCollins, 1984

Barton, T. S., *Power and Knowledge: Astrology, Physiognomics and Medicine under the Roman Empire*, University of Michigan Press, 1994

Beard, M., and North, J., *Pagan Priests*, Duckworth Press, 1990

Beard, M., North, J., and Price, S., *Religions of Rome: Vol. I, A History*, Cambridge University Press, 1998

Benac and Oto, *Bogomil Sculpture*, Braun et Cie, 1975

Bernal, M., *Black Athena*, Free Association Books, 1987

Bernstein, A. E., *The Formation of Hell*, UCL Press, 1993

Bickerman, E. J., *The Jews in the Greek Age*, Harvard University Press, 1988

Bihalji, O. M., and Benac, A., *The Bogomils*, Thames and Hudson, 1962

Birks, W., and Gilbert, R. A., *The Treasure of Montségur*, Crucible, 1987

Boardman, J., Griffin, J., Murray, O., *The Oxford History of the Classical World*, Oxford University Press, 1986

Boethius, *The Consolation of Philosophy*, Penguin Classics, 1969

Bouché-Leclercq, A., *L'Astrologie grecque*, 1899

Bousset, W., *Hauptprobleme der Gnosis*, Göttingen, 1907

Bouyer, L., *The Christian Mystery: From Pagan Myth to Christian Mysticism*, St Bede's Publications, 1990

Boyd, C. A., *Cynic Sage or Son of God?*, Bridge Point, 1995

Brandon, S. G. F., *Religion in Ancient History*, George Allen & Unwin, 1969

Branham, R. B., and Goulet-Caze, M.-O., eds, *The Cynics: The Cynic Movement in Antiquity and Its Legacy*, University of California, 1996

Buber, M., *Jewish Mysticism*, J. M. Dent and Sons, 1931

Bultmann, R., *Theology of the New Testament*, trans. K. Grobel, 2 vols, SCM Press, 1955
— , *The Gospel of John: A Commentary*, Basil Blackwell, 1971
Burckhardt, J., *The Life of Constantine*, Deutsche Verlags-Anstalt, 1929
— , *The Age of Constantine the Great*, Dorset Press, 1949
Burkert, W., *Lore and Science in Ancient Pythagoreanism*, Harvard University Press, 1972
— , *Greek Religion: Archaic and Classical*, Blackwell Publishers, 1985; originally published in German as *Griechische Religion der archaischen und klassischen Epoche*, 1977
— , *Ancient Mystery Cults*, Harvard University Press, 1987
— , *The Orientalising Revolution*, Harvard University Press, 1992
Butler, T. W., *Let Her Keep It*, Quantum Leap Publisher, 1998

C

Campbell, J., *The Hero with a Thousand Faces*, Paladin, 1949
— , *Papers from the Eranos Yearbooks*, Routledge & Kegan Paul, 1955
— , *Occidental Mythology*, Arkana, 1964
Carpenter and Faraone, *Masks of Dionysus*, Cornell University Press, 1993
Cartledge, P., *The Greeks: A Portrait of Self and Others*, Oxford University Press, 1993
Cherniss, H., *The Riddle of the Early Academy*, University of California Press, 1945
— , *Selected Papers*, E. J. Brill, 1977
Churton, T., *The Gnostics*, Weidenfeld and Nicolson, 1987
Cicero, *On the Good Life*, Penguin Classics, 1971
— , *The Nature of the Gods*, Penguin Classics, 1972
Clark, J. M., and Skinner, J., *Meister Eckhart: Selected Treatises and Sermons*, Fount, 1994
Clark, R. J., *Catabasis Vergil and the Wisdom-Tradition*, B. R. Grüner Publishing Company, 1979
Clement of Alexandria, *Clement of Alexandria*, Loeb Classical Library, no. 92, 1919
Cohn, N., *The Pursuit of the Millennium, Revolutionary Millenarians and Mystical Anarchists of the Middle Ages*, London, 1957
Copenhaver, B. P., *Hermetica*, Cambridge University Press, 1992
Corbin, H., *Creative Imagination in the Sufism of Ibn Arabi*, London, 1970
— , *The Man of Light in Iranian Sufism*, Omega, 1971
— , *Cyclical Time and the Ismaili Gnosis*, Kegan Paul International, 1983
— , *Spiritual Body, Celestial Earth: From Mazdean Iran to Shiite Iran*, London, 1990
Cornford, F. M., *The Unwritten Philosophy*, Cambridge University Press, 1950
Cowell, F. R., *Cicero and the Roman Republic*, Pelican Books, 1948
Cramer, F. H., 'The Caesars and the Stars', *Seminar* 9 (1951), 1–35
Cranston, S., *Reincarnation Phoenix Fire Mysteries*, Theosophical University Press, 1977
Cronin, V., *The Florentine Renaissance*, Pimlico, 1967; reissued 1992
Cross, F. L., *The Oxford Dictionary of the Christian Church*, Oxford University Press, 1958
Crossan, J. D., *The Historical Jesus: The Life of a Mediterranean Peasant*, 1991

Cumont, F., *The Mysteries of Mithras*, Dover Books, 1903

— , *Oriental Religions in Roman Paganism*, Dover Publications, 1911

— , *Astrology and Religion among the Greeks and Romans*, 1912

— , *After Life in Roman Paganism*, Yale University Press, 1922

Curry, P. (ed.), *Astrology, Science and Society: Historical Essays*, 1987

D

D'Alviella, G., *The Mysteries of Eleusis*, The Aquarian Press, 1981

Davidson, J., *The Gospel of Jesus: In Search of His Original Teachings*, Element Books, 1995

Davies, S. L., *The Gospel of Thomas and Christian Wisdom*, Seabury Press, 1983

de Boer, E., *Mary Magdalene: Beyond the Myth*, Trinity Press International, 1996

de Santillana, G., *The Renaissance Philosophers*, Mentor, 1956

de Santillana, G., and von Dechend, H., *Hamlet's Mill: An Essay Investigating the Origins of Human Knowledge and its Transmission through Myth*, Nonpareil David R. Godine Publisher, Inc., 1977

De Vogel, C. J., *Pythagoras and Early Pythagoreans*, Royal VanCorcum Netherlands, 1966

Denomy, A. J., *The Heresy of Courtly Love*, D. X. McMullen, 1947

Dicks, D. R., 'Astronomy and Astrology in Horace', *Hermes* 91 (1963), 60–73

Dillon, J., *The Golden Chain: Studies in the Development of Platonism and Christianity*, Variorum, 1990

Diodorus of Sicily, *Books 1–2*, Loeb Classical Library no. 279, 1933

Dodd, 'The Interpretation of the Fourth Gospel', *CHP*, 1970, 274–7

Dodds, E. R., *The Greeks and the Irrational*, University of California Press, 1951

Doherty, E., *The Jesus Puzzle: Did Christianity Begin with a Mythical Christ?*, Canadian Humanist Press, 1999

Doran, R., *Birth of a Worldview*, Westview Press, 1995

Douglas-Klotz, N., *Desert Wisdom: The Middle Eastern Tradition from the Goddess to the Sufis*, Thorsons, 1995

Dower, E. S., *The Secret Adam*, Oxford, 1960

Downing, F. G., *Christ and the Cynics: Jesus and Other Radical Preachers in First Century Tradition*, Sheffield Academic Press, 1988

— , *Cynics, Paul and the Christian Churches*, Routledge, 1988

— , *Cynics and Christian Origins*, T&T Clark, 1992

Drews, A., *The Christ Myth*, Westminster College, 1910; reissued Prometheus Books, 1998

Dunlap, S. F., *The Mysteries of Adoni*, Williams and Norgate, 1866

E

Meister Eckhart: Selected Writings, selected and trans. Oliver Davies, Penguin, 1994

Eddy, P. R., 'Jesus as Diogenes? Reflections on the Cynic Jesus Thesis', *JBL* 115 (1996), 449–69

Edinger, E. F., *The Psyche in Antiquity, Book 2: Gnosticism and Early Christianity*, Inner City Books, 1999

Ehrenberg, V., *From Solon to Socrates*, Methuen and Co., 1968

Eisler, R., *Orpheus the Fisher*, Kessinger Publishing, 1920

—, *The Messiah Jesus and John the Baptist*, The Dial Press, 1931

Eisler, R., *The Chalice and the Blade: Our History, our Future*, Harper & Row, 1987

Eliade, M., *The Myth of the Eternal Return*, Arkana, 1954

—, *Essential Sacred Writings around the World*, HarperSanFrancisco, 1967

Ellegard, A., *Jesus: One Hundred Years Before Christ*, Century, 1999

Ellerbe, H. E., *The Dark Side of Christian History*, Morningstar and Lark, 1995

Ellis, N., *Awakening Osiris*, Phanes Press, 1988

Engelsmann, J. C., *The Feminine Dimension of the Divine*, Westminster Press, 1972

Epictetus, *The Teachings of Epictetus*, Walter Scott Library, n.d.

Erskine, A., *The Helleistic Stoa: Political Thought and Action*, Cornell University Press, 1990

Euripides, *The Bacchae*, Penguin Classics, 1954

Eusebius, *History of the Early Church*, Penguin Classics, 1965

F

Farrington, B., *Greek Science*, Pelican Books, 1944

Faulkner, R. O., *The Book of the Dead*, British Museum Press, 1972

Feeney, D. C., *The Gods in Epic*, Clarendon Press, 1991

Festugière, *La Révélation d'Hermes Trismegiste, II: Le Dieu Cosmique*, 1958

Fidler, D., *Jesus Christ: Sun of God*, Quest Books, 1993

Fiorenza, E. S., 'Wisdom Mythology and the Christological Hymns of the New Testament', *Aspects of Wisdom in Judaism and Early Christianity*, ed. Robert Wilken, Notre Dame University Press, 1974

—, 'Feminist Theology and New Testament Interpretation', *JSQT* 22 (1982)

—, *In Memory of Her: A Feminist Theological Reconstruction of Christian Origins*, SCM Press, 1983

Foerster, W., *Gnosis: A Selection of Gnostic Texts, 1. Patristic Evidence; 2. Coptic and Mandean Sources*, 1974

Framroze, D., and Bode, A., *Songs of Zarathushtra*, George Allen & Unwin Ltd, 1952

Frazer, J., *The Golden Bough*, Wordsworth Reference Books, 1922

Freke, T., *The Illustrated Book of World Scripture*, Thorsons, 1997

—, *Rumi Wisdom*, Godsfield Press, 2000

Freke, T., and Gandy, P., *The Complete Guide to World Mysticism*, Piatkus Books, 1997

—, *The Hermetica*, Piatkus Books, 1997

—, *Wisdom of the Pagan Philosophers*, Journey Editions, 1998

—, *The Jesus Mysteries: Was the 'Original Jesus' a Pagan God?*, Thorsons, 1999

Friedman, R., *Who Wrote the Bible?*, Jonathan Cape, 1988

G

Garin, E., *Astrology in the Renaissance*, Routledge Kegan Paul, 1976

Garsonian, N. G., *The Paulican Heresy*, Mouton, 1967

Gaus, A., *The Unvarnished New Testament*, Phanes Press, 1991

Gibbon, E., *The Decline and Fall of the Roman Empire*, Penguin Classics, 1796

Gilbert, R. A., *Casting the First Stone: The Hypocrisy of Religious Fundamentalism and its Threat to Society*, Element Books, 1993

Gimbutas, M., *The Goddesses and Gods of Old Europe 6500–3500 BC*, University of California Press, 1982

— , *The Language of the Goddess*, HarperSanFrancisco, 1991

Godwin, J., *Mystery Religions in the Ancient World*, Thames and Hudson, 1981

Goldin, F., *Lyrics of the Troubadours and Trouvères: An Anthology and History*, Anchor-Doubleday, 1973

Grant, R. M., *Gnosticism: A Sourcebook of Heretical Writings*, Harper & Brothers, 1961

— , *Gnosticism and Early Christianity*, New York, 1966

— , *Jesus after the Gospels: The Christ of the Second Century*, SCM Press, 1990

Graves, R., *Greek Myths*, Pelican Books, 1955

— , *The White Goddess*, Faber and Faber, 1961

Gregory, J., *The Neoplatonists*, Kylie Cathie, 1987

Grenfell, B. P., and Hunt, A. S., *New Sayings of Jesus and Fragment of a Lost Gospel from Oxyrhynchus*, London, 1904

Gruber and Kersten, *The Original Jesus*, Element Books, 1985

Gruen, E. S., *Heritage and Hellenism: The Reinvention of the Jewish Tradition*, University of California Press, 1998

Guthrie, K. S., *The Pythagorean Sourcebook*, Phanes Press, 1987

Guthrie, W. K. C., *Orpheus and Greek Religion*, Princeton University Press, 1952

— , *History of Greek Philosophy*, Cambridge University Press, 1962

H

Hamilton, B., *The Albigensian Crusade*, The Historical Association, 1974

— , *Monastic Reform: Catharism and the Crusades*, Variorum, 1979

Hanratty, G., *Studies in Gnosticism and in the Philosophy of Religion*, Four Courts Press, 1997

Happold, F. C., *Mysticism*, Penguin Books, 1963

Harrington, D. J., *Wisdom Texts from Qumran*, Routledge, 1996

Harrison, J., *Prologemena to the Study of Greek Religion*, Princeton University Press, 1922

— , *Themis*, Merlin Press, 1963

Haskins, S., *Mary Magdalene: Myth and Metaphor*, HarperCollinsPublishers, 1993

Hayman, Peter, 'Monotheism – A Misused Word in Jewish Studies', *Journal of Jewish Studies* 42 (1990), 1–15

Hedrick, C., and Hodgson, R. (eds), *Proceedings of the International Colloquium on Gnosticism and Early Christianity*, details in R. T. Wallis, *Neoplatonism and Gnosticism*, State University of New York Press, 1992

Hegel, G. W. F., *The Phenomenology of Mind*, Harper and Row, 1967

Hengel, M., *Jews, Greeks and Barbarians: Aspects of the Hellenization of Judaism in the pre-Christian Period*, SCM Press, 1980

Herodotus, *The Histories*, Penguin Classics, 1954

Hesiod, *Theogony and Works and Days*, World's Classics, 1988

Highbarger, E. L., *The Gate of Dreams*, Johns Hopkins Press, 1940

Hoeller, S. A., *Jung and the Lost Gospels: Insights into the Dead Sea Scrolls and the Nag Hammadi Library*, Quest Books, 1989

Hoffmann, J., *Celsus on the True Doctrine*, Oxford University Press, 1987

Hollroyd, S., *Gnosticism*, Element Books, 1994

Holmes, G., *Dante*, Oxford University Press, 1980

Horace, *The Satires of Horace and Perseus*, Penguin Classics, 1973

Hornung, E., *Conceptions of God in Ancient Egypt: The One and the Many*, Cornell University Press, 1982

Huxley, A., *The Perennial Philosophy*, Chatto & Windus, 1946

I

Inge, W. R., *Christian Mysticism*, Methuen, 1899

J

Jaroslav, P., *The Tanakh*, The Jewish Publication Company, 1985

Jay, P., *The Greek Anthology*, Penguin Classics, 1973

Jonas, H., *Gnostic Religion: The Message of the Alien God*, Beacon Press, 1958

Josephus, *The Life and Contra Apion*, Harvard University Press, 1926

—, *The Jewish War*, Penguin Classics, 1959

Jung, C. G., *Psychology and Alchemy*, Routledge, 1953

—, *Mysterium Coniunctionis*, Routledge & Kegan Paul, 1957

—, *Aion*, Routledge, 1959

—, *On the Nature of the Psyche*, Princeton University Press, 1960

—, *Memories, Dreams, Reflections*, Random House, 1961

—, *The Psychology of the Transference*, Ark, 1983

—, *Selected Writings*, Fontana, 1983

—, *The Spirit in Man, Art and Literature*, Ark, 1984

—, *Synchronicity: An Acausal Connecting Principle*, Ark, 1985

—, *Man and his Symbols*, Arkana, 1990

K

Kahn, C. H., *The Art and Thought of Heraclitus*, Cambridge University Press, 1979

Kaplan, R., *The Nothing That Is: A Natural History of Zero*, Allen Lane, 1999

Kasher, A., *Jews and Hellenistic Cities in Eretz-Israel: Relations of the Jews in Eretz-Israel with the Hellenistic Cities during the Second Temple Period (332 BCE–70 CE)*, J. C. B. Mohr, 1990

Kennedy, H. A. A., *St Paul and the Mystery Religions*, Hodder and Stoughton, 1960

Kerenyi, C., *Heroes of the Greeks*, Thames and Hudson, 1959

—, *Eleusis*, Bollingen Press, 1967

—, *Dionysos*, Bollingen Press, 1976

Kermode, F., *The Genesis of Secrecy: On the Interpretation of Narrative*, Harvard University Press, 1977

King, C. W., *Gnostics and their Remains*, David Nutt, 1887

Kingsland, W., *The Gnosis*, Phanes Press, 1937

Kingsley, P., *Ancient Philosophy Mystery and Magic: Empedocles and Pythagorean Tradition*, Oxford University Press, 1995

—, *In the Dark Places of Wisdom*, Element Books, 1999

Kirk, G. S., and Raven, J. E., *The Presocratic Philosophers*, Cambridge University Press, 1957

Kloppenborg, 'Isis and the Book of Wisdom', *HTR* 75 (1982), 57–84

Koester, H, *Introduction to the New Testament*, 2 vols, Gruyter, 1980, 1982

—, 'The History and the Development of Mark's Gospel: From Mark to Secret Mark and "Canonical" Mark', *Colloquy on NT Studies: A Time for Reappraisal and Fresh Approaches*, ed. B. Corley, Mercer University Press, 1983, 35–57

—, *Ancient Christian Gospels*, SCM Press, 1990

L

Lacarrière, J., *The God-Possessed*, Allen & Unwin, 1963

—, *The Gnostics*, Peter Owen Ltd, 1973; reprinted City Lights Books, 1989

Lamy, L., *Egyptian Mysteries*, Thames and Hudson, 1981

Lane, E. N., *Cybele, Attis and Related Cults*, E. J. Brill, 1996

Lane-Fox, R., *Pagans and Christians*, Penguin Books, 1986

—, *The Unauthorised Version: Truth and Fiction in the Bible*, Penguin Books, 1992.

Layton, B., *The Gnostic Scriptures: Ancient Wisdom for the New Age*, Doubleday & Co., 1987

Leedom, T. C. (ed.), *The Book your Church Doesn't Want You to Read*, Kendall/Hunt Publishing Company, 1993

Lemprierre, J., *A Classical Dictionary*, Routledge & Kegan Paul, 1949

Lerner, R. E., *The Heresy of the Free Spirit in the Later Middle Ages*, California University Press, 1972

Lietzmann, H., *The History of the Early Church*, 4 vols, Lutterworth Press, 1961

Lieu, S. N. C., *Manichaeism*, Manchester University Press, 1985

Lieu, North and Rajak, *The Jews among Pagans and Christians*, Routledge, 1992

Lindsay, J., *Origins of Alchemy in Graeco Roman Egypt*, Frederick Müller, 1970

Linforth, I. M., *The Arts of Orpheus*, University of California Press, 1941

Lloyd, G. E. R., *Polarity and Analogy*, Cambridge University Press, 1966

Louth, A., *Early Christian Writings*, Penguin Classics, 1968

Lucian, *Satirical Sketches*, Indiana University Press, 1961

Lucius Apuleius, *The Golden Ass*, Penguin Classics, 1950

Lucretius, *The Nature of the Universe*, Penguin Classics, 1951

Lüdemann, G., *Heretics*, SCM Press, 1995

M

MacDonald, D. R., *The Homeric Epics and the Gospel of Mark*, Yale University Press, 2000

MacMullen, R., *Enemies of the Roman Order*, Oxford University Press, 1966

McEvedy, C., *The Penguin Atlas of Ancient History*, Penguin Books, 1967

Macchioro, V. D., *From Orpheus to Paul*, Constable and Company, 1930

Mack, B. L., *A Myth of Innocence: Mark and Christian Origins*, Fortress Press, 1988
— , *The Lost Gospel*, Element Books, 1993

Magnien, V., *Les Mystères d'Eleusus*, Payot, 1938

Maitland, S. R., *Facts and Documents Illustrative of the History, Doctrine and Rites of the Ancient Albigenses and Waldeneses*, 1832

Marcovich, M., *Studies in Graeco-Roman Religion and Gnosticism*, Leiden, 1988

Marcus Aurelius, *Meditations*, New University Library, n.d.

Marlowe, J., *The Golden Age of Alexandria*, Victor Gollancz, 1971

Martin, L. H., *The Hellenistic Religions*, Oxford University Press, 1987

Matthews, C., *Sophia: Goddess of Wisdom*, The Aquarian Press, 1992

Mayor, Fowler, Conway, *Virgil's Messianic Ecologue*, John Murray Publishers, 1907

Mead, G. R. S., *Fragments of a Faith Forgotten*, The Theosophical Publishing Society, second edition, 1906
— , *The Gnostic Crucifixion*, The Theosophical Publishing Society, 1907
— , *The Mysteries of Mithra, Echoes of the Gnosis: Vol. 5*, The Theosophical Publishing Society, 1907
— , *The Chaldaean Oracles, Echoes of the Gnosis: Vol. 8*, The Theosophical Publishing Society, 1908
— , *The Doctrine of the Subtle Body in the Western Tradition*, Solos Press, 1919
— , *Pistis Sophia: A Gnostic Gospel*, Garber Communications, first published 1921; reissued Spritual Science Library, 1984

Merkur, D., *Gnosis: An Esoteric Tradition of Mystical Visions and Unions*, State University of New York Press, 1993

Metzger, B. M., *The Canon of the New Testament*, Oxford University Press, 1987

Meyer, M. W., *The Ancient Mysteries Sourcebook*, HarperCollins*Publishers*, 1987

Momigliano, A., *Alien Wisdom*, Cambridge University Press, 1971

Mourelatos, A. P. D. (ed.), *The Pre-Socratics: A Collection of Critical Essays*, Anchor Books, 1974

Murray, M. A., *Egyptian Religious Poetry*, John Murray, 1949

Mylonas, G. E., *Eleusis and the Eleusinian Mysteries*, Princeton University Press, 1961

N

Nicholson, R. A., *The Mathnawi of Jalalu-ddin Rumi*, vols I & II, The Trustees of the E. J. W. Gibb Memorial, 1926

Nock, A. D., 'Astrology and Cultural History', *Essays on Religion and the Ancient World*, vol. I., Harvard University Press, 1972
— , 'Gnosticism', *Essays on Religion and the Ancient World*, vol. II, Harvard University Press, 1972

North, J. D., *Horoscopes and History*, London, 1986

Novak, P., *The Division of Consciousness: The Secret Afterlife of the Human Psyche*, Hampton Roads Publishing Co., 1997

Novalis, *Pollen and Fragments*, ed. A. Versluis, Phanes Press, 1989

O

Oblonesky, D., *The Bogomils: A Study in Balkan Neo-Manichaeism*, Cambridge University Press, 1960

Oldenbourg, Z., *Massacre at Montségur*, New York, 1961

O'Meara, D. J., *Pythagoras Revived: Mathematics and Philosophy in Late Antiquity*, Clarendon Press, 1989

Osman, A., *Out of Egypt: The Roots of Christianity Revealed*, Arrow, 1998

Otto, W. F., *Dionysos Myth and Cult*, Spring Publications, 1965

Ouvaroff, M., *Essay on the Eleusinian Mysteries*, Rodwell and Martin, 1817

Ovid, *Metamorphoses*, Penguin Classics, 1955

Owen-Lee, M., *Virgil as Orpheus*, State University of New York Press, 1996

P

Pagels, E., *The Gnostic Paul*, Trinity Press International, 1975

—, *The Gnostic Gospels*, Penguin Books, 1979

—, *Adam, Eve and the Serpent*, Random House, 1988

Pelikan, J., *Mary through the Centuries: Her Place in the History of Culture*, Yale University Press, 1996

Perkins, P., *Gnosticism and the New Testament*, Fortress Press, 1993

Philip, J. A., *Pythagoras and Early Pythagoreanism*, University of Toronto Press, 1966

Philo of Alexandria, *Book IX*, Loeb Classical Library no. 363, 1941

Plato, *Collected Dialogues*, Princeton University Press, 1961

—, *Timaeus* and *Critias*, Penguin Classics, 1965

—, *Phaedrus* and *Letters vii and viii*, Penguin Classics, 1973

Plutarch, *The Fall of the Roman Republic*, Penguin Classics, 1958

—, *The Rise and Fall of Athens*, Penguin Classics, 1960

—, *Makers of Rome*, Penguin Classics, 1965

—, *The Moral Essays*, Penguin Classics, 1971

—, *De Iside et Osiride*, Oxford University Press, 1993

Pollitt, J. J., *Art and Experience in Classical Greece*, Cambridge University Press, 1972

Polybius, *The Rise of the Roman Empire*, Penguin Classics, 1979

Porphyry, *On the Cave of the Nymphs*, Phanes Press, 1991

Potter, D., *Prophets and Emperors*, Harvard University Press, 1994

Potter, H., *Hanging in Judgement: Religion and the Death Penalty in England*, 1993

Powell, A., *Poetry & Propaganda in the Age of Augustus*, Bristol Classical Press, 1992

Price, R. M., *Deconstructing Jesus*, Prometheus Books, 2000

Price, S. R. F., *Rituals and Power: The Roman Imperial Cult in Asia Minor*, Cambridge University Press, 1984

Pritchard, J. B. (ed.), *Ancient Near Eastern Texts Relating to the Old Testament*, Princeton University Press, second edition, 1955

Proclus, *The Elements of Theology*, Oxford University Press, 1963

Pseudo-Dionysius, *The Complete Works*, trans. C. Luibheid, Paulist Press, 1987

Ptolemy, *Tetrabiblos*, trans. and introduction by F. E. Robbins, Loeb Classical Library, 1940

R

Raven, J. E., *Pythagoreans and Eleatics*, Cambridge University Press, 1948

Reedy, J., *The Platonic Doctrines of Albinus*, Phanes Press, 1991

Ringgren, H., *Word and Wisdom: Studies in the Hypostatisation of Divine Qualities and Functions in the Ancient Near East*, 1947; University Microfilms International Reprints, 1980

—, *The Faith of Qumran: Theology of the Dead Sea Scrolls*, Crossroad Publishing Company, 1995

Roberts, A., and Donaldson, J. (eds), *Ante Nicene Fathers*, Wm. B. Eerdmans Publishing Co., 1975

Robinson, J. M., *The Nag Hammadi Library*, HarperSanFrancisco, paperback edition, 1978

Robinson, J. M., and Koester, H., *Trajectories through Early Christianity*, Fortress Press, 1971

Rohl, D. M., *A Test of Time: The Bible from Myth to History*, 1995

Rudolph, K., *Gnosis: The Nature and History of Gnosticism*, Harper and Row, 1987

Runia, D. T., *Philo in Early Christian Literature*, Fortress Press, 1993

S

St Augustine, *Confessions, City of God, Christian Doctrine*, William Benton, 1952

Sallustius, *Concerning the Gods and the Universe*, Cambridge University Press, 1926

Samuel, A. E., *Greek and Roman Chronology*, Oscar Beck, 1972

Scarre, C., *Chronicle of the Roman Emperors*, Thames and Hudson, 1995

Schafer, P., *Judeophobia: Attitudes toward the Jews in the Ancient World*, Harvard University Press, 1997

Schaup, S., *Sophia: Aspects of the Divine Feminine*, Nicolas-Hays, 1997

Scholem, G., *Major Trends in Jewish Mysticism*, Schocken Books, 1946

—, *Origins of the Kabbalah*, Jewish Publication Society, 1987

Schweitzer, A., *The Quest of the Historical Jesus: From Reimarus to Wrede*, 1910

Scott, M., *Sophia and the Johannine Jesus*, Sheffield Academic Press Ltd, 1992

Scott, W., *Hermetica*, Solos Press, 1992

Segal, R. A., *The Gnostic Jung*, Routledge, 1992

Seneca, *Letters from a Stoic*, Penguin Classics, 1969

Shanks, H., *Understanding the Dead Sea Scrolls*, SPCK, 1992

Sheldon, H. C., *Mystery Religions and the New Testament*, Kessinger Publishing, 1918

Shlain, L., *The Alphabet versus the Goddess: Male Words and Female Images*, Allen Lane, The Penguin Press, 1999

Smith, J. Z., *Drudgery Divine: On the Comparison of Early Christianities and the Religions of Late Antiquity*, SOAS, University of London, 1990

Sophocles, *The Theban Plays*, Penguin Classics, 1947

Stanton, G., *Gospel Truth?*, HarperCollins*Publishers*, 1995

Stevenson, J., *A New Eusebius*, SPCK, 1957

Stone, M., *When God was a Woman*, Harvest, 1976

Stoyanov, Y., *The Hidden Tradition in Europe*, Penguin Arkana, 1994
  —, *The Other God: Dualist Religions from Antiquity to the Cathar Heresy*,
      Yale University Press, 2000

Suetonius, *The Twelve Caesars*, Penguin Classics, 1957

Syme, R., *The Roman Revolution*, Oxford University Press, 1948

T

Tacitus, *The Annals of Imperial Rome*, Penguin Classics, 1956
  —, *The Histories*, Penguin Classics, 1968

Taylor, L. R., *The Divinity of the Roman Emperor*, The American Philological
      Association, 1931

Taylor, T., *The Works of Plato*, vol. III, first published 1804; The Prometheus Trust, 1996
  —, *The Eleusinian and Bacchic Mysteries*, J.W. Bouton, 1891
  —, *Collected Writings on the Gods and the World*, The Prometheus Trust, 1994
  —, *Oracles and Mysteries*, The Prometheus Trust, 1995
  —, *The Theology of Plato by Proclus*, The Prometheus Trust, 1995
  —, *Iamblichus on the Mysteries and Life of Pythagoras*, The Prometheus Trust, 1999

Taylour, L. W., *The Mycenaeans*, Thames and Hudson, 1964

Tcherikover, V., *Hellenistic Civilization and the Jews*, The Jewish Publication Society of
      America, 1959

Temple, R. K. G., *Conversations with Eternity*, Rider, 1984

Thesleff, H., *An Introduction to the Pythagorean Writings of the Hellenistic Period*,
      Acta Academiae Aboensis, 1961

Thompson and Griffith, *The Leyden Papyrus*, Dover Books, 1974

Thucydides, *The Peloponnesian War*, Penguin Classics, 1954

Toynbee, A., *A Study of History*, 1939

Trevelyan, G. M., *English Social History*, Longman, 1944

Turcan, R., *Cults of the Roman Empire*, Blackwell Publishers, 1992

U

Ulansey, D., *Origin of the Mithraic Mysteries*, Oxford University Press, 1989

Usher, S., *The Historians of Greece and Rome*, Bristol Classical Press, 1969

V

Van Voorst, R. E., *Jesus outside the New Testament: An Introduction to the Ancient
      Evidence*, 2000

Virgil, *The Pastoral Poems*, Penguin Classics, 1949

W

Wakefield, W. L., *Heresy, Crusade and Inquisition in Southern France, 1100–1250*, Allen & Unwin, 1974

Walbank, F. W., *The Hellenistic World*, Fontana Press, 1981

Walker, B., *The Woman's Encyclopedia of Myths and Secrets*, Harper and Row, 1983

Walker, D. P., *The Ancient Theology*, Duckworth, 1972

Wallace-Hadrill, A., *Augustan Rome*, Bristol Classical Press, 1993

Wallis Budge, E. A., *Egyptian Religion*, 1899, reprinted Arkana

—, *Egyptian Magic*, 1899, reprinted Arkana

Wallis, R. T., *Neoplatonism and Gnosticism*, State University of New York Press, 1992

Warner, H. J., *The Albigensian Heresy*, SPCK, 1922

Watson, D., *A Dictionary of Mind and Spirit*, André Deutsch, 1991

Welburn, A., *Gnosis, the Mysteries and Christianity*, Floris Books, 1994

Wells, G. A., *Did Jesus Exist?*, Pemberton Publishing Company, 1975

—, *The Jesus Legend*, Open Court, 1996

—, *The Jesus Myth*, Open Court, 1999

Wilber, K., *A Brief History of Everything*, Shambhala, 1996

—, *The Marriage of Sense and Soul*, Broadway Books, 1998

Willoughby, H. R., *Pagan Regeneration*, University of Chicago Press, 1929

Wilson, I., *Jesus: The Evidence*, Weidenfeld and Nicolson, 1984

Wright, M. R., *The Presocratics*, Bristol Classical Press, 1985

X

Xenophon, *Conversations of Socrates*, selection, introductions and translations by R. Waterfield and H. Tredenick, Penguin Classics, 1990

Y

Yates, F. A., *Giordano Bruno and the Hermetic Tradition*, University of Chicago Press, 1964

—, *The Art of Memory*, Routledge & Kegan Paul, 1966

—, *The Rosicrucian Enlightenment*, Routledge & Kegan Paul, 1972

Yonge, C. D., *The Works of Philo*, Hendrickson Publishers, 1993

Z

Zanker, P., *The Power of Images in the Age of Augustus*, Michigan University Press, 1988

Zuntz, G., *Persephone: Three Essays on Religion and Thought in Magna Graecia*, Oxford, 1971

WEBSITES

These websites are either referred to in the footnotes, offer texts for download or provide a useful starting-point for further investigation. Live links to all these sites can be found at our website: www.jesusmysteries.demon.co.uk.

The Nag Hammadi Gnostic Library – download the texts
http://www.webcom.com/~gnosis/naghamm/nhl.html

Plotinus, *Enneads* – download the text
http://classics.mit.edu/Plotinus/enneads.html

The Complete Works of Plato – download the texts
http://phd.evansville.edu/links.htm

Hippolytus, *Refutationis Omnium Haeresium* – download the text
http://www.webcom.com/~gnosis/library/hyp_refut1.htm

Irenaeus, *Adverses Haereses* – download the text
http://www.webcom.com/~gnosis/library/advh1.htm

Tertullian, *De Praescriptione Haereticorum* – download the text
http://www.webcom.com/~gnosis/library/ter_persc.htm

Clement of Alexandria, *Stromata* – download the text
http://www.webcom.com/~gnosis/library/strom1.htm

Augustine, *Against Faustus the Manichaean* – download the text
http://www.webcom.com/~gnosis/library/contf1.htm

Patristic polemical works against the Gnostics listed by author
http://www.webcom.com/~gnosis/library/polem.htm

The Ante-Nicene Fathers, Volume I
http://www.ccel.org/fathers2/ANF-01/

The Ante-Nicene Fathers, Volume II
http://www.ccel.org/fathers2/ANF-02/

The Ante-Nicene Fathers, Volume III
http://www.ccel.org/fathers2/ANF-03/

The Gnostic Society Library
http://www.webcom.com/gnosis/library.html

The Gnosis Archive
http://www.gnosis.org/welcome.html

Gnosticism website
http://www.kheper.auz.com/topics/Gnosticism/Gnosticism.htm

Gnosis discussion forum
http://www.hermetic.com/gnostic-list/index.html

Gnostic links and resources
http://www.academicinfo.net/gnostic.html

Elaine Pagels, *The Gnostic Gospels*
http://www.pbs.org/wgbh/pages/frontline/shows/religion/story/pagels.html

The Gospel of Thomas homepage
http://home.epix.net/~miser17/Thomas.html

Gnosis – origins and beliefs
http://members.tripod.com/~aos/general/gnostic.html

Gnosis links
http://www.lumen.org/about_gnosis/links_we_like/links_we_like.html

Excerpts of Theodotus
http://www.ccel.org/fathers2/ANF-08/anf08-20.htm#P711_194933

Valentinus and the Valentinian Tradition
http://www.cyberus.ca/~brons/valentin.htm

The Center for Marcionite Research
http://www.geocities.com/Athens/Ithaca/3827/

The Mysteries of Sophia
Scriptures
http://home.sol.no/~noetic/scrsoph.htm
Articles
http://home.sol.no/~noetic/sophart.htm

'The Sorrow of Sophia' – web lecture of The Gnostic Society
http://www.webcom.com/~gnosis/961018.htm

Mary Magdalene
http://www.magdalene.org/gnostic.htm

Mary Magdalene – author of *St John's Gospel*?
http://www.beloveddisciple.org
http://www.bibletexts.com/terms/bd.htm

The Gospel of Mariam and the Sacred Marriage
http://www.scitec.auckland.ac.nz/~king/Preprints/book/hieros/hieros2.htm

Simon Magus
http://www.kheper.auz.com/topics/Gnosticism/Simon_Magus.htm

Manicheism
http://home.online.no/~noetic/maex.htm

Allegorizations of the Active and Contemplative Lives in Philo, Origen, Augustine and Gregory
http://www2.evansville.edu/ecoleweb/articles/allegory.html

Docetism
http://www2.evansville.edu/ecoleweb/articles/docetism.html

The Mystery of the Bridal Chamber
http://www.hermeticgoldendawn.org/Feminine.htm

Women in the Early Church
http://www.bibletexts.com/women.htm

Article by Karen King, 'Women in the Early Church'
http://www.pbs.org/wgbh/pages/frontline/shows/religion/first/women.html

The Feminine Soul
http://www.fireplug.net/~rshand/streams/gnosis/soul.html

Cathars
http://www.kenyon.edu/projects/margin/cathy11.htm

Cathar scriptures
http://home.sol.no/~noetic/cathtx.htm

Medieval heresy – links page, Inquisition, Cathars, etc.
http://www.fordham.edu/halsall/sbook1s.html#Medieval%20Heresy

Medieval heresy – Beguines, Bogomils, Cathars, Albigensians, etc.
http://www.ptsem.org/heresy/hernet3.htm

The Inquisitor Bernard Gui on the Albigensians
http://www.fordham.edu/halsall/source/gui-cathars.html

Raynaldus, *On the Accusations against the Albigensians*
http://www.fordham.edu/halsall/source/heresy1.html

The Eleusinian Mysteries
http://www.uwec.edu/academic/philrel/beach/eleusis.html

The Mysteries of Eleusis
http://www.san.beck.org/Eleusis-Intro.html#1

Hermetica
http://www.gnosis.org/hermes.htm

The Hermetica, Books 1–13
http://www.gnosis.org/library/hermes1.html (through to: /hermes13.html)

Mithras
http://www2.evansville.edu/ecoleweb/articles/mithraism.html

Iamblichus, *On the Mysteries*
http://www.esotericism.co.uk/iamblichus-and-porphyry.htm

Alexandria: cosmology, philosophy, myth and culture
http://www.cosmopolis.com/index.html

Alchemy website
http://www.levity.com/alchemy

Boethius
http://ccat.sas.upenn.edu/jod/boethius/boethius.html

Philo of Alexandria
http://www.leidenuniv.nl/philosophy/studia_philonica/index.html
http://www.hivolda.no/asf/kkf/philopag.html
on the Therapeutae
http://www.fordham.edu/halsall/ancient/philo-ascetics.html

Essenes
http://religion.rutgers.edu/iho/texts4.html#Essenes

Josephus
http://religion.rutgers.edu/iho/josephus.html
on the *Testimonium Flavium*
http://www.concentric.net/~Mullerb/appe.shtml

The Odes of Solomon
http://www.magi.com/~oblio/jesus/supp04.htm

Thecla
http://www.pbs.org/wgbh/pages/frontline/shows/religion/maps/primary/thecla.html

The Secret Gospel of Mark
http://www.globaltown.com/shawn/secmark.html

Who were the Jews?
http://www.jesusmysteries.demon.co.uk/judaism.html

David Ulansey, *The Heavenly Veil Torn*
http://www.well.com/user/davidu/veil.html

Gnosis and Sufism
http://www.mullasadra.org/article_7.htm

International Association of Sufism
http://www.ias.org/

The Works of Thomas Taylor the Platonist
http://www.users.globalnet.co.uk/~sonoko/index.htm

Guide to Early Church Documents
http://www.iclnet.org/pub/resources/christian-history.html

Historic Documents of the Church
http://www.gty.org/~phil/writings.htm

Ecole Initiative – *Encyclopedia of Early Church History*
http://www2.evansville.edu/ecoleweb/

Christian Classics Ethereal Library
http://www.ccel.org/

The Internet Classics Archive
http://classics.mit.edu/Browse/index.html

Encyclopedia Coptica
http://www.coptic.net/

INDEX

LECTURES AND SEMINARS

Timothy Freke and Peter Gandy are now offering lectures and seminars exploring the ancient Gnosis and its relevance in the modern world. To find out about forthcoming events or to invite them to your venue:

E-MAIL: info@jesusmysteries.demon.co.uk
WEBSITE: http://www.jesusmysteries.demon.co.uk